424

Report writing for business

Report writing
for business

RAYMOND V. LESIKAR, Ph.D.

Professor and Head
Department of Management and Marketing
Louisiana State University

Third edition

1969
Richard D. Irwin, Inc., Homewood, Illinois
Irwin-Dorsey Limited, Georgetown, Ontario

Third Edition
First Printing, February, 1969
Second Printing, December, 1969

Library of Congress Catalog Card No. 69–17156
Printed in the United States of America

Preface

Like its predecessor, this third edition has the primary goal of preparing the student to write the reports he must write in business. That this goal is essential in preparing one for business was logical speculation at the time the first edition appeared. With the appearance of the second edition, the necessity of this goal was more apparent. Today as we view the ever-increasing needs for communication in our rapidly developing technological world of business, the need for report-writing proficiency is unmistakably evident. Without question, today's business students must learn to write reports if they are to meet the needs of today's business world. Hopefully, this book will help them to achieve this goal.

As most report-writing teachers want it, the text places major emphasis on the organizing and writing of reports. In addition to this traditional coverage, it strives to meet the demands of the forthcoming research-minded business world by placing adequate stress on the research methodology which precedes report preparation. And it strives to meet the ever-increasing demand for higher educational standards by challenging the student with realistic, mind-stimulating problems.

The text fully recognizes the fact that reports differ widely by organization and company. In overcoming this problem, it approaches the subject of report preparation from a general viewpoint. It follows the assumption that although reports may differ, the principles of their construction (writing, organizing, and such) are universal. Thus, the general teachings of the book may be adapted easily to the specific report requirements of any organization. At the same time, however, the text contains sufficient specific instruction to enable one to construct the conventional reports.

In planning this third edition, I was guided primarily by the many comments and suggestions received from those who used the second edition. Especially was I guided by the suggestions of Professors Max L. Waters, Brigham Young University; and J. L. Quicksall,

Texas Technological College. Each of these professors made extensive reviews of the book and numerous worthwhile suggestions for change. Their contributions are evident throughout this work. As one would expect, however, many of the suggestions I received contradicted others. Although I could not use them all, I sincerely feel that I have made the changes which make the maximum improvement in the book.

One deserving very special mention for his assistance is Dr. John Pettit, my former student and colleague, now at Texas Technological College. His numerous suggestions proved to be most valuable, and his long hours of labor on Chapter 4 and on certain areas of problem construction were genuine contributions to this work. For these efforts as well as his friendly encouragement throughout the project I am most grateful.

For the feedback they gave me on the preceding edition, I am grateful to my many students of past years. I am grateful, also, to Dr. J. Lincoln DeVillier, West Georgia College, for the corrections he pointed out in the preceding edition. With parental pride I acknowledge the assistance of my son, Ray, whose efforts in pasting up copy saved me valuable time. With gratitude I acknowledge the typing help of my loyal secretary, Mrs. Gloria Armistead. And last but not least, I am grateful for the contribution of my wife. As she has done so often in the past, she provided the love, patience, and understanding I needed to complete the task.

Baton Rouge, Louisiana   RAYMOND V. LESIKAR
January, 1969

Table of contents

terpretation. *Comparison of noncomparable data. Cause–
effect confusion. Unreliable data. Unrepresentative data.
Neglect of important factors.* Attitudes and practices conducive to sound interpreting: *Cultivation of a critical point
of view. Maintenance of the judicial attitude. Consultation
with others. Testing of interpretations.* Statistical aids to
interpretation: *Measures of central tendency. Descriptions of
dispersion. Comparisons by ratios.* Interpreting for the reader.
Orderly procedure in interpreting: *Relate information to the
problem. Make all practical interpretations. Reevaluate interpretations. Select interpretations with most merit. Derive
conclusions from the interpretations.*

The process of communication: *Sensory receptors and the
sensory world. The preverbal stage. The symbolizing stage.
The cycle repeated. The model and written communication.
Some basic truths.* Fundamental need for adaptation. The
essential quality of readability: *Development of readability
formulas. The Gunning Fog Index. Critical appraisal of the
formulas.* The essential quality of objectivity: *Objectivity as
a basis for believability. Objectivity and the question of impersonal versus personal writing.* Logic of present time viewpoint. Structural aids to report coherence: *The use of
introductory, concluding, and summarizing sections. Communication value of transition.* The role of interest in report
communication.

Word selection: *Selecting words the reader understands.
Bring the writing to life with words. Selecting words for
precise communication.* Sentence construction: *Keep the
sentences short. Use words economically. Give the facts
proper emphasis. Arrange the words correctly for clarity.
Place related words close together.* Care in paragraph design:
*Give the paragraph unity. Keep the paragraphs short. Put
topic sentences to good use. Make the paragraphs move
forward.*

General information on physical presentation: *Choice of
cover. Care in paper selection. Conventional page layout.
Special page layouts. Choice of typing form. Patterns of in-*

CHAPTER 1

Orientation to business reports

What are reports? Why should I learn how to write them? These two questions logically come to the mind of the beginning student of report writing. It is fitting that they be answered as the first step in studying the subject.

THE WHAT AND WHY OF REPORT WRITING

What are reports?

The answer to the first question appears to be easy, for reports are commonplace in 20th-century business life. Businesses, civic groups, government agencies, churches, and all such major organizations use reports to some extent. Most use them extensively. In fact, it is unlikely that any modern-day organization of size could function without them. Yet, the very fact that reports are now commonplace probably adds to the confusion in defining them.

Definitions in current use range from one extreme to the other. By the broadest definition, reports are almost any presentation of information ranging from the extremely formal to the highly informal. Narrower definitions limit reports to the more formalized presentations of information. For the student of business reports, a definition approaching the narrower ones is best. Such a definition is the following: A business report is an orderly and objective communication of factual information which serves some business purpose.

Careful inspection of this definition reveals the identifying characteristics of the business report. As an *orderly* communication, a report is given some care in preparation. And care in preparation distinguishes a report from the casual, routine exchanges of information that continually occur in business. This is not to say that all

1

reports are carefully prepared, but it does mean that at least something above minimum care is given in their preparation. Everyday, oral exchanges of information, for example, do not classify as reports. Nor do the most casual handwritten notes.

The *objective* quality of a report is its unbiased approach to the facts presented. The report seeks truth, regardless of its consequences. Because few people can be thoroughly objective, perhaps this quality seldom is realized. Nevertheless, it must be striven for in the report. Certainly, some papers disguised as reports are heavily persuasive, but they represent a specialized form of administrative writing. They are not true reports.

The word *communication* is broad by definition, covering all ways of transmitting meaning (speaking, writing, drawing, gesturing, etc). For all practical purposes, however, business reports are either written or oral. And for reasons that will be given shortly, in today's complex business operations the more significant reports are written.

The basic ingredient of the report is *factual* information—events, records, and the various forms of data that are communicated in the conduct of business. In no way is the content fictional. Nor is there major stress on opinions, except in those rare cases when in the absence of facts authoritative opinions are the best information available. This statement does not mean that interpretations, recommendations, and conclusions (which may border on opinions) may not be included. They can and should be a part of most reports. But it does mean that they should be either supported by fact or clearly labeled as opinion. As far as possible, the emphasis should be on fact.

Not all reports are business reports. Research scientists, medical doctors, ministers, students, and many others write reports. Thus, the need for the final phrase of the definition is obvious. To be classified as a business report, a report must *serve* some *business purpose*.

This purpose may be to solve a problem: Should X Company diversify its line? How can Y Company increase sales in the Northeast district? How can Z Company profitably use an electronic computer? The purpose may be to present information needed in the conduct of business: a weekly report of a salesman's activities, a summary of the day's production, an explanation of expenditures on a particular project, a description of the condition of a piece of equipment. In general, the purpose could concern the thousand and one areas of information a business needs in its operation.

Even though this definition of a business report is specific enough to be meaningful, it is broad enough to take into account the variations to be found in reports. For example, some reports do nothing more than present facts. Others go a step further by including interpretations. Still others proceed to conclusions and recommendations. There are reports formally dressed both in writing style and in physical appearance. And there are reports that evidence a high degree of informality. The definition given permits all these variations.

Why study business report writing?

The question, "Why Study Business Report Writing?" may be answered from two standpoints. One is the standpoint of the company for which the student will work some day. The other is the personal standpoint of the student. Convincing argument supports both positions.

From a business standpoint. In answering the question from the organization's position, one need only point to the major role reports play in today's business. Because reports play a major role, it stands to reason that they sould be well done. The better they are prepared, the better they are likely to perform their role. In other words, business wants good reports, and it wants good report writers.

One can appreciate the vital role played by reports from a brief review of their historical development. This review need not emphasize the conventional historical summary of facts, for such facts are secondary in importance. Of more importance are the conditions that led to the need for reports.

To trace the development of the conditions that gave rise to reports, one must trace the progress of man. The early story of man's progress, of course, is a matter of unrecorded history. But one can safely assume that it was marked by cooperative effort. No doubt, early man discovered that by working together a group could do things that the individual members could not do alone. And they learned that group effort required leadership to guide the progress toward a common goal.

While the operations remained simple, the group leaders were able personally to look into any special problems that came up. When they wanted to know the status of things, they called in a subordinate and asked him. If the information was available, the subordinate reported it. If the information was not available, the subordinate looked for it, and reported it later. Generally the report was oral, for it was easier and more practical that way.

Over the ages, as these organized groups (organizations) became larger and larger and their operations more and more complex, oral reporting became increasingly less practical. Leaders learned that they could keep in personal touch with only a limited number of subordinates. They learned that as their organizations expanded and their geographic areas of operations increased, their need for information also increased; and they found that person-to-person communication became impractical, if not impossible. In time, as civilization advanced and the written report came into being, they began using written reports.

Thus, the origin and development of written reports followed close on the heels of the expansion of organized activity. Probably the armies of the first literate civilization (perhaps the Greeks, Romans, and Egyptians) were among the first to use written reports significantly, for these were among ahe first organized groups engaged in large-scale activity. It is likely, too, that some of the early businessmen of these civilizations also used reports in their more complex and widespread operations. Even so, such reports as these were distinctly different from their modern counterparts; but reports they were, nevertheless.

From this early period the extent of use of written reports followed closely the growth of organized activity. For many centuries, this growth was slow. In fact, only in the past century did it accelerate sharply. But how very, very sharp was this acceleration.

The past century witnessed the phenomenal growth of organization, especially the giant corporation with its mergers, holding arrangements, widespread operations, multiple activities, and such. From regional operations, businesses expanded to national and even worldwide activities. From a one-plant or one-office operation, companies expanded to 10, 20, and more. Employment by a single company increased from a handful to thousands—even tens of thousands for some. Obviously, business operations became increasingly complex.

Added to this complexity of growth was the rapid expansion of technology during this period. With the improvement of technology came a general increase in the sophistication of procedures. New techniques replaced old techniques, and still newer techniques replaced the new. Likewise, new products replaced old products, new materials replaced old materials, new procedures replaced old procedures. In general, this technological advancement produced an increasingly more complex and sophisticated operating procedure.

In dealing with the complexities of operation brought about by increased size and technological advancement, organizations found an increasing need for information. In fact, today's typical organization virtually feeds on information. This is no overstatement, and one needs only to inspect the operations of any of today's business organizations to prove it.

When one inspects a typical business organization of today, probably he sees first the more tangible parts of its existence—land, buildings, machinery, and inventory. And when he visualizes man in this organization, probably he sees man working with these tangible things. Probably he sees men operating lathes, working on assembly lines, inspecting parts, selling goods, handling packages, and the like. But this is only a part of the work that goes on in the organization—frequently a smaller part than one suspects. In addition to the productive work, processing information makes up a major part of the work that goes on in the organization.

Throughout the organization, people send and receive information. Salesmen send in orders and weekly reports, and they receive instructions and sales information from the home office. Production supervisors receive work orders, and they prepare production reports. Order department workers receive purchase orders, and they supply sales and inventory records to the scheduling department. Inspectors prepare reports on their work. Research specialists write up the results of their investigations for those who may use the information. It is like this in every niche of the organization—people receiving information and sending information.

The information received and sent serves as the basis for the bulk of administrative action needed to make the organization an effective production operation. With information, administrators are able to coordinate the activities of the organization. It provides them the bases for the planning they must do. It is the vehicle administrators use in exercising control of the organization. And it provides the intelligence with which they direct the activities of the organization.

The information flow in an organization, of course, is comprised of many forms of communication. Included is all of the oral communication that goes on—the orders, instruction, inquiries, personal conversation, and such. Included are all the records and forms that are kept and exchanged. Included, also, are the vast information storage and retrieval facilities that modern organizations now provide with electronic computers. In addition, there is the information flow handled through written reports, which, of course, is the objective of this investigation. Without question, written reports play a very major role in the conduct of an organization's activities. And as organizations and technology become more complex, the role of written reports is likely to increase further.

The mushrooming role of importance played by reports in the economy is generally accepted by 20th-century business leaders. Statements of general acceptance, however, are not convincing to the traditionally wary student who is convinced only by more concrete data. Fortunately, such data are not hard to find, although they pertain generally to the entire field of business communications, of which reports comprise a major segment.

Among the more convincing areas of evidence available are the surveys conducted by academic and other interested groups. Perhaps the most convincing of these surveys are two published in the *Harvard Business Review*. The first,[1] conducted by its editors, sought to learn what courses are most suitable for educating tomorrow's business leaders. The cross section of leading executives interviewed rank report writing at the top of the list and decidedly ahead of the next ranking course. The second survey sought to learn what determines the promotability of executives. The nearly 2,000 corporate executives interviewed ranked the ability to communicate as the prime requisite of a promotable executive.[2]

Another convincing survey[3] is one taken by Professor Clarence E. Vincent of Southern Illinois University. This survey of personnel executives found that among the most important courses outside the major field that business students should take, writing courses lead the list. Similar findings were made in a survey of women executives, conducted by Margaret H. Thompson[4] of U.C.L.A. This study of 171 female executives listed in Dun & Bradstreet's *Million Dollar Directory* found the business writing courses to be the most useful

---

[1] "Educating Tomorrow's Executive," *Harvard Business Review*, November–December, 1960, pp. 2 ff.

[2] "What Helps or Harms Promotability," *Harvard Business Review*, January–February, 1965, pp. 8–10.

[3] Clarence E. Vincent, "Personnel Executives Examine the College Graduate," *Collegiate News and Views*, Volume XIX, No. 3 (March 1966), p. 13.

[4] Margaret H. Thompson, "Business Women Recognize the Importance of Communication," *The American Business Writing Association Bulletin*, Volume XXIX, No. 3 (April 1965), pp. 25–26.

among the conventional business courses and essential to preparation for managerial work.

Echoing this conclusion are similar studies made by various academic or professional groups. When asked to rank courses outside their major field that they hold most important to business success, former business students of the University of Texas placed business writing well up on the list. Studies of ex-students of Michigan State University and the University of Washington produced almost identical results. So did a survey of small business leaders in Louisiana. In all these studies, business writing was second only to basic accounting. The writing courses soundly outstripped such old business standbys as management, marketing, economics, and finance. This evidence, of course, should not be interpreted to discredit the value of the basic subject courses. Rather, it should be accepted as an indicator of the presence of an area of study urgently in need of more attention.

Further evidence of the value business places on writing skill is the great number of companies that are taking steps to improve their employees' writing. Business writing is a common subject for instruction in company trainee programs. Writing improvement programs for veteran employees are commonplace. Such programs consist of numerous instruction and control devices—formal courses, close direction and supervision, manuals, quality checks, conferences, writing clinics, and the like. All these efforts lend mute testimony to the value of writing in business and to the general writing inadequacy found in business.

Some may suggest that the general writing instruction students received in other courses should be adequate to meet their needs in business. But the studies show a strong preference for specialized course work in business writing. To be sure, all forms of writing have much in common. They all use the same language, the same grammar, the same rules of structure, and such. As is so ably pointed out by John S. Fielden, writing in the *Harvard Business Review*,[5] however, the needs of business writing are somewhat unique. Business writing does not attempt to impress. It does not attempt to entertain. Its primary objective is to communicate— quickly and clearly.

From a personal point of view. Convincing as the foregoing facts

---

[5] John S. Fielden, "What Do You Mean I Can't Write?" *Harvard Business Review*, May–June 1964, pp. 144–56.

tend to be, it is from the personal advantage standpoint that the strongest argument for the study of business writing can be made. That is, if the individual student can be shown how he, personally, stands to profit through improving his writing ability, the argument is won.

Proof of personal gain is easily made from a logical interpretation of fact. The fact is that writing is important to business. Thus, those employees with writing skills are apt to be rewarded personally. This conclusion, however, is more convincing when made through another line of reasoning.

This reasoning, too, begins with a simple statement of fact: the promotions an employee receives are determined largely by the impressions he makes on his superiors. He impresses his superiors in many ways, but mainly by his personal characteristics, appearance, job performance, and intellectual capacity for work. It is in this last-named area, intellectual capacity for work, that the writing skills come in.

Satisfactory performance of the work assigned usually is enough to communicate a worker's intellectual capacity for promotion to a rank-and-file position. For promotion to high-level assignments, however, the employee must impress his superiors with his intellectual capacity for the task. Such impressions are made largely through the employee's ability to communicate to others. And in business, this communicating often must be done in writing. Thus, the ability to write good reports and other business papers is a requisite for business advancement. Without this ability, the employee is likely to be doomed to a mediocre role in business. This is true even if the employee happens to be intellectually capable in his field, for he must be judged mainly by the intellectual capacity he is able to communicate. What he cannot communicate is known only to him. The old adage, "Who is to say what the deaf-mute knows?" could be appropriately adapted to this situation.

Proof of the value of writing in business could go on and on, for there is no shortage of supporting evidence. To the student, however, the foregoing presentation of fact and reason should be sufficiently convincing. Certainly, there can be no denial that good writing is needed in business. Nor should there be doubt that writing skills can lead to personal gain. Possibly, these observations will serve as incentives for the student as he progresses through the chapters that follow.

A REVIEW OF REPORT CLASSIFICATION

Since the first organized efforts to study the subject, scholars of report writing have advanced many classifications of reports. Each of these classification plans proposes to divide all reports written into distinct categories. A review of these classifications provides an appropriate introduction to the study of report writing. Such a review is appropriate for two main reasons.

First, discussion of the ways of classifying reports illustrates the variation in approaches to the subject. Reports are far from standardized. With tens of thousands of companies writing them and unknown scores of authorities determining their construction, they could not be otherwise. A knowledge of report classification gives some insight into this complex picture.

A second benefit derived from reviewing report classification is that the various classification terms are used in discussing report writing. As with most subjects, report writing has its own specialized terms—the technical language of the field, so to speak. Logically, a student of report writing should be acquainted with the vernacular of his subject. The terms used in classifying reports comprise much of this vernacular.

Subject matter as a basis for classification

Possibly the simplest of all report classifications used is one by subject matter. Obviously, all reports concern some subject. It is equally obvious that reports can be classified on the basis of some logical grouping of subjects.

The possibilities of grouping by subjects are almost limitless, being bound only by the infinite differences among report topics. Subject classifications, therefore, could be based on minute differences in content, or they could follow broader and more general lines. For example, in the field of accounting, distinctions in subject matter could provide classifications such as *cost, audit, tax,* and *finance*. But such divisions generally are not practical. A more practical and more widely used subject classification is one that follows broader lines—for example, one based on broad subject fields such as *accounting, management, economics, finance, engineering,* and *marketing*.

Classification by time interval

One often-used means of classifying reports is by the frequency of their occurrence. Some reports are written regularly—daily, weekly, monthly, or annually. These may be referred to as *periodic* reports. Examples of this type are the routine weekly and monthly reports made by salesmen, the periodic summaries of progress in any large-scale operation, and the corporation's typical annual report of operations. Completing this classification are the *special* reports—reports prepared for a special assignment. By special assignment is meant an assignment that is not likely to be repeated with any degree of regularity.

Functional classification of reports

Possibly the most popular classification in use is that based on the function of reports. By this plan, reports are classified by what they do. On this functional basis, it is practical to classify reports into three groups—*informational, examination,* and *analytical.*[6]

As the term implies, the *informational* report is little more than a bare presentation of fact on the subject. It contains no attempt at analysis, and any decision or interpretation that comes from the data presented must be drawn by the reader himself.

The *examination* report carries the problem one step further than does the informational report. In the examination report, in addition to presenting the facts about the problem, the writer analyzes and interprets the data. But the writer's assistance stops here. There is no effort to follow the analysis to the point of concluding or of recommending. Any possible conclusion or recommendation to be derived from the information must be made by the reader, but doubtless the reader will be guided in these efforts by the writer's presentation of fact.

The *analytical* report does all that the examination report does, and more. Like the examination report, it presents and analyzes data. But it also draws conclusions from the data, and when the problem warrants, it may even arrive at recommendations. It is the most complete of all reports, covering all phases of a particular problem. It presents a problem in its entirety, beginning with an

---

[6] Sometimes referred to as problem-solving reports.

orientation and description of the problem, proceeding to the gathering of facts, thence to the analysis and examination of the data, and finally to a presentation of definite steps toward solving or concluding the problem.

Formality as a division criterion

Still another area of variation that lends to classification is the formality of the report. It is easy to see that the same degree of formality is not required in all report situations. A study addressed to an august body such as the United States Senate would logically be strictly formal in its makeup. On the other hand, a report written by one employee for the use of another employee of equal rank might be extremely informal. The differences between these two reports is sufficient to serve as a basis for classification. Two groups are commonly represented in this classification—*formal* and *informal*. By this classification, the term *formal* applies to all those reports that are dressed up physically and are appropriately worded to fit the requirements of a formal occasion. The term *informal* includes all reports with the makeup and wording requirements of an informal occasion. Obviously, there is a hazy and indefinite dividing line between the two types.

Division of reports by physical factors

The physical makeup of reports provides a simple and logical basis for grouping. It may be noted, however, that physical makeup is largely influenced by the formality of the situation and the length of the report. These two factors should be kept in mind as the following classification is reviewed.

At the bottom of the formality and length scale is the *memorandum* report. Generally, it concerns a routine matter that must be transmitted within an organization. In the typical business situation, memorandum reports are written on specially prepared forms. Most common of these forms is one that begins with the headings "To, From, Subject," and has space provided below for informal presentation of the subject. Other variations resemble questionnaires, providing space for routine presentation of specific information.

Short topics with some need for formal or semiformal presentation are frequently submitted in the form of a *letter* report. From all outward appearances, they are letters, with all the physical properties of a typical business letter. They are classified as reports principally because of the nature of their content.

Topics that are of medium or moderate length and have no great need for formal presentation usually are submitted in a form classified as a *short* report. Although there is no one set makeup of the short report, usually it is one that is minus much of the prefatory pages (contents pages, epitome, title fly, and such) associated with more formal works.

At the top of this classification scale in formality and length is the *long* report. Long reports, as the term implies, concern presentations of relatively large problems. As a rule, such topics have some need for formal presentation. The typical long report is well supplemented with prefatory parts. Its contents are carefully organized and marked with captions. It may even require such supplementary parts as an appendix, bibliography, or index.

Writer–reader relationship as a basis for grouping

Classification arrangements have also been constructed on the basis of the relation between reader and writer. Although there is wide variation in the terms used in this division, possibly the most common are *administrative,*[7] *professional,* and *independent.*[8] *Administrative* reports are those reports officially written within a business organization to facilitate operations. *Professional* reports are submitted to an organization by outside specialists. For example, an outside management consultant may be called in to study a particular problem of a company. His findings, when presented in written form, would constitute a professional report. *Independent* reports are written for no particular group or person. Such reports frequently are written by nonprofit research organizations, which write up and publish the results of a project for public review.

Classification by status of authorship

A commonly used classification is one that distinguishes reports by the employment status of their authors. Reports written by those engaged in private business are logically referred to as *private* reports. Reports that originate through employees of public institutions (government groups, professional societies, colleges, and

---

[7] Administrative reports are also known as *internal* reports.

[8] Professional and independent reports are sometimes referred to as *external* reports.

such) are known as *public* reports. Completing this classification is the *independent* report—one written by an individual without the authorization of any public or private group. For example, a research scholar working on his own authority would present his findings in an independent report.

Miscellaneous report types

In addition to the terms used in the preceding classifications, scholars use numerous other terms to describe specific report types. Many in this group are well-known only within the narrow confines of a particular field, industry, or business. A few in this group, however, are so widely used as to warrant special review of them.

The *progress* report is one of the best-known types used in industry. Actually, it is strictly an informational type report. The information it presents is limited to the progress of some undertaking such as the construction of a bridge, an advertising campaign, or the operation of production machinery.

In recent years, much use has been made of the term *justification* report. It is a type of report that presents a decision to a particular problem—usually a short one. The text of the report is devoted to a logical review of the points that affect the decision. This review, of course, justifies the author's decision.

Frequently in report-writing discussion there is reference to the *recommendation* report. A recommendation report is nothing more than a variety of the analytical report referred to previously. Specifically, it is an analytical report that concludes with a recommendation. Another name for this type is the *improvement* report, although some authorities draw minor distinctions between the two terms.

The role of classification in studying reports

As noted previously, the conventional report classifications are useful in describing reports. And they show something of the wide variations that exist in approaches to the subject. It would not be logical, however, to study reports by types, as perhaps these classifications suggest.

In truth, there is little difference in the basic principles used in any good report. With small exception, the basic writing principles, the rules of logical organization, techniques of writing style and tone, and so on, remain the same in all reports. Thus, any plan to study the subject by report types would be plagued with needless repetition. A more workable approach to the subject is one that treats all reports as being integrally related. Such an approach is followed in this book.

QUESTIONS

1. Critically review the definition of reports given in the text. Bring out the key words in this definition, and discuss their significance in the study of report writing.
2. Discuss the role of information in the operation of a business. How do reports fit into this role?
3. Trace the historical development of business reports.
4. Explain the recent increase in emphasis on reports in business. Is this increase likely to continue through the years ahead?
5. Discuss how the ability to write reports may be vital to you in your professional progress.
6. Discuss critically the statistical evidence supporting courses in report writing.
7. Why should students be concerned with report classification?
8. Classify each of the reports described below on the basis of each of the classification schemes described in the chapter. You may make any assumptions that are logical, but include them with your answers.

   a) A building contractor submits a monthly report of the progress made on a large construction project. The reports are four to six pages in length and are sent to those for whom the building is being built.

   b) A marketing consultant submits a 45-page report to a client on a survey he has conducted concerning consumer preferences of certain style goods. The report includes an analysis of findings as well as a recommended course of action for the client.

   c) The supervisor of a certain department in a manufacturing plant writes a two-page report recommending and justifying the firing of a subordinate.

   d) A college professor working as a labor relations consultant to a company writes a report recommending that the company revise its seniority policy. The report consists of 21 pages of text, including tables.

   e) On the first of each month, the supervisor of a production department fills out the blanks on a form designed for reporting inventories of raw materials used in his department.

9. Which of the report classification schemes are most useful? Defend your selection.
10. Discuss critically the author's point of view regarding report classification.
11. Inspect the reports at the ends of Chapters 6 and 7. Classify each by the classification schemes discussed in the chapter.

CHAPTER 2

Determining the problem and planning the investigation

As in all forms of endeavor, orderly and logical procedure is vital to business reporting. Just what this procedure should be in any given instance depends on the nature of the particular problem involved. The problem possibilities are so varied and complex that no uniform and detailed procedure can be given. It is possible, however, to relate a very general procedural guide—one that serves as an over-all plan into which the specific steps required in a given problem may be placed. A description of such a procedural guide follows.

ORIGIN OF A REPORT

Before work on a business report begins there should be a need for information, and someone in a position of sufficient authority should recognize this need. Usually, this someone is not the report writer. More than likely it is someone higher up the administrative ladder—someone in a position to recognize the need and with the authority to have something done about it.

A subjective process

Recognizing needs is not a task for which meaningful instruction can be given. It is a highly subjective process, requiring an intimate knowledge of the subject. Authorities in every field know what topics need further investigation, whereas the novice does not know. A competent chemist, for example, knows what areas of his field need further analysis. So does a physicist, a geologist, or a psychologist. And so does a competent business administrator know the research needs in his field. He knows the boundaries of business knowledge and where these boundaries should be pushed back. He knows his own business and its needs for information. Armed with this knowledge, he subjectively determines the needs for reports.

Two types of needs for reports

Needs for business reports generally are of two types. First, a company may have a special problem to be solved. For example, a company may be faced with problems such as determining which of two machines to buy, why sales in certain districts have dropped, whether a change in inventory method should be made, or what is the root of labor unrest at X Plant. To solve such problems, someone would need to gather all pertinent information, analyze it, and from the analysis arrive at an answer.

A second need for business reports is that of supplying the information a business must have in order to function properly. As noted in Chapter 1, proper functioning of today's complex business organizations requires vast quantities of information—production records, sales statistics, activity descriptions, personnel reviews, and the like. Modern business needs such information to facilitate decision making, to regulate production, to measure progress, and generally to coordinate and control its multiphased operations. Without adequate transmittal of information, modern business could not function. Reports serve as a major medium in transmitting this vital information.

Three ways of assigning reports

The report writer may receive his assignment in one of three basic ways. First, someone or some group may ask specifically for the information. In doing so, they may make the request in writing, usually in the form of a letter or an interoffice memorandum, or they may make it orally. Second, the report situation could be the result of a company's standard operating procedure. As noted previously, many companies require that reports be used to transmit certain types of information within the organization. Third, the writer could originate the report on his own initiative. For example, an administrator may see a problem need, investigate the situation, collect information, analyze this information and write his findings as a record of his work. An employee may see a need for collecting and passing on information. Or an independent researcher may conduct an investigation on a topic of his interest and record his findings for any who might be interested.

DETERMINING THE BASIC PROBLEM

After receiving his assignment, the researcher makes certain that he has the problem clearly in mind. In some situations, this is a simple and routine step, requiring little effort. The researcher may, for example, have worked on similar problems before; he may be intimately acquainted with the specific problem situation; or the problem may be a simple one. In other situations, the problem may be vaguely defined or complex. The more intricate and generally sophisticated such problems are, the more likely the researcher is to misinterpret his objective. It is for problems such as these that the following suggestions for problem determination procedure are given.

Getting the problem clearly in mind

The researcher begins the task of getting the problem in mind by carefully reviewing the information available to him. If the problem was assigned in writing, he carefully studies the written words for their most precise and likely meanings. In this effort, he may want to communicate further with those who originated the problem. If the problem was orally assigned, the researcher probes and questions the authorizer until he is certain of the authorizer's intent. If, perhaps, the problem was originated by the researcher, then he has the task of clearing the thoughts in his own mind.

The informal investigation

Problem determination is not always the task of merely interpreting words. It may well involve a search for hidden meanings and an effort to clear up vague thinking. Thus, at least in the more complex situations the investigator would do well to conduct a preliminary investigation in order to gather the facts to guide him. In addition to helping the researcher understand his problem, an informal investigation provides the foundation of knowledge that guides him through the remaining stages of planning the investigation.

The informal investigation may take many forms. It could involve informal talks with those associated with the problem, with authorities in the field, with colleagues, and the like. It could involve a preliminary review of library material, or perhaps an inspection of company records. In any event, the investigator should review as much of the information available to him as is necessary for him to have a clear understanding of his problem.

Clear statement of the problem

After he has the basic problem clearly in mind, the investigator should put it in writing. Putting the problem in writing is good for many reasons. A written statement is permanently preserved; thus, it may be referred to time and again without danger of changes occurring in it. In addition, other people can review, approve, and evaluate a written statement, and their assistance may sometimes be valuable. Most important of all, putting the problem in writing forces the researcher to do, and to do well, this basic initial task of getting the problem in mind. In this way, this requirement serves as a valuable form of self-discipline.

The problem statement normally takes one of three forms. One is the infinitive phrase: To determine the cause of decreasing sales at store X. Another and equally good form is the question: What are the causes of decreasing sales at store Y? A third and less popular form is the declarative statement. Although somewhat dull and not so solution-oriented as the other two, this form nevertheless gives a good indication of the problem. An example of it is the following: Company X sales are decreasing and it wants to know the cause for this decline.

DETERMINING THE FACTORS

From the problem statement, the investigator turns to the mental task of determining its needs. Within the framework of his logical imagination, he looks for the factors of the problem. That is, he looks for the subject areas that must be investigated in order to satisfy the overall objective. Specifically, these factors may be of three types. First, they may be merely subtopics of the broader topic about which the report is concerned. Second, they may be hypotheses that must be subjected to the test of investigation and objective review. Third, in problems that involve comparisons they may be the bases on which the comparisons are made.

Obviously, this process is a mental one, involving the intricate workings of the mind. Thus, it may be described only in the most general way. The investigator begins the process by applying his best logic and comprehensive abilities to the problem. The same mental processes that helped him to comprehend his problem now should assist him in determining the structure of the solution.

Use of subtopics in information reports

If the problem concerns primarily a need for information, the researcher's mental effort should produce the main areas about which information is needed. Illustrating this type of situation is the problem of presenting for Company X a report that reviews the company's activities during the past quarter. Clearly, this is a routine and informational type of problem—that is, it requires no analysis, no conclusion, no recommendation. It requires only that information be presented. The mental process in this case is concerned simply with determining which subdivisions of the overall subject should be covered. After thoroughly evaluating the possibilities, the investigatior may come up with the following factor analysis.

Problem statement: To review operations of company X from January 1 through March 31.

Factors:
1. Production.
2. Sales and promotion.
3. Financial status.
4. Plant and equipment.
5. Product development.
6. Personnel.

Hypotheses for problems of solution

Some problems by their nature seek a solution. Typically, such problems seek an explanation of a phenomenon or the correction of a condition. In analyzing such problems, the researcher must seek possible explanations or solutions. Such explanations or solutions are termed *hypotheses*. Once they are determined, hypotheses are tested and their applicability to the problem is either proved or disproved.

Illustrating problem analysis for this type of situation is the problem of a department store chain that seeks to learn why sales at one of its stores are dropping. In preparing this problem for investigation, the researcher logically would think of the possible explanations (hypotheses) of the decline in sales. He would be likely to think of more explanations than would be workable, so his task would be one of studying, weighing, and selecting. After such a study session, he may come up with explanations such as these.

Problem statement: Why have sales declined at the Milltown Store?

Factors:
1. Change in competition in the area.
2. Exceptional changes in area economy.
3. Merchandising deficiency.

Logically, in the investigation that follows the researcher would test each of the above hypotheses. Perhaps he would find that one, two, or all apply. Or perhaps he would find that none is logical. Then he would have to advance additional hypotheses for further evaluation.

Bases of comparison in evaluation studies

When the problem concerns evaluating something, either singularly or in comparison with others, the researcher seeks to determine the bases for the evaluation. That is, he seeks to determine what characteristics he will evaluate. In some cases, the procedure may concern more than naming the characteristics. It may include also the criteria to be used in evaluating each characteristic.

The problem of a company that seeks to determine which of three cities would be best for opening a new factory illustrates this technique. Such a problem obviously involves a comparison study of the cities, and the bases for the comparison are the factors that determine success for the type of factory involved. After careful mental search for these factors, the investigator will be likely to come up with a plan such as the following.

Problem statement: To determine whether Y Company's new factory should be built in City A, City B, or City C.

Factors:
1. Availability of labor.
2. Abundance of raw material.
3. Tax structure.

4. Transportation facilities.
5. Nearness to markets.
6. Power supply.
7. Community attitude.

Need for subbreakdown

Each of the factors selected for investigation may have factors of its own. In the last illustration, for example, the comparison of transportation in the three cities may well be covered by subdivisions such as water, rail, truck, and air. Labor may be compared by categories such as skilled and unskilled. These breakdowns may go still further. Skilled labor may be broken down by specific skills: machinists, plumbers, pipefitters, welders, and such. The subdivisions could go on and on, and they should be made so far as it is helpful to the investigator.

The value of this step of finding the factors of the problem is obvious: it serves as a guide to the investigation that follows. In addition, it gives the problem the first semblance of order, and the value of order in any complex process cannot be questioned.

CONSTRUCTING THE RESEARCH PLAN

After deciding what information he needs for his problem, the investigator turns his energies to the task of planning his research. In all but the simplest and most routine investigations, he should construct this plan in step-by-step detail.

The value of a detailed plan is apparent. Certainly, a plan serves to bring order to the investigation, and the larger, more complex investigations cannot be made without order. By thinking out a course of action, the investigator is likely to see the possible errors before he has the chance to make them. A plan serves generally to clarify the investigator's thinking. In addition, it serves as a blueprint to be followed throughout the investigation.

The investigator's plan may be either mental or written. In simple investigations, such as those that require only library research or research through company files, this plan may be made in the mind of the investigator. But when more complex problems are concerned and more complex research techniques are employed, the plan is best written (see illustration at end of chapter). Although the content and arrangement of the written plan need not follow any prescribed pattern, the plan usually is arranged in the order in which the investigation progresses. The following checklist outline shows one acceptable arrangement.

A Suggested Arrangement of the Working Plan

1. The Problem

Statement of the problem; its scope and limitations.

Factors (working hypotheses) or areas of information to be investigated.

Background material.

Limitations to the investigation (money, time, qualified people, etc.).

2. Methodology

Complete yet concise description of how the research is to be conducted.

If secondary research is to be employed: Would include description of basic sources to be consulted. May include a tentative bibliography.

If primary research is to be used: Would consist of a how-to-do-it description that goes through the procedure step by step. Contains sufficient detail to permit one to follow. For a survey, for example, may include topics such as sample design, selecting and training of workers, conduct of investigation, plan for pilot study, controls and checks, and time schedule of work.

3. Handling the Findings

A description of how the finding will be prepared for application to the problem. Covers such activities as editing, classifying, tabulating, and verifying results.

4. Reporting the Results

Any preliminary thinking concerning the procedure to be used in giving meaning to the findings and applying them to the problem. May include a tentative outline and a discussion of approach for final report.

Important as the tenative working plan is to the analysis of a problem, it is unnecessary to discuss it further at this point. Logically, the investigator must be familiar with basic research techniques before he can wisely construct a plan for solving report problems. Chapters 3 and 4 summarize this material.

Illustration of a research plan

A PRELIMINARY SURVEY PLAN

TO DETERMINE EFFECTS OF SURGEON GENERAL'S

SMOKING REPORT ON ATTITUDES

AND PRACTICES

Prepared for

The Research Advisory Board

Mr. Otis Compton, Chairman

Prepared by

William J. Bradford, Director

Division of Research

United States Tobacco Institute

2311 Baker Road

Raleigh, North Carolina

May 30, 1968

This report illustrates the planning that should precede any major investigation. As this plan is preliminary, it does not include the minute details that must be worked out before the study is completed. Although not submitted as a model in all respects, the report does illustrate the orderly and thorough planning that marks the scientific method.

A PRELIMINARY SURVEY PLAN
TO DETERMINE EFFECTS OF SURGEON GENERAL'S
SMOKING REPORT ON ATTITUDES
AND PRACTICES

I. ORIENTATION TO THE PROBLEM AND THE PLAN

A. Authorization of the Project

The following preliminary research plan is submitted May 30, 1968, to the Research

Advisory Board as a means of determining changing attitudes and practices concerning

cigarette smoking since release of the Surgeon General's report. Prepared by William J.

Bradford, Director of Research, this proposal generally conforms to the plan agreed upon

by Mr. Bradford and the Board at their May 15th meeting. As anticipated at this meeting,

some modifications in the plans had to be made. All of these changes, however, were

made with the approval of Mr. Otis Chambers, Chairman of the Board.

B. The Problem of Determining Changes in Smoking Practices and Attitudes

As summarized at the Board meeting the basic problem concerns the general effect

of all anti-smoking reports and campaigns, of which the Surgeon General's report is the

most recent and most significant. Prior to 1962 per capita cigarette consumption increased

steadily. In 1962, however, this trend stopped; and since publication of the Surgeon

General's Report on Smoking and Health the trend has been reversed.

As a result of the downward trend in cigarette smoking, the industry has become con-

cerned about the public's attitude toward smoking. In order to assist the industry in its

planning, the Institute has decided to conduct a national survey. As outlined by the Re-

search Advisory Board of the Institute, the following are the objectives of this survey:

(1) To determine the nature of the actual changes in
smoking practice.

Research plan, continued

(2) To determine any change in attitude toward smoking.

(3) To gather sufficient classification data to permit meaningful analysis and trend projections to be made from (1) and (2) above.

C. General Plan of the Survey

The Institute's own staff will conduct this research, although by prior agreement with Waltham and Associates, the part-time professional interviewers on call for this research firm will be available for conducting the interviews. To get the information needed to meet these objectives, the Institute tentatively appropriated $50,000 for a nationwide survey. Logically, the survey will seek to cover a representative cross-section of the universe involved. Although the number of interviews needed to get reliable results is better answered after the returns are in, the Board did express a desire to work within the funds budgeted for the study.

II. DESIGN OF THE SAMPLE

Proper design of the sample for this problem involves three considerations. First is the question of who is to be interviewed. Second is the question of how many. And third is the selection of procedure to be implemented.

A. Determination of the Universe

Logically, the universe involved in any question concerning cigarette smoking is the entire adult population. For very practical reasons, however, the proposed survey will exclude two groups.

First, all under 18 years of age will be excluded. Although many in this age bracket smoke, they rarely do so with parental knowledge and approval. Since the interviews will be conducted in the home, perhaps in the presence of other members of the family, these young people are not likely to respond truthfully. Should information on opinions and practices of this group be needed, another and different form of survey could be conducted.

Research plan, continued

Second, no rural people will be included in the sample. Obviously, considerable time and travel is consumed in interviewing rural people; and, as noted previously, the survey is being conducted on a limited budget. Also, there appears to be little difference in smoking habits and preferences between rural and urban areas. At least, past surveys tend to bear out this statement. Thus, there is little justification of the disproportionate expense that rural interviews would involve.

B. Area Analysis as Basis for Sample Selection

State economic areas, as developed by Donald J. Bogue and Calvin L. Beale,[1] will serve as the major geographic divisions for the sample design. These areas are relatively homogeneous with respect to a large number of characteristics. The delineation of the areas takes into account demographic, physiographic, and cultural factors. Commercial and industrial activities were taken into account.[2] Used in connection with this book was the Census of Population.

The specific steps recommended for constructing the area sample from this material are as follows:

(1) Assign a percentage[3] of the sample size to each Province as shown in Appendix A, Map 1.

(2) Assign a percentage of the Province sample to each Region.

(3) Assign a percentage of each Region sample to each Subregion as shown in Appendix A, Map 2.

----

[1] Donald J. Bogue and Calvin L. Beale, Economic Areas of the United States, The Free Press of Glencoe, Inc., New York, 1961, 1162 pp.

[2] U.S. Department of Commerce, State Economic Areas, U.S. Government Printing Office, Washington 25, D.C., 1960, p. 7.

[3] All percentages used are based on the segment's percentage of population relationship to the whole.

Research plan, continued

(4) Assign a percentage of each Subregion sample to each State Economic Area as shown in Appendix A, Map 3.

(5) In each State Economic Area, randomly select one city with a population of over 2,500. However, if the State Economic Area is a Metropolitan State Economic Area, make no selection and sample the whole area.

(6) Obtain maps for each city selected. If a Census Tract Map is available, use it; otherwise, obtain a detailed map. Using a random number table, number each block in the city. Choose blocks until the number of blocks chosen equals the number of people to be interviewed.

(7) Instruct interviewers to go, after 6 p.m., to the first house on the right as they move into the area. If for some reason they are unable to interview at the house, the house on each side and the one directly across the street from the original house may serve as alternatives. If an interviewer twice fails to find the respondent, or if the people do not qualify, he may use an alternative. The interviewer interviews whomever answers the door if they are 18 years of age or over. If the person is not 18 years old, the interviewer is to ask for anyone of the household who is over 18.

Selection by this procedure assures a sample which will include the true proportionate share of all economic areas of the nation. Although there is little knowledge available on the effects of economic status on smoking, there is good reason to believe that a proportionate representation by economic status assures a proportionate representation of other characteristics likely to be significant.

C. Determination of Sample Size

Ideal sample size is, of course, determined by the need for accuracy and the practical matter of finances. Tentatively, the recommended sample size is 10,000, although after returns from the pilot study are tabulated there may be need to revise this figure. This estimate is based on commonly used statistical techniques. Assuming the critical

need of the study to concern a dichotomous question with a near-equal split of answers
(the situation requiring the greatest number of interviews), one can apply the test of
the standard error of the percentage. Application of this measure shows that a sample
of 10,000 for such a question would assure with ninety-five per cent certainty a variation from the true value of not more than one per cent. Such a probability appears
to be well within the requirements of this problem.

III. CONDUCT OF THE SURVEY

Although the interviewers to be used are experienced, there still is need for
training and checking them. Not to exercise diligence in these vital areas would
be to invite error.

A. The Training Plan

Because of the need for economy and the widespread geographic location of the
interviewers all training must be handled by mail. A week before the surveys begin,
each interviewer will receive detailed instruction sheets along with the questionnaires
he is to use. The instruction sheets, which will be written after an initial pilot study,
will cover at least the following points:

> (1) The need for following scientific procedure in general
>   and the percentage study in particular.
>
> (2) Procedure for locating interviewees, as previously
>   discussed.
>
> (3) Procedure for determining alternates, as discussed
>   earlier.
>
> (4) Instructions on how to conduct the interview--how
>   to introduce oneself, how to answer respondents'
>   questions, how to record findings, and generally
>   how to handle all problems which will be brought
>   out by the pilot study.
>
> (5) Instructions on proper use of cards in reducing per-
>   sonal effect of answers to classification questions.

Research plan, continued

(6) Proper attire for interviewers (appropriate business wear).

(7) Emphasis on the fact that checks will be made of all interviewers.

(8) Procedure for submitting questionnaires as described below.

B. Questionnaire Collection and Interview Remuneration Procedure as Control Instruments

At the end of each work day the interviewers will mail in all questionnaires completed that day. This practice will enable the office staff to control and evaluate the interviewers. To encourage the interviewer to turn in complete and accurate information, his remuneration will be made only after he turns in the questionnaires and after they have been judged acceptable by the survey editor. In addition to this control measure, there will be a checkback on the interviewers.

C. Checkback to Insure Interviewer Honesty

After the questionnaires are in, every tenth person interviewed will be checked by means of a postal card. This card (see Appendix C) will seek to confirm the interviewer's work. Should the check prove the dishonesty of the interviewer, his services will be terminated and his interviews rejected. Certainly not all of those interviewed will return the cards. However, a sufficient number should return cards to provide an efficient check on the interviewer. In addition, the mere fact that the interviewers know that such a check will be made is assurance that they will comply strictly with the survey instructions.

IV. THE HOME OFFICE OPERATION

As this study is typical of others done by this agency, the home office procedure already is established.

A. Editing to Provide Comparable Information

After the questionnaires come in they will be edited by the staff members assigned
to this task. The editors will follow their usual procedures for detecting discrepancies
and will make corrections whenever possible. Also, with the coordination of the research supervisor they will have the duty of reporting to the research director any errors
or shortcomings in the interviewer's work. In addition, the editors will have the task
of coding the answers and preparing them for tabulation. This last named assignment
will, of course, be coordinated with the electronic data processing director.

B. Electronic Data Processing Tabulation for Accuracy

The data will be tabulated by the IBM 1401 which the Royal Cigarette Company
has made available on a cost-of-operations basis. As this survey is somewhat complex and the analysis will require several cross-classifications, electronic processing
is justified. Especially is it justified in view of the low cost of the equipment in
this instance. Institute personnel will punch all cards on Institute equipment. The
code used for punching will be determined by the research director and editor after
consultation with the data processing personnel.

Through a formal comprehensive report the research director will present the
findings of this study. The report will, of course, contain a tabular summary of
findings. In addition, it will include analyses of all significant findings as well
as any conclusions and recommendations which the data justify. As previously
agreed, each of the member companies of the Institute will receive five copies
of the report. Also by agreement, all companies will give the report confidential
treatment. No company or person will be authorized to divulge any findings,
significant or otherwise, without the majority approval of the Institute members.

Research plan, continued

V. RECOMMENDATION OF A PILOT STUDY

As previously mentioned, this is a preliminary plan; and many of its details need to be worked out. In addition, the plan itself may need to be altered after additional information has been gathered. Much of this work can be facilitated through conduct of a limited-scale pilot study.

For this study, an urban area outside the tobacco belt will be the test city. This study will follow closely and realistically the plan to be used in the actual study. This trial will test the questionnaire. It will provide realistic tests for all interviewer training and checking procedures for the survey plan in general. Approximately 100 interviews will constitute the pilot study.

APPENDIX A
Example of Region and Subregion Divisions Used in Sample Design

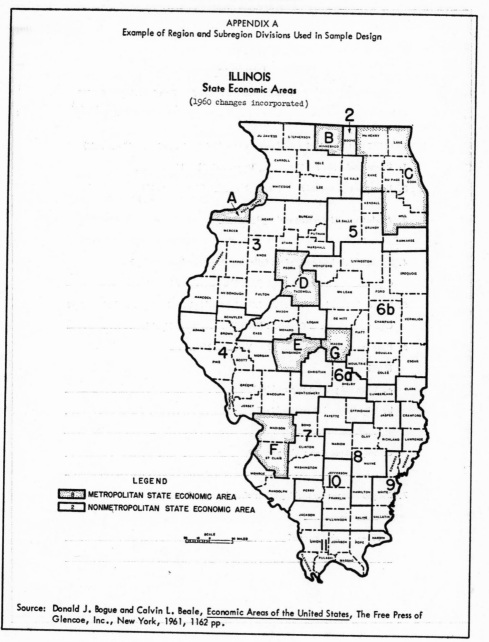

ILLINOIS
State Economic Areas
(1960 changes incorporated)

LEGEND

METROPOLITAN STATE ECONOMIC AREA

NONMETROPOLITAN STATE ECONOMIC AREA

Source: Donald J. Bogue and Calvin L. Beale, Economic Areas of the United States, The Free Press of Glencoe, Inc., New York, 1961, 1162 pp.

<u>APPENDIX B</u>

1968 CIGARETTE SURVEY   Time Interview   CIRCLE
                                             Started:_____   AM   PM

(DO NOT start interviewing until you are sure the interviewee is over 18 years old)

1. Do you smoke now?   Yes_____ (If <u>yes,</u> omit 2)   No _____

2. Have you ever smoked?   Yes____ No ____   (If <u>no,</u> go to 11)
                                               (If <u>yes,</u> omit 4-7)

3. At what age did you start smoking?_____

4. Approximately how many of the following did you smoke yesterday?

   Cigars_____Cigarettes (PACKS)_____ Pipefuls _____

5. Six months ago, how many of the following would you estimate you smoked per day?

   Cigars_____ Cigarettes (PACKS)_____ Pipefuls _____

6. Have you ever stopped smoking?   Yes_____ No_____

   IF YES

   a. When did you last stop smoking?_____

   b. Why did you last stop smoking?_____

   _____

   c. Why did you start smoking again?_____

   _____

7. Did you change your smoking habits after the report?

   Yes_____ No _____

   IF YES--, in what manner?_____

   _____

(Ask questions 8 through 10 only if the interviewee once smoked but does not smoke now)

8. When did you last stop smoking?_____

9. When you did smoke about how many of the following would you estimate you smoked per day?

   Cigars _____ Cigarettes (PACKS) _____ Pipefuls _____

10. Why did you stop smoking?_____

    _____

(Ask of all interviewees)

11. What has been the effect of the Government's report on smoking and cancer on your attitude toward smoking?_____

    _____

    _____

12. About how far did you go in school?_____Grade Level (in years)

13. Sex:_____Male,_____Female

14. USE CARD 1
    Please tell me the letter showing your marital status.

    _____ A. Single
    _____ B. Married
    _____ C. Widowed, divorced, separated, etc.

15. USE CARD 2
    Please indicate which income bracket your family falls in by telling me the letter that shows where you are this year.

PER WEEK		PER MONTH	
_____ A.	Under $20	_____ F.	Under $500
_____ B.	$20 to $39	_____ G.	$500 to $1000
_____ C.	$40 to $79	_____ H.	$1001 to $1500
_____ D.	$80 to $119	_____ I.	$1501 to $2000
_____ E.	$120 or more	_____ J.	More than $2000

16. USE CARD 3
    Please tell me the letter showing the age bracket you are in.

_____ A.	18–21	_____ D.	46–65
_____ B.	22–30	_____ E.	66 and over
_____ C.	31–45		

Research plan, concluded

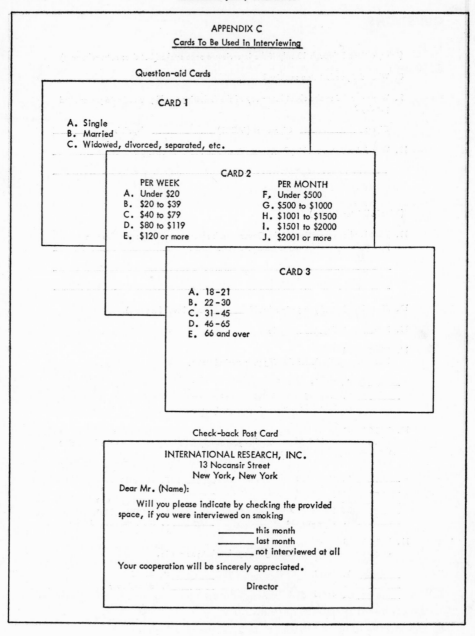

APPENDIX C

Cards To Be Used In Interviewing

Question-aid Cards

CARD 1

A. Single
B. Married
C. Widowed, divorced, separated, etc.

CARD 2

PER WEEK		PER MONTH	
A.	Under $20	F.	Under $500
B.	$20 to $39	G.	$500 to $1000
C.	$40 to $79	H.	$1001 to $1500
D.	$80 to $119	I.	$1501 to $2000
E.	$120 or more	J.	$2001 or more

CARD 3

A. 18-21
B. 22-30
C. 31-45
D. 46-65
E. 66 and over

Check-back Post Card

INTERNATIONAL RESEARCH, INC.
13 Nocansir Street
New York, New York

Dear Mr. (Name):

Will you please indicate by checking the provided space, if you were interviewed on smoking

_____ this month
_____ last month
_____ not interviewed at all

Your cooperation will be sincerely appreciated.

Director

QUESTIONS

1. Discuss the origin of needs for reports in business.
2. Illustrate each of the three basic ways in which a report may be assigned in business.
3. For each of the following problem situations, write a clear statement of the problem and list the factors involved. When necessary, you may use your imagination logically to supply any additional information needed.

   a) A manufacturer of camping equipment wants to know what the future holds for his business.

   b) A major corporation seeks to determine the causes of unrest among its employees.

   c) A motel chain seeks to determine which of three types of roofing it should specify for the new facilities it is building.

   d) In designing an advertising campaign for Brand X automobiles, an advertising agency attempts to learn what brand X customers are like.

   e) Each store manager in a chain of ladies dress shops submits at the beginning of each quarter a summary report of his operations during the quarter.

   f) Each year, Smith Manufacturing Company, Incorporated, prepares a summary of its operations for its stockholders.

   g) A major oil company wants to learn what determines the success of service stations.

   h) A marketing consultant wants to learn how members of a certain economic group spend their incomes.

   i) A grocery chain wants information that will guide it in selecting employees who are most likely to become good and permanent workers.

   j) A professor of advertising seeks to explain what determines the success of magazine advertising campaigns.

4. Select and analyze one problem each for hypothetical situations with factors that consist of (*a*) subtopics of information needed, (*b*) hypotheses, and (*c*) bases of comparison.
5. Point out and discuss the basic differences in approaches to analyzing the problems proposed in question 4.
6. Defend the logic of writing a detailed research plan.

CHAPTER 3

Collecting information: primary research

With the problem analyzed, the investigator has learned just what his objective is. He has learned, too, what information he will need to achieve his objective. Next, as pointed out in Chapter 2, he must make careful plans for collecting the information needed.

FIVE BASIC METHODS OF BUSINESS RESEARCH

In this task the investigator may make use of one or more of five basic research methods.

1. Search through company records.
2. Experimentation.
3. Observation.
4. Interrogation.
5. Use of printed sources.

The last-named method is a means of secondary research. That is, it involves research through printed material for information that someone else has recorded. The remaining four methods are used on occasions when there is insufficient reliable published information on the topic of concern. On such occasions, the investigator must uncover firsthand the information he seeks.

Although there are times when report writers need only to be skilled in one type of research, more often they must know the rudiments of all the major methods. And while it would be well beyond the scope of this book to thoroughly cover all possible methods, nevertheless a quick review of the five basic techniques is appropriate.

SEARCH THROUGH COMPANY RECORDS

The nature of the information needed for each problem will, of course, govern the research procedures employed. As many of today's problems concern various phases of company operations, frequently the information needed for presentation may be gleaned from the company's internal records. Production data, sales records, merchandising information, accounting records, and the like frequently are sources of report information.

Instruction on how to go about gathering and seeking information through company records, however, cannot logically be given. Company records vary much too widely to facilitate orderly discussion of the topic. But one simple standing rule should be kept in mind by those who engage in research through this type of information. On no occasion should research through company records ever be attempted without the close cooperation of one thoroughly familiar with the records concerned, except, of course, when the investigator himself is intimately acquainted with the information.

THE EXPERIMENT

The experiment is a research technique that is becoming more and more useful in the business areas. Originally a technique perfected in the sciences, the experiment is an orderly form of testing. In general, it is a form of research in which an investigator systematically manipulates one variable factor of a problem while holding constant all the others. The investigator measures quantitatively or qualitatively any changes resulting from these manipulations. Then he applies these findings to his problem.

A general form of the experiment is illustrated by an investigation to determine whether a new package design would lead to more sales than the old. In such a case, the investigator might first select two test cities. He would take care to select cities as nearly alike as possible on all characteristics that might affect the problem. First, he would secure information on sales in the two cities for a specified period of time before the experiment. Then, in one city he would introduce the new package design. In the other city, he would continue to sell the product in the old package. For a second specified period of time, he would keep sales records for the two cities. During this time, he would take care to keep constant all other factors that might have some effect on the experiment. Specifically, he would check to see whether advertising, economic conditions, competition, and such remained unchanged in the two cities. In the end, any differences he would find in sales in the two cities he could attribute to the package design.

The need for keeping constant all variables other than those that are the subject of the experiment cannot be overemphasized. All too frequently, this fundamental precept is unwittingly violated, thereby leading to false conclusions. There are times, too, when it is impossible to keep constant all the variables concerned. In such instances, the investigator has no choice but to try in some logical way to compensate for the unwanted variations. At best, conclusions arrived at in such instances should be qualified with an explanation of any variations.

Design of the experiment

Each experiment should be designed individually to fit the requirements of the problem. Nevertheless, the general procedures one may use fall into a few basic designs. A review of the two basic experiment designs provides a workable framework for understanding and using this research technique.

The before–after design. The simplest form of the experiment is the before–after design. In this plan, the investigator selects a test group of subjects. Then, he measures the variable in which he is interested. Next, he injects the experimental factor. After the experimental factor has had time to make its effect, the investigator again measures the variable in which he is interested. The investigator assumes that any difference he finds in the first and second measurements is caused by the experimental factor. Perhaps this diagram more clearly explains the before–after design.

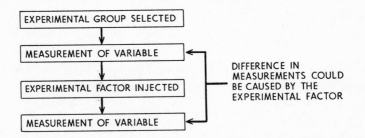

An experiment to determine the effect of point-of-sale advertising in a retail store illustrates this design. First, the experiment group must be selected. In this case, the selection is Y brand of razor blades. Sales of Y blades are recorded for one week in which no point-of-sale advertising is used. Then, the razor blades are displayed with point-of-sale advertising, which, of course, is the experimental factor in this case. Next, sales of Y blades are recorded for a week during which the point-of-sale advertising is used. Any increase in sales from the first to the second week may be explained by the point-of-sale advertising. That is, if 500 packages of blades are sold the first week and 600 the second, one may attribute the increase to the advertising.

This conclusion points up a major shortcoming of this design. The assumption that the experimental factor explains all the difference in sales in the two periods simply is illogical. Sales could change for a number of other reasons—changes in weather, holiday and other seasonal influences on business activity, other advertising, and such. At best, one could conclude only that point-of-sale advertising *could* have some influence on sales.

Controlled before-after design.   In order to account for influences other than the experimental factors, designs more complex than the before–after plan are used. These designs attempt to measure the other influences by means of some form of control. Simplest design of this group is one that may be called the controlled before–after design.

In the controlled before–after design, two groups, rather than one, are selected. One is the experimental group; the other is the control group. Measurements are made in both groups before the experimental factor is injected. Then, the experimental factor is injected into the experimental group only. Next, measurements are made in both groups. The difference between the two measurements made in the experimental group is explained by two possible causes—the experimental factor and other influences. The difference between the two measurements made in the control group is explained only by other influences, for this group was not subjected to the experimental factor. Thus, comparisons of these findings give a measure of the influence of the experimental factor and the other influences. In diagram form, this design appears as follows:

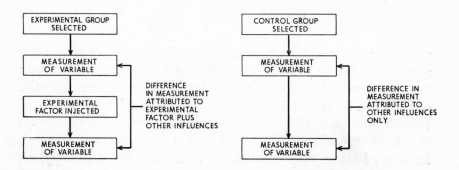

The point-of-sale advertising problem also serves to illustrate this design. First, two groups must be selected. One in Y blades; the second is another brand, X blades. Sales of both blades are recorded for one week. Then, point-of-sale displays are used with Y blades but not with X blades. Next, a record of sales for the following week is made. Comparisons of the sales for the two groups over the two periods give a fair measure of the effect of the experimental factor as well as of outside influences. For example, if 400 packages of X blades were sold during the first week and 450 packages during the second, the 12.5 percent increase is attributed to influences other than the experimental factor. If 500 packages of Y blades were sold the first week and 600 the second, the increase of 100 is attributed to other influences as well as the experimental factor. Other influences accounted for a 12.5 percent increase in X sales, so they can be assumed to have a similar influence on Y sales. An increase of 12.5 percent from 500 is 63. This leaves 37 additional sales, which are explained by the point-of-sale advertising.

High in accuracy but limited in use

The experiment is the most reliable and accurate of all research methods. Developed to a fine degree in the fields of the sciences, this technique greatly reduces the possibility of human error. With this the major source of all error reduced, there is little wonder that through this technique almost all technological and scientific advancement has been made. As a technique in business research, however, the experiment is limited to problems concerned with the effects of change on a given set of conditions. Unfortunately, most business research problems are not of this type.

Illustrations of business experimentation

Examples of the use of experiments in business serve to prove the value of the technique. For years, advertisers have experimented with copy and layout. In determining the best of two or more copy approaches, for example, an advertiser may prepare advertisements that are identical in layout, size, artwork, and the like. Only the copy differs. Then, he takes great care to run the ads under identical conditions. He does all in his power to make certain that the ads are read by comparable groups under comparable conditions. In short, he works hard to keep constant all variables other than copy, although complete success in this undertaking obviously is unlikely. Finally, he measures the effects of the advertisements on sales. It should be noted, however, that this description of procedure has been greatly simplified. Each of the foregoing steps involves numerous complex problems, some of which cannot be definitely solved.

As an additional example, a number of possible production techniques may also be tested through experimentation. Each technique can be tested under similar conditions and for a comparable time period. A measure of the effects of overall production then indicates the relative values of the production methods.

Similarly, experiments may be made to determine the best location of departments or counters in a retail store. Each of the locations in question can be tested in actual practice. Great care is taken to make certain that each location is tested under comparable conditions. In this task, such variables as store traffic, the weather, and the season are considered. In addition to these illustrations, there are the numerous examples of experiments generally associated with the design and production end of a business, but most of these types are well out of the realm of business research.

OBSERVATION AS A RESEARCH TECHNIQUE

Like the experiment, observation is a form of originating research. Although it is not widely used in business, the potential value of observation as a research technique makes it worthy of careful study.

Recording observations of physical phenomena

Simply stated, observation is seeing with a purpose. It consists of watching certain phenomena involved in a problem and recording systematically what is seen. The observer watches the physical phenomena exactly as they occur. He makes no attempt to manipulate them as he would do in an experiment.

This last point is made to clear some confusion that may exist in some minds. Because some experiments do make use of observation in determining results, sometimes the two methods are confused. The distinguishing point to keep in mind is this: in the observation method, the investigator makes no attempt to manipulate data; he observes the real situation. This is the whole procedure. In the experiment, the investigator may use some form of watching to gather his information, but this task is only a part of his whole procedure.

Practical use in business situations

Although observation is not widely used in business research, there is no shortage of illustrations of its possible uses. One good example is that of the shoe manufacturer who seeks to learn the shoe preferences of ladies. To get this information, the manufacturer can use observation to good advantage. Observers stationed at selected traffic centers can record on a simple tally sheet the shoe styles, colors, heel heights, and such as the wearers pass by. Or, possibly, observers can be stationed at points of sale to record actual purchases.

A research group that seeks to learn the canned vegetable brand preferences of different consumer groups may also use observation. Rather than use the conventional and somewhat biased system of asking housewives what brands they buy, the investigator can observe their purchases of canned vegetables at grocery stores. Or they may go to the homes, get permission to check the canned vegetables stored in the pantry, and record the brands they see.

Plan of the observation

The procedure for planning an observation study is not easily summarized, for each problem presents its unique requirement. In general, however, the investigator's planning efforts involve two steps. First, he constructs a recording form. Second, he designs a systematic procedure for observing and recording the information.

The investigator designs the observation recording form through the logical use of his imagination, for the form may be any tabular arrangement that permits quick and easy recording of the information observed. Although observation forms are far from standardized, one commonly used arrangement (see Figure 1) provides a separate line for each observation. Captions at the top of the page mark the columns in which the observer will place the appropriate marks.

In designing the observation procedure, the investigator determines whatever steps are necessary in order to accurately record the observations made. As few problems are likely to have anything in common, again the investigator must make use of his logical imagination. His work perhaps is best explained by illustration. In a problem of determining what style of clothing men wear in a certain city, the plan would have to produce a detailed schedule of observation for all appropriate parts of the city in proportion to the part's influence on the whole. It would specify times for the observations, with provisions made for weather and other complicating factors. It would include detailed observing instructions, telling each observer precisely what to do, and it would cover all possible complications

Figure 1.   Excerpt of a common type of observation recording form

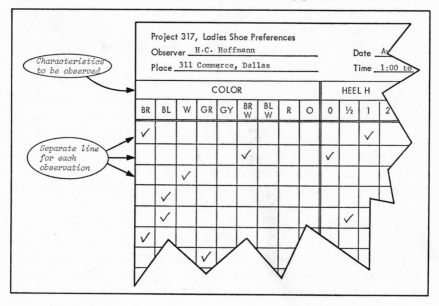

the observer might encounter. It would be so thorough that it would not leave a major question of procedure unanswered.

Possibility of complexities

Although observation in general is a relatively simple technique, it can become complex by the occurrence of various limiting factors. For example, in the aforementioned study of shoe style preferences, observations made at a busy downtown street intersection might differ sharply from those made at a suburban shopping center or at a point across the tracks. Thus, care should be exercised in selecting the sites of observation.

In addition, the actual recording of observations could become complex, particularly when the rate of traffic exceeds the speed of recording. Too, time would have to be reckoned with. Styles of wear differ with the hour of the day and with the season. The effects of the weather on shoe wear would add still further to the complex situation—and on, and on. There is no formula that can be used to overcome such problems. Only the foresight and logic of the investigator can be used to cope with the situation.

Merits and demerits of observation

Like the experiment, the method of observation greatly reduces the possibility of human error. Thus, the chief advantage of the technique is in its objectivity and resulting accuracy. Although it may be claimed that the observer is human and thereby subject to typical human shortcomings, he is likely to be an individual well trained in objective study and in the subject matter of the study. Also, the accuracy of his work can be enhanced through a simple system of checks and controls.

The high objectivity and accuracy of observation are partially offset by two major limitatons of the technique. First, observation is limited to only those physical phenomena that can be seen. It is especially limited in studies of human behavior. It cannot be used to pry into the human mind for information on attitudes, opinions, and the like. The technique is useful only for recording overt acts. But it may sometimes be possible to interpret the psychological significance of the overt acts. This practice, however, is highly dangerous, for seldom is there sufficient grounds to conclude that all overt actions have definite psychological explanations.

Second, the technique can be costly when compared with other methods. Its cost is largely set by frequency of occurrence of the phenomena to be observed. If the thing to be observed occurs frequently, cost of observing is low. For example, observing characteristics of ladies' shoes on a busy downtown street would keep the observer busy. Most subjects of observation, however, do not occur so rapidly. Some, in fact, are so infrequent in occurrence as to make costly any attempt to observe them. As an illustration, an observer stationed at a jewelry store to record actions concerning the sale of diamond rings would be likely to spend many idle and costly hours waiting.

RESEARCH THROUGH INTERROGATION

Certain types of information may be gathered simply by asking questions. The techniques of interrogation, as these methods of research may generally be referred to, vary greatly. In some instances, interrogation may comprise conversations with a few authorities in the field of inquiry. This type of research is a preliminary step in many research problems, but it could constitute the whole of the research work. More often, however, interrogation follows systematic and scientific procedure. The people interrogated are carefully determined through exacting statistical procedure, generally referred to as sampling. As a rule, these investigations follow a uniform list of questions (the questionnaire). The questioning itself may be conducted through various means—personal interview, the telephone, and the mail being the most common.

Sampling theory as a basis for interrogation

The theory of sampling forms a basis for most types of interrogation. This commonly accepted theory should require little explanation, for already it is an accepted basis of logical procedure in many areas of work. Buyers of grain, for example, judge the quality of the grain by examining a small part of the whole. Buyers of cotton base their bids on the quality of a bit of cotton cut from each bale. Judges of jelly at a county fair base their decisions on the taste of a small portion of each entry. All these examples illustrate the theory of sampling. Behind each of the acts is the belief that the part inspected is representative of the whole. This belief, with some refinement, illustrates the theory of sampling.

The general law of sampling. More specifically stated, the theory of sampling is based on the general law that a sufficiently large number of items taken at random from a larger number of items will have the characteristics of the larger group. It should be noted that the law is applicable only when the whole is comprised of a large number of items. But it is only when the whole is large that there is real need for short cuts in determining overall characteristics. Small quantities can be analyzed item by item. From the remaining words of this general law, two fundamental principles are logically derived.

Principle of sample reliability.   First of these is the principle that samples taken must be sufficient in number to be reliable. Small samples are apt to contain chance errors. But as the number of items selected increases, these errors tend to offset. This tendency for the sample errors to level off is called stabilization. Thus, in all sampling studies as many items should be observed as are needed to produce stable results.

A researcher may use various methods to determine sample reliability. Each of these methods tests reliability of only one finding of the investigation at a time. That is, in a survey covering 10 questions, 10 tests for sample reliability could be made—one for each question. Although it is seldom necessary to test every question in such a study, the investigator should test a sufficient number to assure a reasonable degree of reliability for the whole. At least, he should test the questions that require the most accuracy.

Among the methods available are some statistical as well as some less technical techniques. As the statistical techniques are beyond the scope of this book (the statistically inclined reader may want to consult Appendix B for a summary of this method), a review of one of the less technical ones is appropriate. This one is the cumulative frequency test.

The investigator begins the cumulative frequency test by arranging his questionnaires in random order and dividng them into equal groups of 50, 100, or whatever number appears to be appropriate. Then he counts for the first group the answers to the questions he has selected for the test and he works out the percentage (or mean) for his total. He then counts the answers for the second group, adds this total to the preceding group total, and computes the percentage (or mean) for the cumulative total. He does the same with the third group and with each succeeding group until all groups are included. Finally, he plots the cumulative percentages (or means) on a grid.

At first, the percentages are likely to plot in an erratic pattern. As the group totals are accumulated, however, the plot will tend to stabilize. When the plot line straightens out and begins to run parallel to the base line, one may assume that the answer is reliable.

To illustrate this technique, assume the case of a survey of 1,200 housewives. The investigator feels that the one most significant question in his questionnaire is one asking whether the respondent prefers Product A to Product B. Obviously, this is a question with a simple yes, no, and no opinion answer.

In applying the cumulative frequency test, the investigator decides to work with groups of 100, giving him 12 test groups. And he decides to plot the yes answers. (He could just as easily apply the test to the no answer.) In the first group of 100 questionnaires, he finds 74 yes answers, or 74 percent. He plots this percentage on a grid. In the next group of 100, he finds 56 yes answers. When he adds this group total to the preceding group total, he has a cumulative total of 130 yes answers, or 65 percent. He then plots this percentage on the grid. For the third group, he counts 59 affirmative answers. His cumulative total now becomes 189, for a percentage of 63, which he plots on his grid. As shown in the accompanying chart and table (Figure 2 and Table 1), he continues to record, cumulate, and plot his findings. As he cumulates his 10th total and plots the final cumulative percentage, he knows from visual inspection of his plot that he has a reliable finding.

Principle of representativeness. The second principle derived from the general law of sampling is that the sample must be representative of the universe (the group under study). Large numbers alone do not ensure representativeness. A basic error in selection favoring one segment of the universe is apt to continue, regardless

Figure 2. Cumulative frequencies plotted (illustrating tendency to flatten out as stability reached)

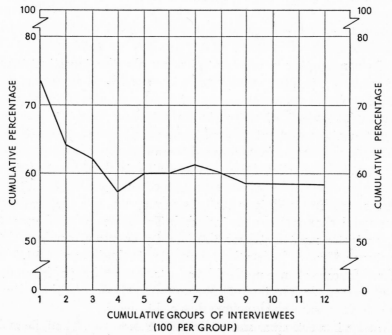

CUMULATIVE GROUPS OF INTERVIEWEES
(100 PER GROUP)

TABLE 1

APPLICATION OF CUMULATIVE FREQUENCY TEST

(12 groups of 100, yes answers to product preference question)

Group Number	Yes Answers in Group	Cumulative Yes Answers	Cumulative Percentage of Yes Answers
1...............74		74	74
2...............56		130	65
3...............59		189	63
4...............44		233	58
5...............66		299	60
6...............57		356	60
7...............68		424	61
8...............52		476	60
9...............49		525	58
10...............57		582	58
11...............63		645	58
12...............56		701	58

of how many individuals are included in the sample. A sample selected from telephone directories, for example, would contain a disproportionately small number of very low-income families. And this disproportionate distribution would be present regardless of whether the sample selected includes 100, 1,000, or 10,000 families.

The techniques of sampling

In constructing a representative sample, the investigator may select from a number of basic techniques. Each of these techniques has its advantages in certain situations and its limitations in others. The investigator's prime task in designing a sample is to select the one technique best suited for his problem and to adapt this technique to the special conditions of his case.

Random sampling. Random sampling is the ideal and is the technique assumed in the general law of sampling. By definition, it is the sampling technique that gives every member of the universe an equal chance of being included. To assure equal chance, the investigator must first have the identity of every member of the universe. Usually, he has this information in the form of a list. Then, through some chance method he selects the members of his sample.

For example, the investigator may record on individual slips of paper the names of every member of his universe. Next, he places the slips in a container and mixes them thoroughly. Then, he makes a chance drawing of a predetermined number of the slips. Since each slip in the container has an equal chance of being drawn, the resulting sample is random.

Stratified random sampling. A special form of random sample is made by dividing the universe into subgroups and making a random selection within these subgroups. Stratified random sampling, as this technique is called, ensures the investigator that each subgroup is represented in the sample in whatever proportion is appropriate. Usually, this desired proportion is the actual share of the universe the subgroups comprise. In some cases, however, an investigator may choose to get a disproportionately large number from a small subgroup in order to get meaningful findings about the subgroup. In such instances, he would take care to deflate this disproportionately large subgroup sample to its true portion of the universe when he is concerned with statistics on the whole group rather than the subgroup.

A problem of determining religious preferences of a group of workers illustrates this technique. In constructing a sample for this problem, the investigator might first divide his list of workers by religious affiliation—Catholic, Methodist, Baptist, Church of Christ, and so on. Then, he would draw a random sample from each of these denomination groups. He would take care that the number drawn from each subgroup was the same as that subgroup's share of the whole. That is, if 31 percent of the universe was Catholic, 31 percent of his sample would be Catholic. If 22 percent of his universe was Baptist, 22 percent of his sample would be Baptist, and so on throughout the sample. Thus, his final sample would have the same makeup as the whole.

Systematic sampling. Although not random in the strictest sense, systematic sampling is random for all practical purposes. It is the simple technique of taking selections at constant intervals (every *n*th unit) from a list of the universe. The interval used is, of course, a matter of the size of the list available and the sample size desired. For example, if an investigator wants a sample of 1,000 from a list of 10,000, he selects every 10th member of the list.

The technique approaches randomness if the investigator makes his first selection purely a matter of chance. Thus, the investigator in the aforementioned problem may by some equal chance process determine whether his sample will begin with number 1, 2, 3, and so on. If, for example, number 7 were selected, the sample would be made up of the 7th, 17th, 27th, 37th . . . 9,997th names on the list.

And it could reasonably be assumed that all numbers had an equal chance of being selected.

Frequently, systematic sampling and the other random techniques are difficult or impossible to use. Obviously, one can use these techniques only when he has a list of all members of the universe. But in actual practice, such a list is not likely to exist. Even if complete lists were available for a particular group, the usefulness of the list would be short-lived. Because people are forever moving about and changing, lists quickly become obsolete. Thus, the investigator frequently must find a technique that substitutes for a random one.

Quota sampling. A nonrandom technique that assures that a sample will have the same characteristics as the universe is quota sampling (or controlled sampling). This technique may be used whenever a proportionate makeup of characteristics of the universe is available. Knowing the proportionate makeup of the universe, the investigator can design his sample so that it has the same makeup of characteristics. Specifically, he sets quotas for each characteristic, and he makes certain that each quota is met. Of course, the characteristic selected for determining proportionality should have some bearing on the problem.

For example, suppose an investigator wants to survey a college student body of 4,000 and that he decides to use a sample of 400. He may derive quotas for the sample as follows:

	Number in Universe	Percent of Total	Number to Be Interviewed
Total student enrollment	4,000	100	400
Sex:			
Men students	2,400	60	240
Women students	1,600	40	160
Fraternity, sorority membership:			
Members	1,000	25	100
Nonmembers	3,000	75	300
Marital status:			
Married students	400	10	40
Single students	3,600	90	360
Class rank:			
Freshmen	1,600	40	160
Sophomores	1,000	25	100
Juniors	800	20	80
Seniors	400	10	40
Graduates	200	5	20

Area sampling. One of the most widely used sampling techniques is area sampling. Area sampling consists of drawing the units for the sample in a series of stages. The units used normally are successively smaller divisions of geographic areas. For example, in drawing an area sample for a certain city, the investigator begins by dividing the city into homogeneous districts. (Census as well as *Sales Management* data provide very useful information for this division.) Next, through some random process he selects some of these districts for his sample. Then, he divides each of the districts selected into subdistricts. (He may use city blocks for this division.) Next, he again uses a random selection technique to select some of the blocks in each district. Finally, for each of the blocks drawn he lists the household units, and again through a random process he selects some of these households. The households selected make up his sample.

A survey of the workers in an industry illustrates the flexibility of this technique. In constructing an area sample of this universe, the researcher could first get a list of the individual companies in the industry. Then, for the first step in the selection process, he could randomly select some of them. Next, he could use the organization units (divisions, departments, sections, or such) of the companies selected as the bases for the next random selection, and he could randomly select some of them. Finally, in each of the divisions selected he could randomly select specified numbers of workers. Those individuals selected would make up the sample.

Construction of the questionnaire

Most orderly interrogation follows a definite plan of inquiry. Usually, this plan is worked out in a printed form called the questionnaire. The questionnaire is simply an orderly arrangement of the questions and information needed, with appropriate spaces provided for answers. But simple as the questionnaire may be in finished form, it is the subject of careful planning. It is, in a sense, the outline of the analysis of the problem. In addition, it must be constructed so as not to violate certain fundamental rules. These rules are many, and sometimes they vary with the problem. The more general and by far the more important ones follow.

Avoid leading questions. An ever-present possibility of error in questionnaire construction is the leading question. A leading question is one that in some way suggests an answer. Violations of this rule range from the obvious and deliberate attempts to distort truth in the results to the subtle and innocent violations. An illustration of obvious attempts to lead the respondent are questions of the type,

"Is Ivory your favorite soap?" The question leads the respondent's mind toward favoring Ivory. Many people would answer yes, whereas, if they were asked simply, "What is your favorite brand of bath soap?" they may give another brand.

On the more subtle side are those leading questions that may not at first glance appear to be leading. Foremost in this group is the checklist—an arrangement for easy recording of answers by listing the most likely answers. Unless all likely answers have been included in the checklist, some bias will be present. The respondent's memory may be assisted by the list of possible answers, whereas if he were left entirely to his own thoughts, an entirely different answer might be given. If a checklist is used, plenty of space should be left for other answers a respondent may want to fill in.

Subtle bias may also be brought into a questionnaire by any hint that may name or imply the group conducting the study. As a rule, people are inclined to be agreeable. Thus, they may tend to give the answers they believe the investigators would like to receive.

Make the questions easy to understand. Questions not clearly understood by all respondents lead to error. In other words, one simply cannot supply information unless he knows what information is wanted. Unfortunately, it is difficult to determine in advance just when the question is not clearly understood, for few writers can see the error in their own wording. Possibly the best means of detecting such errors in advance is through preliminary testing of questions before they are used for intense investigation. It is possible, however, to be on the alert for a few general sources of confusion.

Sometimes, this confusion is the result of a general awkwardness and vagueness of expression. The ridiculous question, "How do you bank?" well illustrates this type of error. Who other than its author knows the question's meaning?

Question confusion may also be traced to the use of words that are not understood by the respondent—technical words, unusual words, words with multiple meanings, and the like. A good illustration of this error is the question, "Do you read your house organ regularly?" The trouble here lies in the words used. The term "house organ" is technical and is not likely to be understood by those outside the publications field. "Regularly" is a word of multiple meanings. Some who answer the question may consider anything short of 100 percent as not regular; others may have in mind a proportion much smaller.

Sometimes, two questions may be unintentionally combined into one. Although the second question usually requires subtle detection, it nevertheless leads to error. In some instances, some respondents may see one question; some may see the other; and some may see both. To say the least, confusion would abound. An illustration is the question, "Why did you buy a Ford?" The answer may involve two questions: "What do you like about Fords?" and "What don't you like about the other makes of automobiles?"

Avoid questions that touch on personal prejudices or pride.   For reasons of pride or prejudices, people cannot be expected to answer accurately in certain areas of information. In these areas are such topics as age, income status, morals, and personal habits. How many people, for example, would answer no to the question, "Do you brush your teeth daily?" How many middle-aged spinsters would give their ages correctly? How many solid citizens would admit to fudging a bit on their tax returns? The answers are obvious.

But one may ask, "What if such information is essential to the solution of the problem?" The answer is to use more devious means of inquiry. In determining age, for example, the investigator could first ask for dates of high school graduation, marriage, or the like. Then, from this information he could approximate age. Or he could approximate through observation, although such a procedure would be wise only if the investigator needed broad categories. He could approximate income by first getting such harmless information as occupation, residential area, and standard of living. Admittedly, such techniques are sometimes awkward and difficult. But they could not help but improve on the biased results that interrogation would bring about.

Stick to facts as much as possible.   Although some studies must involve opinion, it is far safer to seek fact when possible. Human beings simply are not accurate reporters of their opinions. Oftentimes, they are limited in their ability to express themselves. Frequently, they report opinions erroneously simply because they have never before been conscious of having these opinions.

Usually, when opinions are needed it is safer to record facts and from these facts judge the thoughts behind them. This technique, too, is hazardous, for it is only as good as the investigator's judgment. But a logical analysis of fact made by a trained investigator is preferable to a spur-of-the-moment opinion.

One frequently occurring violation of this rule is made through the use of generalizations. Respondents are sometimes asked to generalize an answer from a large number of experiences over time. Although this fallacy touches on other rules, it nevertheless fits here. The question, "Which magazines do you read regularly?" serves as good illustration. Aside from the confusion that the word "regularly" would bring about, and the fact that the respondent's memory may be taxed, the question forces the reader to generalize. Would it not be better, for example, to phrase the question thus: "What magazines have you read this month?" The question could then be followed by an article-by-article check of the magazine to determine the extent of readership.

Ask only for information that can be remembered.   The memory of all humans is limited. So it is important that the questionnaire asks only for information that can be easily remembered. In order to determine just what can be remembered, a knowledge of certain fundamentals of memory should be understood.

Recency is the foremost fundamental. Insignificant events occurring within the past few hours may be remembered at the moment. Some of them may be forgotten a day later. Possibly none will be remembered with the passing of a month. One might well remember, for example, what he had for lunch on the day of inquiry. Possibly he would remember what he had eaten a day, or two, or three previously. But he would be unlikely to know what he had eaten for lunch one year earlier.

Significant events may be remembered over long periods of time. This second fundamental of memory is easily illustrated. One may long remember his first day of school, the day of his marriage, an automobile accident, a Christmas Day, and the like. In each of these examples there was an intense stimulus—a requisite for retention in memory.

Some fairly insignificant facts may also be remembered over long periods of time. Usually such information is retained in the mind through a third memory fundamental—association with something significant. Although one would not normally know what he had for lunch a year earlier, for example, he might remember such information if that date happened to be his wedding day, Christmas Day, or his first day at college. Obviously, it is not the meal itself that stimulates the memory. Rather, it is the association of the meal with something more significant.

Plan the physical layout with foresight.   The overall design of the questionnaire should be planned to facilitate recording, analyzing, and tabulating the answers. Three major considerations are involved in this planning.

First, sufficient recording space must be allowed for all answers. When practical, a system for checking answers may be set up. Such a system must always provide for all possible answers, including conditional answers. For example, a direct question may provide for three possible answers: Yes——, No——, and Don't know——.

A second layout objective is to provide adequate space for identification and description of the respondent. Information such as the age, sex, and income bracket of the respondent is sometimes vital to the analysis of the problem and should be recorded. In other instances, little or no identification is necessary.

A third problem of design common to most questionnaires is that of determining the sequence of questions. Sometimes, there may be psychological advantages for starting with a question of high interest value. In some instances, it may be best to follow some definite order of progression. Frequently, some questions must precede others because they help to explain the others. Whatever the individual case requirements may be, however, the best possible sequence is determined only through careful and logical analysis.

Research by personal interview

Of the numerous techniques that may be used in interrogation, the most common one is the personal interview. Personal interviewing, as the terminology implies, consists simply of gathering information through formal oral questioning. Questions are asked of a group determined by the rules of sound sampling previously described. In large surveys, the questions are asked by a carefully supervised field force of interviewers, but in small studies a single investigator may do all of the work. Usually, the interview follows the pattern of questions established in the questionnaire. In recent years, however, informal, conversational type questioning by skilled interviewers has been used, but this technique (depth interviewing) is in the field of the psychologist and is beyond the scope of this book.

Need for care in interviewing. Just as with any technique in orderly research, personal interviewing should not be conducted haphazardly. Instead, great care constantly needs to be exerted to assure accurate returns. And although the need for precautionary steps is not likely to be the same for any two problems, some common safety measures should be considered.

One of these safety measures concerns the need for extreme care in selecting the people to make interviews. Foremost of the requisites of the interviewer is the willingness to work, honesty, and general intelligence. In addition, the interviewer should be well suited to meet the type of people concerned. A city man, for example, may not be able to get so much out of a farmer as a man who can talk the farmer's language. In selecting just the right individual for the task, frequently it is wise to first determine the job requirements in terms of characteristics such as age, physical appearance, social background, education, and sex. Each problem, of course, will differ in these requirements.

A second safety measure is to take great care in having all interviewers follow the same procedure. Variation in the opening introduction, the order and technique of questioning, explanations to the questions, and the like could affect the accuracy of the answers. Further, in instances when the interviewers are required to observe and interpret in addition to asking questions, lack of uniformity in procedure would be hazardous. Uniformity in procedure can be accomplished best through the foresight and planning of the chief investigator. All probable situations the interviewers may encounter should be considered and instructions for covering them made. These instructions must be understood by all those who use them. In most instances, the plan is put in writing as a detailed and simple instruction sheet distributed to all the investigators.

Even if investigators are selected carefully and clear instructions are prepared, the chances of major errors are good. Most such errors are made by the investigators, either intentionally or unintentionally. Investigators' errors are best controlled by a third safety measure—adequate supervision. Only in exceptional cases should the investigator be allowed to work without supervision. In large research operations, the investigators are separated into teams, and a supervisor is selected for each group. It is the supervisor's task to teach his team the techniques of interviewing. He explains to them the written instructions. He makes assignments, gives out advice, and generally controls work standards. And, most important, he checks the work of each interviewer at regular intervals. Were it not for such checks, a lazy or dishonest investigator could wreck the accuracy of the investigation.

Strong and weak points of the personal interview.   Like all research techniques, personal interviewing is properly used only in certain instances. Just when conditions are right for its use is best determined by a review of its limitations and strong points.

Personal interviewing is best used when the group to be sampled is located in a compact geographic area. If much time is lost traveling between interviews, the technique can become expensive. A sample taken from the entire population of a large city, for example, would be relatively inexpensive. A sample of the tree surgeons of the United States, on the other hand, would require much expensive travel between interviews.

The speed and expense with which interviews may be made is additionally controlled by the accessibility of the subjects. If interviews can be made at random on a busy street corner, costs will be low. But if the investigators must work their ways into the busy offices of doctors, lawyers, or business executives, costly time will be spent in waiting.

Only certain types of information can be gathered through the personal interview. Largely, the technique is limited to factual data that can be remembered. But opinion surveys and interpretive studies have also made use of personal interviewing. These two types of studies are criticized because they involve hazardous human interpretation. But usually such information cannot be gathered by any other means.

Inaccurate answers sometimes are recorded through personal interviewing. In most groups, there are a few chronic jokers who willfully distort their answers. Then there are those people who, for reasons of bias, give the answers that tend to elevate their positions, please the interviewers, or support their own prejudices. It is a general practice to eliminate these respondents from the sample when they are discovered. But the fact that there can be no certainty of detecting all such errors serves to limit the accuracy of the technique.

Possibly the greatest of all limitations of personal interviewing is the human factor. It is human to err; thus, when a human being asks questions of another human being, the possibilities of error are great. This deficiency is corrected, in part, because one of the human beings involved—the interviewer—may be well trained in objective and accurate reporting. There is little question that the limitations of the human factor vary with the quality of the interviewer.

The telephone as a research medium

Interrogation by telephone has become increasingly popular in recent years. Actually, it is a form of personal interview. But the technique has distinct limitations and advantages that sharply distinguish it from personal interviewing.

Advantages of telephone interviewing. Telephone interviewing is particularly commendable for its speed. It can quickly reach large numbers of people, for it loses little time between interviews. And because of the possibility for speedy work, its cost per interview can be reduced. Unless the group being surveyed is located in compact geographic areas, however, cost is likely to rise. Obviously, long-distance calls would not be advisable in most instances.

With telephone interviewing, a truly random sample becomes a possibility, provided that telephone subscribers make up all of the group being studied. When all of the group is known, it becomes a simple process to devise a representative sample of the whole. The exactness of procedure allowed in such instances is far higher than it is in instances when the group to be studied cannot be so clearly defined.

In reaching certain select groups, however, the telephone saves valuable time. With groups such as lawyers, doctors, and business executives, personal interviewers often spend long and costly hours working for appointments and waiting in outer offices. With the telephone, the same investigator may be able to make the interview in a fraction of the time.

Disadvantages of telephone interviewing. The technique is not all good, however. In fact, its limitations make its use prohibitive in many studies.

Foremost of the limitations is that the telephone subscribers are not truly representative of the whole of American society. Not all families have telephones. Although the condition is improving rapidly, the low-income group is not proportionately represented. Thus, any study of the whole of society could not make use of the telephone method.

Telephone interviewing is limited in the amount of information that can be obtained. Only in rare instances is it likely that a long questionnaire can be covered. The number of questions that can be asked by telephone, however, varies with the subject and the respondents.

In addition, the telephone method does not allow observation, which sometimes is necessary to determine economic condition of the respondent or to judge his sincerity. Similarly, explanations of questions are made much better when facial expressions and gestures can be seen.

Finally, widespread use of telephones for selling and promotion as well as for research has turned many people against such practices. It is simple for these people to hang up the receiver without answering questions.

Interrogation by mail

A third popular form of interrogation is the use of mail question-naires. In this technique, rather than ask questions personally or by telephone the investigator simply mails the questionnaires to the respondents. He then hopes that a good number of those receiving the questionnaires will write in the answers and mail back the questionnaires. Usually, the questionnaire is accompanied by a let-ter to explain the purpose of the study and by a stamped return envelope.

Mail survey advantages. The mail questionnaire has strong ad-vantages, two outstanding: (1) wide geographic coverage is possi-ble at (2) comparatively little cost. For these two reasons, the method is particularly good in reaching small and widely scattered groups. A widely scattered group such as United States tree sur-geons, for example, could be reached for personal interviewing only with great loss of time and travel expense. Telephone interrogation likewise would be costly in reaching them. Chances are the mails would be the most economical method of the three.

There is some reason to believe that the mail questionnaire, by eliminating some of the human element, tends to eliminate some of the human error in research. Whereas the telephone and personal interview methods involve two human beings in each interrogation, the mail method involves only one. This one, however, is likely not to be skilled in objective and accurate reporting. Thus, a good possibility of human error remains.

Questionnaires that require care and time in answering may be answered more accurately by mail than by other methods. Particu-larly is this true if the topic of study is highly specialized and is high in the interest of the respondents. Too often, personal interviews are rushed by time conflicts of one kind or another. Mail questionnaires, on the other hand, may be answered at the leisure of the respond-ent.

Like the telephone, the mail questionnaire encounters little diffi-culty in entering doors not easily accessible to personal interview-ers. But, of course, entry alone does not assure an answer.

A final advantage is that the mail questionnaire lends to sound sampling technique, provided that mailing lists available are repre-sentative to the group to be studied. As is pointed out in the following section, however, the selection of a sound sample for mailing does not assure a sound sample of returns.

Weaknesses of the mail questionnaire. Offsetting these advantages are some significant weaknesses of the mail questionnaire. In many instances, these weaknesses are strong enough to make the method impractical.

One such disadvantage is the possibility of biased or nonrepresentative returns. Although it is true that questionnaires may be mailed to a representative sample scientifically drawn from the group under study, unfortunately not all those who receive questionnaires can be expected to return them. As a rule, questionnaires are most likely to be returned by the people who feel strongly in one way or another toward the topic of study. Usually, such people are not representative of the group under study. Thus, the representative quality of the original mailing list is likely to be lost.

The mail questionnaire, although inexpensive in problems when wide geographic coverage is necessary, can be quite costly. For example, assuming that the cost of each questionnaire mailed (including postage two ways, processing, handling, and cost of stationery) is a conservative 15 cents, a return of 10 percent (about average) would mean a cost of $1.50 per return. A return of 5 percent would raise the cost to $3.00. Such returns and even lower are not uncommon. On the other hand, with some select groups and with a problem in their fields of interest, much higher returns and a resulting lower cost may be expected.

Like the telephone method, the mail survey affords no opportunity for observation. And observation is sometimes essential in obtaining information like age, economic status, and nature of employment. Similarly, the elimination of personal contact in turn eliminates the possibility of explaining and interpreting questions.

Still another disadvantage of the mail questionnaire is the possibility of its slowness. The mails do not work instantaneously. Nor do respondents all reply without delay. But even though the mail method may not be a quick means of finding an answer, it may be relatively fast in some instances. Certainly, the mails would be a faster means of reaching a small and widely scattered group than would personal interviewing.

The panel survey

A special form of interviewing is the panel survey. This research method involves interviewing the same group of people more than once on the same subject. Frequently, the panel is a continuing study with the same group serving an indefinite period of time.

As in conventional interviewing, the researcher in a panel survey forms a group of people who can give information on his problem. He may form the group in two general ways. First, if his problem is the usual type concerning the action, feelings, or reactions, of a universe, the researcher may use conventional sampling techniques in forming his group. In a problem to determine consumer preferences for laundry detergents, for example, he may follow quota, random, area, or any other standard technique in constructing a sample of the consuming public. Second, in special cases when the investigator seeks expert opinion rather than information from the public, the researcher may form his panel through careful and subjective selection. A national manufacturer, for example, may carefully select a panel of psychologists to help predetermine public reaction to advertising appeals, product designs, and sales techniques.

In practice, two general forms of the panel interview are used. One is in a sense a form of experiment. In it, the researcher interviews his panel on the subject of concern. Then, he makes the phenomenon of the problem occur. Finally, he makes another interview with the same group to detect any changes brought about by the phenomenon. To illustrate, a panel group might be interviewed on its feelings relative to a certain company's public image. Next, the company might begin an intensive public relations campaign (the phenomenon). After sufficient elapsed time, the researcher could again interview the panel. Any changes in their answers from the first to the second contact might be explained by the public relations campaign.

The second and more popular form of panel is the continuing study. In this form, the participants serve as a sounding board or as a means of providing continuing consumer (or other) data. The Marketing Research Corporation of America, for example, gets information monthly from its standing panel of families on such topics as expenditures by product, by brand, and by geographic area.

Perhaps the most significant advantage of the panel is that it permits measurements of change over time. In addition, it can be a relatively inexpensive survey form, since usually it involves relatively small groups. Also, because the sample group remains available and willing for interviewing, information can be successfully gathered by this technique.

Of the disadvantages of the panel survey, two stand out. One is the tendency of the group selected to become nonrepresentative. The panel may be representative of the universe at the time it is selected. But its representativeness may change quickly. A panel made up of married couples representing all ages would be without young couples as time passed by. Of course, the problem is not so important in short-run studies. Also, this shortcoming can be offset by adding new members as the old drop off.

A second disadvantage of the panel is the artificial effect panel membership has on the members. Members are likely to become more self-conscious of the subject matter involved and thus become atypical. Or they tire of the questioning and become somewhat less accurate and comprehensive in their reporting.

QUESTIONS

1. List some of the topics of information that research through company records could produce. Discuss the major obstacle to this method of research.
2. What is an experiment?
3. Explain the significance of keeping constant all factors other than the experimental variable of an experiment.
4. Give one example each of problems that can best be solved through (a) before-after designs and (b) controlled before-after designs. Explain your choices.
5. Discuss the limitations in using experiments in business.
6. Select an example of a business problem that can be solved best by observation. Explain your choice.
7. Explain the basic difference between experimentation and observation.
8. For the problem you selected in question 6, explain the complexities you would be likely to encounter in your research.
9. Using your imagination to supply any missing facts you may need, develop a plan for the experiment you would use in the following situations.

    a) The Golden Glow Baking Company has for many years manufactured and sold cookies packaged in attractive boxes. It is considering packaging the cookies in plastic bags and wants to conduct an experiment to determine consumer response to this change.
    b) The Miller Brush Company, manufacturers of a line of household goods, has for years sold its products on a house-to-house basis. It now wants to conduct an experiment to test the possibilities of selling through conventional retail outlets.

c) A national chain of food stores wants to know whether it would profit by using trading stamps. It is willing to pay the cost of an experiment in its search for an answer.

d) The True Time Watch Company is considering the use of automated sales displays ($9.50 each) instead of stationary displays ($4.50 each) in the 2,500 retail outlets that sell True Time watches. The company will conduct an experiment to determine the relative effects on sales of the two displays.

e) The Marvel Soap Company has developed a new cleaning agent that is unlike current soaps and detergents. The product is well protected by patent. The company wants to determine the optimum price for the new product through experimentation.

f) National Cereals, Incorporated, wants to determine the effectiveness of advertising to children. Until now, it has been aiming its appeal at the housewife. The company will support an experiment to learn the answer.

10. Using your imagination to supply any missing facts you may need, develop a plan for research by observation for these problems.

   a) A chain of department stores wants to know what causes differences in sales by departments within stores and by stores. Some of this information it hopes to get through research by observation.

   b) Your university wants to know the nature and extent of its automobile parking problem.

   c) The management of an insurance company wants to determine the efficiency and productivity of the workers in its typing pool.

   d) Owners of a shopping center want a study to determine shopping patterns of their customers. Specifically, they want to know such things as what parts of town the customers come from, how they travel, how many stores they visit, and so on.

   e) The director of your library wants a detailed study of library use (what facilities are used, when, by whom, and so on).

   f) The management of a restaurant wants a study of its workers' efficiency in the kitchen.

11. Using your imagination to supply any missing facts you may need, develop a plan for research by survey for these problems.

   a) The American Restaurant Association wants information that will give its members a picture of its customers. The information will serve as a guide for a promotion campaign designed to promote restaurant eating. Specifically, it will seek such information as who eats out, how often, where they go, how much they spend. Likewise, it will seek to determine who does not eat out and why.

   b) The editor of your local daily paper wants a readership study of his publication. That is, he wants to know just who reads what.

c) An organization of tobacco companies wants to learn the current trend in tobacco use. They want to know such information as how many people are smoking, how many have stopped, how many new smokers there are, and so on.

d) The American Association of Publishers wants a survey of reading habits of the American people. They want to know who reads what, how much, when, where, and so on.

12. Give examples of sampling problems that can make best use of random sampling. Do the same for controlled and area sampling.

13. Construct three leading questions. Explain why they are leading.

14. Rewrite the questions in 13, above, so that they do not lead the reader.

15. What can the researchers do to avoid asking questions that are not understood by all respondents?

16. Assume that you need information on the following subjects, and that you have reason to believe the people in your sample will be reluctant to give it to you. How would you attempt to get this information?

    a) Family income.
    b) Age.
    c) Reading habits.
    d) Morals.
    e) Personal cleanliness.

17. Give an illustration of how a question asking for opinion could be substituted by one asking for fact.

18. What would be the effect of the laws of memory on questions concerning these matters?

    a) Articles read in a periodical.
    b) Expenditures for recreation.
    c) Clothing worn at one's wedding.
    d) Reasons for purchasing an automobile.
    e) An automobile accident.

19. Discuss the pros and cons of using telephone, personal interview, and mail survey techniques for each of the problems listed in question 11.

20. Point out violations of the rules of good questionnaire construction in the following questions. The questions do not come from the same questionnaire.

    a) How many days on the average do you wear a pair of socks before changing? _____

    b) (The first question in a survey conducted by Fortune cigarettes) Have you ever smoked a Fortune cigarette?

Yes _____ No _____
Don't know or no answer _____

c) Do you consider the ideal pay plan to be one based on straight commission? _____ Or straight salary? _____

d) What kind of gasoline did you purchase last time? _____

e) How much did you pay for clothing in the past 12 months? _____

f) Check the word below that best describes how often you eat dessert with your noon meal.

Always   _____
Usually   _____
Sometimes _____
Never   _____

21. A major manufacturer of soaps and detergents maintains a panel of housewives to give it information on products in the field. Discuss the problem it is likely to have with this group. How should these problems be handled?

CHAPTER 4

Collecting information: library research

Frequently, the information needed to solve a report problem exists in printed form. But as is known by anyone who has ever observed the great bulk of printed matter shelved in any respectable library, locating one particular bit of information could be compared to finding the proverbial needle in the haystack. The possible blind alleys that the untrained investigator could run into in his search for information are all too numerous to count. Thus, unless the investigator is thoroughly schooled in the procedure of locating printed data, the difficulty of the research task is increased many times.

Although trained investigators vary in their working habits, one acceptable procedure of conducting research through printed sources is presented in the following pages.

LOCATION OF PUBLICATION COLLECTIONS

The first step in orderly research for printed information is to determine where the search should begin. The natural place to start looking for published material, of course, is a library, but libraries differ in their content. Although the investigator is not always fortunate enough to have a choice of libraries, if he does have a choice he should be familiar with the numerous types of libraries that exist and with specific differences in their content.

Foremost among the libraries available to most investigators are the *general* libraries. This group includes the best-known ones, consisting mainly of college and university libraries plus the great bulk of public libraries. These libraries are general to the extent that they contain data of all descriptions. Many in this group, however, have, in certain specialized areas, voluminous collections that are more complete than numerous so-called specialized libraries that are discussed in following paragraphs. As a rule, libraries in the general group are accessible to the investigator.

In addition to the easily accessible general libraries, a number of lesser known collections of a specialized nature may be used as sources of printed information. Unfortunately, many of these *specialized* libraries are private collections not generally available to outside investigators. While many such libraries do not openly invite public use of their collections, they frequently are extremely cooperative to investigators working on worthwhile projects.

Included in the specialized group are the libraries of private businesses. As a rule, these collections are especially designed to serve the sponsoring company; consequently, the collections provide excellent information in the specialized areas of the company's operations. Unfortunately, company libraries are not so accessible as are other specialized types.

Frequently, specialized libraries are maintained by various types of associations—trade, professional, and technical groups; chambers of commerce; labor unions; and such. Like the company libraries, these collections frequently provide excellent coverage of highly specialized areas. And although they are founded principally for their memberships and occasionally research staffs, the association libraries frequently open their doors to those engaged in reputable research.

Libraries of a specialized nature are also kept by some public and private research organizations. Foremost in this group are the research divisions of big-city chambers of commerce and bureaus of business research of the major universities. To investigate some of the information sources from these types of organizations, the *Research Centers Directory* is available. Formerly the *Directory of University Research Bureaus and Institutes,* this revised directory lists more than 3,000 nonprofit information centers. It is updated quarterly by *New Research Centers.* Many chambers of commerce and bureaus of business research maintain extensive collections of material, covering statistics and general information for a local area. In many states, various state agencies maintain similar collections.

Specialized libraries are so numerous that the Special Libraries Association has found it desirable to publish guides to them. One of these guides, *Special Library Resources,* lists in four volumes the nation's best special libraries. It also lists some of the special collections in the general libraries. A second guide published by the Association is the *Special Libraries Directory.* This publication lists about 2,000 special libraries, but it is not so extensive in its description of the libraries as is *Special Library Resources*. Another careful guide is the *Directory of Special Libraries and Information Centers*, published by the Gale Research Company of Detroit. Edited by Anthony T. Kruzas, this publication contains information on 10,500 special libraries, information centers, and documentation centers in this country and Canada.

EMPLOYMENT OF DIRECT APPROACH WHEN PRACTICAL

After he has found an appropriate library, the investigator faces the task of finding what he needs from the great mass of information available to him. To the untrained investigator, this task can be complex and confusing to an extreme degree. On the other hand, the investigator who knows the orderly arrangement of library material will find his task routine.

The experienced investigator's steps could follow two basic patterns in library research. In some instances, the investigator may be able to proceed directly to the source of the information needed. More often, however, he must take a more indirect and time-consuming approach.

In research situations where the information sought is of a quantitative or factual nature, the investigator may be able to go directly to the source. The extent to which the research man will be able to move directly to the source will, of course, depend on his acquaintance with published material in the field of inquiry. While it would be impossible for a good research man to know all possible sources, even within specialized fields, it is not only possible but also desirable that he be acquainted with certain basic sources.

Encyclopedias

Possibly the best known sources of general information are the encyclopedias. Although encyclopedias provide an authoritative and wide coverage of factual information, frequently they are too scant and general for use on specialized topics. Particularly they are good for general background information and for the list of reading material they frequently present on the subject.

A number of good encyclopedias are in general use, but three may be singled out for special mention. These are the *Encyclopedia*

Americana, Encyclopædia Britannica, and the *New International Yearbook.* The *Encyclopedia Americana* is exceptionally good for American use, particularly with its coverage of statistical and technological material. All three are supplemented with yearbooks that summarize the happenings of each year and are designed generally to keep the series up-to-date. In addition to the more popular encyclopedias, some specialized types exist. Among this group, the *Encyclopedia of the Social Sciences* stands out. As its name implies, the publication covers such related fields as economics, history, sociology, statistics, and commerce. Also, the *Encyclopedia of Associations,* published in three volumes, may prove helpful for locating information from the 12,910 organizations it lists.

Yearbooks and almanacs

Needs for general, factual, and statistical information frequently can be met by publications known as yearbooks and almanacs. The information presented in both types of publications is similar, although yearbooks may be distinguished from almanacs by their fuller and more analytical coverage. Of the almanacs available, the *World Almanac,* published by the New York World-Telegram, is without peer as a general source of factual and statistical information. Almanacs serving limited geographic areas, however, frequently are best for very specific data.

Like almanacs, yearbooks are limited to varying areas of geographic coverage. The *Statesman's Year-Book,* a British publication, provides general statistical and factual coverage from 1865 for all countries of the world. The *Europa Yearbook* provides general coverage of the European countries. Yearbooks devoted principally to coverage of individual countries are available for some of the major nations. Among this group are *The American Year Book, The Canada Yearbook, Official Year Book of the Commonwealth of Australia, The New Zealand Official Year-Book, Mexican Yearbook,* and *The Times of India Directory and Year Book Including Who's Who.* Some of these publications, particularly those covering countries with backward economies, should be used with extreme caution, as they are apt to be biased or contain statistically unreliable estimates.

Although it does not fit specifically into a yearbook or almanac classification, *Statistical Sources,* another publication of Gale Research Company, does provide a useful reference for much of the information given in such publications. Using more than 8,000 subject captions, it records 12,000 sources of statistical data.

Biographical directories

If it is biographical information about leading personalities of today or the past that is needed, a number of biographical directories may be consulted. Best known in this group is the currently popular *Who's Who in America,* which summarizes the lives of the living Americans who have achieved some degree of prominence. Similar publications provide coverage of Americans by limited geographic regions. For information concerning prominent Americans of the past, the *Dictionary of American Biography* may be used. In addition to these general sources, biographical information on individuals in particular professions may be found in a number of specialized publications. *Who's Who in Commerce and Industry,* for example, gives wide coverage to prominent businessmen, as does *Poor's Register of Corporations, Directors and Executives,* although the Poor's publication is the more exclusive of the two. Other similar sources include *Who's Who in the Motor Industry, Who's Who in Advertising, Rand McNally Bankers Directory, Who's Who in Engineering, American Men of Science, Directory of American Scholars, Leaders in Education,* and on and on. Few areas of economic activity are not covered by some such directory.

Information on well-known personalities may also be found through the *Biography Index.* Published quarterly, this index is a guide to current biographical material in books and magazines. Its references are arranged alphabetically by the names of the personalities covered.

Trade directories

For information about specific businesses (their operations; the products they buy, sell, or manufacture; and other useful facts and statistics) numerous directories are available. So many of these directories exist, in fact, that guides to them have been published. One guide, *Trade Directories of the World,* is a loose-leaf service that keeps current lists of directories covering foreign as well as domestic companies. Another, *Guide to American Directories,* contains information on more than 3,000 United States and foreign directories covering 250 fields of endeavor. Compiled by Bernard Klein and published by Klein and Company, this popular directory was in its seventh edition in 1968. Especially valuable to the marketing man are two directories published by Dun & Bradstreet. The *Million Dollar Directory* identifies the 25,000 United States companies with a net worth of $1 million or more. Its companion publication, *Middle Market Directory*, identifies the 15,000 companies with a net worth of $500,000 to $1 million.

Government publications

A wide range of general statistical information is released by various departments, bureaus, and agencies of the federal government. Although these data are so numerous and complex as to require an indirect method of research in uncovering them, the qualified investigator should be able to proceed directly to some of the more important sources. The importance of these sources obviously varies with the specific problems concerned and in the minds of the investigators. Nevertheless, the following review of the information made available by agencies of the federal government is presented as a summary of major government contributions to general research. The investigator should at least know that such data are available.

Possibly the most widely used of government-collected data are the censuses taken by the Bureau of the Census, a division of the Department of Commerce. Best known of the census series is the decennial count of population, which dates back to 1790. The results of this census are published in two parts, each of which is broken down by volumes. Lesser supplements and special reports are released from time to time. For example, *Current Population Reports* provides an annual updating for the years between census counts. Titles for the major publication necessarily vary to fit the period—for example, *United States Census of Population: 1960* and *United States Census of Housing: 1960*. The information is available by cities, counties, and states. A national summary also is presented.

In addition to the population count, the Bureau of the Census conducts censuses of agriculture and business. The compilations of both studies are made available in published form. The *Census of Business* has been compiled for the years 1929, 1933, 1935, 1939, 1948, 1954, 1958, 1963, and 1968. This census covers by states and by cities such areas as retail trade, wholesale trade, service businesses, and construction. The bureau's *Census of Agriculture* has been published regularly at five-year intervals. The data presented cover a wide range of agricultural activity. Tabulations are broken down geographically by county and by state. The bureau also publishes the *Census of Manufacturing*, the *Census of Transportation*, the *Census of Mineral Industries*, and the *Census of Government*. Since the early 1950's, the bureau has been considering censuses of insurance and utilities.

Another Bureau of the Census publication vital as a basic source to the investigator is the *Statistical Abstract of the United States*. Compiled in this work is a large portion of the statistics collected by the branches of the federal government. For selected data on cities and counties, the publication is supplemented by *The County and City Data Book*. Another publication that brings together great volumes of economic statistics is *The Economic Almanac*, a publication of the National Industrial Conference Board.

A source of current data of major concern to one engaged in business research is *Survey of Current Business*, a release of the Office of Business Economics of the Department of Commerce. This periodical brings together the best of current business statistics collected by various government agencies. Coverage is given to areas such as prices, construction, trade, employment and population, finance, manufacturing, and transportation. General business indicators such as national income and gross national product also are constructed. In addition, analyses of these data are presented.

This summary of basic sources with which the skilled investigator should be familiar is by no means complete. In every area of research there are additional direct sources that the trained research man working in that field should be familiar with. The investigator will find many such sources in the annotated bibliography presented later in this chapter.

MORE GENERAL USE OF INDIRECT METHODS

If the systematic investigator cannot move directly to the source of the information he needs (and this is the usual case), he must then find the data through indirect steps. His first move in indirect research is to construct a bibliography—a list of publications likely to contain the information he seeks. After the bibliography is constructed, he gathers the publications listed. Then, he systematically checks each of them for the information he needs. Only the first of these steps—preparation of a bibliography—needs to be discussed. The final two steps are routine and simple.

Preliminary search for prepared bibliographies

Obviously, the difficulty of his task would be lessened if the investigator could find already prepared for him a bibliography on his subject. And frequently, prepared lists of published material in specific areas do exist. Academic groups, associations, government agencies, and others are forever contributing bibliographies in all major areas. Thus, in most areas of research the investigator is wise to search first for a bibliography on his topic.

In searching for a prepared bibliography, the researcher could pursue a number of courses. He could start by looking through master's and doctor's theses, research reports, trade and textbooks, and such, for many of these writings contain lists of publications in the specific fields covered. Of special importance in searching for business bibliographies are various books on business research. *How to Use the Business Library,* by H. Webster Johnson and Stuart W. McFarland, is one of the more recent of these books. Another recent source is Robert W. Murphey's *How and Where to Look It Up.* In addition to including bibliography information, this publication is a comprehensive guide to library research in general. The *Executive's Guide to Information Sources* is another convenient guidebook for investigating prepared bibliographies as well as periodicals, year-books, directories, organizations, and such that may be associated with timely business subjects. Edwin T. Coman's voluminous work, *Sources of Business Information,* a valuable bibliography source, was revised in 1964 by Edwin T. Coman, Jr. A useful guide to the great bulk of government publications available is the book *United States Government Publications.* Originally written by Anne M. Boyd, the book was later revised by Rae Elizabeth Rips.

Use of the card catalog

If search for a bibliography already prepared is fruitless, or if those found are inadequate, the investigator must then construct a bibliography of his own. His first step in this endeavor may well be to consult the card catalog.

Learning to use the card catalog is the key to the resources of the library and to the location of the books and periodicals it contains. The card catalog lists the books and all other sources that can be found in the library. The material is listed by authors, titles, and subject matter. When the author's name is not known but the title is known, the card can serve as a guide to finding the book or other source desired, as the title card is a duplicate of the author card but with the title typed in black above the author's name. Subject cards tell what sources are in the library on any certain subject. An example of an author card appears below.

```
 651.      Lesikar, Raymond Vincent
               Report writing for business. Rev. ed.
           R.D. Irwin 1965
           viii, 414p illus biblio




           1 Report writing     I Title          651.

                         ( )
```

An explanation of the author card is as follows.

```
 Cat. No.  Author's Name
 Book No.     Title of book....Edition of book....
           Name of publisher...Date of publication
           Pages numbered with Roman numerals...
           Number of pages in text....Illustrations,
           diagrams....Bibliography

           Notes on book

           1 Subject entry  I Title entry   Catalog No.
                                                of book
           Wilson Co. No.   (W) The H. W. Wilson Company

                         ( )
```

The call number in the upper left-hand corner of the card is based on the Dewey Decimal System. This subject classification divides human knowledge in nine main classes, numbered one to nine. Encyclopedias, periodicals, and other sources of general information are marked zero and form a 10th class. Each class is similarly separated into nine divisions; general works belong to no division and have a zero in place of a division number.

Divisions are similarly divided into nine sections. This process is repeated as often as necessary. Thus 651 means Class 6 (Applied Science), Division 5 (Business Communication), Section 1 (Office Economy). All phases of office economy such as equipment, correspondence, and organization are numbered 651.

The following is a breakdown of the division of classes of the Dewey Decimal System.

000	General Works
100	Philosophy
200	Religion
300	Social Sciences
400	Philology
500	Pure Science
600	Useful Arts—Applied Science
700	Fine Arts
800	Literature
900	History

Although the Dewey system is quite adequate for some libraries, its use by the larger libraries is limited. In each division, class, or section, the number of division possibilities is restricted. Since this limitation creates rather complex indexing techniques for the larger libraries, many institutions of such character are presently adopting the Library of Congress System. And because business researchers should display skill in using all types of research facilities, an understanding of both systems is essential.

Whereas the Dewey system was initiated for use by all libraries, the Library of Congress method was developed for use only by the Library of Congress and for entries it had and expected to receive. Basically, the plan combines an alphabetical series with a numbering pattern to potentially provide a more expansive classification system. However, its major advantage (expansiveness) is also a disadvantage. The system can be applied to a large collection of entries in many ways, and all may vary slightly.

Even though the specific adaptation of the Library of Congress method may differ somewhat from library to library, the base of the system is consistent enough to allow business researchers to understand any particular variation. The following divisions, corresponding to letters of the alphabet, are the rudiments of the system.

A   General Works—Polography
B   Philosophy—Religion
C   History—Auxiliary Sciences
D   History and Topography (except America)
E   F—America
G   Geography—Anthropology
H   Social Sciences
J   Political Science
K   Law
L   Education
M   Music
N   Fine Arts
P   Language and Literature
Q   Science
R   Medicine
S   Agriculture—Plant and Animal Industry
T   Technology
U   Military Science
V   Naval Science
Z   Bibliography and Library School

Divisions are made within each of these categories by additional letters and numbers. Thus, the books numbered 650–659 (Business) in the Dewey system would be replaced by the Library of Congress symbols HF (Commerce, General). Special works would be further indexed by additional numbers and letters.

Indexes as a guide to information

All too frequently, the card catalog is too general a guide to be of value for specific research topics. In such instances, the researcher should make use of one or more appropriate indexes to published material. These indexes are numerous and are available for most general topics and many specialized ones as well. No research library of significance operates without at least some of them. A few of these indexes are so generally used as to deserve special mention.

Perhaps the most useful index in business research is the *Business Periodicals Index.* Issued monthly (except July) and cumulated yearly, this index serves as a guide to major periodicals in the business areas of accounting; advertising; banking and finance; general business; insurance, labor, and management; marketing and purchasing; office management; public administration, taxation; and specific businesses, industries and trades. Although the *Business Periodicals Index* began only in 1958, its predecessor, the *Industrial Arts Index*, goes back to 1913. Together these indexes cover the bulk of authoritative periodical writings in business for these years.

The *Readers' Guide to Periodical Literature*, as its name implies, is a guide to material printed in magazines. Its coverage is limited to a definite group of widely known periodicals, which are listed in the prefatory pages of the index. Listings are arranged alphabetically by subject, by author, and by title. Compilations are made monthly and cumulated semiannually and annually. The series dates back to 1900.

Poole's Index to Periodical Literature may be used for periodical literature dated prior to 1900. This service covers major publications for the period 1802–1906, thereby overlapping the *Readers' Guide.*

Another periodical index of interest to the business investigator is the *International Index*. Published quarterly, this guide to periodical literature in the social sciences and the humanities is indexed by subject and author. Because of the increasing application of the other social sciences to business, this index is becoming more and more valuable to the business investigator.

As the preceding indexes are devoted primarily to periodicals, they provide scant coverage of the great volume of bulletins, pamphlets, special reports, and the like that are issued by various government groups, associations, individuals, and business houses. *The Public Affairs Information Service* fills much of this gap with its weekly index, which summarizes publications in the general field of public affairs. Although the service is devoted primarily to the general field of public affairs, the subject field is interpreted broadly. Coverage is especially good in the areas of commerce.

For information likely to have been newsworthy, the *New York Times Index* and the *Wall Street Journal Index* are the best generally available sources. Published semimonthly and cumulated annually, the *New York Times Index* is primarily good for national and international happenings occurring since 1913. *The Wall Street Journal Index* divides its references into two general areas—corporate news and general news. The publication, available by edition of the *Wall Street Journal,* was started on a monthly basis, with yearly cumulations beginning in 1957. For earlier events of international significance, the *Times* [London] *Official Index* may be used. Information on events of only local significance usually may be obtained from the files of local papers. Many such files are quite complete, although newspapers generally are not sufficiently staffed to allow extensive public use of their collections.

Information that appears in book form may be traced through the *United States Catalog,* an index that was compiled in 1928 and lists English language books. Listings in this index are made by general subject as well as by author and title. For more recent information on books, the *Cumulative Book Index* may be used. This monthly index is cumulated semiannually and in larger cumulations. In addition to the usual subject, author, title information, it gives complete buying information plus library card numbers. The index has been continuous since 1898.

ORDER IN NOTE-TAKING

As the researcher finds the publications he seeks, logically he looks through them for the information he needs. And when he locates such information, he takes notes for future reference.

At first glance, note-taking may appear to be a simple chore that deserves little comment. It may appear to involve only the simple mechanics of writing down the information found, but the task really involves far more than this. It involves care in selecting that information likely to be usable. It involves careful determination of what parts should be recorded verbatim (word for word), what parts should be paraphrased (in the researcher's words), what parts should be recorded in detail, and what parts should be summarized. Most important of all, good note-taking involves order in recording this information.

To not take notes by a predetermined, orderly plan is to invite chaos. Unfortunately, too many researchers experience this kind of chaos. They may search through great numbers of sources and diligently write down an abundance of vital information. After exhaustive research, they may end up with reams of note paper or thick stacks of note cards. Perhaps they have recorded in these voluminous notes all the information they need. But finding the information they want in these overample notes becomes a task of frustrating paper shuffling that resembles the proverbial search for a needle in a haystack. An orderly note-taking procedure would eliminate much of this confusion.

One such orderly procedure is presented in the following paragraphs. It is not presented as a one best plan, for doubtless there are others. For the novice researcher who has not yet devised a plan of his own, this one should prove to be helpful. Its logic and value are apparent from its description.

Two sets of note cards (or papers) are used in this procedure. On one set, the investigator records the bibliography descriptions; on the other, he records the information he finds in the sources.

Bibliography cards keyed with notes

For recording bibliography information, small cards are best (about 3 × 5). On separate cards, the researcher writes the com-

Figure 3. Illustration of bibliography cards keyed with note cards

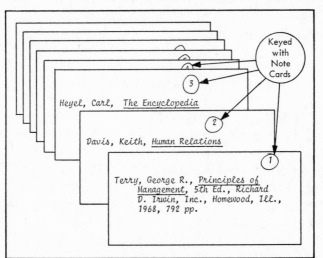

plete bibliography description (as described in Chapter 12). Then, he numbers each card consecutively (see Figure 3). As will be described later, these numbers are used as keyed references to the note cards.

Note cards arranged by topics

The investigator uses the second set of cards for recording his findings. For this set, he should use large cards (about 5 × 7). At the beginning of the research, he anticipates the topics and subdivisions of these topics on which he hopes to find information. For each

Figure 4.   Illustration of note cards keyed with bibliography cards

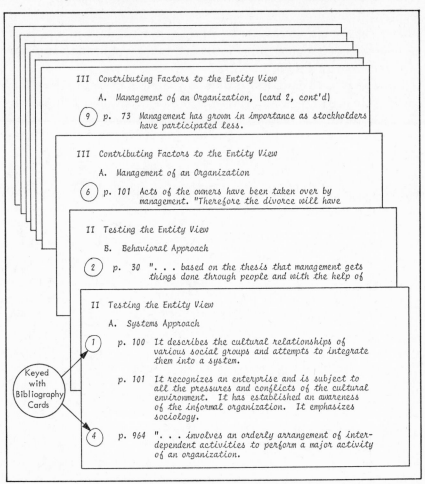

topic and subtopic, he sets up a card, placing the topic and subtopic titles at the top (see Figure 4).

As he conducts the research, the investigator records each bit of pertinent information on the appropriate card. Should he find topics he did not anticipate, he sets up cards for them. And when he fills up any one card, he starts another card with the same topic heading and continues note-taking. At the end of his research efforts, he has all his findings on cards with all like information together.

So that the source of each note can be easily determined, the investigator writes by each entry on the cards the number he has given the source in the bibliography cards. Thus, he is spared the chore of writing a complete bibliography description each time he records information.

Two practical advantages of the system are apparent, and both are related to the fact that cards are easily arranged. First, the investigator can quickly and easily put the information collected into the order in which he will present it in his report. Second, he can prepare the bibliography for final typing simply by arranging the bibliography cards alphabetically by types of publications. Both advantages lead to significant reductions in costly, long hours of work time.

A BIBLIOGRAPHY OF BUSINESS INFORMATION

The search for secondary information need not always be so involved or complex as the preceding discussion may imply. As previously noted, the experienced researcher should have a working acquaintance with at least the major sources of information in his field. Thus, he may be able to proceed directly to the source of information he seeks. So that the beginning researcher may have a quick guide to such sources, the following annotated bibliography is presented.

Certainly, this bibliography is too extensive to be kept in mind in detail. But the business researcher would do well to look through the entries and to note the basic sources that all business investigators should know and the sources of special interest to one in his field of specialization.

A BIBLIOGRAPHY OF BASIC BUSINESS SOURCES

(With Brief Annotations)

ACCOUNTING

Books

Accountant's Encyclopedia, Prentice-Hall, Inc., Englewood Cliffs, N.J., 1962, 4 vols.
A valuable guide for accountants, accounting students, treasurers, controllers, lawyers, engineers, and anyone who seeks information concerning accounting.

Fiske, Wyman P., and John A. Beckett, *Industrial Accountant's Handbook*, Prentice-Hall, Inc., New York, 1954, 1,072 pp.

A comprehensive coverage of the uses and limitations of accounting. Gives emphasis in depth and breadth to specialized aspects of industrial cost accounting.

Kohler, Eric L., *A Dictionary for Accountants*, 3rd ed., Prentice-Hall, Inc., Englewood Cliffs, N.J., 1963, 523 pp.
Translates the language of the accountant into words that have established meanings in other fields.

Lang, Theodore, editor, *Cost Accountant's Handbook*, Ronald Press Co., New York, 1952, 1,482 pp.
A comprehensive review of the fundamental principles, methods, and techniques of cost accounting used primarily in manufacturing industries.

Lasser, J. K., editor, *Handbook of Auditing Methods*, Van Nostrand, New York, 1953, 756 pp.
A book about auditing mechanics within individual industries and businesses. Chapters individually written by specialists cover the procedures and problems of auditing in 70 industries or businesses.

———, *Handbook of Tax Accounting Methods*, Van Nostrand, New York, 1951, 897 pp.
A guide to tax accounting practices in the various industries. Presents tax principles applicable to all industries as well as those pertaining to specific industries. Has an extensive bibliography.

Williams, Robert I., and Lillian Doris, editors, *Encyclopedia of Accounting Systems*, Prentice-Hall, Inc., Englewood Cliffs, N.J., 1957, 2,005 pp.
Five preference volumes describing and illustrating accounting systems for diversified industries, professions, and businesses. Each system is presented by a specialist in the particular field.

Wixon, Rufus, editor, and Walter G. Kell, staff editor, *Accountant's Handbook*, 4th ed., Ronald Press Co., New York, 1957, 1,453 pp.
A reference book recognized as a standard source of authoritative information in commercial and financial accounting.

Periodicals

The Accountant, Gee and Co., Ltd., London, Weekly.
A recognized weekly organ for chartered accountants and accountancy throughout the world.

The Accountants Digest, L. L. Briggs, Burlington, Vt., Quarterly.
A digest of outstanding articles selected from leading accounting periodicals in the English language.

The Accountants' Journal, Gee and Co., Ltd., London, Monthly.
Contains helpful articles for the practitioner and discussions of timely subjects in the field of accounting.

The Accounting Review, American Accounting Association, Published by the School of Commerce, University of Wisconsin, Madison, Wis., Quarterly.

A collection of timely articles that reflect the thinking and experience of leading accountants.

Accounting Trends and Techniques, American Institute of Accountancy, New York, Annually.

An annual cumulation of surveys of accounting phases of corporate annual reports.

The Canadian Chartered Accountant, The Canadian Institute of Chartered Accountants, Toronto, Ontario, Monthly.

Contains theoretical and practical selected articles on new developments in taxes, accounting, and auditing, written by leading Canadian accountants.

Financial Executive, Financial Executives Institute, Inc., New York, Monthly.

A presentation of accounting and related topics at the executive level of controllership and treasurership.

The Federal Accountant, The Federal Government Accounting Association, Washington, D.C., Quarterly.

Presents articles pertaining to accounting theory and practice in governmental auditing and accounting.

The Internal Auditor, Institute of Internal Auditors, Burlington, Vt., Quarterly.

A selection of articles on the theories and practices of internal auditing.

The Journal of Accountancy, American Institute of Certified Public Accountants, New York, Monthly.

Presents a wide selection of timely articles in all areas of accounting. Includes theoretical as well as practical works.

Journal of Accounting Research, The Institute of Professional Accounting, Graduate School of Business, University of Chicago and the London School of Economics and Political Science, University of London, Baltimore, Maryland, Semiannually.

A presentation of scholarly research of interest to the accounting profession.

Management Accounting, National Association of Accountants, New York, Monthly.

A collection of professional activities devoted to internal accounting methods for management decision making.

The New York Certified Public Accountant, New York State Society of Certified Public Accountants, New York, Monthly.

Articles discussing current accounting thought, methods, and standards of the profession, written by prominent accountants and businessmen.

Miscellaneous

Accountancy Law Reporter, Commerce Clearing House in cooperation with the American Institute of Accountants, Chicago.
A summary of the regulations of all the various states relating to the practice of the public accountant. Includes the various statutes, regulations, forms, code of ethics, and decisions and rulings of some court cases.

Kane, Robert L., Jr., editor, *CPA Handbook,* Special Edition, American Institute of Certified Public Accountants, New York, 1956, 2 vols.
A reference work designed for use by practitioners engaged in the public accounting profession, their staff and office personnel, and students who expect to engage in public accounting.

BUSINESS EDUCATION

Books

Dames, J. Frank, and Albert R. Brinkman, *Guidance in Business Education,* 3rd ed., South-Western Publishing Company, Cincinnati, Ohio, 1962, 297 pp.
Provides assistance to secondary business teachers in the vocational guidance of students.

Douglas, Lloyd V., *Business Education,* The Center for Applied Research in Education, Inc., Washington, D.C., 1963, 115 pp.
A philosophical account of the past, present, and future status of business education.

———, editor, *The Business Education Program in the Expanding Secondary School,* United Business Education Association, Washington, D.C., 1957, 160 pp.
A guidebook and collection of experiences related to business education in secondary schools. Gives special emphasis to the role of business education in the total education effort.

Green, Helen Hinkson, *Activities Handbook for Business Teachers,* McGraw-Hill Book Company, New York, 1958, 369 pp.
Deals with extracurricular activities of business teachers, such as commercial clubs, business programs, field trips, and community projects.

Harms, Harm and B. W. Stehr, *Methods in Vocational Business Education,* South-Western Publishing Company, Cincinnati, Ohio, 1963, 522 pp.

A reference source for business teachers with suggestions for preparing office workers.

Haynes, Benjamin R., M. E. Broom, and Mathilde Hardaway, *Tests and Measurements in Business Education*, South-Western Publishing Company, Cincinnati, Ohio, 1940, 400 pp.
A comprehensive treatment of testing programs in business education for more effective measurement procedures.

Kightlinger, Toma S., *Business Education Teaching Tricks*, Interstate Printers and Publishers, Inc., Danville, Illinois, 1954, 143 pp.
A supplement for effective teaching methods, which should add extra incentives to business education programs.

Liles, Parker, editor, *Administration and Supervision in Business Education*, National Business Education Association, Washington, D.C., 1965, 357 pp.
A collection of works associated with the problems of administration of business education programs at secondary and collegiate levels. Presents discussions from the state, city, and school positions.

Nolan, C. A., C. K. Hayden, and D. R. Malsbary, *Principles and Problems of Business Education*, 3rd ed., South-Western Publishing Company, Cincinnati, Ohio, 1967, 681 pp.
A text concerned with the planning and implementing of effective business education programs at all educational levels.

Tonne, Herbert A., L. Estelle, and Herbert M. Freeman, *Methods of Teaching Business Subjects*, McGraw-Hill Book Company, New York, 1957, 427 pp.
Provides teaching materials for basic methods courses in business education at the college level.

Periodicals

American Business Education, Joint Publication Commission of the Eastern Business Teachers Association and the National Business Teachers Association, Somerville, New Jersey, Quarterly.
Contains a timely presentation of articles of interest to American business education, such as distributive education, typewriting, education, curriculum, teaching techniques, and problems of teaching.

American Vocational Journal, American Vocational Association, Washington, D.C., Monthly.
Offers articles on topics of business and office education as well as many other vocational subjects.

The Balance Sheet, South-Western Publishing Company, Cincinnati, Ohio, Monthly.
For business and economics teachers, this publication gives discussion

to current problems of teaching and the profession of business education.

Business Education Forum, National Business Education Association, Washington, D.C., Monthly.
A periodical that covers such areas as bookkeeping, filing, basic business, distributive education, and typewriting.

Business Education World, Gregg Publishing Division of McGraw-Hill Book Company, New York, Monthly.
A presentation of current articles that should benefit teachers, supervisory personnel, and administrators who are engaged in business education.

The Business Teacher, Gregg Publishing Division, McGraw-Hill Book Company, New York, Five times per year.
Contains articles for practical use of business teachers concerning the subjects they teach.

Delta Pi Epsilon Journal, Delta Pi Epsilon, Denver, Colorado, Quarterly.
A professional journal designed to promote theory, practice, and research in business education.

The Journal of Business Education, Trethaway Publishing Company, Wilkes-Barre, Pennsylvania, Monthly.
A journal devoted to covering the various interests of business education teachers and administrators.

National Business Education Quarterly, National Business Education Association, Washington, D.C., Quarterly.
Gives particular emphasis to research activities on business education subjects.

The Office Executive, National Office Management Association, Willow Grove, Pennsylvania, Monthly.
Presents articles related to the problems and development of office administration.

Review, Catholic Business Education Association, San Antonio, Texas, Quarterly.
A timely account of business education in Catholic schools. Contains philosophical, denominational, and professional reviews of Catholic business education.

The Secretary, National Secretaries Association (International), Kansas City, Missouri, Monthly.
Reports professional articles which are of interest to the modern secretary.

Today's Secretary, Gregg Publishing Division, McGraw-Hill Book Company, Inc., New York, Monthly.
A periodical that covers areas of general interest to secretarial training and skill.

Miscellaneous

American Business Education Yearbook, Eastern Business Teachers Association and the National Business Teachers Association, Sommerville, New Jersey, Annually.
Covers a wide range of topics related to business education over several years. Each issue is devoted to a particular phase of business education.

Collins, Marion Josephine, *Handbook for Office Practice Teachers,* South-Western Publishing Company, Cincinnati, Ohio, 1954, 57 pp.
Provides suggestions for secondary school teachers of office practice, with coverage in such areas as physical provisions, organizational plans, and instructional procedures.

Erickson, Lawrence W., and Mary Ellen Oliverio, *Evaluative Criteria for Survey Instruments in Business Education,* South-Western Publishing Company, Cincinnati, Ohio, 1964, 89 pp.
A detailed study of the survey as a method of collecting information for solution of business education problems.

Lomax, Paul S., and W. Harman Wilson, *Improving Research in Business Education,* South-Western Publishing Company, Cincinnati, Ohio, 1962, 21 pp.
An analysis of research methodology in business education for the improvement of curriculum and classroom methods.

Olson, Milton C., and Eugene L. Swearingen, editors, *Business and Economic Education for the Academically Talented Student,* National Education Association and the United Business Education Association, Washington, D.C., 1961, 80 pp.
This booklet covers the topic of basic economic understandings in secondary schools.

Wyllie, Eugene Donald, *An Evaluation Plan for Business Education Programs in High Schools,* South-Western Publishing Company, Cincinnati, Ohio, 1963, 34 pp.
Provides guidelines and implementation programs for evaluating business education in high schools.

FINANCE

Books

Credit Research Foundation, editors, *Credit Management Handbook,* Richard D. Irwin, Inc., Homewood, Ill., 1958, 776 pp.
A basic and detailed analysis of all phases of credits and collections.

Credit Management Year Book, National Retail Merchants Association, New York, Annually.
Selected articles by specialists in the field on all phases of credit and management.

New York Stock Exchange Factbook, Department of Public Relations and Market Development, New York Stock Exchange, New York, Annually.
Presents a summary of the year's facts and figures pertaining to the stock market.

Periodicals

Banking Law Journal, Warren Gôrham & Lamont, Inc., New York, Monthly.
A publication that contains a wide assortment of articles of interest to bankers.

Bankers Monthly, Rand McNally and Co., New York, Monthly.
A journal of current articles and timely news of interest to bankers.

Banking, American Bankers Association, New York, Monthly.
Presents current basic data pertaining to the nation's financial analyses.

Barron's, Dow Jones and Co., Inc., New York, Weekly.
Presents current basic data pertaining to the nation's financial and business activities. Contains stock listings, and financial analyses.

Board of Governors of the Federal Reserve System, *Federal Reserve Bulletin,* United States Government Printing Office, Washington, D.C., Monthly.
A publication that presents statistics on banking, finance, money rates, and security markets, funds, savings, national product and income, production, department store sales, prices, international finance and trade.

Bulletin of the American Institute of Banking, American Institute of Banking Section of American Bankers Association, New York, Quarterly.
Selected articles pertaining to all areas of banking.

Burroughs Clearing House, Burroughs Clearing House, Detroit, Monthly.
Contains articles relating to the general areas of banking as well as timely notes on banking organizations.

The Commercial and Financial Chronicle, William B. Dana Co., New York, Semiweekly.
Contains news and articles in the general area of finance, including stock listings, security prices, and various economic and financial data.

Credit and Financial Management, National Association of Credit Management, New York, Monthly.
This journal presents news of the association as well as articles on all areas of credit and financial management.

The Credit World, International Consumer Credit Association, St. Louis, Monthly.
Presents a wide variety of articles pertaining to credit at the retail level.

Federal Reserve Bank of New York, Federal Reserve Bank of New York, New York, Monthly.
Presents articles in the areas of finance and business. Analyzes and forecasts business conditions.

Financial Analysts Journal, National Federation of Financial Analysts Societies, New York, Bimonthly.
Selected articles for those interested in investment management and in the profession of security analysis.

Financial World, Guenther Publishing Corp., New York, Weekly.
Containing various articles in the area of investments and data, and analyses pertaining to investment opportunities, this publication is designed especially for the investor.

Forbes, Forbes Inc., New York, Semimonthly.
Carries articles on all areas of finance and related business activities.

The Journal of Finance, American Finance Association, New York, Quarterly.
A publication that carries scholarly articles in the various areas of finance.

The Journal of Taxation, Journal of Taxation, Inc., New York, Monthly.
A national journal of current news and comment for professional tax men.

The Magazine of Wall Street and Business Analyst, Ticker Publishing Co., New York, Biweekly.
Includes articles relating to the economic situation, information on investment opportunities, and statistical data concerning company operations.

Miscellaneous

Bank Clearings, Dun & Bradstreet, Inc., New York, Weekly.
Reports bank changes for 26 leading cities.

The Federal Reserve Bulletin, Board of Governors of the Federal Reserve System, United States Government Printing Office, Washington, D.C., Monthly.
A periodical that contains a variety of articles pertaining to money,

banking, and the national economy in general. Carries current statistical series useful in measuring levels of economic activity.

Monthly Bank Clearings, Dun & Bradstreet, New York, Monthly.
Summarizes bank clearings in leading cities.

Moody's Investors Service, New York.
This service consists of a number of publications in the areas of finance and investments. The major service is the weekly and semiweekly investment data on the nation's business organizations. Their reports cover five areas: Transportation, Industrials, Public Utilities, Banking and Finance, and Municipal and Government. Moody's other publications include *Moody's Stock Survey, Moody's Bond Survey, Moody's Bond Record, Moody's Handbook of Widely Held Common Stocks, Moody's Investors Advisory Service, Moody's Dividend Record.*

Munn, Glenn G., revised by F. S. Garcia, *Encyclopedia of Banking and Finance,* 6th ed., Banker Publishing Co., Boston, 1962.
Defines and explains in detail the terms used in banking. Bibliographies follow the major topics.

GENERAL BUSINESS AND ECONOMICS

Books

The Economic Almanac, National Industrial Conference Board, New York, Biennially.
A fact-filled handbook, covering the subjects of business, government, and labor.

Reference Book of Dun & Bradstreet, Dun & Bradstreet, Inc., New York, Bimonthly.
A reference book that gives names, lines of business, Standard Industrial Classification code numbers, and credit and financial ratings of businesses in the United States and Canada. Sectional editions of the *Reference Book* are available.

Thomas Register of American Manufacturers, Thomas Publishing Co., New York, Annually, 5 vols.
This is a listing of manufacturers by product classifications.

The World Almanac, New York World-Telegram, New York, Annually.
A compilation of general economic, sociological, educational, and other facts relating to all parts of the world.

Periodicals

American Economic Review, American Economic Association, Menasha, Wis., Five times a year.

A journal that publishes scholarly, mostly theoretical, articles in the field of economics.

The American Journal of Economics and Sociology, The American Journal of Economics and Sociology, Inc., Lancaster, Pa., Quarterly.
A journal devoted to synthesizing the social sciences. Publishes articles primarily related to sociology and economics.

Business History Review, Harvard University Graduate School of Business Administration, Boston, Quarterly.
A publication of historical articles pertaining to the institutions and concepts of American business.

Business Week, McGraw-Hill Publishing Company, Inc., New York, Weekly.
A periodical presenting business news and timely reports of interest to the business executive.

The Canadian Journal of Economics and Political Science, University of Toronto Press, Toronto, Canada, Quarterly.
Contains articles in the fields of economics, political science, sociology, and related areas of the social sciences.

Conference Board Record, National Industrial Conference Board, Inc., New York, Monthly.
A publication of current data on the business situation.

Dun's Statistical Review, Dun & Bradstreet Publication Corporation, New York, Monthly.
Contains detailed breakdowns of the data carried in *Dun's Review and Modern Industry.* Features detailed data on bank debits, wholesale prices, building permits, business failure, and regional trade.

Econometrica, North-Holland Publishing Co., Amsterdam-C, Netherlands, Quarterly.
A publication dedicated to the advancement of economic theory, particularly in its relation to quantitative methods.

Economic Development and Cultural Change, The University of Chicago Press, Chicago, Quarterly.
Contains scholarly articles on subjects relating to economic development and cultural change.

Economic Geography, Clark University, Worcester, Mass., Quarterly.
A publication that carries articles in the field of economic geography and related topics.

The Economic Journal, Macmillan and Co., Ltd., London, Quarterly.
This official publication of the Royal Economic Society presents scholarly articles in economics.

Fortune, Time, Inc., Chicago, Monthly.
A popular periodical that contains various articles of interest to the business executive. Presents current reviews of business conditions.

Harvard Business Review, Harvard University Graduate School of Business Administration, Boston, Bimonthly.
A publication of authoritative, selected articles of interest to the business executive. Presents current reviews of business conditions.

Journal of Business, University of Chicago Press, Chicago, Quarterly.
Contains scholarly articles and research in business.

Journal of Farm Economics, The American Farm Economic Association, Madison, Wis., Five times a year.
A journal of articles and current notes in agricultural economics.

Land Economics, University of Wisconsin, Madison, Wis., Quarterly.
A journal of articles on the related subjects of utilities, planning, and housing.

The Magazine of Wall Street and Business Analyst, Ticker Publishing Co., New York, Monthly.
A periodical that analyzes business conditions and carries articles of interest to the business executive.

The Quarterly Journal of Economics, Harvard University Press, Cambridge, Mass.
A journal devoted to current articles, both practical and theoretical, in economics.

Quarterly Review of Economics and Business, Bureau of Economic and Business Research, College of Commerce and Business Administration, University of Illinois, Urbana, Ill., Quarterly.
Presents factual information and interpretative comment on economic and business questions.

Taxes, Commerce Clearing House, Inc., Chicago, Monthly.
Published to promote sound thought in economics, legal, and accounting principles relating to all federal and state taxation.

Trade Review of the Week, Dun & Bradstreet, New York, Weekly.
Interprets the week's developments in retailing, wholesaling, and manufacturing. Includes national and regional estimates of retail volume changes, 10 significant weekly statistics, and other such information.

The Wall Street Journal, Dow Jones and Co., Inc., New York, Daily except Saturdays and Sundays.
A daily business newspaper that covers the current happenings in the business world. Discusses many topics of timely interest to the business executive.

Government publications

United States Bureau of the Census, *Catalog of United States Census Publications,* United States Government Printing Office. Washington, D.C., Quarterly.
All available Census Bureau data is indexed in this catalog.

————, *Census of Housing,* United States Government Printing Office, Washington, D.C., 1960, published every 10 years.

A publication that gives detailed information about housing and household characteristics of the United States population.

United States Bureau of the Census, *Census of Population,* United States Government Printing Office, Washington, D.C., 1960, published every 10 years.

A publication that gives detailed information about the United States population.

————, and Bureau of Old Age and Survivor's Insurance, *County Business Patterns,* United States Printing Office, issued periodically.

This publication classifies over 3 million reporting business units into more than 1,000 kinds of classifications, and shows their state and county locations. Statistics about these businesses are included.

————, *The Cities Supplement,* United States Government Printing Office, Washington, D.C., issued periodically.

A supplement to the *Statistical Abstract* containing selected data for cities of over 25,000 population.

————, *County Data Book,* United States Government Printing Office, Washington, D.C., issued periodically.

A book that gives summary statistics for small geographic areas.

————, *Historical Statistics of the United States: Colonial Times to 1957,* United States Government Printing Office, Washington, D.C., 1960, 789 pp.

A summary of historical statistical data that covers periods from 1789 to 1957.

————, *Statistical Abstract of the United States,* United States Government Printing Office, Washington, D.C., Annually.

An annual compilation of the major statistics on the United States. Includes all major statistics compiled by federal agencies, with detailed explanations.

————, *United States Census of Manufacturers,* United States Government Printing Office, Washington, D.C., 1963.

Presents data compiled on manufacturing in the nation. Data presented include number and size of establishments, employment and payrolls, inventories, value of production. Their data are presented by industry, product, state, and industrial area.

————, *United States Census of Business,* United States Government Printing Office, Washington, D.C., 1968.

Taken at irregular intervals, *The Census of Business* contains data on most phases of business activity. Covered are data such as number of establishments, receipts by commodity lines, employment and payroll. The data are arranged by type of business (wholesale, retail, service) and geographic component (city, county, state).

United States Bureau of Labor Statistics, *Monthly Labor Review,* United States Government Printing Office, Washington, D.C., Monthly.
Contains current statistics on labor and articles pertaining to labor. Labor statistics include employment, turnover, earnings and hours, prices (consumer and wholesale), work stoppage, and work injuries.

United States Department of Agriculture, *Agricultural Statistics,* United States Government Printing Office, Washington, D.C., Annually.
An annual compilation of the nation's agricultural statistics plus some data on world production.

United States Economic Research Service, Department of Agriculture, *Agricultural Outlook Digest,* United States Government Printing Office, Washington, D.C., Monthly.
Presents current reports on conditions of the agricultural economy of the nation.

United States Office of Business Economics, Department of Commerce, *Business Statistics,* United States Government Printing Office, Washington, D.C., Biennially.
Contains a compilation of historical series going back 30 years.

————, Department of Commerce, *Survey of Current Business,* United States Government Printing Office, Washington, D.C., Monthly.
A periodical that presents articles and current data on business conditions. Statistical series covered include national income, prices, finance, construction, trade, employment and wages, finance, and transportation.

Miscellaneous

Dun & Bradstreet, Inc., Business Economics Department, New York.
Statistical reports on the areas generally recognized as early sensitive indicators of business trends. Includes reports such as *Business Failures* (weekly), *Building Permit Values* (monthly), *Business Men's Expectations* (quarterly), *Monthly Business Failures* (monthly), *New Business Incorporations* (monthly), *Wholesale Commodity Prices* (weekly), and *Wholesale Food Prices* (weekly).

Editor & Publisher Market Guide, Editor & Publisher, New York, Annually.
A guide to over 1,500 newspaper markets and pertinent data about those markets.

J. Walter Thompson Co., *Population and Its Distribution: The United States Markets,* 8th ed., McGraw-Hill Book Co., Inc., New York, 1961, 489 pp.
A handbook of marketing facts. The information is gathered from the *1960 United States Census of Population* and other census data on retail trade.

Media-Market Planning Guide, Advertising Publications, Inc., Quarterly.

This quarterly presents basic sales, media, and trade association facts on 67 industrial markets.

Prentice-Hall Loose-Leaf Services, Prentice-Hall, Inc., Englewood Cliffs, N.J.

A group of 42 comprehensive loose-leaf services, giving authoritative information on taxation, government regulation, and business conditions. Included are such services as *American Federal Tax Reports Bank Service, Federal Tax Citator, Labor Policies and Practices, Securities Regulation Service, State and Local Taxes.*

Rand McNally Commercial Atlas and Marketing Guide, Rand McNally & Co., Chicago, Annually.

A complete atlas of the world supplemented with statistics. Monthly supplements provide information on business conditions.

Standard Corporation Records, Standard and Poor's Corporation Services.

An extensive loose-leaf service that provides investors with financial and other information on organizations that offer investment opportunity. Other investment information is given in the Service's many other publications: *The Bond Outlook, Railroad Securities, Listed Bond Report, Industry Surveys, Stock Reports Over-the-Counter and Regional Exchanges, Daily Dividend Record, Facts and Forecasts Service.*

MANAGEMENT

Books

Benn, A. E., *The Management Dictionary,* Exposition Press, New York, 1952, 381 pp.
A standardization of definitions and concepts of terminology in the field of personnel management.

Heyel, Carl, editor, *The Encyclopedia of Management,* Reinhold Publishing Corporation, New York, 1963, 1,084 pp.
A comprehensive reference work to all aspects of management.

The Management Almanac, National Industrial Conference Board, New York, 1946, 340 pp.
A source book of information for the business executive. Primarily covers the fields of personnel and labor relations.

Maynard, H. B., editor, *Top Management Handbook,* McGraw-Hill Book Co., Inc., New York, 1960, 1,236 pp.
A presentation of comprehensive articles prepared by leading executives of the American business world.

Weld, Christopher M., editor, *The Dartnell Office Manager's Handbook,* The Dartnell Corporation, Chicago, 1958, 1,375 pp.
Generally covers all basic areas of office management.

Wylie, Harry L., editor, *Office Management Handbook,* 2nd ed., Ronald
   Press Company, New York, 1958, N.N.
   Covers in separate sections the major areas of office management.
   Each section is written by a specialist in the field.

Yoder, Dale, *et al., Handbook of Personnel Management and Labor
   Relations,* McGraw-Hill Book Co., Inc., New York, 1958, N.N.
   A handbook and source book covering the management areas of
   personnel and labor relations.

Periodicals

Academy of Management Journal, Academy of Management, Eugene,
   Oregon, Quarterly.
   Contains scholarly articles in management theory and research.

Administrative Management, Geyer-McAllister Publications, Inc., New
   York, Monthly.
   Presents articles of interest to the office manager, especially in the
   areas of personnel relations, office methods, and office equipment.

Administrative Science Quarterly, Graduate School of Business and
   Public Administration, Cornell University, Ithaca, N.Y., Quarterly.
   A journal that presents scholarly studies and articles designed to
   further knowledge of administration.

Advanced Management—Office Executive, Society for the Advancement
   of Management, New York, Monthly.
   Contains articles in the general area of management and especially in
   the area of personnel policies and labor relations.

Business Management, Management Magazines, Inc., Greenwich, Conn.,
   Monthly.
   Articles that present practical thinking in all areas of management,
   with special emphasis on office management.

California Management Review, University of California Press, Berkeley,
   California, Quarterly.
   Presents articles for those teachers, researchers, and managers who are
   interested in improving management effectiveness.

Industrial and Labor Relations Review, New York State School of Industrial and Labor Relations, Cornell University, Ithaca, N.Y., Quarterly.
   Presents selected articles and research reports in the fields of industrial
   and labor relations.

Management Record, National Industrial Conference Board, New York,
   Monthly.
   A collection of timely articles covering the current areas of interest in
   management, with emphasis on personnel management and employee
   relations.

The Management Review, American Management Association, Inc., New York, Monthly.
A digest of the best management articles from other publications.

Management Science, Institute of Management Sciences, Baltimore, Quarterly.
A scholarly journal that contains analytical treatises in the areas of management science.

Personnel, American Management Association, Inc., New York, Bimonthly.
A periodical that carries articles relating to all phases of personnel management.

Personnel Journal, The Personnel Journal, Inc., Swathmore, Pa. Monthly.
A publication devoted primarily to articles in the fields of labor relations and personnel practices. Reviews books, presents research findings, and reports conferences in these fields.

Supervision, Supervision Publishing Co., Madison, N.J., Monthly.
Presents articles and news in the fields of industrial relations and operating management.

Supervisory Management, American Management Association, New York, Monthly.
A periodical that covers the general areas of interest to the manager, with articles and digests of articles.

Government publications

United States Small Business Administration, *Management Aids for Small Business,* United States Superintendent of Documents, Washington, D.C., Annually.
Collection of valuable suggestions for small business managers and owners. The subject matter is divided into three classes: Business–Government Regulations, Internal General Management, and External Sources of help, advice, and guidance.

United States Small Business Administration, *Small Business Management Series,* Superintendent of Documents, Washington, D.C.
A series of booklets that cover numerous subjects of interest to small business managers.

MARKETING

Books

Aspley, John Cameron, editor, *The Dartnell Public Relations Handbook,* 3rd ed., The Dartnell Corp., Chicago, 1961, 992 pp.
Contains information basic to all areas of public relations.

————, editor, *The Sales Promotion Handbook,* 3rd ed., The Dartnell Corp., Chicago, 1960, 1,053 pp.

Gives detailed analysis of all phases of sales promotions. Appendix shows distribution of sales dollars of 221 companies.

Barton, Roger, editor, *Advertising Handbook*, Prentice-Hall, New York, 1950, 1,015 pp.
A general coverage by 35 specialists in the basic problems of advertising. Contains a glossary of advertising terms.

Credit Research Foundation, editors, *Credit Management Handbook*, Richard D. Irwin, Inc., Homewood, Ill., 1958, 776 pp.
A basic and detailed analysis of all phases of credits and collections.

Frey, Albert W., with the assistance of Gerald Albaum, *Marketing Handbook*, 2nd ed., Ronald Press Company, New York, 1965, varying pagings.
A useful reference for planning and executive marketing functions. Covers in detail the entire marketing process from planning of the product through channels of distribution to the ultimate consumer.

Graham, Irvin, *Encyclopedia of Advertising*, Fairchild Publishing, Inc., New York, 1952, 606 pp.
Contains more than 1,100 entries related to advertising, marketing, publishing, public relations, and the graphic arts.

Printers' Ink, editors, *Check List of Advertising Essentials*, Printers' Ink Books, Pleasantville, New York, 1955, 336 pp.
This book contains 204 lists of pointers for improving all phases of advertising from copy for newspapers to television programs.

Strand, Stanley, *Marketing Dictionary*, Philosophical Library, New York, 1962, 810 pp.
A reference work that presents the marketing language in concise and comprehensive meanings.

Periodicals

Advertising Age, Advertising Publications, Inc., Chicago, Weekly.
Presents a variety of articles on marketing and selling plus short news items on all phases of advertising and selling. An annual edition, *Advertising Age Market Data Issue* is a good guide to privately published data on markets of the United States by different classifications.

Advertising Agency, Moore Publishing Co., Bristol, Conn., Monthly.
Contains a variety of articles of copy, layout, media, and general techniques of advertising.

Chain Store Age, Lebhar Friedman Publications, Inc., New York, Eleven times a year.
Published in seven editions, each containing general news and statistics. The Administration Edition is slanted toward the executive level

of chain-store merchandising. The remaining six editions are for executives and managers of drug, grocery, and merchandise-variety chains.

Department Store Economist, Chilton Co., Philadelphia, Pa., Monthly.
A publication for department store executives, containing timely articles on all phases of department store operations.

Distribution Age, Chilton Co., Philadelphia, Pa., Monthly.
A publication that covers the field of marketing in a broad sense. Has timely articles on handling, packing, warehousing, financing, insurance, and other phases of the distribution function.

Industrial Marketing, Advertising Publications, Inc., Chicago, Monthly.
Contains a variety of articles on the marketing of industrial goods. Gives good coverage to current happenings and developments in the field.

Journal of Marketing, The American Marketing Association, Chicago, Quarterly.
A collection of scholarly and practical articles in the basic marketing areas. Included is a list and summary of articles from business, economic, and social science periodicals on marketing.

Journal of Marketing Research, American Marketing Association, Chicago, Quarterly.
A scholarly journal devoted to reporting current research efforts and developments in marketing.

Journal of Retailing, New York University School of Retailing, New York, Quarterly.
Presents various articles on the theoretical as well as practical aspects of retailing.

Marketing/Communications, Decker Communications, Inc., New York, Monthly.
A current publication of articles in the general areas of advertising and marketing.

Modern Packaging, McGraw-Hill, Inc., Breskin Publishing Division New York, Monthly.
Contains articles of broad scope relating to packaging and display. Illustrates packaging material and has an index of advertisers and their product specialty.

Purchasing, Conover-Mast Publications, New York, Biweekly.
Contains various timely articles and features in the area of industrial purchasing. Is especially interesting to the purchasing agent.

Reporter of Direct Mail Advertising, The Reporter of Direct Mail Advertising, Inc., Garden City, N.Y., Monthly.
A periodical for those in the direct-mail industry. Covers current happenings and developments, and presents practical articles on all areas of direct-mail advertising.

Sales Management, Sales Management Inc., New York, Semimonthly.

A journal devoted to the areas of sales management and selling. Annually compiles valuable statistics pertaining to population and buying power for all areas of the nation. Gives good coverage to current developments and trends in the sales area.

Standard Rate and Data Service, Standard Rate and Data Service, Inc., Skokie, Ill., Monthly.

A source of information on advertising rates and media data. Published in four volumes by media type: newspapers, business papers, magazines and trade journals, and radio and television.

Stores, National Retail Merchants Association, New York, Eleven times a year.

A report of trends, developments, special studies, and the like in all areas of the industry.

Government publications

United States Bureau of the Census, *Monthly Retail Trade Reports,* United States Government Printing Office, Washington, D.C.

Reports recent data on trends in sales, receipts, and inventories of retail trade. The data are reported by kind of business for selected large cities and for the entire country.

————, *Monthly Wholesale Trade Reports,* United States Government Printing Office, Washington, D.C.

Miscellaneous

Bradford, Ernest S., *Bradford's Directory of Marketing Research Agencies,* Ernest S. Bradford, New Rochelle, New York, Biennially.

A listing of research firms in the United States and abroad, and the information on those firms.

N. W. Ayer & Son's Directory of Newspapers and Periodicals, N. W. Ayer and Son, Inc., Philadelphia, Annually.

A publication that lists over 21,700 newspapers and periodicals, and pertinent data about them.

Standard Advertising Register, National Register Publishing Co., New York, Annually.

A guide to over 16,000 advertisers and essential facts concerning them.

QUESTIONS

1. Suggest a hypothetical research problem that would make good use of a specialized library.

2. What specialized libraries are there in your community? What general libraries?

3. Name the most important library sources in your major field of interest (your college major) to which you would be able to go directly.

4. Distinguish between biographical and trade directories.

5. Distinguish between the contents of encyclopedias and yearbooks.

6. Discuss the major differences between the Dewey Decimal System and the new system of the Library of Congress.

7. In which of the indexes is one most likely to find information on the following subjects.

   a) Labor–management relations.
   b) Innovation in sales promotion.
   c) Accident proneness among workers.
   d) Safety engineering.
   e) Trends in responsibility accounting.
   f) Labor unrest in the late 1800's.
   g) Events leading to enactment of a certain tax measure in 1936.
   h) Textbook treatment of business writing in the 1930's.
   i) Viewpoints on the effect of deficit financing by governments.
   j) New techniques in office management.

8. Select one of the topics listed above and set up for it a tentative note card arrangement and the beginning of a bibliography (at least five sources).

9. Select three government publications useful in business research. Find them in your library and inspect them. Comment on their content and their usefulness.

10. Using the bibliography of basic business sources at the chapter end, point out the sources that generally are most useful to the researcher. If you know any important omissions, name them.

CHAPTER 5

Organizing information

After information has been gathered, it may be in various states of order. If it has been collected through an orderly form of bibliographical research (as described in Chapter 4), it is already arranged by like subjects and is likely to be ready for application to the problem. Information collected through primary research, however, is likely to need classifying, editing, and tabulating before it can be applied.

CLASSIFYING DATA

Classifying data simply means grouping them by some logical basis, such as time, quantity, and place. In primary research problems, the plan for classifying usually precedes the work of editing and tabulating.

The technique of classifying information is best explained by example. A questionnaire survey of 1,000 people would have 1,000 different answers to the question of how many miles the family car was driven during the past years. To make this finding more meaningful, the investigator might arrange the answers by broad quantitative groups. Such a grouping might include these quantitative divisions: under 3,000, 3,000 to under 7,000, 7,000 to under 12,000, and 12,000 miles and over.

Another example is the case of an investigation to determine what housewives like about a certain detergent. Of the many varied answers received, most could be classified into such categories as cleansing ability, mildness on hands, aroma, and sudsing quality.

In either instance, the information is brought together—or reduced so as to be more workable and understandable. Thus, the two

chief reasons for grouping are apparent: (1) significant relationships of the data are brought to light; (2) the data are simplified,
thereby aiding the mental process of interpretation.

Classifying and the corollary tasks of editing and tabulating may
be done while the research is going on or after all the information is
collected. If the investigator elects to classify, edit, and tabulate as
the information is collected, he must either predetermine the grouping plan for the information or base the groupings on early or
incomplete information. With some problems, this early determination of the classification plan is easy. With others, however, it is
difficult and may result in costly and time-consuming corrections.

EDITING AND TABULATING

After the researcher has determined the classifications to be used,
logically he turns to the tasks of editing and tabulating. Editing
generally involves inspecting all the data collected; looking for
possible errors, inconsistencies, and omissions; making corrections
whenever possible; and generally preparing the forms for tabulation. The process of interpreting the forms and looking for error is
largely a subjective one and requires a thorough knowledge of the
subject matter. Obviously, such work is no better or worse than the
quality of the editor.

Preparing questionnaires for tabulation can be a somewhat complex chore, depending on the tabulation system used. In most instances, it involves marking the classifications each answer falls into.
For example, the answer $90 to a questionnaire question asking for
weekly income might fall into an $80–$100 classification; thus the
editor might write $80–$100 in a prominent position near the question. Perhaps he would use red or other colored pencil so that the
proper answer could be clearly seen in the tabulating process.

If machine tabulation is being used, editing may also include
writing a code number for each answer in the margin of the questionnaire. Machine tabulation requires that each likely answer to a
question be given a number or letter designation. The editor then
places the proper number or letter designations on the forms,
usually in the margins near the answers. Later, when the information is punched on cards, the key punch operator has only to read
down the margin and punch the numbers and letters. Admittedly,
the foregoing description of coding for machine tabulation is gen-

eral and scant. A more detailed explanation, however, is beyond the scope of this book.

Tabulation is the procedure of counting the answers recorded on questionnaires onto other forms. It is the procedure of reducing the findings to orderly and understandable form. At the conclusion of a survey, for example, the information collected may be on a few hundred questionnaires. In this form, the information is so voluminous as to be meaningless. To be meaningful, this information must be summarized. It is summarized through tabulation.

The task of tabulating may be done by machine, as mentioned previously. Machine tabulating involves recording the information collected on special cards and then counting the results by high-speed electronic machines. The machines and their operations are highly technical and need only to be mentioned at this time. It should be noted, however, that machine tabulating is economically practical only for large-scale surveys or when the tabulating plan is complex.

For less complex research projects, the researcher can tabulate the results by hand. For this task he may use the old and familiar cross-five technique. Known to every schoolboy, this elementary technique involves counting by marks and making every fifth mark across the preceding four (卌).

CONSTRUCTING THE REPORT OUTLINE

After collecting the information and putting it in a preliminary workable order, the good reporter next makes an outline to guide him in presenting his findings in written form. Such an outline is simply a plan for the writing task that follows. The outline is to the writer what the blueprint is to the construction engineer or what the pattern is to the dressmaker. In addition to guiding his efforts, the outline compels the writer to think before he writes. And when the writer thinks, his writing is likely to be clear.

Although this plan may be either written or mental, it is highly recommended that a written form be used in all but the shortest of problems. In longer reports, where tables of contents are needed, the outline forms the basis of this table. Also, in most long reports, and even in some short ones, the outline topics may serve as guides to the reader when placed within the report text as captions (or heads) to the paragraphs of writing they cover.

Patterns of report organization

After he has made ready his information for outlining, and before he begins the task of outlining, the report writer should decide on which writing sequence, or pattern, to use in his report. The possible sequences are many, but they fall into two basic patterns—logical (or indirect) and psychological (or direct). Some authorities suggest a third order, the *chronological* arrangement. Although it deserves attention here, it really is a special form that can be adapted to either the logical or psychological order. Although the emphasis at this stage of report preparation is on the selection of a sequence for the whole of the report, these patterns may be followed in any writing unit, be it sentence, paragraph, major section, or the whole.

In the *logical* (or indirect) arrangement, the findings are presented in inductive order—moving from the known to the unknown. Preceding the report findings are whatever introductory material is necessary to orient the reader to the problem. Then come the facts, possibly with their analyses. And from these facts and analyses, concluding or summary statements are derived. In some problems, a recommendation section may also be included. Thus, in report form this arrangement is typified by an introductory section, the report body (usually made up of a number of sections), and a summary, conclusion, or recommendation section.

An illustration of this plan is the following report of a short and rather simple problem concerning a personnel action on a subordinate. For reasons of space economy, only the key parts of the report are presented.

Numerous incidents during the past two months appear to justify an investigation of the work record of Clifford A. Knudson, draftsman, tool design department. . . .

The investigation of his work record for the past two months reveals these points:

1. He has been late to work seven times.
2. He has been absent without acceptable excuse for seven days.
3. On two occasions he reported to work in a drunken and disorderly condition.
4. Etc.

The foregoing evidence leads to one conclusion: Clifford A. Knudson should be fired.

Contrasting with the logical sequence is the *psychological* (or direct) arrangement. This sequence presents the subject matter in deductive fashion. Conclusions, summaries, or recommendations come first, and are followed by the facts and analyses they are drawn from. A typical report following such an order would begin with a presentation of summary, conclusion, and recommendation material. The report findings and the analyses from which the beginning section is derived comprise the following sections.

Clifford A. Knudson, draftsman, tool design department, should be fired. This conclusion is reached after a thorough investigation brought about by numerous incidents during the past two months. . . .

The recommended action is supported by this information from his work record for the past two months:

1. He has been late to work seven times.
2. He has been absent without acceptable excuse for seven days.
3. On two occasions he reported to work in a drunken and disorderly condition.
4. Etc.

In the *chronological* arrangement, the findings are presented in the order in which they happened. Obviously, such an arrangement is limited to problems that are of a historical nature or in some other way have a relation to time. The time pattern followed may be from past to present, from present to past, from present to future, or from future to present. A report following an order of time may begin with an introductory section or with a conclusion, summary, or recommendation. In other words, the chronological order is generally combined with either of the two preceding orders. Therefore, it is the arrangement of the findings (the report body) to which the chronological sequence is usually applied.

Clifford A. Knudson was hired in 1966 as a junior draftsman in the tool design department. For the first 18 months his work was exemplary, and he was given two pay increases and a promotion to senior draftsman. In January of 1968, he missed four days of work, reporting illness, which was later found to be untrue. Again, in February. . . .

All of these facts lead to the obvious conclusion: Clifford A. Knudson should be fired.

Systems of outline symbols

Various authorities have prescribed guides and procedures for outlining. The gist of most of this procedure is that the material to be presented should be divided into separate units of thought and that some system of Arabic, Roman, or alphabetical symbols should join the units. The most common system of outline symbols is the conventional form.

I. First degree of division.
   A. Second degree of division.
      a. Fourth degree of division.
         (1) Fifth degree of division.
            (a) Sixth degree of division.

A second system of symbols is the numerical (sometimes called *decimal*) form. This system makes use of whole numbers to designate the major sections of a paper. Whole numbers followed by decimals and additional digits indicate subsections of the major sections. That is, an additional digit to the right of the decimal designates each successive step in the subdivision. Illustration best explains this procedure.

1. First degree of division.
   1.1 Second degree of division.
      1.11 Third degree of division.
         1.111 Fourth degree of division.
2. First degree of division.
   2.1 Second degree of division.
      2.11 Third degree of division (first item).
      2.12 Third degree of division (second item).
         2.121 Fourth degree of division (first item).
         2.122 Fourth degree of division (second item).

Care should be taken with numbers over 10. For example, 1.19 shows that this is item 9 of the third-degree of division, not the 19th item of the second degree, which would be written 1.(19).

The nature and extent of outlining

In general, the outline is built around the objective of the investigation and the findings. With the objective and findings in mind, the writer builds the structure of the report in imagination. In this process, he holds large areas of facts and ideas in his mind, shifting them around until the most workable arrangement comes about. This workable arrangement is that order that will present the findings in their clearest and most meaningful form.

The extent of the outlining task will differ from problem to problem. In fact, in many instances much of the work may be done long before the investigator consciously begins the task of constructing an outline. The early steps of defining the problem and determining its subproblems may lay the groundwork for final organization. If a questionnaire or other form is used in gathering information, possibly its structure has given the problem some order. The preliminary analysis of the problem, the tasks of classifying and tabulating the findings, and possibly preliminary interpretations of the findings may have given to the reporter the general idea of the report story he is to write. Thus, when the investigator begins to construct the outline, the work before him may be in varying degrees of progress. Obviously, the task of outlining will never be the same for any two problems. Even so, a general and systematic procedure for outlining may prove helpful.

Organization by division

This procedure is based on the concept that outlining is a process of dividing. The subject of division is the whole of the information that has been gathered. Thus, the report writer begins the task of organizing by surveying this whole for some appropriate and logical means of dividing the information.

After the report writer has divided the whole of his information into comparable parts, he may further divide each of the parts. Then, he may further divide each of these subparts, and he may continue to divide as far as it is practical to do so. Thus, in the end the writer may have an outline of two, three, or more levels (or stages) of division. The report writer designates these levels of division in the finished outline by some system of letters or numbers, such as the two systems previously discussed.

Division by conventional relationships

In dividing the information into subparts, the report writer has the objective of finding a means of division that will produce equal and comparable parts. Time, place, quantity, and factors are the general bases for these divisions.

Division by time periods. Whenever the information to be presented has some chronological aspect, organization by time is possible. In such an organization, the divisions of the whole are periods of time. Usually, the periods follow a time sequence. Although a past-to-present and present-to-past sequence is the rule, variations are possible. The time periods selected need not be equal in length, but they should be comparable in importance. Determining comparability is, of course, a subjective process and is best based on the facts of the one situation.

A report on the progress of a research committee serves to illustrate this possibility. The time period covered by such a report may be broken down into the following comparable subperiods.

The period of orientation, May–July.
Planning the project, August.
Implementation of the research plan, September–November.

In addition to illustrating a time breakdown of a problem, this example shows a logical division of subject matter. Each of the three time periods contains logically related information (orientation, planning, implementation). Similarly, the following breakdown of a report on the history of a company is made up of logical time periods. As in the preceding example, each of these parts may be further subdivided into smaller time units.

Struggle in the early years (1887–1901).
Growth to maturity (1902–1929).
Depression and struggle (1930–1939).
Wartime shifts in production (1940–45).
Postwar prosperity (1946–present).
The years ahead.

The happenings within each period may next be arranged in the order of their occurrence. Close inspection may reveal additional division possibilities.

Place as a basis for division. If the information collected has some relation to geographic location, a place division is possible. Ideally, the division would be such that like characteristics concerning the problem exist within each geographic area. Unfortunately, place divisions are hampered in that political boundary lines and geographic differences in characteristics do not always coincide.

A report on the sales program of a national manufacturer illustrates a division by place. The information in this problem may be broken down by these major geographic areas.

New England   Midwest
Atlantic Seaboard   Rocky Mountain
South   Pacific Coast
Southwest

Another illustration of organization by place is a report on the productivity of a company with a number of manufacturing plants. A major division of the report may be devoted to each of the company's plants. The information for each of the plants may be further broken down by place—this time by sections, departments, divisions, or such.

The following outline excerpt illustrates one such possibility.

Millville Plant
    Production
        Planning and Production Control
        Production Department A
        Production Department B
        Production Department C
        Etc.
    Sales
        Sales Office A
        Sales Office B
        Sales Office C
        Etc.
    Finance
        Credit and Collection
        Comptroller
        Etc.
    Personnel
        Salary Administration
        Employment
        Etc.
Bell City Plant
    Production
    Etc.

Division based on quantity.   Divisions by quantity are possible whenever the information involved has quantitative values. To illustrate, an analysis of the buying habits of a segment of the labor force could very well be broken down by income groups. Such a division might produce the following sections.

Under $2,000.
$2,000 to under $4,000.
$4,000 to under $7,000.
$7,000 to under $10,000.
$10,000 to under $15,000.
Over $15,000.

Another example of division on a quantitative basis is a report of a survey of men's preferences for shoes. Because of variations in preferences by ages, an organization by age groups might be used. Perhaps a division such as the following would be appropriate:

Youths, under 18.
Young adult, 18–30.
Adult, 31–50.
Senior adult, 51–70.
Elderly adult, over 70.

Factors as a basis for organization.　Factor breakdowns are not so easily seen as the preceding three possibilities. Frequently, problems have little or no time, place, or quantity aspects. Instead, they require that certain information areas be investigated in order to meet the objectives. Such information areas may consist of a number of questions that must be answered in solving a problem. Or they may consist of subjects that must be investigated and applied to the problem.

An example of a division by factors is a report that seeks to determine the best of three cities for the location of a new manufacturing plant. In arriving at this decision, one must compare the three cities on the basis of the factors that affect the plant location. Thus, the following organization of this problem is a logical possibility.

Worker availability.
Transportation facilities.
Public support and cooperation.
Availability of raw materials.
Taxation.
Sources of power.

Another illustration of organization by factors is a report advising a manufacturer whether to begin production of a new product. This problem has little time, place or quantity considerations. The decision on the basic question will be reached by careful consideration of the factors involved. Among the more likely factors are these.

Production feasibility.
Financial considerations.
Strength of competition.
Consumer demand.
Marketing consideration.

Combination and multiple division possibilities

Not all division possibilities are clearly time, place, quantity, or factor. In some instances, combinations of these bases of division are possible. In the case of a report on the progress of a sales organization, for example, the information collected can be arranged by a combination of quantity and place.

Areas of high sales activity.
Areas of moderate sales activity.
Areas of low sales activity.

Although not so logical, the following combination of time and quantity is also a possibility.

Periods of low sales.
Periods of moderate sales.
Periods of high sales.

The previously drawn illustration about determining the best of three towns for locating a new manufacturing plant shows that a problem may sometimes be divided by more than one characteristic. In this example, the information also could have been organized by towns—that is, each town could have been discussed as a separate division of the report. This plan, however, is definitely inferior, for it physically separates the information that must be compared. Even so, it serves to illustrate a problem with multiple organization possibilities. The presence of two characteristics is common. The possibility of finding three or even four characteristics by which the information may be grouped is not remote. As a rule, when multiple division possibilities exist, those not used as a basis for the major division may serve to form the second and third levels of division. In other words, the outline to this problem may look like this.

    II.   Worker availability.
          A. Town A.
          B. Town B.
          C. Town C.
    III. Transportation facilities.
          A. Town A.
          B. Town B.
          C. Town C.
    IV.   Public support and cooperation.
          A. Town A.

B. Town B.
C. Town C.

Or it might look like this.

II. Town A.
   A. Worker availability.
   B. Transportation facilities.
   C. Public support and cooperation.
   D. Availability of raw materials.
   E. Taxation.
   F. Sources of power.
III. Town B.
   A. Worker availability.
   B. Transportation facilities.
   C. Public support and cooperation.
   D. Availability of raw materials.
   E. Taxation.
   F. Sources of power.
IV. Town C.
   A. Worker availability.
   B. Etc.

The plan of organization selected should be the one that best presents the information gathered. Unfortunately, the superiority of one plan over the others will not always be so clear as in the illustration above. Only a careful analysis of the information and possibly trial and error will lead to the plan most desirable for any one problem.

Introductory and concluding sections

To this point, the organization procedure discussed has been concerned primarily with arrangement of the information gathered and analyzed. It is this portion of the report that comprises what is commonly referred to as the report body. To this report body may be appended two additional major sections.

At the beginning of a major report may be an introduction to the presentation (the reason the examples above begin with II rather than I), although some forms of today's reports eliminate this conventional section. Appended to each major report may be a final major section, in which the objective is brought to head. Such a section may be little more than a summary in a report when the objective is simply to present information. In other instances, it may be the section in which the major findings or analyses are drawn together to form a final conclusion. Or possibly it may lead to a recommended line of action based on the foregoing analysis of information.

Wording the outline for report use

As the outline in its finished form is the report's table of contents and may also serve as caption guides to the paragraphs throughout the written text, care should be taken in constructing its final wording. In this regard, a number of conventional principles of construction may be reviewed. Adherence to these principles will produce a logical and meaningful outline to the report.

Topic or talking caption? In selecting the wording for the outline captions, the writer has a choice of two general forms—the topic and the talking caption. Topic captions are short constructions, frequently one or two words in length, which do nothing more than identify the topic of discussion. The following segment of a topic caption outline is typical of its type.

II. Present armor unit.
   A. Description and output.
   B. Cost.
   C. Deficiencies.
III. Replacement effects.
   A. Space.
   B. Boiler setting.
   C. Additional accessories.
   D. Fuel.

Like the topic caption, the talking caption (or popular caption, as it is sometimes called) also identifies the subject matter covered. But it goes a step further. It also indicates what is said about the subject. In other words, the talking captions summarize, or tell the story of, the material they cover, as in the following illustration of a segment of a talking outline.

II. Operation analyses of armor unit.
   A. Recent lag in overall output.
   B. Increase in cost of operation.
   C. Inability to deliver necessary steam.
III. Consideration of replacement effects.
   A. Greater space requirements.
   B. Need for higher boiler setting.

C. Efficiency possibilities of accessories.
D. Practicability of firing two fuels.

A REPORT OUTLINE MADE UP OF CAPTIONS THAT TALK

I. Orientation to the problem.
   A. Authorization by board action.
   B. Problem of locating a woolen mill.
   C. Use of miscellaneous government data.
   D. Logical plan of solution.
II. Community attitudes toward the woolen industry.
   A. Favorable reaction of all cities to new mill.
   B. Mixed attitudes of all toward labor policy.
III. Labor supply and prevailing wage rates.
   A. Lead of San Marcos in unskilled labor.
   B. Concentration of skilled workers in San Marcos.
   C. Generally confused pattern of wage rates.
IV. Nearness to the raw wool supply.
   A. Location of Ballinger, Coleman, and San Marcos in the wool area.
   B. Relatively low production near Big Spring and Littlefield.
V. Availability of utilities.
   A. Inadequate water supply for all but San Marcos.
   B. Unlimited supply of natural gas for all towns.
   C. Electric rate advantage of San Marcos and Coleman.
   D. General adequacy of all for waste disposal.
VI. Adequacy of existing transportation systems.
   A. Surface transportation advantages of San Marcos and Ballinger.
   B. General equality of airway connections.
VII. A final weighting of the factors.
   A. Selection of San Marcos as first choice.
   B. Recommendation of Ballinger as second choice.
   C. Lack of advantages in Big Spring, Coleman, and Littlefield.

A REPORT OUTLINE MADE UP OF TOPIC CAPTIONS

I. Introduction.
   A. Authorization.
   B. Purpose.
   C. Sources.
   D. Preview.
II. Community attitudes.
   A. Plant location.
   B. Labor policy.
III. Factors of labor.
   A. Unskilled workers.

      B. Skilled workers.

      C. Wage rates.

  IV. Raw wool supply.

      A. Adequate areas.

      B. Inadequate areas.

   V. Utilities.

      A. Water.

      B. Natural gas.

      C. Electricity.

      D. Waste disposal.

  VI. Transportation.

      A. Surface.

      B. Air.

 VII. Conclusions.

      A. First choice.

      B. Alternate choice.

      C. Other possibilities.

The choice between topic and talking captions usually is the writer's, although some companies have specific requirements for their reports. Topic captions are the conventional form. Because they have the support of convention, they are most often used in industry, especially in the more formal papers. Talking captions, on the other hand, are relatively new, but they are gaining rapidly in popularity. Because they do the best job of communicating the report information, talking captions are recommended as the superior form. But either form is correct.

Parallelism of construction.   Because of the many choices available to him, the report writer is likely to construct an outline that has a mixture of grammatical forms. Some report writers believe that such a mixture of forms is acceptable and that each caption should be judged primarily by how well it describes the material it covers. The more precise and scholarly writers disagree, saying that mixing caption types is a violation of a fundamental concept of balance.

This concept of balance they express in a simple rule—the rule of parallel construction: all coordinate captions should be of the same grammatical construction. That is, if the caption for one of the major report parts (say part II) is a noun phrase, all equal-level captions (parts III, IV, V, etc.) must be noun phrases. And if the first subdivision under a major section (say part A of II) is constructed as a sentence, the captions coordinate with it (B, C, D, etc.) must be sentences.

The following segment of an outline illustrates violations of the principle of parallel construction.

A. Machine output is lagging (sentence).
B. Increase in cost of operation (noun phrase).
C. Unable to deliver necessary steam (decapitated sentence).

Parallelism may be achieved in any one of three ways, by making the captions all sentences, all noun phrases, or all decapitated sentences. If all noun phrases are desired, such captions as these could be constructed.

A. Lag in machine output.
B. Increase in cost of operations.
C. Inability to deliver necessary steam.

Or as all sentences, they could appear like this.

A. Machine output is lagging.
B. Cost of operations increases.
C. Boiler cannot deliver necessary steam.

Another violation of parallelism is apparent in the following example.

A. Rising level of income (participial phrase).
B. Income distribution becoming uniform (decapitated sentence).
C. Rapid advance in taxes (noun phrase).
D. Annual earnings rise steadily (sentence).

Again, the error may be corrected by selecting any one of the captions and revising the others to conform with it. As participial phrases, they may look like this.

A. Rising level of income.
B. Uniformly increasing income distribution.
C. Rapidly advancing taxes.
D. Steadily rising annual earnings.

When revised as noun phrases, they would take this form.

A. Rise in level of income.
B. Uniform increase in income distribution.
C. Rapid advance in taxes.
D. Steady rise in annual earnings.

As decapitated sentences, they would read this way.

A. Income level rising.
B. Income distribution becoming uniform.

C. Taxes advancing rapidly.
D. Annual earnings rising steadily.

More specifically, the talking caption should be the shortest possible word arrangement that also meets the talking requirement. Although the following captions talk well, their excessive lengths obviously affect their roles in communicating the report information.

Appearance is the most desirable feature that steady college users of cigarette lighters look for.

The two drawbacks of lighters mentioned most often by smokers who use matches are that lighters get out of order easily and frequently are out of fluid.

More dependability and the ability to hold more lighter fluid are the improvements most suggested by both users and nonusers of cigarette lighters.

Obviously, the captions contain too much information. Just what should be left out, however, is not easily determined. Much depends on the analysis the writer has given the material and what he has determined to be most significant. One analysis, for example, would support these revised captions.

Appearance most desirable feature.
Dependability primary criticism.
Fuel capacity most often suggested improvement.

Variety in expression. In the report outline, as in all forms of writing, a variety of expression should be used. Words and expressions should not be overworked, for too-frequent repetitions tend to be monotonous. And monotonous writing is not pleasing to the discriminating reader. The following outline excerpt well illustrates this point.

A. Chemical production in Texas.
B. Chemical production in California.
C. Chemical production in Louisiana.

As a rule, if the captions are made to talk well there is little chance for occurrence of such monotonous repetition, for it is unlikely that successive sections would be presenting similar or identical information. That is, captions that are really descriptive of the material they cover are not likely to make use of the same words. As an illustration of this point, the outline topics in the foregoing example can be improved simply through making the captions talk.

A. Texas leads in chemical production.
B. California holds runner-up position.
C. Rapidly gaining Louisiana ranks third.

QUESTIONS

1. In a survey, automobile owners were asked what influenced them in their selection of brand and model. Using your imagination logically, construct a classification plan for the answers received for this question.
2. In what ways is the task of editing related to the research plan used?
3. What should one consider in deciding between machine and hand tabulation of research data?
4. What are the basic patterns of report organization? Can you see advantages and shortcomings in these patterns? Discuss.
5. Discuss the concept of outlining as a process of division.
6. Illustrate with examples different from those in the text each of the conventional relationships by which report information may be divided.
7. Select a problem (different from the text illustrations) that has at least two division possibilities. Evaluate each of the possibilities.
8. Assume that you are working on a report on the history of manufacturing in the northeastern section of the United States. What division possibilities would you consider in organizing this problem? Discuss the merits of each.
9. What are talking captions? Topic questions? Illustrate each by example (different from those in the text).
10. Point out any violations of grammatical parallelism in the following subheads of a major division of a report.
    a) Sporting Goods Shows Marked Increase
    b) Modest Increase in Hardware Volume
    c) Automotive Parts Remains Unchanged
    d) Plumbing Supplies Records Slight Decline
11. Find any possible error in grammatical parallelism in these captions.
    a) Slow Growth in Early Years
    b) Wartime Demand Accelerates Volume
    c) Steady Prosperity through Postwar Years
    d) Continued Growth for the Near Future
12. Mark the parallelism violations in these captions.
    a) District 1 Not in Running
    b) High Return Loss Evident in District 2
    c) Inadequate Sales Coverage Found in District 3
    d) District 5 Leads in Sales

13. Mark the point of error in the following portion of the report outline. Explain the error.
    a) Initial Costs Differ Little
    b) Brand B Has Best Trade-In Value
        1. Brand A is a close second
    c) Composite Costs Favor Brand B

14. Which one of the following outline captions is not consistent with the others?
    a) Record Sales in New York
    b) Little Change in Chicago
    c) Modest Increase in Los Angeles
    d) Slight Loss in Houston
    e) Production lags behind sales

15. Select an article from a periodical, a chapter from a book, or some other comparable writing that has few or no captions, and write captions for it. First write topic captions; then write talking captions.

16. Assume that you are writing a report on the expenditures of students at your college. Work up a tentative outline for this problem.

CHAPTER 6

Constructing the formal report

After the outline is in finished form, the report writer next turns to the task of planning the makeup of his report. This task is complicated by the fact that reports are far from standardized in regard to their physical arrangement. The variations among reports are countless. In fact, report types in use are so numerous as to almost defy meaningful classification. Even so, if the report writer is to determine the makeup of a specific report he must be generally acquainted with the possibilities of choice available to him. Thus, he should be acquainted with some workable approach to a summary of all reports.

AN APPROACH TO REPORT MAKEUP

Such an approach is presented in the following paragraphs. It should be pointed out, though, that the concept of this approach is quite general. It does not account for all possible reports nor the countless variations in report makeup. But it does serve to help the student grasp the relationship of all reports.

Structural relationships of all reports

To understand this relationship, one may view the whole of reports as resembling a stairway, as illustrated in Figure 5. At the top of this stairway is the formal, full-dress report. This is the form used when the problem is long and the problem situation is formal. In addition to the report text (usually introduction through conclusion), this formal report has a number of parts. They appear before the report text in the same way the prefatory parts appear before the text material of this or almost any other book. Such pages are included primarily for reasons of length and formality. Although there is no standardized set of prefatory ingredients, these parts are traditional to the typical long, formal report: title fly, title page, letters of transmittal and authorization, table of contents, and synopsis. Detailed descriptions of the content and form of these papers appear elsewhere in this book.

As the need for formality decreases and the problem becomes

Figure 5.   Progression of change in report makeup as formality requirements and length of the problem decrease

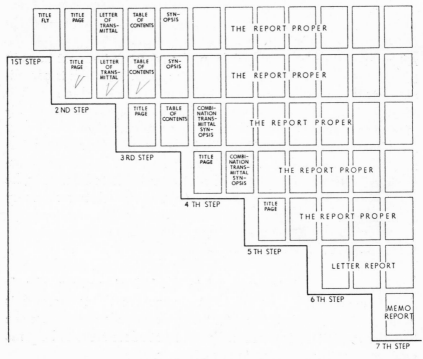

smaller, the makeup of the report also changes. Although these changes are far from standardized, they follow a general order. First, the somewhat useless title fly drops out. This page contains nothing other than the title, and the title information appears on the next page. Obviously, the page is used strictly for reasons of formality. Next in the progression, the synopsis (summary) and the transmittal letters are combined. When this stage is reached, the report problem usually is short enough to permit its summary in relatively short space. A third step down, the table of contents drops out. The table of contents is a guide to the report text, and such a guide serves little value in a short report. Certainly, a guide to a 100-page report is necessary, and a guide to a 1-page report is illogical. Somewhere between these extremes a dividing point exists. The report writer should follow the general guide of including a table of contents whenever it appears to be of some value to the reader.

Another step down as formality and length requirements continue to decrease, the combined letter of transmittal and synopsis drops out. Thus, the report now has only a title page and report text. The title page remains to the last because it serves as a very useful cover page. In addition, it contains the most important of the identifying information. Below this short-report form is a report that reinstates the letter of transmittal and summary and presents the entire report in the form of a letter—thus, the letter report. And finally, for short problems of even more informality the memorandum (informal letter) form may be used. The first of these steps is illustrated at the end of this chapter. Some of the steps at the opposite end of the stairway are displayed in Chapter 7.

As previously mentioned, this analysis of report change is at best general, and perhaps it oversimplifies changes in report structure. Few of the reports actually written coincide exactly with its steps. Most of them, however, fit generally within the framework of the diagram. Knowledge of this relationship of length and formality should be helpful to the investigator as he begins to plan the report for his problem.

Ingredients of the formal report

In a sense, the report writer's task of designing a report is much like the task of the architect. Both have a number of possible ingredients with which to work. Both seek to select and arrange the ingredients to meet the requirements of a given situation. And in order to do their respective tasks skillfully, both must know well the ingredients at their disposal.

For the report writer, these ingredients are the report parts. Because the traditional long, formal report contains the most common of these parts, it is described in the following pages. In addition, one such report is illustrated at the chapter end, and the mechanics of some of the parts are illustrated in Chapter 11. Less formal and shorter reports are described in Chapter 6. The following outline of the parts of a traditional long, formal report serve as a preview to the discussion that follows. For convenience, the parts are arranged by groups. First are the prefatory parts—those that are most related to the formality and length of the report. Then comes the report proper, which, of course, is the meat of all reports. It is the report story. The parts before and after it are to some extent mainly trappings. The final group consists of appended parts. These contain supplementary materials. As a rule, these materials are not essential to the report presentation. They are included largely to serve any special interests the reader may have in the problem or to help the reader in his use of the report.

Prefatory parts:
  Title fly.
  Title page.
  Letter of authorization.
  Letter of transmittal, preface, or foreword.
  Table of contents and table of illustrations.
  Synopsis.
The report proper.
  Introduction.
  The report findings (usually presented in two or more major divisions).
  Conclusions, recommendations, or summaries.
Appended parts.
  Bibliography.
  Appendix.
  Index.

CONSTRUCTION OF THE PREFATORY PARTS

Construction of the prefatory parts of a report is somewhat routine and mechanical. In some companies, precise arrangements for these pages are prescribed. As the following pages illustrate, however, some room remains for the application of good logic and imagination.

Title fly

First among the possible prefatory report pages is the title fly. As a rule, it contains only the report title (see page 137). The wording of the title should be so carefully selected that it tells at a glance what is covered in the report. That is, it should fit the report like a glove, snugly covering all the report information—no more, no less.

For completeness of coverage, the report writer may build his title around the five W's of the journalist: *who, what, where, when, why.* Sometimes *how* may be added to this list. In some problems, however, not all of the W's are essential to complete identification; nevertheless, they serve as a good checklist for completeness. For example, a title of a report analyzing the Lane Company's 196— advertising campaigns might be constructed as follows:

Who: Lane Company.
What: Analysis of advertising campaigns.
Where: (not essential).
When: 196—.
Why: (implied).

Thus, the title emerges: "Analysis of the Lane Company's 196— Advertising Campaigns."

Obviously, a completely descriptive title cannot be written in a few words—certainly not in a word or two. Extremely short titles are usually vague. They cover everything; they touch nothing. Yet, it is the report writer's objective to achieve conciseness in addition to completeness, so he must also seek the most economical word pattern consistent with completeness. Occasionally, in the attempt to achieve conciseness and completeness at once, it is advisable to make use of subtitles.

Title page

Like the title fly, the title page presents the report title, But, in addition, it displays other information essential to the identification of the report (see page 138). Usually, it presents the complete identification of the writer and authorizer or recipient of the report. Normally, such identification includes titles (or roles), companies and/or departments, street and city addresses. The date of writing may also be included, particularly if the time identification is not made clear in the report title. As was pointed out earlier, it is the last of the prefatory parts to drop out as the report changes form. It remains to the last because the part contains some vital identification material. The page is mechanically constructed and may take any of a number of forms. Two such forms are illustrated in Chapter 11.

Letter of authorization

As discussed in Chapter 2, a report may be authorized orally or in writing. If a written authorization is used, a copy of this document (usually a letter or memorandum) may be inserted after the title page. If the report is authorized orally, the letter of transmittal and/or the introductory section of the report may review the authorization information.

The primary objective of the letter of authorization is that of authorizing the investigator to begin the investigation. In addition, the letter contains a brief statement of the problem with some indication of the limiting factors, together with the scope of the investigation and the limitations (if there are any). Perhaps the use of the report may also be mentioned, as well as when the report is needed and how much the cost of preparation is to be. The letter may follow any of a number of acceptable organization patterns. The following outline describes one acceptable arrangement and content.

1. Direct, clear authorization of the investigation.
2. Explanation of the objective in clear, unmistakable words.
3. Description of areas of the problem that require investigation. This description may be an explanation of the subdivisions of the problem.
4. Limitations (such as time and cost) and special instructions.

Letter of transmittal

Most formal reports contain some form of personal communication from writer to reader. In most business cases, the letter of transmittal makes this contact (see page 139). In some formal cases, particularly when the report is written for a group of readers, a foreword or preface performs this function.

The letter of transmittal, as its name implies, is a letter that transmits the report to the intended reader. Since this major message is essentially positive, the letter is preferably written in direct style. That is, the letter beginning transmits the report directly, without explanation or other delaying information. Thus, the opening words say, in effect, "Here is the report." Tied to or following this statement of transmittal usually comes a brief identification of the subject matter of the study and possibly an incidental summary reference to the authorization information (who assigned the report, when, etc.).

If the letter is combined with the synopsis, as may be done in some forms of reports, the opening transmittal and identification may be followed by a quick review of the report highlights, much in the manner described in the following discussion of the synopsis. But whether the letter of transmittal does or does not contain a synopsis of the report text, generally the writer uses the letter to make helpful and informative comments about the report. He may, for example, make suggestions about how the report information may be put to use. He may suggest follow-up studies, point out special limitations, or mention side issues of the problem. In fact, he may include anything that helps the reader to understand or appreciate the report.

Except in very formal instances, the letter affords the writer an opportunity to more or less chat with the reader. Such letters might well reflect the warmth and vigor of the writer's personality. Generally, good use of personal pronouns (*you, I, we,* etc.) is made. A warm note of appreciation for the assignment or a willingness and desire to further pursue the project traditionally marks the letter close.

Minor distinctions sometimes are drawn between forewords and prefaces, but for all practical purposes they are the same. Both are preliminary messages from writer to reader. Although usually they do not formally transmit the report, forewords and prefaces do many of the other things done by letters of transmittal. Like the letters of transmittal, they seek to help the reader appreciate and understand the report. They may, for example, include helpful comments about the report—its use, interpretation, follow-up, and such. In addition, prefaces and forewords frequently contain expressions of indebtedness to those helpful in the research. Like the letters of transmittal, they usually are written in first person, but seldom are they as informal as some letters. Arrangement of the contents of prefaces and forewords follows no established pattern.

Table of contents and list of illustrations

If a report is long enough for a guide to its contents to be helpful, it should have a table of contents (see page 140). This table is the report outline in its finished form (as discussed in Chapter 5) with page numbers. If the report has a number of tables, charts, illustrations, and the like, a separate table of contents may be set up for them. The mechanics for construction of both of these contents units are fully described in Chapter 11.

Synopsis

The synopsis (also called summary, abstract, epitome, and precis) is the report in miniature. It concisely summarizes all the essential ingredients of the report. It includes all the major facts, as

Figure 6.   Diagram of the synopsis in normal order and in direct order

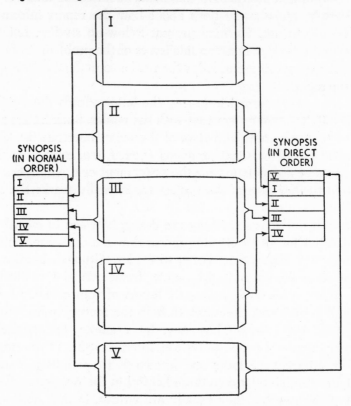

well as major analyses and conclusions derived from these facts. Primarily, it is designed for the busy man who may not have time to read the whole report, but it may also serve as a preview or review for those who very carefully read the report text.

In constructing the synopsis, the report writer simply reduces the parts of the report in order and in proportion. As his objective is to cut the report to a fraction of its length (usually less than one eighth), much of the writer's success will be determined by his skill in directness and word economy. With space at a premium, obviously loose writing is costly. But in his efforts to achieve conciseness, the writer is likely to find his writing style dull. Thus, he must work hard to give this concise bit of writing a touch of color and style interest to reflect the tone of the main report.

Although most synopses simply present the report in normal order (normally from introduction to conclusion), there is now some usage of a more direct opening (see Figure 6). Such a plan shifts the major findings, conclusions, or recommendations (as the case may be) to the major position of emphasis at the beginning. From this direct beginning, the summary moves to the introductory parts and thence through the report in normal order.

CONTENT OF THE REPORT PROPER

Presentation of the report contents may follow any of a number of arrangements. Some companies prefer to prescribe a definite arrangement for all reports, particularly for the technical ones. As may be expected, these arrangements vary with the needs and whims of the companies involved. Descriptions of two such reports, the technical research report and the staff study, appear later in the chapter.

Other companies prefer to follow the traditional, time-honored arrangements. The best known of these is the *logical* arrangement. This order of presenting the report material begins with whatever introductory comments are needed to prepare the reader for the information that follows (see the long, formal report at the chapter end). Next comes the information gathered. Here, the information collected is applied to the problem. It is analyzed and interpreted. The final section of a report written in logical order achieves the report objective. Depending on the objective, this section may summarize, conclude, and/or recommend.

The *direct* (or psychological) arrangement is a second conventional pattern of report structure. It differs from the logical arrangement mainly by its beginning. Instead of introducing the problem, the direct order of report leads off with the major message of the report. That is, the report may begin with a recommendation, conclusion, or summary of findings, whichever the objective of the report happens to involve.

All these variations in the form of the report body are largely rearrangements of the contents of the conventional logical pattern. Thus, the following review of the makeup of the logical report arrangement should equip the student to adapt to the other patterns.

Introduction

The purpose of the introduction of the report is to orient the reader to the problem at hand. In this undertaking, it may include scores of possible topics, for anything may logically be included to help the reader to understand and appreciate the problem. Although the possible contents are varied, certain general topics of coverage should be considered.

Origin of the report. In many reports, the first part of the introduction is devoted to a review of the facts of authorization. In this section are such facts as when, how, and by whom the report was authorized; who wrote the report; and when the report was submitted. This section is particularly useful in reports that have no letter of transmittal, but some writers prefer its inclusion in all report introductions, even though duplication of information is the result.

Purpose. The first section of many report introductions is a description of the purpose of the investigation. Called by other names (objective, problem, object, aim, goal, mission, assignment, proposal, project, etc.), the purpose of the report is the value to be attained by solving the problem. That value may be a long- or short-term value or a combination of both.

The purpose of a report may be stated in various ways. For example, it may be stated in an infinitive phrase (. . . to propose standards of corporate annual reports), or in the form of a well-phrased question (What retail advertising practices do Centerville consumers disapprove of?). Usually, no more than a single sentence is needed for this major purpose.

Collateral, or secondary, purposes should also be stated in this section. If a major problem is solved, collateral values are achieved. By stating these values, the writer helps to convince the reader of the worthwhileness of his report. In other words, he uses a positive approach by telling what the solved problem can do for the reader.

Scope. If the scope of the problem is not clearly covered in any of the other introductory sections, a separate section may be devoted to it. By *scope* is meant the boundaries of the problem. In good, clear language, the problem is described in regard to its exact coverage. Thus, the reader is led to know exactly what is and what is not a part of the problem.

Sources and methods of collecting data. It is usually advisable to tell the reader how the report information has been collected, whether through bibliographical research, through interviewing, and such. If bibliographical research has been used, for example, the library sources consulted may be given and the major publications consulted may be presented. If the publications list is long, however, a bibliography appended to the report may be a better means of listing. Or, another example, if interviewing has been employed, the description would cover such areas of the survey as sample determination, construction of the questionnaire, procedures followed in interviewing, facilities for checking returns, and so on. Whatever the technique used, it should be described in sufficient detail to allow the reader to evaluate the quality of the work done.

Limitations. With some problems, there are limitations of sufficient importance to warrant their presentation as a separate section of the introduction. By *limitations* is meant anything that in some way has worked to impede the investigation or in some way has a deterring effect on the report. An illustrative list of limitations to a report investigation problem may include an inadequate supply of money for conducting the investigation, insufficient time for doing the work, unavoidable conditions that hampered objective investigating, or limitations within the problem under investigation.

Historical background. Sometimes, a knowledge of the history of the problem is essential to a thorough understanding of the problem. Thus, a section on the problem's history is frequently made a part of the report introduction. The general aim of this part is to acquaint the reader with some of the issues involved, some of the principles raised, and some of the values that may be received if more research is done. Too, this section orients the reader and helps to give him a better understanding of the problem. This better understanding will theoretically help the reader and writer to solve similar problems that may arise in the future.

Definitions. If a report is to make use of words likely to be unfamiliar to the reader, these words should be defined somewhere in the report. One practice is to define each such word at the time of its first use in the report text. A more common practice, however, is to set aside in the introduction a special section for definitions.

Report preview. In many reports, a final introductory section is used to preview the report presentation. In this section, the reader is told how the report will be told—what topics will be taken up first, second, third, and so on. And of even greater importance, the reasons this plan is followed may be given. Thus, the reader is given a clear picture of the road ahead so that he may logically relate the topics of the report as he comes to them.

As previously noted, the sections discussed are listed only for the purpose of suggesting possible introduction contents. In few reports will all of the topics mentioned be needed. And in some instances, some of the topics may be combined; in other instances, they may be further split into additional sections. In summary, each introduction should be individually tailored to fit each report.

The report body

The part of the report that presents the information collected and relates it to the problem is the report body. Normally, it comprises the bulk of the content of a report. In fact, this part is, in a sense, the report. With the exception of the conclusion or recommendation section that follows, the other parts of the report are merely trappings.

Specifically, the report body consists of the presentation of findings of the research. It includes the analysis of these findings and application of them to the problem. It is all that appears in the logical order report between the introduction and conclusion sections, including the supporting tables and charts that relate to this part. Truly, it is the heart of the report. Because it is so very important, it is the subject of many of the remaining chapters of this textbook.

The ending of the report

The ending of a report usually consists of a summary, a conclusion, a recommendation, or a combination of the three.

Summary. For some reports, particularly those that do little more than present fact, the end may consist of a summary of the major findings. Frequently, these reports follow the practice of having minor summaries at the end of each major division of the report. When this practice is followed, the final summary simply recaps these summaries. This form of summary, however, should not be confused with the synopsis. Like the summary, the synopsis presents a summary of major findings, but unlike the summary it contains a gist of the major supporting facts.

Conclusions. Conclusions are drawn by inference (induction or deduction) from the facts and discussion in the body. They follow facts, even though in some reports they are placed at the beginning (the psychological arrangement).

Conclusions should flow logically from the facts, but since this is a human process of interpretation, faulty conclusions may result.

Consequently, conclusions are subject to opinions, be it rightly so or not.

For easy reference, conclusions may be tabulated. Their arrangement is open to question. Sometimes, the most important are placed first; sometimes they are listed according to the arrangement discussed in the findings. They also may be combined with the recommendations. In some cases, when the conclusion is obvious it is omitted and only a recommendation is presented.

Recommendations. The recommendations are the writer's section. Here he states his opinion based on the conclusions. Of course, he may not state his recommendations if he is not asked to; but if he is asked, he states them completely, including who should do what, when, where, why, and sometimes how.

Alternative courses of action may be included. But the writer should state his preference. Since he is familiar with the findings, he should not leave his reader on the horns of dilemma. He should state his desired action and then leave the reader to choose his own course of action. Since the writer is usually in a staff position, he should give his advice for a line person to accept.

APPENDED PARTS

Sometimes, it is desirable that special sections be appended to the report. The presence of these parts is normally determined by the specific needs of the problem concerned.

Appendix

The appendix, as its name implies, is a section tacked on. It is used for supplementary information that supports the body of the report but has no logical place within the body of the report. Possible contents include questionnaires, working papers, summary tables, additional references, other reports, and so on.

As a rule, the charts, graphs, sketches, and tables that directly support the report should not be in the appendix. Instead, they should be in the body of the report where they support the findings. Reports are best designed for the convenience of the reader. Obviously, it is not convenient for the reader to thumb through many pages in order to find an appendix illustration to the facts he reads in the report body.

Bibliography

Investigations that make heavy use of bibliographical research normally require a bibliography (an identifying list of the publications consulted). The construction of this formal list is described in detail in Chapter 12.

Index

An index is an alphabetical guide to the subject matter of a piece of writing. It is used primarily with long manuscripts in which it would be difficult to find a specific topic were a subject guide not available. But few reports are of a length sufficient to justify use of the index.

SUMMARY REVIEW OF REPORT CONSTRUCTION

In summary, it is with these ingredients that the report writer builds the report described at the top step in the diagram (Figure 5). By systematically dropping and changing some of them, he can adapt his report to meet the formality needs of his one situation. The description, of course, is oversimplified. Many companies prescribe differing report arrangements. Some, for example, may remove acknowledgements from the letter of transmittal or preface and place them in a separate section. They may break up the synopsis and present conclusions, recommendations, and findings in separate prefatory sections. And some may include special prefatory sheets for intercompany routing purposes. Nevertheless, the progression described captures the nature of the relationship of all reports. And it should serve as a good general guide in planning them.

(*Questions for Chapter 6 appear on page 158.*)

Illustration of a long, formal report

RECOMMENDATIONS FOR 196- REPLACEMENTS

IN ALLIED DISTRIBUTORS, INC., SALES FLEET

BASED ON A COMPARATIVE STUDY OF BRANDS A, B, AND C

The illustration that appears in the following pages typifies the long, formal report. Although this report is competently constructed and well illustrates this traditional form, it is not submitted as a model in all respects. Because of the need to disguise the names of the branded products involved, perhaps the report has lost some of its realism. Nevertheless, it represents an orderly, thorough, and objective solution to a somewhat complex problem.

RECOMMENDATIONS FOR 196X REPLACEMENTS

IN ALLIED DISTRIBUTORS, INC., SALES FLEET

BASED ON A COMPARATIVE STUDY OF BRANDS A, B, AND C

Prepared for

Mr. Norman W. Bigbee, Vice-President
Allied Distributors, Inc.
3131 Speedall Street, Akron, Ohio 44717

Prepared by

George W. Franklin, Associate Director
Midwestern Research, Inc.
1732 Midday Avenue, Chicago, Illinois 60607

April 13, 196X

Long, formal report, continued

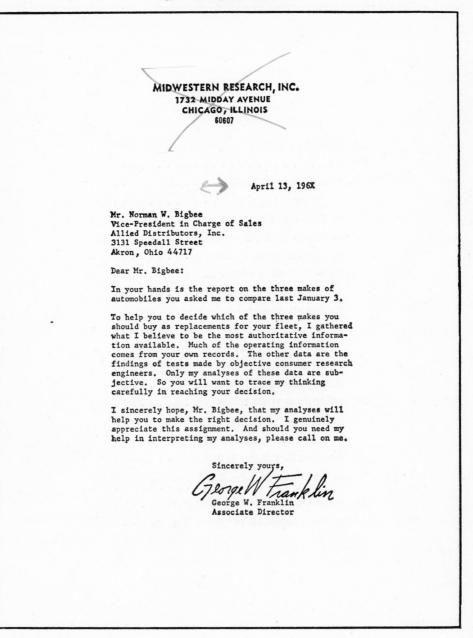

MIDWESTERN RESEARCH, INC.
1732 MIDDAY AVENUE
CHICAGO, ILLINOIS
60607

April 13, 196X

Mr. Norman W. Bigbee
Vice-President in Charge of Sales
Allied Distributors, Inc.
3131 Speedall Street
Akron, Ohio 44717

Dear Mr. Bigbee:

In your hands is the report on the three makes of
automobiles you asked me to compare last January 3.

To help you to decide which of the three makes you
should buy as replacements for your fleet, I gathered
what I believe to be the most authoritative information available. Much of the operating information
comes from your own records. The other data are the
findings of tests made by objective consumer research
engineers. Only my analyses of these data are subjective. So you will want to trace my thinking
carefully in reaching your decision.

I sincerely hope, Mr. Bigbee, that my analyses will
help you to make the right decision. I genuinely
appreciate this assignment. And should you need my
help in interpreting my analyses, please call on me.

Sincerely yours,

George W. Franklin

George W. Franklin
Associate Director

Long, formal report, continued

TABLE OF CONTENTS

Long, formal report, continued

Long, formal report, continued

<u>Epitome</u>

That Car B is the best buy for Allied Distributors, Inc., in
replacing its present sales fleet is the recommendation of this
study. Authorized by Mr. Norman W. Bigbee, Vice-President, on
February 3, 196-, this recommendation is submitted on April 23,
196-, to give the company an insight into the problem of replacing the approximately 50 two-year-old model cars in its present
sales fleet. The basis for this recommendation is an analysis
of cost, safety, and construction factors of three makes of cars
(designated as Makes A, B, and C).

The three cars show little difference in ownership cost (initial
cost less trade-in allowance after two years). On a per-car
basis, Make B would cost $795 for two years, which is $10 under
Car C and $25 below Make A. These differences become more mean-
ingful, however, when interpreted in terms of a 50-car fleet
purchase. Purchase of 50 Make B's would save $1,250 over Make A
and $500 over Make C. Operating costs also favor Car B. Its
cost per mile estimate is $.04126 as compared with $.04157 for
Make C and $.04323 for Make A. A composite of all costs for 50
cars over the two years the cars would be used shows Make B to
be least costly at $113,465. A close second at $114,318 is Make
C; and Make A is a distinct third at $118,883.

On the qualities pertaining to driving safety, Makes B and C are
about equal and are superior to Make A. Although Make A has the
most safety devices built into its cars, it lags in all the other
safety features. Make C, closely followed by B, accelerates best
on both level and grade terrains. Too, Make C has the best weight
distribution of the three. Its 48 per cent (Institute ideal is
50 per cent) is significantly superior to the 44 per cent recorded
for Make B and the 42 per cent for Make A. Car B has the best
braking quality, scoring 95 per cent on the Institute's test as
compared with Make A's 88 per cent and Make C's 85 per cent.

Construction features of both B and C assure a good ride and good
performance. Over-all riding quality is nearer Institute standards
for Car B than for the other makes (94 per cent conformity versus
84 per cent and 86 per cent for Makes C and A, respectively).
Make C is the easiest car to handle. Its score of 95 per cent
conformity with Institute standards is slightly over the 92 per
cent given to Make B and well ahead of the 82 given Make A. Car B

Long, formal report, continued

is tightly built and has fewer rattles and squeaks than either
A or C.

Certainly, all three makes of automobile have outstanding
qualities. A weighting of these factors, however, places Make
B first. Make C ranks a close second; and Make A is a clear
third.

Long, formal report, continued

RECOMMENDATIONS FOR 196- REPLACEMENTS

IN ALLIED DISTRIBUTORS, INC., SALES FLEET

BASED ON A COMPARATIVE STUDY OF BRANDS A, B, AND C

I.   ORIENTATION TO THE PROBLEM

A.   The Authorization Facts

This comparison of the qualities of three brands of automobiles
is submitted April 13, 196-, to Mr. Norman W. Bigbee, Vice-
President, Allied Distributors, Inc. Authorized by Mr. Bigbee
at a meeting in his office January 3, 196-, this investigation
has been made under the direction of George W. Franklin, Associate Director of Midwestern Research, Inc.

B.   Problem of Selecting Fleet Replacements

The objective of this study is to determine which model of automobile Allied Distributors, Inc., should select for replacements
in its sales fleet. The Company's policy is to replace all two-
year-old models in its sales fleet annually, and approximately
fifty automobiles will be replaced this year.

As the replacements involve a major capital outlay, and as the
sales fleet expenses constitute a major sales cost, the proper
selection of the new model presents an important problem. The
model selected must be economical, dependable, and safe. Three
light automobiles, referred to as Makes A, B, and C, are being
considered as replacement possibilities.

C.   Reports and Records as Sources of Data

The selection of the replacement brand is based on a comparative
analysis of the merits of Makes A, B, and C. Data for the comparisons were obtained from both company records and statistical
reports. Operating records of ten representative cars of each
model provide information on operating costs. These reports are
summaries compiled by salesmen-drivers and represent actual per-

1

2

formance of company cars under daily selling conditions. Additional material enumerating safety features, over-all driving quality, and dependability was acquired from the reports of the Consumption Research Institute and the National Automotive Safety Association. Mr. Bigbee furnished price quotations on the new models and trade-in allowances granted on the old models From this material extensive comparisons of the three models are presented.

D. A Preview to the Presentation

The findings in this report are presented in logical order. Comparative analyses treat three major fields: operating costs, safety features, and durability and over-all driving quality. Operating costs constitute the major consideration in comparison and therefore command primary attention. This category is broken down into single cost areas with comparisons of the three models in each area. The most efficient and economical model in each area is signified

Safety features constitute the second field of comparison. Again the field is subdivided into single areas, and the outstanding automobile in each area is noted. Finally, the over-all riding quality and durability of the three models is considered. Throughout the report graphic displays emphasize particular comparisons and analyses

In formulating a final recommendation, the outstanding qualities of each model are tabulated, and the three models are objectively compared. The embodiment of the greatest number of outstanding qualities in one particular model determines the selection of that model for the replacements

II. THE MAJOR FACTOR OF COST

Conceivably, an adequate and logical breakdown of the problem should be followed; and it is, therefore, natural to begin where the ordinary American buyer begins--at cost. First interest is in original cost, "How much will the car cost stripped down except for heater, windshield wipers, oil filter, and a few such Class A accessories?" Of second interest in a natural thinking process, figures of prime concern are the cash differences after trade-in allowances for the old cars. These figures clearly indicate the cash outlay for the new fleet.

3

A. Initial Costs Differ Little

From Table I it is evident that Car B has the lowest stripped-
down cost before and after trade-in allowances. It has a $25
margin which must be considered in the light of what features
are standard on Car B in comparison with those standard on Cars
A and C. That is, Car B may have fewer standard features included in its original cost and, therefore, not be worth as much
as Cars A and C.

	Stripped-down prices*	Trade-in value for two-year-old models	Cash costs after trade-in allowance
TABLE I ORIGINAL COST OF THREE BRANDS OF LIGHT CARS IN 196X			
Make A	$1,824	$1,004	$820
Make B	1,795	1,000	795
Make C	1,810	1,015	805

*Uniformly 5% lower than those paid for the two-year-old
cars now in use.
Source: Primary

It is clear that where features are listed as standard they do
not add to original cost, but where listed as optional they do.
It is seen in Table IV that Car A gives a buyer more safety
features than either other make as standard equipment. As
shown in the table, safety belts are optional on all cars and
are, as a result, an addition to original cost of $25. In
addition to a study of standard features, a close look at trade-
in values and operating costs will also be necessary to properly
evaluate original cost. Further discussion of these facets will
be postponed until they are fitted into our comprehensive study
of optional safety features and operation cost-per-mile estimate.

B. Trade-in Values Show Uniformity

As a logical follow-up of original cost, trade-in values usually
offer some conclusive data for consideration. Trade-in values
are the variable in determining original cost when stripped
prices are fairly uniform. In this study the trade-in values
are fairly uniform, varying only by $15 from highest of $1,015
for Make C to lowest cost of $1,000 for Make B (Table I).

Long, formal report, continued

4

Although fairly uniform, these figures appear to be more significant when converted to total amounts involved in the fleet
purchases. A fleet of 50 cars of Make B would cost $39,750. The
same fleet with Make C cars would cost $40,250, and with Make
A's the cost would be $41,000. Thus, $1,250 could be saved by
purchasing Make B cars over Make A cars, or $500 could be saved
by purchasing Make B cars over Make C cars.

C   Operating Costs Indicate B's Economy

Makes C and B Have Lowest Maintenance Costs. Make C has the lowest maintenance cost of the three, .00661 cents per mile; but
Car B is close behind with .00733 cents. Both costs are well
below Make A's .00901 cents per mile. The components of these
values, as shown in Table II, are repairs and resulting loss of
working time, miscellaneous expense, and battery and tire replacement

It should be stressed here how greatly repair expense influences
the estimate. Actually, two expenses are involved, for to the
costs of repairs must be added the expense of lost working time.
Obviously, a salesman without a car is unproductive. Each hour
lost by car repairs adds to the cost of the car's operation.

As shown in Table II, the hours lost per repair for each make
are the same (five hours). Thus, the important consideration is
the number of repairs and the costs of these repairs. On this
basis, Car C has the lowest total cost burden at $202. Car B
ranks second with a cost total of $236, and Car A is well ahead
with $318.

TABLE II
COMPARISON OF REPAIRS AND RELATED
LOST WORKING TIME FOR THREE MAKES
OF CARS FOR TWO YEARS

	Number of Repairs	Repair Expense	Working Hours Lost*	Total Burden
Car A	8	$234	40	$318
Car B	6	176	30	236
Car C	5	154	25	202

*Based on hourly wage of $2.
Source: Allied Distributors, Inc., Operating Records

Long, formal report, continued

5

Gas and Oil Economy Is Best with Make A. As shown in Table
III, Make A has the best record for oil and gas economy with
a per-mile cost of .01779 cents. Make B, with a cost of .01866
cents, is second; and Make C trails with a cost of .01958 cents
per mile. Computed on the basis of 55,000 miles (the two-year
mileage average for company cars), these costs mean a $98.45
margin per car for Make A over Make C, or $4,923 for the fleet
of 50 cars. Compared with Make B, Make A would show a gas-and-
oil saving of $47.85 per car, or a fleet total of $2,393.

D. Composite Cost Picture Favors Car B

Consolidation of all the cost figures (see Table III) shows
Car B to be slightly more economical than Car C. Total cost
per mile for Car B is .04126 cents, as compared with .04157
cents for Car C and .04323 cents for Car A. These figures take
a more meaningful form when converted to total fleet costs over
the two-year period the cars will be owned. As shown in Chart
I, a fleet of 50 Make B cars would cost Allied a total of
$113,465, which is slightly ($853) under the $114,318 total
cost of Make C. Make A, with a total cost of $118,883, would
cost $5,418 more than Make B.

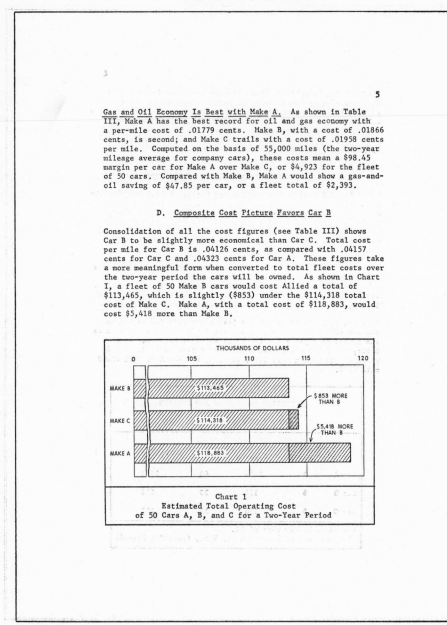

Chart 1
Estimated Total Operating Cost
of 50 Cars A, B, and C for a Two-Year Period

Long, formal report, continued

6

TABLE III COST-PER-MILE ESTIMATE OF OPERATION BASED ON COMPANY RECORDS FOR THIRTY CARS*			
	Car A	Car B	Car C
Depreciation	$ 0.01583	$ 0.01527	$ 0.01538
Gas	0.01657	0.01754	0.01852
Oil	0.00122	0.00112	0.00106
Tires	0.00106	0.00098	0.00086
Repairs and lost time	0.00568	0.00418	0.00357
Miscellaneous expense	0.00227	0.00216	0.00208
Total	$ 0.04323	$ 0.04126	$ 0.04157

*Expenses were calculated at:
  gas...............30 cents per gallon
  oil...............40 cents per quart
  labor.............$2 per hour
  tires.............$30 per each
  Source: Allied Distributors, Inc., Operating Records

III. EVALUATION OF SAFETY FEATURES

Although operating costs receive major consideration in the
selection of replacement models, the safety features of each
model must also be analyzed. In fact, as salesmen spend a large
part of their time traveling and thus need maximum protection from
the hazards encountered in driving, the lowest operating expenses
may be sacrificed in order to obtain added safety features.

A. Car A Is Best Equipped with Safety Devices

In considering the safety features included in each model, all of
the more common safety devices are provided in Make A.   Although
the attachment of a safety belt is optional, Make A is fully
equipped with the padded dashboard, the non-crush steering wheel,
the punchout windshield, and non-shatter glass, as enumerated in
Table IV. The addition of these devices undoubtedly increases the
safety qualities of Make A.   However, Make B also provides adequate driving protection with fewer safety features.

Although it is not as completely equipped with added safety
features as Make A, Make B does embody non-shatter glass and
the electric eye automatic dimmer switch. Safety belts may be

Long, formal report, continued

7

installed. With these features, Make B would be safe for the
extensive driving to which salesmen are subjected. Make C, on
the other hand, is extremely limited in modern safety devices.

TABLE IV
LIST OF APPROVED AVAILABLE
SAFETY FEATURES

	Make A	Make B	Make C
Padded dashboard	X		
Non-crush steeling wheel	X		
Safety belt	X*	X*	X*
Electric-eye switch		X	
Punch-out windshield	X		
Non-shatter glass	X	X	X

*Optional equipment
 Source: National Automotive Safety Association list
          of approved features

In comparison with Makes A and B, Make C, equipped only with
non-shatter glass, seems to lack most of the modern safety devices. The safety belt may be attached. However, the failure
of Make C to have these safety devices does not render the car
unsafe for driving. Good over-all construction of the car body
would compensate for these safety deficiencies.

B. Acceleration Adds Extra Safety to C

A life saving factor that differs greatly among the three brands
is acceleration. It is important as a safety "on-the-spot" need--
something good to have when in a pinch. When needed, acceleration
should be available in the safest car. It should never be depend-
ed on by a driver to the extent of his taking chances because he
knows that it is available, but it must be included in any brand
comparison.

Car C's acceleration is the best of the three makes on both level
and grade terrain (see Charts 2 and 3). Although the charts do
not show it, top speed on the grade climb also goes to Car C with
a speed of 66 mph. Cars A and B attained speeds of 62 and 59
miles per hour respectively. Car C leads in level acceleration
by a 1.8 second difference over Car B (14.4-12.6); thus it is
consistently ahead in over-all acceleration performance.

Long, formal report, continued

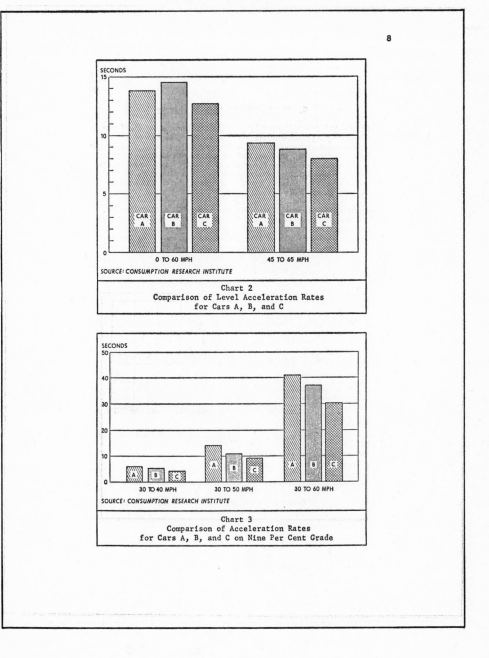

8

SECONDS
15

10

5

0

CAR A   CAR B   CAR C   CAR A   CAR B   CAR C

0 TO 60 MPH   45 TO 65 MPH

SOURCE: CONSUMPTION RESEARCH INSTITUTE

Chart 2
Comparison of Level Acceleration Rates
for Cars A, B, and C

SECONDS
50

40

30

20

10

0

A   B   C   A   B   C   A   B   C

30 TO 40 MPH   30 TO 50 MPH   30 TO 60 MPH

SOURCE: CONSUMPTION RESEARCH INSTITUTE

Chart 3
Comparison of Acceleration Rates
for Cars A, B, and C on Nine Per Cent Grade

9

C. Weight Distribution Is Best in C

Acceleration is affected by weight distribution on the frame which in turn influences braking quality. The proportion of weight on rear wheels balances the car and in doing so controls body skidding and sway on instant starts and stops. It presents a problem due to placement of heavier items such as the motor in the front of the automobile. The placement of the other essential heavy items at various spots on the chassis results in the best distribution.

As shown in Chart 4, Car C has the best weight distribution. Its 47 per cent is near the 50 per cent automotive engineers consider to be ideal. In contrast, Car A carries a relatively low proportion (42%) of weight on rear wheels. This low percentage of weight is not good from the standpoint of traction on slippery roads such as the high crown black-top found in this section of the state. The distribution shown by Car B (44%) is slightly better.

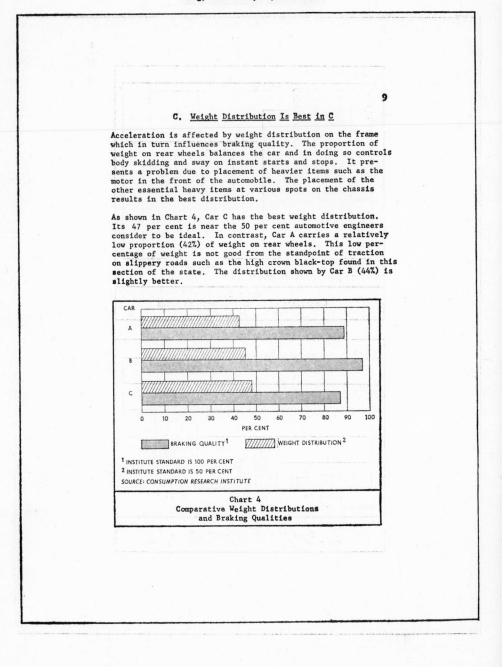

[1] INSTITUTE STANDARD IS 100 PER CENT
[2] INSTITUTE STANDARD IS 50 PER CENT
SOURCE: *CONSUMPTION RESEARCH INSTITUTE*

Chart 4
**Comparative Weight Distributions
and Braking Qualities**

10

D. Braking Quality Makes Safest Stop Possible in B

The direct effect of weight distribution upon braking quality
is seen in Chart 4, which shows that Make A has a braking quality
(88%) comparatively equal to its distribution rating. Its brakes
are adequate both as to power and performance, but they have a
slight tendency to overheat.

Make B contrasts somewhat from Make A in brake efficiency. Although it occupies a second place in weight distribution, Make
B is far ahead in braking quality (95% conformity). Its brakes
are both adequate and well-behaved in normal use, never overheat-
ing excessively.

An over-all review of safety qualities shows Make C to have a
slight advantage over the other cars. Its braking and acceleration are the best of the three, and these factors are the most
vital to safe driving. Make B, although leading only in weight
distribution, is second in all other qualities. For its consistency it ranks a close second. Although Make A is best equipped
in safety devices, it is well back in the important qualities of
acceleration and braking

IV. RIDING COMFORT AND OVER-ALL CONSTRUCTION

Few things affect the day's work of a traveling salesman more
than the ride he gets in his car. Thus, the factors of handling
ease and general riding quality should be considered in selecting his car. Somewhat related to these factors are the over-
all qualities of construction of the cars in question.

A. Car C Ranks First on Handling Ease

Make C, with ball-jointed steering, is the best handling car of
the three. As shown by Institute standards in Chart 5, Make C
scores 95 per cent out of a possible 100 on steering qualities.
The steering standards are based on the automobile's performance
over all types of roads and under all types of driving conditions.
Furthermore, according to Institute reports, Make C has good road
sense.

Make A handles well on the road as far as roadability and behavior
in taking turns are concerned, but the steering lacks road sense.
Make A scored 82 per cent on the Institute test. The Institute
also points out that a driver of Make A receives less information

Long, formal report, continued

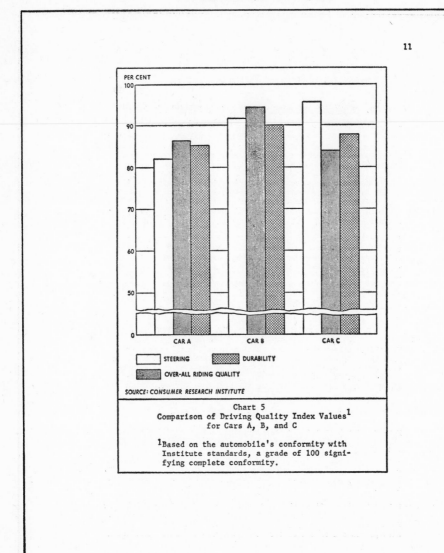

11

Chart 5
Comparison of Driving Quality Index Values[1]
for Cars A, B, and C

[1]Based on the automobile's conformity with
Institute standards, a grade of 100 signi-
fying complete conformity.

12

than he should from the front wheels as to how well he is steering.

On the other hand, Make B handles very well and offers extremely
easy and smooth steering, but it is under Institute standards for
maximum acceptable amount of wheel turning. On the steering
test Make B scored 92 per cent.

B. Make B Gives Best Ride

Make B gives a ride so much better than the other two cars that
it is in a class by itself on this quality. Its suspension is
soft and free of annoying jars, although some rapid vertical
vibration is felt on washboard types of roads. This car takes
corners with more roll than either A or C, but its other features
more than compensate for this shortcoming. Its seats are extremely comfortable and allow the driver to sit more erect than
in the other cars Makes A and C, on the other hand, fall short
of Institute standards on nearly all of these points. The Institute index for over-all riding comfort shows Make B with 94 per
cent, which is well ahead of Make A's 85 per cent and Make C's
84 per cent.

C. Most Durable Is Make B

A quality affecting many of the other qualities discussed is durability of construction. Certainly, the quality of construction
of a car relates to the car's operating costs, especially to repair expense. It relates to safety, for mechanical failure can
be a cause of accident, and mechanical failure is related to
construction. And as signs of weak construction (noise, squeaks,
rattles) are annoying to a driver, construction may affect driving comfort. Thus, the general construction of the three cars,
as reported by Institute researchers, is analyzed as another
factor to be considered in selecting the best car.

Make B tops both A and C in durability of construction It has
fewer squeaks and rattles and a tighter body. A close second
is Make C, which also is tightly built. This car is relatively
free of squeaks and rattles and is well above the average in resistance to shake on rough roads. In third place and below the
Institute's satisfactory shake level is Car A. According to
Institute engineers, this car is willowy and loose. Its height
is good for country driving but is of little value elsewhere.

The superiority of Make B on this point plus its ranking on the
qualities of riding comfort and construction keep the car ahead on

Long, formal report, continued

the basis of these qualities combined. Car C, however, is a
close second; and Car A clearly appears to be in third place.

V. RECOMMENDATION OF MAKE B

The evaluations presented thus far have been significant only as
individual items. It is the summation of these evaluations which
will determine the decision as to which car Allied should buy.
This summation, however, cannot be merely a count of rankings (see
Table V) on the various evaluations made, although such a summation helps to present the whole picture. Obviously, each of
the qualities compared must be weighted, and here subjective
evaluations must be made. But this course cannot be avoided.

From a business standpoint, money costs are primary considerations
in most business decisions. In this problem they appear to deserve major emphasis. As previously concluded, Makes B and C
clearly are superior in over-all matters of cost, with Make B
holding a slight advantage. Which of these two should be purchased, then, is best determined by how each ranks on the secondary
considerations of safety and the operating qualities relating to
construction.

On the question of safety, Make C has an edge over Make B, although
this difference is slight. In the operating areas relating to construction, the differences are equally slight. Make B has a lead
on riding quality and on over-all durability. And Make A is out
front in handling ease.

Apparently there is little to choose between Makes B and C, for
both rank well in all areas of evaluation. But because Make B
has a slight advantage in cost and gets no lower than a draw on
the remaining qualities, this car appears to be the best buy. On
this basis, therefore, Allied should buy Make B automobiles as
replacements for its sales fleet.

Long, formal report, concluded

14

	Make A	Make B	Make C
TABLE V RECAST OF PURCHASE FACTORS OF THREE CARS			
Cost Factors:*			
Original cost (less trade-in)	1	3	2
Gas	3	2	1
Oil	1	2	3
Repair expense and time lost	1	2	3
Tires	1	3	2
Batteries	1	2	3
Miscellaneous	1	2	3
	9	16	17
Safety Features:			
Safety devices	2	2	2
Acceleration	1	2	3
Weight distribution	1	2	3
Braking Quality	2	3	1
Driver Visibility	3	2	1
	9	11	10
Construction Features:			
Steering and handling quality	1	2	3
Riding quality	2	3	1
Durability	1	3	2
Road clearance	2	2	2
	6	10	8
TOTAL POINTS	24	37	35

*All factors are rated on the basis of 6 total points distributed between three makes, 3 points being best grade; 2 points, second best grade; and 1 point, least best grade.
Source: Primary

QUESTIONS

1. Discuss the model used in the chapter to show progression of report change. Trace the steps in it and explain each.
2. Select three of the report problems at the end of the text (preferably the long ones) and write a report title for each. Use the title checklist to explain and defend your title.
3. Discuss the content of the title page. Why is it the last of the prefatory parts to leave the report?
4. Discuss the objectives and contents of the letter of authorization.
5. Explain the differences in letters of transmittal, forewords, and prefaces. When would you use each?
6. Discuss and justify the differences in writing style in the letter of transmittal and the text of the report.
7. What determines whether a report should have a table of contents?
8. Tell how to construct a synopsis.
9. Select one of the reports illustrated at the end of Chapter 7 and write a synopsis for it.
10. Discuss the objectives of the introduction to a report.
11. How would the introduction of a report written for only one man who knows the problem well differ from that written for a dozen men, some of who know little about the problem?
12. What effect does the life of a report (the time it is kept on file) have on the introduction content?
13. Select one of the report problems at the end of the text and determine the topics that should be covered in its introduction.
14. Discuss each of the introduction topics mentioned in the text, bringing out the considerations that would determine the use of each.
15. Explain the content and role of a preview in the introduction of a report.
16. Discuss the ways in which a long, formal report may end.
17. What is the role of the appendix in a report?

CHAPTER 7

Constructing short and special reports

Most reports written in industry are short, informal types. They are quite different from the long, formal type described in detail in Chapter 6. To be sure, long, formal reports are written—often. But they simply do not compare in number with the less imposing types. Thus, because of their importance this chapter is devoted to a review of these less formal reports. And because certain special report types also are likely to be encountered in business, some of these reports also are covered.

To some, the emphasis that has been placed on the long, formal report may appear to be disproportionate. "If the long, formal report is not among the types most frequently used," they may ask, "Why has it been given such major emphasis? Why has not the major stress been placed on the type most common in day-to-day business activity?"

The answers to these questions should be apparent from the approach taken in Chapter 6. As the diagram in Figure 5, page 124, shows, the long, formal report is related to other types. The relationship of its form to that of the other report types is clear. The techniques of organizing it are much the same as those for the lesser types. The writing that goes into it likewise is similar. In fact, all that goes into the long, formal report has some application in constructing the lesser forms. Thus, by learning to write and to construct this the most complex of all reports, one has prepared himself to work on the lesser types. The process may be likened to the work of a carpenter. Having built a mansion, he finds it easy to build a bungalow, a barn, or a lean-to.

MAJOR DIFFERENCES IN SHORT AND LONG REPORTS

Even though much of what has been learned concerning the long, formal report applies equally well to the other forms, certain differences do exist. By concentrating on these differences, one can quickly adapt his knowledge of report writing to the wide variety of short, informal reports. Four areas of such differences stand out as most significant: (1) less need for introductory material, (2) predominance of direct (psychological) order, (3) more personal writing style, and (4) less need for a coherence plan.

Less need for introductory material

One major content difference in the shorter report forms is their minor need for introductory material. Most reports at this level concern day-to-day problems. Thus, these reports have a short life. They are not likely to be kept on file for posterity to read. They are intended for only a few readers, and these few know the problem and its background. The reader's interests are in the findings of the report and any action it will lead to.

This is not to say that all shorter forms have no need for introductory material. In fact, some have very specific needs. In general, however, the introductory need in the shorter and more informal reports is less than that for the more formal and longer types. But no rule can be applied across the board. Each case should be analyzed individually. In each case, the writer must cover whatever introductory material is needed to prepare his reader to receive the report. In some shorter reports, an incidental reference to the problem, authorization of the investigation, or such will do the job. In some extreme cases, a detailed introduction comparable to that of the more formal report may be needed. There are reports, also, that need no introduction whatever. In such cases, the nature of the report serves as sufficient introductory information. A personnel action, for example, by its very nature explains its purpose. So do weekly sales reports, inventory reports, and some progress reports.

Predominance of direct order

Because usually they are more goal-oriented, the shorter more informal reports are likely to use the direct order of presentation.

That is, typically such reports are written to handle a problem—to make a specific conclusion or recommendation of action. This conclusion or recommendation is of such relative significance that it by far overshadows the analysis and information that support it. Thus, it deserves a lead-off position.

As noted earlier, the longer forms of reports may also use a direct order. In fact, many of them do. The point is, however, that most do not. Most follow the traditional logical (introduction, body, conclusion) order. As one moves down the structural ladder toward the more informal and shorter reports, however, the need for direct order increases. At the bottom of the ladder, direct order is more the rule than the exception.

The decision of whether or not to use the direct order is best based on a consideration of the reader's likely use of the report. If the reader needs the report conclusion or recommendation as a basis for an action he must take, directness will speed his effort. A direct presentation will permit him to quickly receive the most important information. If he has confidence in the work of the writer, he may not choose to read beyond this point, and he can quickly take the action the report supports. Should he desire to question any part of the report, however, it is there for his inspection. The obvious result would be to save the valuable time of a busy executive.

On the other hand, if there is reason to believe that the reader will want to arrive at the conclusion or recommendation only after a logical review of the analysis, the writer should organize his report in the indirect (logical) order. Especially would this arrangement be preferred when the reader does not have reason to place his full confidence in the writer's work. A novice working in a new assignment, for example, would be wise to lead his reader to his recommendation or conclusion by using the logical order.

More personal writing style

Although the writing that goes into all reports has much in common, that in the shorter reports tends to be more personal. That is, the shorter reports are likely to use the personal pronouns *I, we, you,* and such rather than a strict third-person approach.

The explanation of this tendency toward personal writing in short reports should be obvious. In the first place, the situation that gives rise to a short report usually involves more personal relationships. Such reports tend to be from and to people who know each other—

people who normally address each other informally when they meet and talk. In addition, the shorter reports by their nature are apt to involve a personal investigation. The finished work represents the personal observations, evaluations, and analyses of the writer. He is expected to report them as his own. A third explanation is that the shorter problems tend to be the day-to-day routine ones. They are by their very nature informal. It is logical to report them informally, and personal writing tends to produce this informal effect.

As is explained in Chapter 9, the report writer's decision on whether to write a report in personal or impersonal style should be based on the circumstances of the situation. He should consider the expectations of those who will receive the report. If they expect formality, he should write impersonally. If they expect informality, he should write personally. Second, if he does not know the reader's preferences he should consider the formality of the situation. Convention favors impersonal writing for the most formal situation.

From this analysis, it should be apparent that either style can be appropriate for reports ranging from the shortest to the longest type. The point is, however, that short report situations are most likely to justify personal writing.

Less need for coherence plan

As is pointed out in Chapter 9, the longer forms of report need some form of coherence plan to make the parts stick together. That is, because of the complexities brought about by length, the writer must make an effort to relate the parts. Otherwise, the paper would read like a series of disjointed minor reports. What he does is to use summaries and introductory forward-looking sentences and paragraphs at key places. Thus, the reader is able to see how each part of the report fits into the whole scheme of things.

The shorter the report becomes, the less is its need for such a coherence plan. In fact, in the extremely short forms (such as memorandum and letter reports), little in the way of wording is needed to relate the parts. In such cases, the information is so brief and simple that a logical and orderly presentation clearly shows the plan of presentation.

Although coherence plans are less frequently used in the short forms of reports, the question of whether to include them should not be arbitrarily determined by length alone. Instead, the matter of need should guide the writer in his choice. Whenever his presentation contains organization complexities that can be made clear by summaries, introductions, and relating parts, these coherence elements should be included. Thus, need rather than length is the major determinant. But it is clearly evident that need for coherence decreases as the report length decreases.

SHORT FORMS OF REPORTS

Of the conventional short forms of reports, three in particular deserve special attention. They are the three at the bottom of the illustration stairway of report progression (Figure 5, page 124): the short report, the letter report, and the memorandum report. Varying widely in form and arrangement, they make up the bulk of the reports written in industry.

The short report

One of the more popular of the less imposing reports is the conventional short report. Representing the fourth step in the diagram of report progression, this report consists of only a title page and the report text. Its popularity may be explained by the middle-ground impression of formality it gives. Inclusion of the one most essential of the prefatory parts gives the report at least a minimum appearance of formality. And it does this without the tedious work of preparing the other prefatory pages. It is ideally suited for the short but somewhat formal problem.

Like most of the less imposing forms of reports, the short report may be organized in either the direct or indirect order, although direct order is by far the most common plan. As illustrated by the report at the chapter end, this most common plan begins with a quick summary of the report, including and emphasizing conclusions and recommendations. Such a beginning serves much the same function as the synopsis of a long, formal report.

Following the summary are whatever introductory remarks are needed. As noted previously, sometimes this part is not needed at all. Usually, however, there follows a single paragraph covering the facts of authorization and a brief statement of the problem and its scope. After the introductory words come the findings of the investigation. Just as in the longer report forms, the findings are presented, analyzed, and applied to the problem. From all this comes a final conclusion and, if needed, a recommendation. These last two elements—conclusions and recommendations—may be presented at the end, even though they are also presented in the beginning summary. Sometimes, to not do so would end the report abruptly. It would stop the flow of reasoning before reaching its logical goal.

The mechanics of constructing the short report are much the same as those for the more formal, longer types. As illustrated in Chapter 11, this report uses the same form of title page and the same layout requirement. Like the longer reports, it makes use of captions. But because of the report's brevity, the captions rarely go beyond the two-division level. In fact, one level of division is most common. Like any other report, its use of graphic aids, appendix parts, and bibliography is dependent on its need for them.

Letter reports

As the wording implies, a letter report is a report written in letter form. Primarily, it is used to present information to someone outside the company, especially when the report information is to be sent by mail. For example, a company's written evaluation of one of its credit customers may well be presented in letter form and mailed to the one who requests it. An outside consultant may write his analysis and recommendations in letter form. Or an organization officer may elect to report certain information to the membership in letter form.

Normally, letter reports are used to present the shorter problem —typically, those that can be presented in three or four pages or less. But no hard and fast rule exists on this point. Long letter reports (10 pages and more) have often been used successfully.

As a general rule, letter reports are written personally (using *I, you, we* references). Exceptions exist, of course, as when one is preparing such a report for an august group, such as a committee of the United States Senate or a company's board of directors. Other than this point, the writing style recommended for letter reports is much the same as that for any other report. Certainly, clear and meaningful expression is a requirement for all reports.

Letter reports may be arranged either in the direct or indirect order. If the report is to be mailed, there is some justification for using an indirect approach. As such reports arrive unannounced, an initial reminder of what they are, how they originated, and such is in order. A letter report written to the membership of an organization, for example, may appropriately begin with these words.

As authorized by your Board of Directors last January 6th, the following review of member company expenditures for direct-mail selling is presented.

If one elects to begin a letter report in the direct order, he would be wise to use a subject line. The subject line consists of some identifying words, which appear at the top of the letter, usually immediately after or before the salutation. Although they are formed in many ways, one acceptable version begins with the word "Subject" and follows it with descriptive words that identify the problem. As the following example illustrates, this identifying device helps to overcome any effect of confusion or bewilderment the direct beginning may otherwise have on the reader.

Subject: Report on direct-mail expenditures of
         Association members, authorized by Board of
         Directors January 1969

Association members are spending 8 percent more on direct-mail advertising this year than they did the year before. Current plans call for a 10 percent increase for next year.

Another possibility is to work the introductory identifying information into the direct opening material.

Regardless of which beginning is used, the organization plan for letter reports corresponds to those of the longer, more formal types. Thus, the indirect order letter report follows its introductory build-up with a logical presentation and analysis of the information gathered. From this presentation, it works logically to a conclusion and/or recommendation in the end. The direct order letter report follows the initial summary-conclusion-recommendation section with whatever introductory words are appropriate. For example, the direct beginning illustrated above could be followed with these introductory words.

These are the primary findings of a study authorized by your Board of Directors last January. As they concern information vital to all of us in the Association, they are presented here for your confidential use.

Following such an introductory comment, the report would present the supporting facts and their analyses. The writer would systematically build up the case that supported his opening comment. With either order, when the report is sent as a letter it may close with whatever friendly goodwill comment is appropriate for the one occasion.

Memorandum reports

Memorandum reports are merely informal letter reports. They are used primarily for routine reporting within an organization, although some organizations use them for external communicating. Because they are internal communications, often they are informally written. In fact, they frequently are hurried, handwritten messages from one department or worker to another department or worker. The more formal memorandum reports, however, are well written and carefully typed compositions (see page 171) that rival some more imposing types in appearance.

As far as the writing of the memorandum is concerned, all the instructions for writing letter reports apply. But memorandum reports tend to be more informal. And because they usually concern day-to-day problems, they have very little need for introductory information. In fact, they frequently may begin reporting without any introductory comment.

The memorandum report is presented on somewhat standardized interoffice memorandum stationery. The words *From, To,* and *Subject* appear at the page top (see page 171), usually following the company identification. Sometimes, the word *Date* also is included as a part of the heading. Like letters, the memorandum may carry a signature. In many offices, however, no typed signature is included, and the writer merely initials after his typed name in the heading.

SPECIAL REPORT FORMS

As noted previously, this review describes only generally the forms of the reports used in business. Countless variations exist. Of these variations, a few deserve special emphasis.

The staff report

One of the most widely used reports in business is the staff report. Patterned after a form traditional to the technical fields, the staff report is well adapted to business problem-solving. Its arrangement follows the logical thought processes used in solving the conventional business problems. Although the makeup of this report varies by company, the following arrangement recommended by a major metals manufacturer is typical.

Figure 7.   Military form of staff study report*

DEPARTMENT OF THE AIR FORCE
HEADQUARTERS UNITED STATES AIR FORCE
WASHINGTON 25, D.C.

REPLY TO
ATTN OF AFODC/Colonel Jones

SUBJECT Staff Study Report

TO:

PROBLEM

1. --.

FACTORS BEARING ON THE PROBLEM

2. Facts.

    a. --.

    b. --.

3. Assumptions.

4. Criteria.

5. Definitions.

DISCUSSION

6. --.

7. --.

8. --.

CONCLUSION

9. --.

ACTION RECOMMENDED

10. --.

11. --------------------------.

JOHN J. JONES, Colonel, USAF   2 Atch
Deputy Chief of Staff, Operations   1. --------------------------
                                    2. --------------------------

Use only those portions of this format necessary for your particular report. If you omit certain paragraphs, renumber subsequent paragraphs accordingly.

Only long enough for identification.

Normally this caption is left blank on the staff study report.

Clear, but brief, statement of the problem.

Pertinent facts, assumptions (if necessary), criteria, and definitions (if necessary) used to solve the problem.

Briefly state background of problem.

List possible solutions that are most probable; test each possible solution, using criteria listed under "FACTORS BEARING ON THE PROBLEM", compare all solutions; and select the best possible solution, giving reasons for choice. No set number of paragraphs is prescribed.

Restate the best possible solution to the problem, using only one paragraph.

Indicate clearly the action necessary to implement the solution.

Preparation of Written Communication, Air Force Manual 10-1, Department of the Air Force, Washington, D. C., 1 February 1960, p. 27.

Identifying information: As the company's staff reports are written on intercompany communication stationery, the conventional identification information (To, From, Subject, Date) appears at the beginning.

Summary: For the busy executive who wants his facts fast, a summary begins the report. Some executives will read no further. Others will want to trace the report content in detail.

The problem (or objective): As in all good problem-solving procedures, the report text logically begins with a clear description of the problem—what it is, what it is not, what are its limitations, and such.

Facts: Next comes the information gathered in the attempt to solve the problem.

Discussion: Analyses of the facts and applications of the facts and analyses to the problem follow. (Frequently the statement of facts and the discussion of them can be combined.)

Conclusions: From the preceding discussion of facts comes the final meanings as they apply to the problem.

Recommendation: If the problem's objective allows for it, a course of action may be recommended on the basis of the conclusions.

Perhaps the major users of staff study reports are the branches of the Armed Forces. In all branches, this report is standardized. As shown in Figure 7, the military version differs somewhat from the business arrangement just described.

The corporate annual report

Although they are not likely to participate in writing them, business students should know the general forms and contents of corporate annual reports. These reports, which are prepared for most of the nation's leading corporations, tell the operations stories for the companies concerned. The reports are designed to help the investor, the employees, and the public to understand and appreciate the business enterprise. And as the business student will some day fall into one or more of these categories, he would do well to be able to understand these reports.

Originally designed to present only the financial operating facts of the firm, annual reports now cover all areas of a company's operations. (See the annual report illustration at the chapter end.) Most companies prepare these reports by choice, for although annual reports are required by regulations of the Securities and Exchange Commission and by listings agreements with stock exchanges, these companies want to keep the public closely informed of their activities. They see in the annual report both a public service and a public relations tool. The following words of the General Electric Company explain well this concept of the annual report.

It should be clear that even today the formal requirements which apply to annual reports can be satisfied with a brief and simple financial statement. The modern annual report follows the spirit rather than the letter of these requirements. More than this, the modern report takes on a number of communications objectives over and beyond those required by the rules.

For the share owner, the modern annual report attempts to provide the information needed as the base for sound investment decisions. The investor is concerned with whether he should continue to hold his stock or to divest himself of his holdings. Does he look to his investment primarily for income or for appreciation? The annual report is the keystone in corporation communications, facilitating the share owner's investment decisions.

Financial information is still the prime staple of the annual report. In most modern reports the addition of color photographs has not been in place of, or at the expense of, financial data. Today's report generally offers more financial information than its predecessors. The data are usually presented on a year-to-year comparative basis, with useful ratios worked out, and with charts to facilitate quick comprehension.

But share owners have come to realize increasingly that the balance sheet and operating statements do not tell the whole corporate story. Equally important in forming judgments about a business are evidences of the competence or excellence of its management, the extent and quality of its research, the boldness and foresight of its investment in potential growth areas, the vision shown in supplying new productive facilities and equipment, the excellence of its products, and the presence of a healthy and mutually respectful spirit in relations between managers and other employees.

In recent years still another significant element had begun to appear in annual reports. This is the recognition that the welfare and progress of a business enterprise are affected by such external forces as economic, social and political issues—the ideological "climate" in which business must operate. The past tendency to take purely an intramural view of the business is giving way to the belief that share owners cannot look to management alone to protect and enhance their investment but must themselves accept a share of the responsibility in issues affecting the usefulness of the enterprise in the interests of all the groups it must serve.

The attempt to provide investors with information enabling them to make sound judgments concerning their ownership increases the task of the modern annual report and swells its content.

Finally, management recognizes that a pubilc broader than the share owners has strong and valid reasons for interest in a major company's welfare. This public includes customers, employees, suppliers, independent distributors and dealers, neighbors in communities where the company has plants, and other groups as well as share owners. A well-rounded, comprehensive annual report has become one of business' major channels for communicating to these other members of the public. The growth of this extra audience for the annual report is indicated by the fact that the distribution of General Electric's annual report to share owners of record is only about half the total distribution of the report.[1]

---

[1] *Transition in Annual Reports*, Educational Relations and Support Service, General Electric Company, Ossining, New York, 1960, pp. 5–7.

The audit report

The short-form and long-form audit reports are well known to accountants. The short-form report is perhaps the most standardized of all reports—if, indeed, it can be classified as a report. Actually, it is a stereotyped statement verifying an accountant's inspection of a firm's financial records. Its wording seldom varies much from that illustrated on page 190.

Composition of the long-form audit report is as varied as the short form is rigid. In fact, a national accounting association, after studying practices, concluded that no typical form exists. Although it covers a somewhat simple and limited audit, the audit report illustrated at the chapter end shows one acceptable form.

The technical report

Although often treated as a highly specialized form of report, the technical report differs primarily in its subject matter. Its form variations correspond to most of those discussed in this and the preceding chapter (see pages 175–76). Even so, a somewhat conventional arrangement of the more formal research report has emerged.

This conventional arrangement begins much like the traditional formal report described in Chapter 6. First come the title pages, although frequently a routing or distribution form for intercompany use may be worked into them, or perhaps added to them. A letter of transmittal is likely to come next, followed by a table of contents and illustrations. From this point on, however, the technical report is likely to differ from the traditional one. These differences are mainly in the treatment of the information usually presented in the synopsis and the introduction of the conventional formal report.

Instead of the conventional synopsis, the technical report may present the summary information in various parts, such as findings, conclusions, and recommendations. Parts of the conventional introductory material also may be presented in prefatory sections. The objective is the most likely part in this area, although method is also a widely used section. The text usually begins with introductory information with remaining information organized much as any conventional report. It may follow a predetermined and somewhat mechanical arrangement as: facts, discussion, conclusions, and recommendations.

(*Questions for Chapter 7 appear on page 196.*)

Illustration of a memorandum report

MEMORANDUM   THE **M**URCHISON **C**O. **I**NC.

July 21, 1969

FROM: James C. Colvin, Manager
             Millville Sales District

TO: William T. Chrysler
             Director of Sales

SUBJECT: Quarterly Report for Millville Sales District

SUMMARY HIGHLIGHTS

After three months of operation I have secured office facilities, hired and developed
three salesmen, and cultivated about half the customers available in the Millville Sales
District. Although the district is not yet showing a profit, at the current rate of development it will do so this month. Prospects for the district are unusually bright.

OFFICE OPERATION

In April I opened the Millville Sales District as authorized by action of the Board of
Directors last February 7th. Initially I set up office in the Three Coins Inn, a motel
on the outskirts of town, and remained there three weeks while looking for permanent
quarters. These I found in the Wingate Building, a downtown office structure. The office
suite selected rents for $340 per month. It has four executive offices, each opening into
a single secretarial office, which is large enough for two secretaries. Although this
arrangement is adequate for the staff now anticipated, additional space is available in
the building if needed.

PERSONNEL

In the first week of operations, I hired an office secretary, Miss Catherine Kruch.
Miss Kruch has good experience and has excellent credentials. She has proved to
be very effective. In early April I hired two salesmen--Mr. Charles E. Clark and
Mr. Adam E. Knapper. Both were experienced in sales, although neither had worked in apparel sales. Three weeks later I hired Mr. Otto Strelski, a proven salesman
who I managed to attract from the Hammond Company. I still am searching for someone for the fourth subdistrict. Currently I am investigating two good prospects and
hope to hire one of them within the next week.

PERFORMANCE

After brief training sessions, which I conducted personally, the salesmen were assigned the territories previously marked. And they were instructed to call on the accounts
listed on the sheets supplied by Mr. Henderson's office. During the first month

Memorandum report, continued

Memorandum   -2-   July 21, 1969

Knapper's sales totaled $17,431 and Clark's reached $13,490, for a total of $30,921. With three salesmen working the next month, total sales reached $121,605. Of the total, Knapper accounted for $37,345, Clark $31,690, and Strelski $52,570. Although these monthly totals are below the $145,000 break-even point for the three subdistricts, current progress indicates that we will exceed this volume this month. As we have made contact with only about one half of the prospects in the area, the potential for the district appears to be unusually good.

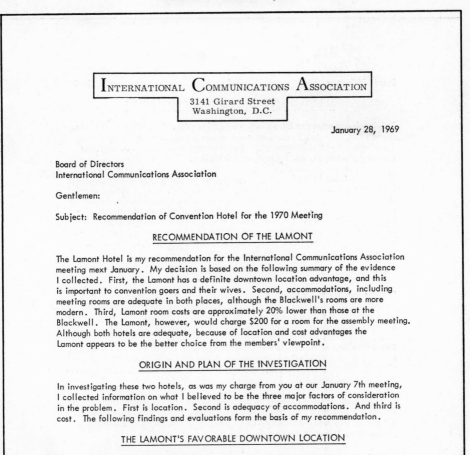

INTERNATIONAL COMMUNICATIONS ASSOCIATION
3141 Girard Street
Washington, D.C.

January 28, 1969

Board of Directors
International Communications Association

Gentlemen:

Subject: Recommendation of Convention Hotel for the 1970 Meeting

RECOMMENDATION OF THE LAMONT

The Lamont Hotel is my recommendation for the International Communications Association meeting mext January. My decision is based on the following summary of the evidence I collected. First, the Lamont has a definite downtown location advantage, and this is important to convention goers and their wives. Second, accommodations, including meeting rooms are adequate in both places, although the Blackwell's rooms are more modern. Third, Lamont room costs are approximately 20% lower than those at the Blackwell. The Lamont, however, would charge $200 for a room for the assembly meeting. Although both hotels are adequate, because of location and cost advantages the Lamont appears to be the better choice from the members' viewpoint.

ORIGIN AND PLAN OF THE INVESTIGATION

In investigating these two hotels, as was my charge from you at our January 7th meeting, I collected information on what I believed to be the three major factors of consideration in the problem. First is location. Second is adequacy of accommodations. And third is cost. The following findings and evaluations form the basis of my recommendation.

THE LAMONT'S FAVORABLE DOWNTOWN LOCATION

The older of the two hotels, the Lamont is located in the heart of the downtown business district. Thus it is convenient to the area's two major department stores as well as the other downtown shops. The Blackwell, on the other hand, is approximately nine blocks from the major shopping area. Located in the periphery of the business and residential area, it provides little location advantage for those wanting to shop. It does, however, have shops within its walls which provide virtually all of the guest's normal needs. Because many members will bring wives, however, the downtown location does give the Lamont an advantage.

Letter report, continued

Board of Directors   -2-   January 28, 1969

ADEQUATE ACCOMMODATIONS AT BOTH HOTELS

Both hotels can guarantee the 600 rooms we will require. As the Blackwell is new (since 1967), however, its rooms are more modern and therefore more appealing. The 69-year-old Lamont, however, is well preserved and comfortable. Its rooms are all in good repair, and the equipment is modern.

The Blackwell has 11 small meeting rooms and the Lamont has 13. All are adequate for our purposes. Both hotels can provide the 10 we need. For our general assembly meeting, the Lamont would make available its Capri Ballroom, which can easily seat our membership. It would also serve as the site of our inaugural dinner. The assembly facilities at the Blackwell appear to be somewhat crowded, although the management assures me that it can hold 600. Pillars in the room, however, would make some seats undesirable. In spite of the limitations mentioned, both hotels appear to have adequate facilities for our meeting.

LOWER COSTS AT THE LAMONT

Both the Lamont and the Blackwell would provide nine rooms for meetings on a complimentary basis. Both would provide complimentary suites for our president and our secretary. The Lamont, however, would charge $200 for use of the room for the assembly meeting. The Blackwell would provide this room without charge.

Convention rates at the Lamont are $10-$13 for singles, $12-$16 for double-bedded rooms, and $13-$17 for twin-bedded rooms. Comparable rates at the Blackwell are $12-$15, $15-$20, and $16-$22. Thus the savings at the Lamont would be approximately 20% per member.

Cost of the dinner selected would be $7.50 per person, including gratuities, at the Lamont. The Blackwell would meet this price if we would guarantee 600 plates. Otherwise, they would charge $8. Considering all of these figures, the total cost picture at the Lamont is the more favorable one.

Respectfully yours,

Willard K. Mitchell

Willard K. Mitchell
Executive Secretary

Illustration of a technical memorandum report

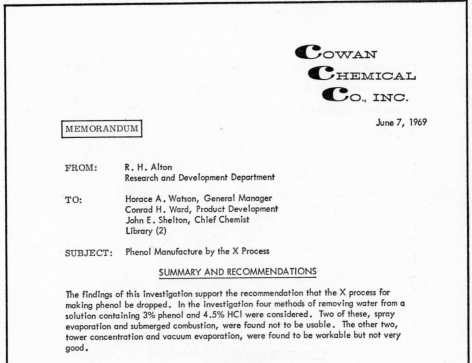

COWAN
CHEMICAL
Co., INC.

June 7, 1969

MEMORANDUM

FROM: R. H. Alton
                 Research and Development Department

TO: Horace A. Watson, General Manager
                 Conrad H. Ward, Product Development
                 John E. Shelton, Chief Chemist
                 Library (2)

SUBJECT: Phenol Manufacture by the X Process

SUMMARY AND RECOMMENDATIONS

The findings of this investigation support the recommendation that the X process for making phenol be dropped. In the investigation four methods of removing water from a solution containing 3% phenol and 4.5% HCl were considered. Two of these, spray evaporation and submerged combustion, were found not to be usable. The other two, tower concentration and vacuum evaporation, were found to be workable but not very good.

INTRODUCTION

Authorized by Mr. Horace A. Watson January 17, 1969, an investigation was conducted to evaluate four methods of concentrating a solution of 3% phenol and 4.5% hydrochloric acid obtained in the X process of manufacturing phenol. Previous investigation has indicated that the X process is the only practical process available to the company for making phenol.

The X process consists of passing chlorobenzene vapor and water through a tube maintained at a temperature of about 165°C. From this mixture a solution forms, consisting of about 3.5% phenol, 4.5% hydrochloric acid, and 90% water. Included, also, is a small amount of unreacted chlorobenzene. Previous investigations have worked out all steps in the process except the final one of concentrating the weak phenol solution. Because of the presence of hydrochloric acid, ordinary evaporation equipment cannot be used. This chemical would attack any metal sufficiently inexpensive to use.

DISCUSSION OF RESULTS

In an effort to find a practical solution to the problem, the four possibilities were considered: (1) spray evaporation, (2) submerged combustion, (3) tower concentration, and (4) vacuum evaporation.

Technical memorandum report, continued

Memorandum   -2-   June 7, 1969

Spray evaporation was eliminated as a possibility on the advice of Dr. Charles E. Coward, consultant to the company. Dr. Coward advised that the presence of hydrochloric acid constituted an insurmountable obstacle.

The method of submerged combustion consists of operating a gas burner submerged beneath the liquid to be concentrated. When tested in the laboratory this method resulted in a high loss of phenol during the evaporation (see report on Research Project 2143). Since Drake and Bolen Manufacturing Company, manufacturers of submerged equipment, could not suggest any corrective change in equipment, this method was rejected.

The method of concentrating phenol solutions by passing hot combustion gases from propane up a tower against a descending stream of solution was tried (Project 3171). Because of the combustion of phenol, this method proved to be ineffective. Apparently the combustion resulted largely from incomplete wetting of the packing by the small liquid flow. Further trials (Project 3190) attempted to use a recirculating system in order to increase the liquid flow. Yield values gave evidence that a maximum process yield of 90% could be expected by using this method.

The method of vacuum concentration was tried by flashing a hot phenol solution into a steam-jacketed tube maintained at a moderately high vacuum (Project 3011). The method produced a process yield of 96% phenol. This method, however, has the disadvantage of requiring expensive equipment and of possibly giving smaller process yields when carried out in large-scale equipment, since experiment showed that heat-transfer coefficients decreased as the diameter of the tube increased.

CONCLUSIONS AND RECOMMENDATIONS

From the results of these experiments the apparent conclusion is that, of all the methods investigated, only the tower concentration and vacuum evaporation methods are usable. Neither one is particularly good. Of the two, the former is the better. It produces lower yields, but these are compensated for by cheap equipment.

It is therefore recommended that consideration of the X process be dropped.

Illustration of a long-form audit report

From: Auditing Department   Date: May 3, 1969

To: William A. Karnes

Subject: Annual Audit, Spring Street Branch

Introduction

Following is the report on the annual audit of the Spring Street branch. Reflecting conditions existing at the close of business May 1, 1969, this review covers all accounts other than Loans and Discounts. Specifically, these accounts were proofed:

Accounts Receivable	Savings
Cash Collateral	Suspense
Cash in Office	Series "E" Bonds
Collections	Tax Withheld
Christmas Club	Travelers Checks
Deferred Charges	

Condition of Accounts

All listing totals agreed with General Ledger and/or Branch Controls except for these:

Cash in Office	$1.17 short
Tax Withheld	.21 short
Travelers Checks	.97 short

Exceptions Noted

During the course of the examination the following exceptions were found:

Analysis. The branch had 163 unprofitable accounts at the time of the audit. Losses on these accounts, as revealed by inspection of the Depositors Analysis Cards, ranged from $7.31 to $176.36 for the year. The average loss per account was $17.21.

Proper deductions of service charges were not made in 73 instances in which the accounts dropped below the minimum.

Bookkeeping. From a review of the regular checking accounts names were recorded of customers who habitually write checks without sufficient covering funds. A list of 39 of the worst offenders was submitted to Mr. Clement Ferguson.

The long-form audit report that appears in the following pages is a special form of memorandum. Traditionally, this type is more conservatively written and more formal than are most memorandum reports. Although this illustration concerns a relatively small audit, it does illustrate the techniques and procedures of this specialized type.

Long-form audit report, continued

A check of deposit tickets to the third and fourth regular checking ledgers revealed six accounts on which transit delays recorded on the deposit tickets were not correctly transferred to the ledger sheets.

During the preceding month on 17 different accounts the bookkeepers paid items against uncollected funds without getting proper approval.

Statements. Five statements were held by the branch in excess of three months:

Account	Statement Dates
Curtis A. Hogan	Sept. through April
Carlton I. Breeding	Dec. through April
Alice Crezan	Nov. through April
Jarvis H. Hudson	Jan. through April
W. T. Petersen	Dec. through April

Paying and Receiving. During the week of April 21-27, tellers failed to itemize currency denominations on large (over $100) cash deposits 23 times. Deposits were figured in error 32 times.

Savings. Contrary to instructions given after the last audit, the control clerk has not maintained a record of errors made in savings passbooks.

The savings tellers have easy access to the inactive ledger cards and may record transactions on the cards while alone. When this condition was noted in the last report, the recommendation was made to set up a system of dual controls. This recommendation has not been followed.

Safe Deposit Rentals. Rentals on 164 safe deposit boxes were in arrears. Although it was pointed out in the last report, this condition has grown worse during the past year. Numbers of boxes by years in arrears are as follows:

2 to 3 years	87
3 to 4 years	32
4 to 5 years	29
over 5 years	17
Total	165

Stop Payments. Signed stop payment orders were not received on three checks on which payment was stopped:

Account	Amount	Date of Stop Payment
Whelon Electric Company	$317.45	Feb. 7, 1969
George A. Bullock	37.50	April 1, 1969
Amos H. Kritzel	737.60	Dec. 3, 1969

Long-form audit report, concluded

Over and Short Account. A $23.72 difference between Tellers and Rack Department was recorded for April 22. On May 1 this difference remained uncorrected.

William P Bunting

William P. Bunting
Head, Auditing Department

Copies to:

W. F. Robertson
Cecil Ruston
W. W. Merrett

Illustration of a short report

RECOMMENDATIONS FOR DEPRECIATING DELIVERY TRUCKS

BASED ON AN ANALYSIS OF THREE PLANS

PROPOSED FOR THE BAGGET LAUNDRY COMPANY

Submitted to

Mr. Ralph P. Bagget, President
Bagget Laundry Company
312 Dauphine Street
New Orleans, Louisiana 70102

Prepared by

Charles W. Brewington, C.P.A.
Brewington and Karnes, Certified Public Accountants
743 Beaux Avenue, New Orleans, Louisiana 70118

April 16, 1969

In the following pages is a short report written in the direct order (recommendation and summary first). As its introduction reviews the background facts of the problem, most of which are known to the immediate reader, the report apparently is designed for future reference. For reasons of convention in the accounting field, the writing style of the report is somewhat reserved and formal.

RECOMMENDATIONS FOR DEPRECIATING DELIVERY TRUCKS

BASED ON AN ANALYSIS OF THREE PLANS

PROPOSED FOR THE BAGGET LAUNDRY COMPANY

I. Recommendations and Summary of Analysis

The Reducing Charge method appears to be the best method to depreciate Bagget Laundry Company delivery trucks. The relative equality of cost allocation for depreciation and maintenance over the useful life of the trucks is the prime advantage under this method. Computation of depreciation charges is relatively simple by the Reducing Charge plan but not quite so simple as computation under the second best method considered.

The second best method considered is the Straight Line depreciation plan. It is the simplest to compute of the plans considered, and it results in yearly charges equal to those under the Reducing Charge method. The unequal cost allocation resulting from increasing maintenance costs in successive years, however, is a disadvantage that far outweighs the method's ease of computation.

Third among the plans considered is the Service Hours method. This plan is not satisfactory for depreciating delivery trucks primarily because it combines a number of undesirable features. Prime among these is the complexity and cost of computing yearly charges under the plan. Also significant is the likelihood of poor cost allocation under this plan. An additional drawback is the possibility of variations in the estimates of the service life of company trucks.

II. Background of the Problem

Authorization of the Study. This report on depreciation methods for delivery trucks of the Bagget Laundry Company is submitted on April 16, 1969, to Mr. Ralph P. Bagget, President of the Company. Authorization for this report was given orally by Mr. Bagget to Mr. Charles W. Brewington, Brewington and Karnes, Certified Public Accountants, on March 15, 1969.

Statement of the Problem. Having decided to establish branch agencies, the Bagget Laundry Company has purchased delivery trucks to transport laundry back and forth from the central cleaning plant in downtown New Orleans. The problem is to select the most advantageous method to depreciate the trucks. The trucks have an original cost of $2500, a five-year life, and a trade-in value of $500.

Method of Solving the Problem. Study of Company records and a review of the authoritative writings on the subject have been used in seeking a reliable solution to the Bagget Laundry Company's problem. Alternative methods of depreciating delivery trucks have been selected through the experience and study of the writer. Conclusions are based on generally accepted business principles as set forth by experts in the field of depreciation.

Short report, continued

Steps in Analyzing the Problem. The depreciation methods evaluated in this report are discussed in order of their rank as a solution to the problem. No attempt has been made to isolate the factors discussed under each method. Since each method contains fixed factors, a comparison of them directly would be meaningless, because they cannot be manipulated. The method of computation, amount of depreciation each year, and effect of maintenance costs are the factors to be considered. The Reducing Charge method will be discussed first.

III. Marked Advantages of the Reducing Charge Method

The Reducing Charge method, sometimes called the Sum–of–the–Digits method, is an application of a series of diminishing fractions to be applied over the life of the trucks. The fractions to be applied to the five-year life of the delivery trucks are computed by adding the sum of the years (the denominator) and relating this to the number of position of the year (the numerator). Each fraction is applied against the depreciable value of the trucks. Computation of the depreciable value is made by subtracting the trade-in value from the original cost. The depreciable value for the delivery trucks is $2000 ($2500 – $500).

This method results in larger depreciation costs for the early years, with subsequent decreases in the latter years. Since maintenance and repair costs can be expected to be higher in later years, however, this method provides a relatively stable charge for each year as shown in Table I.

Table I

DEPRECIATION AND MAINTENANCE COSTS FOR
DELIVERY TRUCKS OF BAGGET LAUNDRY FOR 1963-1967
USING REDUCING CHARGE DEPRECIATION

End of Year	Depreciation	Maintenance	Sum
1	5/15 ($2000) = $ 667	$ 33	$ 700
2	4/15 ($2000) = 533	167	700
3	3/15 ($2000) = 400	300	700
4	2/15 ($2000) = 267	433	700
5	1/15 ($2000) = 133	567	700
	Totals $2000	$1500	$3500

However, since in actual practice the maintenance charges will not be exactly proportionate, the periodic charges shown will not be exactly the same.

The Reducing Charge method combines the most desirable combination of factors to depreciate the delivery trucks. The equalization of periodic charges is considered to be the prime factor. Although computation of this method is relatively easy, it is slightly more complicated than Straight-Line depreciation, which is the next method discussed.

IV. Runner-up Position of Straight-Line Method

Compared to the Reducing Charge method, Straight-Line depreciation is easy to compute. The depreciable value of each truck ($2000) is divided by the five-year life of the truck to arrive at an equal depreciation charge each year of $400.

Since the maintenance cost of operating the truck will increase in later years, however, this method will result in much greater periodic charges in the last years. As illustrated in Table II, the inequality of the periodic charges is the major disadvantage of this method. This method is very popular in the business world today, but where it is shown that maintenance costs will grow in later years, it is not usually recommended. The stand taken by many authorities is similar to the following:

> Straight-Line depreciation is the method most widely used in business today. It has the advantage of simplicity and under normal plant conditions offers a satisfactory method of cost allocation. For a plant to have normal conditions two factors must exist: (1) accumulation of properties over a period of years so that the total of depreciation and maintenance costs will be comparatively even, and (2) a relatively stable amount of earnings each year so that depreciation as a percentage of net income does not fluctuate widely.[1]

Table II
DEPRECIATION AND MAINTENANCE COSTS FOR DELIVERY TRUCKS OF BAGGET LAUNDRY FOR 1963-1967 USING STRAIGHT-LINE DEPRECIATION

End of Year	Depreciation	Maintenance	Sum
1	1/5 ($2000) = $ 400	$ 33	$ 433
2	1/5 ($2000) = 400	167	567
3	1/5 ($2000) = 400	300	700
4	1/5 ($2000) = 400	433	833
5	1/5 ($2000) = 400	567	967
	Totals $2000	$1500	$3500

However, the trucks considered in this report have not been purchased over a period of years. Consequently, the Straight-Line method of depreciation will not result in equal periodic charges for maintenance and depreciation over a period of years. Although this method is used by many companies in preference to more complex means, it is selected as second choice for depreciating delivery trucks. The prime disadvantage cited is the unsatisfactory cost allocation it provides. The Service-Hours method which will be discussed next has this same disadvantage.

---

[1]Wilbur E. Karrenbrock and Harry Simons, *Intermediate Accounting*, South-Western Publishing Company, Cincinnati, Ohio, 1958, p.44.

V. <u>Poor</u> <u>Rank</u> of <u>Service-Hours</u> <u>Depreciation</u>

The Service-Hours method of depreciation combines the major disadvantages of the other ways discussed. It is based on the principle that a truck is bought for the direct hours of service that it will give. The estimated number of hours that a delivery truck can be used efficiently according to automotive engineers is one-hundred thousand miles. The depreciable cost ($2000) for each truck is allocated pro rata according to the number of service hours used.

The difficulty and expense of maintaining additional records of service hours is a major disadvantage of this method. The depreciation cost for the delivery trucks under this method will fluctuate widely between first and last years. It is reasonable to assume that as the trucks get older more time will be spent on maintenance. Consequently, the larger depreciation costs will occur in the initial years. As can be seen by Table III, the periodic charges for depreciation and maintenance hover between the two previously discussed methods.

The periodic charge for depreciation and maintenance increases in the latter years of ownership. Another difficulty encountered is the possibility of a variance between estimated service hours and the actual service hours. The wide fluctuations possible make it impractical to use this method for depreciating the delivery trucks.

The difficulty of maintaining adequate records and increasing costs in the latter years are the major disadvantages of this method. Since it combines the major disadvantages of both the Reducing Charge and Straight-Line methods it is not satisfactory for depreciating the delivery trucks.

Table III

DEPRECIATION AND MAINTENANCE COSTS FOR
DELIVERY TRUCKS OF BAGGET LAUNDRY FOR 1963-1967
USING SERVICE-HOURS DEPRECIATION

End of Year	Estimated Service-Hours	Depreciation	Maintenance	Sum
1	30,000	$ 600	$ 33	$ 633
2	25,000	500	167	667
3	20,000	400	300	700
4	15,000	300	433	733
5	10,000	200	567	767
	100,000	$2000	$1500	$3500

ANNUAL
REPORT

RICHARD D. IRWIN, INC.
HOMEWOOD, ILLINOIS

FISCAL YEAR ENDED FEBRUARY 29, 1968

Because of space considerations, the corporate annual report selected for illustration in the following pages had to be moderate in length. It is well under the magazine-length report published by some of today's giant corporations, and it is well above the two- and four-page reports put out by some. In addition, the illustration selected does not match some reports in elaborate art work, photography, and detailed review of company progress; yet, it is more comprehensive than the bare financial statements of other reports. In general, it represents a form about midway between the extremes.

Corporate annual report, continued

FINANCIAL HIGHLIGHTS

Year Ended February 29/28

	1968	1967
Net Sales	$8,627,498	$8,127,645
Net Income	806,551	987,361
Earnings per Share[1]	.65	.80
Dividends per Share	.32	.2225
Common Shares Outstanding (end of year)	1,256,349	1,241.318
Working Capital	2,339,867	2,267,721
Common Shareholders' Equity	4,731,009	4,240,203

[1] On average shares outstanding

Corporate annual report, continued

May 20, 1968

TO OUR SHAREHOLDERS:

In submitting this annual report, I would like to indicate areas in which we have moved ahead with definite plans for the future growth and development of the company.

Our Canadian subsidiary, Irwin-Dorsey Limited, started operations in Nobleton, Ontario, last August and is rapidly establishing itself as an important adjunct to the Irwin company. It gives full sales coverage in all Canadian schools for Irwin and Dorsey publications, as well as providing a base for both sales and the editorial phases of publishing. We also anticipate issuing a number of Canadianized versions of some of our present titles with particular applications to the Canadian market. The results of this new venture even in the short period of time that it has been operating have been most encouraging.

To give more depth and concentration to our domestic sales force, a new and fifth field division was created last July. Each of these divisions is headed by a vice president responsible for the creation and development of sales volume and manuscript work. Because of this expansion, further additions were needed for our field force, not only for Irwin but for the Dorsey Press as well. I am more than satisfied with the early results of this expansion, and I am confident that this increase in personnel will add to our position during the new fiscal year, as well as in the years to come.

Plans are now being made to establish an international sales force designed to give us further coverage all over the world. Our Irwin and Dorsey lists have grown, and we feel that international exposure is now more important than ever. There is an increasing demand for our books overseas, and the creation of our worldwide sales force will, I am sure, increase our potential greatly in the international markets.

I am particularly pleased to announce that the fiscal year just ended marked the largest production year that we have ever experienced. In all, ninety new books and revisions were published during this twelve-month period—73 for Irwin and 17 for Dorsey. These new books and revisions, along with our backlist, gives us a strong and balanced group of titles for promotion during the coming 1968-69 school year. We anticipate an even stronger program for the 1969-70 academic year. In this respect we will publish a great many important revisions, plus a number of promising new titles, such as an entirely programmed series of books in mathematics for business schools.

It is significant that for the first time our Dorsey Press came close to equaling the Irwin manuscript program in new book contracts. During the fiscal year just ended, thirty-five new manuscripts were acquired by Dorsey and thirty-six by Irwin. This is indeed indicative of the growth trend and future contribution of our Dorsey Division.

For the fiscal year just ended, I invite your attention to the financial highlights contained in the following pages. You will note that earnings for the past fiscal year declined from 80 cents per share to 65 cents per share. We attribute this in part to returns from college bookstores unprecedented to us as well as the entire textbook industry. This was due to the concern of bookstore personnel well over a year ago that a printing shortage was in the making and, consequently, these stores overordered earlier and in quantities larger than they could hope to absorb. Also, world unrest had a negative effect on involvements, but as in the past, we fully expect returning servicemen to resume their education.

More important, however, is the position that was taken by Irwin management during the past twelve months. In this instance we felt that it was essential to invest in the developments mentioned; namely, the Canadian subsidiary, additions to our sales force, and making plans for an international sales organization, even though these commitments might be reflected temporarily in decreased current earnings. It is felt that this investment in building for the future will meet with the approval of the stockholders. To this end, I wish to point out that the first two and one-half months of the first quarter of the new fiscal year, not shown in the report, are running approximately twenty percent ahead of the same period of time for the fiscal year just ended.

I also invite your attention to some additional publishing highlights described in the succeeding pages of this report. Each of these important developments will play a major role in our future growth.

Lastly, I would like once again to extend my personal thanks to our employees, editors, authors, and friends for their unwavering support this past year.

Richard D. Irwin
Chairman of the Board

1

Corporate annual report, continued

PUBLISHING HIGHLIGHTS

During the past fiscal year, there were a number of significant developments that took place which we feel are worthy of your attention, and these are as follows:

PROGRAMMED INSTRUCTION

ACCOUNTING: A PROGRAMMED TEXT by Edwards, Hermanson and Salmonson has at this date completed its first full school year of classroom use. This unique two-volume approach designed especially for elementary accounting courses has enjoyed acceptance in 108 institutions throughout the country. We are pleased with these results, and early indications this spring point toward a number of new users beginning next fall.

As mentioned previously in this report, a completely programmed approach to mathematics for business schools will be available in January 1969. Also, a programmed volume in the field of Fortran is scheduled for publication in June 1968. As a result of this, we are presently planning to move ahead in other areas with additional programmed materials.

DOW JONES-IRWIN, INC.

Dow Jones-Irwin, Inc., the equally owned subsidiary of Dow Jones and Co., Inc., and Richard D. Irwin, Inc., continued to progress with its trade publishing program. A number of important new books are scheduled for publication during the next twelve-month period, and new contracts recently negotiated give further depth to this program for succeeding years. Two very important handbooks will soon be published under the Dow Jones-Irwin, Inc., imprint; namely, the FINANCIAL EXECUTIVE'S HANDBOOK and the STOCK AND SECURITIES HANDBOOK. Other potentially strong titles are underway to supplement the backlist of this organization which has received strong support and acclaim in the trade book market.

RESEARCH AND DEVELOPMENT

Our new research and development department, created during the summer of 1967, has proven to be most helpful in assisting management in its plans for the future. A number of significant research reports have been completed and others are presently underway, each of which will give us important guidelines to follow in planning product for the future growth of our existing list and the development of new materials. This department continues to furnish our marketing and product development personnel with valuable information pertaining to the growing junior college and community college markets.

2

Corporate annual report, continued

THE IRWIN SERIES IN INFORMATION PROCESSING

In order to keep abreast of the growing demand for educational materials emphasizing quantitative aspects for education, we recently inaugurated the Irwin Information Processing Series which will be announced formally to the public in September 1968. Professors Robert B. Fetter, Yale University, and Richard L. Van Horn, Carnegie-Mellon University, have agreed to serve as editorial advisors for this important series of educational materials. This new group of books, now in the developmental stage, along with our existing Irwin Series in Quantitative Analysis for Business, will give us added strength and balance in the quantitative approach to instruction.

NEW BOOKS AND REVISIONS

As was previously stated, our Irwin and Dorsey publishing program for the fiscal year just ended involved ninety new books and revisions. These would be far too numerous to list at this point but a few of the significant new volumes for Irwin are as follows: FORMAL ORGANIZATION: A SYSTEMS APPROACH by Carzo and Yanouzas; INVESTMENT ANALYSIS AND PORTFOLIO MANAGEMENT by Cohen and Zinbarg; BUSINESS COMMUNICATION by Devlin; PRODUCTION-INVENTORY SYSTEMS: PLANNING AND CONTROL by Buffa; and PROMOTION: PERSUASIVE COMMUNICATION IN MARKETING by Tillman and Kirkpatrick. Some of Irwin's important revisions of highly successful publications included PERSONNEL MANAGEMENT, Sixth Edition, by Jucius; RETAILING: PRINCIPLES AND METHODS, Seventh Edition, by Duncan and Phillips; COST ACCOUNTING: PRINCIPLES AND PRACTICE, Seventh Edition, by Neuner and Frumer; MATHEMATICS: WITH APPLICATIONS IN MANAGEMENT AND ECONOMICS, Revised Edition, by Bowen; and MANAGERIAL ECONOMICS: TEXT, PROBLEMS, AND SHORT CASES, Third Edition, by Spencer.

New books from the Dorsey program included INTERPRETING EUROPEAN HISTORY, a two-volume paperback series by Gooch with excellent prospects in the large first and second year European history courses. AN INTERPRETIVE HISTORY OF AMERICAN FOREIGN RELATIONS by Cole, CONTEMPORARY POLITICAL THOUGHT: A CRITICAL STUDY by Meehan, and THE LANGUAGE OF MODERN POLITICS: AN INTRODUCTION TO THE STUDY OF GOVERNMENT by Roelofs represent other new Dorsey publications that have enjoyed immediate acceptance. Important revisions supplementing this program include Bell's MARRIAGE AND FAMILY INTERACTION, Johnson's CRIME, CORRECTION, AND SOCIETY, Mangone's THE ELEMENTS OF INTERNATIONAL LAW, and STUDIES IN PERSONNEL AND INDUSTRIAL PSYCHOLOGY by Fleishman.

Shortly after the close of the fiscal year covered by this Annual Report, a number of new books and revisions for both Irwin and Dorsey were

3

Corporate annual report, continued

published that will have a definite effect on our sales picture during the next twelve months. For Irwin, PRINCIPLES OF ECONOMICS by Royall Brandis, published for the first time in March 1968, has been well received, and early indications suggest its use in a number of elementary economics courses. The new Third Edition of McCarthy's BASIC MARKETING, long acclaimed the leading text in this field, gives every appearance of being even more successful than previous editions. PRINCIPLES OF MANAGEMENT, Fifth Edition, by Terry, appeared in March of 1968, and early reactions point toward increased acceptance and success with this basic volume.

Important March and April publications for Dorsey, which at this writing appear to have strong support for fall classes, include the Revised Edition of MAIN PROBLEMS IN AMERICAN HISTORY, a highly popular two-volume paperback compiled for the large freshman and sophomore courses, the Third Edition of COMPARATIVE POLITICS by Macridis and Brown, along with the new PERSONALITY THEORIES: A COMPARATIVE ANALYSIS by Maddi.

ACCOUNTANTS' REPORT

ERNST & ERNST
231 SOUTH LA SALLE STREET
CHICAGO, ILL 60604

To the Board of Directors and Shareholders
Richard D. Irwin, Inc.
Homewood, Illinois

We have examined the statement of consolidated financial condition of Richard D. Irwin, Inc. and Canadian subsidiary as of February 29, 1968, and the related statements of consolidated income, retained earnings, and changes in working capital for the year then ended. Our examination was made in accordance with generally accepted auditing standards, and accordingly included such tests of the accounting records and such other auditing procedures as we considered necessary in the circumstances. We previously made a similar examination of the financial statements for the preceding year.

In our opinion, the financial statements identified above, present fairly the consolidated financial position of Richard D. Irwin, Inc. and Canadian subsidiary at February 29, 1968, and the consolidated results of their operations and changes in working capital for the year then ended, in conformity with generally accepted accounting principles applied on a basis consistent with that of the preceding year.

Chicago, Illinois
April 26, 1968

Ernst & Ernst

STATEMENT OF CONSOLIDATED FINANCIAL CONDITION

ASSETS

	February 29 1968	February 28 1967
CURRENT ASSETS		
Cash and certificates of deposit	$ 272,446	$ 285,135
Trade accounts receivable, less allowances for collection losses and book returns (1968—$208,350; 1967—$182,200)	1,912,048	1,740,582
Inventories—Note B	1,887,133	2,032,194
Prepaid expenses	80,318	95,738
TOTAL CURRENT ASSETS	4,151,945	4,153,649
INVESTMENT AND OTHER ASSETS		
Investment in 50% owned company—at cost— Note C	—	—
Notes and accounts with officers	73,205	47,863
Miscellaneous accounts and deposits	346,048	214,721
	419,253	262,584
PROPERTY, PLANT, AND EQUIPMENT—on the basis of cost		
Land	153,768	153,768
Building	748,086	748,086
Plates	1,890,288	1,636,927
Equipment and airplanes	926,929	682,449
Leasehold improvements	257,349	257,349
	3,976,420	3,478,579
Less allowances for depreciation and amortization ..	1,187,912	997,174
	2,788,508	2,481,405
	$7,359,706	$6,897,638

LIABILITIES

CURRENT LIABILITIES		
Notes payable to bank	$ 350,000	$ 200,000
Accounts payable	672,281	725,613
Royalties to authors	413,409	323,491
Dividend payable	100,536	99,653
Federal income taxes	209,664	470,983
Portion of 5% notes payable due within one year ..	66,188	66,188
TOTAL CURRENT LIABILITIES	1,812,078	1,885,928
5% NOTES PAYABLE TO BANK, less portion classified as current liability—Note D	359,641	425,829
DEFERRED FEDERAL INCOME TAXES	456,978	345,678
SHAREHOLDERS' EQUITY		
Common Shares—par value $.50 a share— Notes E and F: Authorized 1,275,942 shares Issued: 1968—1,256,349 shares; 1967—1,241,318 shares	628,175	347,711
Additional paid-in capital—Notes E and F	376,273	571,641
Retained earnings—Note D	3,726,561	3,320,851
	4,731,009	4,240,203
	$7,359,706	$6,897,638

See notes to financial statements.

5

Corporate annual report, continued

STATEMENTS OF CONSOLIDATED INCOME AND RETAINED EARNINGS

STATEMENT OF CONSOLIDATED INCOME

	Year Ended	
	February 29 1968	February 28 1967
Income:		
Net sales	$8,627,498	$8,127,645
Other	25,115	22,725
	8,652,613	8,150,370
Costs and expenses:		
Production cost of books sold	2,175,512	1,950,296
Royalties to authors	1,531,098	1,474,205
Provision for depreciation and amortization (straight-line method)	700,151	584,905
Selling, shipping, general, and administrative expenses	2,625,628	2,235,974
Interest	68,173	50,629
	7,100,562	6,296,009
INCOME BEFORE FEDERAL INCOME TAXES	1,552,051	1,854,361
Federal income taxes:		
Current	634,200	807,600
Deferred	111,300	59,400
	745,500	867,000
NET INCOME	$ 806,551	$ 987,361
Net income per share—Note E	$ .65	$ .80
STATEMENT OF CONSOLIDATED RETAINED EARNINGS		
Balance at beginning of year	$3,320,851	$2,609,155
Net income for the year	806,551	987,361
	4,127,402	3,596,516
Cash dividends—$.32 a share in 1968 and $.2225 a share in 1967—Notes D and E	400,841	275,665
BALANCE AT END OF YEAR	$3,726,561	$3,320,851

See notes to financial statements.

STATEMENT OF CHANGES IN CONSOLIDATED WORKING CAPITAL

	Year Ended	
	February 29 1968	February 28 1967
Additions:		
From income:		
Net income for the year	$ 806,551	$ 987,361
Provision for depreciation and amortization	700,151	584,905
Provision for deferred federal income taxes	111,300	59,400
	1,618,002	1,631,666
Proceeds from stock options exercised	85,096	51,279
Proceeds from sale of Common Shares in treasury	—	10,004
Decrease in notes and accounts with officers	—	211,294
TOTAL ADDITIONS	1,703,098	1,904,243
Deductions:		
Additions to property, plant, and equipment—net	1,007,254	1,070,646
Increase in notes and accounts with officers	25,342	—
Increase in miscellaneous accounts and deposits	131,327	4,333
Cash dividends	400,841	275,665
Payments on 5% notes payable to bank	66,188	66,188
TOTAL DEDUCTIONS	1,630,952	1,416,832
INCREASE IN WORKING CAPITAL	72,146	487,411
Working capital at beginning of year	2,267,721	1,780,310
WORKING CAPITAL AT END OF YEAR	$2,339,867	$2,267,721

See notes to financial statements.

6

Corporate annual report, continued

NOTES TO CONSOLIDATED FINANCIAL STATEMENTS
February 29, 1968

NOTE A — CONSOLIDATION POLICY:
The consolidated financial statements include the accounts of the Company and its wholly-owned Canadian subsidiary, Irwin-Dorsey Limited, with operations of the Canadian subsidiary from the date of incorporation (July 25, 1967). The net current assets and operations of the Canadian subsidiary were translated at the current rate of exchange, and the translation of the property accounts was based on rates in effect at dates of acquisition. Intercompany accounts and transactions have been eliminated in consolidating the financial statements.

NOTE B — INVENTORIES:
Inventories were stated at the lower of cost (first-in, first-out method) or market as follows:

	February 29 1968	February 28 1967
Bound books	$1,087,225	$ 905,551
Work in process and sheet stock	133,906	408,184
Paper and cloth	666,002	718,459
TOTAL	$1,887,133	$2,032,194

NOTE C — INVESTMENT IN 50% OWNED COMPANY:
The Company owns a 50% interest in Dow Jones-Irwin, Inc., which publishes and sells books to the noncollege market. The Company acquired its interest in Dow Jones-Irwin, Inc. in exchange for the exclusive right to use the copyrights on certain manuscripts or works and plates therefor in the noncollege market. Dow Jones-Irwin, Inc. commenced operations in the latter part of 1965 and the accumulated losses to February 29, 1968 were not significant. In the event Dow Jones-Irwin, Inc. is liquidated or sold prior to August 28, 1968, the assets contributed by the Company will be returned.

NOTE D — 5% NOTES PAYABLE TO BANK:
The 5% notes payable to bank are payable in quarterly installments of $16,547 with the balance maturing on August 1, 1969. The Company has agreed, among other things, to maintain minimum working capital of $1,000,000, maintain minimum tangible net worth of $1,900,000, and annually limit the payment of dividends to the lesser of 50% of net income or $320,000 (dividend limitation waived by bank for year ended February 29, 1968).

NOTE E — STOCK SPLIT AND CHANGES IN COMMON SHARES:
On March 27, 1967, the authorized Common Shares of the Company were increased from 1,000,000 to 1,500,000 shares and a 2-for-1 stock split was effected. Appropriate adjustments to give effect to the stock split were made in the financial statements, including per share information.
On June 5, 1967, the Company, an Illinois corporation, was merged into a wholly-owned subsidiary incorporated on April 14, 1967, under the laws of the State of Delaware. The outstanding no-par Common Shares of the Illinois Corporation were converted into Common Shares of the Delaware Corporation having a par value of $.50 per share (1,275,942 shares authorized). In connection with the foregoing merger, an amount of $275,501 was transferred from additional paid-in capital to the Common Shares account.

NOTE F — Stock Options:
The changes during the year in Common Shares optioned to employees under the Company's stock option plan, adjusted for the 2-for-1 stock split on March 27, 1967, are summarized as follows:

	Shares Under Options	Shares Available for Future Options
At March 1, 1967	34,624	—
Options exercised at an average price of $5.66 a share	(15,031)	
Options canceled	(1,150)	1,150
At February 29, 1968 (all options exercisable)— average option price of $10.49 a share	18,443	1,150

Options become exercisable six months after date of grant and may be exercised over a period of five years from the date of grant. The option price is the fair market value on the date the option was granted.
An amount of $80,133 was added to additional paid-in capital in respect of shares issued during the year under the stock option plan.

NOTE G — Lease Commitment:
The Company's offices are occupied under a lease agreement expiring in 1973 with renewal rights for an additional five years. The lease provides for minimum annual rentals of $33,600, plus additional amounts based upon net sales, the total rental not to exceed $58,000 a year. Taxes, maintenance, insurance, and other costs of occupancy are payable by the Company.

NOTE H — PENSION PLAN:
An insured-type contributory retirement plan provides retirement benefits for all employees of the Company who meet certain service requirements. The total retirement plan expense for 1968 and 1967 was $68,723 and $60,177, respectively. The expense for the year represents the annual premium paid to the insurance company which includes an amount for past service cost.

7

TEN YEAR STATISTICAL SUMMARY

Fiscal Year Ended February 28 (29)

	1968	1967	1966	1965	1964	1963	1962	1961	1960	1959
Net sales	$8,627,498	$8,127,645	$6,681,565	$5,753,784	$4,845,845	$3,871,672	$3,669,525	$3,362,295	$2,886,358	$2,264,877
Gross profit (1)	4,220,737	4,118,239	3,416,648	2,889,006	2,411,303	1,880,740	1,818,603	1,659,109	1,394,474	1,111,023
Income before federal income taxes	1,552,051	1,854,361	1,412,865	1,143,528	866,124	445,028	522,923	502,329	308,663	229,678
Net income	806,551	987,361	732,865	571,428	412,724	221,828	258,273	244,629	151,063	113,578
Earnings per share —on the basis of shares outstanding at year end (3)	$ 0.64	$ 0.80	$ 0.60	$ 0.47	$ 0.35	$ 0.19	$ 0.22	$ 0.22	$ 0.14	$ 0.10
—on the basis of average monthly weighted shares outstanding (3)	0.65	0.80	0.60	0.47	0.35	0.19	0.23	0.22	0.14	0.10
Dividends per share (3)	0.32	0.2225	0.16	0.10	0.10	0.085	0.035	0.025	0.015	0.015
Working capital	2,339,867	2,267,721	1,780,310	1,744,865	1,464,355	1,363,373	1,347,828	697,360	606,206	614,913
Common stockholders' equity	4,731,009	4,240,203	3,467,224	2,883,533	2,379,792	2,083,985	1,984,321	1,287,165	1,070,086	932,798
Current ratio	2.3	2.2	2.3	2.6	2.5	3.8	3.9	1.9	1.8	2.1
Common shares outstanding (end of year) (3)	1,256,349	1,241,318	1,224,668	1,211,454	1,195,728	1,194,940	1,200,940	1,095,940	1,095,940	1,095,940
Percent return on net sales	9.3	12.1	11.0	9.9	8.5	5.7	7.0	7.3	5.2	5.0
Percent return on common stockholders' equity (yearly average)	18.0	25.6	23.1	21.7	18.5	10.9	15.8	20.8	15.1	12.9
Titles published (2)	90	88	78	73	72	64	64	43	40	38
Titles in publication	525	480	441	397	343	307	273	235	203	183
Number of employees	173	164	121	115	110	105	104	92	91	74
Number of authors	592	546	505	451	392	368	334	296	260	239

(1) Gross profit represents net sales less production cost of books sold, royalties to authors, and provision for depreciation and amortization.
(2) Includes in any year both new and revised titles generally on an approximately equal basis.
(3) After giving retroactive effect to 3 for 2 stock split on May 24, 1965 and to 2 for 1 stock split on March 27, 1967.

Corporate annual report, concluded

OFFICERS AND DIRECTORS

Richard D. Irwin	*Chairman of the Board of Directors*
Irvin L. Grimes	*President and Director*
John K. Franklin	*Vice President-Finance,*
	Secretary-Treasurer, and Director
John H. Bishop	*Assistant Secretary, Director,*
Bishop, Burdett, Falasz	*and Legal Counsel*
& Ericson	
Davis W. Gregg	*Director*
President, American College	
of Life Underwriters	
John F. Mee	*Director*
Dean, Division of General	
and Technical Studies,	
Indiana University	
Leslie J. Buchan	*Director*
Distinguished Service	
Prof. of Administration,	
Washington University	
Robert Bottorff	*Director*
Vice President, Dow Jones	
and Company, Inc.	
William D. Crawford	*Vice President and Director*
Frank G. Griffin	*Vice President, The Dorsey Press,*
	and Director
Richard E. Willis, Jr.	*President, Irwin-Dorsey Limited*
Robert W. Bingham	*Vice President, Midwest Division*
Robert C. Boozer	*Vice President, Southern Division*
Norman Dorian	*Vice President, Northeastern Division*
Oliver A. Ryder	*Vice President, Western Division*
William H. Schoof	*Vice President, Eastern Division*

STOCK TRANSFER AGENT

American National Bank and Trust Company of Chicago

REGISTRAR

Continental Illinois National Bank and Trust Company of Chicago

GENERAL COUNSEL

Bishop, Burdett, Falasz, and Ericson

INDEPENDENT ACCOUNTANTS

Ernst & Ernst

EXECUTIVE and EDITORIAL OFFICES

1818 Ridge Road, Homewood, Illinois

Richard D. Irwin, Inc.

Printed in U.S.A.

QUESTIONS

1. What are the major differences in the construction of the short and long reports?
2. Why do the shorter forms of reports usually require less introductory material than do the longer reports?
3. Defend the use of direct order in the shorter forms of reports.
4. What should determine whether one should use the direct order in a report?
5. Explain the logic of using personal style in some reports.
6. What should determine whether one should use personal style in a report?
7. What should determine whether one should use a coherence plan in a report?
8. Describe the structure of a typical short report.
9. Distinguish between letter and memorandum reports.
10. Discuss and illustrate (with examples other than those in the text) two contrasting types of beginnings for the letter report.
11. Describe the makeup of the traditional staff study report. Can you think of any advantages of this plan?
12. Discuss the purposes of the typical corporate annual report.
13. How do technical reports differ from other business reports? How are they similar?

CHAPTER 8

Interpreting information

Before the report can be put in words, and frequently even before the report can be organized, meaning must be given to the information collected. Normally, the information collected consists of facts, and facts alone do not solve a problem. If the problem is to be solved, the facts must be examined as they relate to the one case. From this examination must be derived logical meaning—meaning that helps to solve the problem. This highly subjective process is the process of interpretation.

AN APPROACH TO INTERPRETATION

Any review of so subjective a process as interpretation must be quite general. Obviously, interpretation is largely a mental process; and the human mind works in complex and diverse ways. Because of this complexity and diversity, the following discussion makes no effort to reduce interpretation to a formula or to a set of hard and fast rules. To do so would be folly, for no formula or set of rules could possibly fit all the varying human minds and all the varying interpretation situations.

Because interpretation is a mental process, the ability to interpret is closely correlated with one's mental capability. And like most mental functions, interpretation is improved with knowledge. Normally, the analyst will gain interpretation knowledge through experience. But such knowledge may also be acquired from a review of the fundamentals of interpretation—fundamentals that ordinarily would be learned through experience. These fundamentals may logically be grouped into five areas.

1. Human frailties that lead to interpretation error.
2. Fallacious procedures in interpretation.

3. Attitudes and practices conducive to sound interpretation.
4. Statistical aids to interpretation.
5. Techniques in interpreting for the reader.

HUMAN FRAILTIES AND INTERPRETATION ERROR

Because interpretation is a product of the mind, it is affected by the limitations of the mind. It is common knowledge that the mind is subject to quirks of peculiarity, irrationality, and inconsistency. Certainly, it would be impractical to review all such quirks, for such a review would encompass the field of psychology. It is possible, however, to list the major limitations to interpretation. Thus, the following review of the three major limitations is presented. Possibly by knowing the nature of human frailties one will be better prepared to guard against them.

Desire for the spectacular

Inside all human beings there is a love for the unusual—the spectacular. Sometimes, this tendency is a result of wishful thinking. At other times, it is the result of a belief that true events usually are not sensational enough to kindle human interest. Whatever the cause, this tendency is frequently revealed in everyday human living. The 5-pound bass, for example, may gain to 7 pounds between the time it is caught and the time the fisherman describes his catch to the boys downtown. A simple neighborhood tale will grow in intensity as it is relayed over backyard fences. Tales of athletic achievement tend to grow in incredibility each time they are related.

Occasionally, this tendency leads to exaggeration in the interpretation of report material, particularly in the reports of the less experienced analysts. For this, just as for most of the other human frailties, there is but one cure. The analyst must be continuously aware of this possibility of error, and he must make conscious effort to avoid it.

Belief that conclusions are essential

Another cause of error in interpretation is a prevailing belief that there must be an answer to every question—that absolute finality and certainty is desirable in all cases. This belief is wrong. Few areas of information can be interpreted definitely. Even so, the inexperienced analyst frequently makes definite interpretations simply because he believes that not to do so would be evading a basic issue.

This form of error is well illustrated by the following example. In a consumer survey made for a soap company, 3 percent of the people interviewed voiced disapproval of the aroma of one of the company's toilet soaps. This information, however, was not asked for in the questionnaire used in the survey but was submitted voluntarily. Thus, not all those interviewed had an opportunity to express their opinions on this point. Yet, the writer of this report, probably feeling that a definite interpretation was necessary, concluded that the objection to the characteristic was negligible. A second survey, this one asking all respondents to comment on the soap's aroma, proved him wrong.

The experienced analyst will recognize that oftentimes interpretation must be qualified with explanation. Sometimes, more than one possible interpretation may be presented. Then, there are occasions when the analyst is incapable of interpreting some information. On such occasions, he should accept his incapability rather than make a wild guess simply because he believes to not interpret is an indicator of loose and illogical thinking.

Acceptance of lack of evidence as proof to contrary

Prevailing in the minds of many beginning analysts is a belief that when a proposition cannot be proved the opposite must be true. Obviously, this belief is fallacious. It is a rare case, indeed, when the lack of evidence to support one proposition can be used as evidence to support a contrary proposition. For example, the absence of data proving that a proposed advertising campaign will be successful does not prove that it will fail. Because there is no evidence available to prove that a man is a good credit risk does not make him a bad risk.

The experienced analyst consciously works on the proposition that evidence must support every conclusion. He knows that conclusions that cannot be supported cannot be made. He recognizes the truth that evidence is not capable of being stretched or turned around. And he takes great care to make certain that all evidence is used logically.

FALLACIOUS INTERPRETATION PROCEDURES

Interpretation errors may also be the result of fallacious interpretation procedures. Perhaps a review of some of the more common errors of this type will enable the analyst to learn from the experiences of others rather than by the trial-and-error teachings of his own efforts.

Bias in interpretation

Bias in interpretation may be unconscious or deliberate. In neither case is it excusable. Deliberate bias is unethical by any measure. Unconscious bias reflects on the mentality of the analyst. Of the two, however, unconscious bias is the more dangerous, for it is both difficult to detect and to correct.

For example, consider the case in which two accountants were assigned identical tasks of determining the best inventory valuation method for use by a new company. The accountants began the problem with differing personal convictions that one particular method was best. The two men worked diligently and, so they thought, objectively in analyzing all the methods. They used the same supporting information. The two men came up with different decisions. Their decisions supported the convictions they held when they began the study; yet, neither was conscious of any bias in reporting.

Unconscious bias is extremely difficult to detect and equally difficult to control. There is but one corrective measure that can be used against it, and that one is maintenance of constant mental alertness to detect bias. But this prescription is by no measure a panacea for bias. As is the case with many of today's wonder drugs, many people are allergic to such a prescription.

Comparison of noncomparable data

In most forms of reports, various comparisons of the collected information are made. As a rule, most such comparisons are logical and assist in developing a conclusion. Occasionally, however, the data compared are not really comparable. A recent journal article, for example, reported on the success of typical graduates of a number of American colleges. The data pointed to the fact that the earning power of graduates of one particular school was well above that of the graduates of any other school in the study. Without further explanation, however, this comparison is fallacious. In truth, the groups of graduates are not comparable. The school with the high-earning graduates is one traditionally attended by the sons of the very wealthy. These men would be likely to have high earnings even if they never attended college.

Cause–effect confusion

Interpretation error sometimes is the result of a mistaken assumption that a cause–effect relationship exists between sets of data. This interpretation error is a result of a confusion of association with causation. Cause–effect relationships must be based on more than mere association. The association must also be clearly logical. But the problem is intensified because in some instances associations falsely appear to have a cause–effect relationship.

The almost classic illustration of the error concerns the series of data gathered on hourly traffic flow over the Brooklyn Bridge and the tide changes in the water below. Analysis of the two series shows a high correlation in traffic flow and the falling and rising tide. Yet, it would be foolish to contend that one caused the other.

Unreliable data

Unless the information collected is reliable, interpretations made from it are uncertain at best. Reliable data are statistically sound. They are collected through sound research methodology and by competent researchers. Usually, they are facts—that is, they are verifiable truths as contrasted with opinions, which are attitudes of the mind.

Although it is not always possible to determine the reliability of information gathered, it is best to handle questionable information with extreme care. Only that information that is unquestionably reliable is worthy of interpretation. In no case are interpretations better than the data from which they are derived.

The first tests of the vaccine for poliomyelitis, for example, serve to illustrate the necessity for reliability of data. The medical men did not try the vaccine on a mere handful of children. Instead, tens of thousands were used. Had only a few been included in the preliminary tests, the data collected would have been highly unreliable. Most probably none in a small group would have acquired the disease. But who could say whether their good fortune was because of the vaccine or in spite of it?

Unrepresentative data

Oftentimes, interpretations are based on data not representative of the subject of the interpretation. Too often, the analyst is guided by the numerical significance of the information rather than its representativeness. In reality, a small bit of representative data is far superior to great quantities of unrepresentative data.

Classic proof of this example are the election surveys of the 1936 presidential campaign. One survey made by the now defunct *Literary Digest* comprised a sample of 2,376,000 votes. The other, made by *Fortune,* comprised only 4,500 votes. The first survey, however, was not representative of the voting public, being weighted heavily with people in the upper-income group. Its returns were in error 20 percent. The *Fortune* survey, small though it was, missed the actual outcome only 1.2 percent. Needless to say, it was a representative study.

Neglect of important factors

Errors in interpretation may stem from a review of only one factor in a complex problem of many factors. Few problems are so simple that they can be solved by analysis of a single area of information. The complex problem is the rule rather than the exception. The analyst, therefore, must take care to look for all possible factors that affect his problem and to give all of these factors their due weight in his analysis.

This principle is well illustrated by a survey of university students and their grades. The report on this study presented the startling conclusion that a direct correlation exists between high grades and the amount of money spent by the student. This conclusion contradicts the accepted belief that the hard-working poor boy makes a better student than his playboy classmate. But only grades and income were compared in the study. It is apparent that factors other than income determine grades. Isn't it likely that many of the poorer students' grades suffer because of the hours they must devote to outside work? Couldn't it be that the amount of study time available has the major effect on grades earned? Might it not be that the money spent is not a cause of high grades but merely associated with them—that the real cause may be that those with higher incomes have the advantages of higher cultural and academic backgrounds? Obviously, the conclusion was based on only one factor of a complex problem.

ATTITUDES AND PRACTICES CONDUCIVE TO SOUND INTERPRETING

As noted previously, interpretation is the application of clear thinking to the information gathered. Clear thinking, of course, follows the rules of logic. But logic does not come to all men by nature. Nor can its method be reduced to a formula. Generally it is developed through experience and knowledge. Its development can be helped along, however, through the adoption of some attitudes and practices that characterize its use.

Cultivation of a critical point of view

The cultivation of a critical point of view is a requirement for all those who engage in research and reporting work. In report preparation, just as in two-party governments, criticism from an opposing standpoint tends to maintain a balance of reason. But usually in report preparation only one party is engaged in the work, so he must play a dual role. He must be both the critic and the advocate. He must be for and against everything with equal vigor.

Maintenance of the judicial attitude

The analyst would do well to assume the role of the judge. He should try to place himself above the role of ordinary man—without emotion, without prejudice, and with an open mind. His primary objective should be to uncover truth, and he should be determined to leave no stones unturned in his search for truth.

The judicial attitude, as described above, may appear idealistic and out of the reach of the investigator. Possibly it is. Yet, the investigator who honestly attempts to assume such an attitude cannot fail to succeed in part. There is some truth to the adage, "Those whose goal is the stars may never reach them, but they seldom fail to leave the ground."

Consultation with others

Even though the investigator may be well qualified in the field of inquiry, the chances of his knowing all there is to know in the field are slim. Usually, he may profit by talking over his problems, appraisals, and interpretations with others in the field. He may profit, too, by submitting his ideas to an ardent critic. Then, armed with the critic's views, he is in a much better position to interpret his opinions. It is a rare occasion, indeed, in which the work of one mind cannot be improved through the assistance of others. If it does nothing else, talking over the problem with someone helps to give the investigator courage in his convictions.

Testing of interpretations

Often, it is not enough simply to look at all sides of an issue with an eye for criticism. The wise analyst may profit by extending his critical review to actual tests of his interpretations. Unfortunately, few interpretations can be tested conclusively, for the means of testing are largely subjective. But the fact that the interpretations are tested at all should lend support to their logic. Two subjective tests may be given to any interpretation.

First is the test of experience. In interpretation, as in all scientific methods, the dominant method of testing is with the reason. In using this test, the analyst simply ponders on each interpretation, asking himself the question, "Does this appear reasonable in the light of all that I know or have experienced?" This method may be explained best by example.

Numerous times in the primitive past the descent of plagues on villages and countries was interpreted by many a wise man of the day as a form of punishment for the sins of the people affected. It did not matter that their theory did not stand to reason. They were not moved by the failure of the plague to strike against all places of sin or all sinners. They took little cognizance of the fact that the plague struck against saint and sinner alike. Their appeal was to fear rather than to reason.

Their reasoning contrasts sharply with the testing by experience later used by scientists in finding the cause of the diseases. It was the scientists' approach to search through all experience for consistencies in the case patterns of the disease under study. With some diseases, they found that those stricken had drunk polluted water. Consistencies found in the case histories of other diseases led to tracing the causes to carriers such as flies, rats, and mosquitoes. In all cases, the scientists' conclusions were based on facts gathered through experience. Because their conclusions were based on consistencies of experience, they fulfilled the requirement of logic. Thus, their appeal was to the reason.

A second means of subjective examination of interpretation is the negative test. In a sense, it is a corollary to the interpretation fundamental of cultivating a critical point of view. The negative test consists of constructing an interpretation directly opposed to each interpretation made. Then, the opposite interpretation is examined carefully in the light of all available evidence. The analyst may go as far as to build up a case in its defense. Finally, the two opposite interpretations are compared and the stronger one retained. In other words, the pros and cons, the advantages and disadvantages, of each issue are examined.

Illustrating the negative test is an interpretation made of the findings of a survey of student reading habits at a certain state university. The supervisor of the survey hastily interpreted the findings to indicate that the quality of material read by students was high. He pointed to his collection of numerous facts and figures, which showed that most of the literature read by students was that considered good by literary standards. A critic of the study carefully pointed out that some of the data uncovered supported the opposite interpretation, for the data revealed that a sizable group of the students read low-quality literature. Further investigation proved the first conclusion not so clear-cut as was at first supposed. Had the supervisor applied the negative test he would have tried to support both interpretations. Then, he would have favored the one best supported by fact.

STATISTICAL AIDS TO INTERPRETATION

Frequently, the information gathered by the investigator is quantitative—that is, the information uncovered is expressed in numbers. Usually, such data in their raw form are voluminous, consisting of tens, hundreds, even thousands of individual figures. If they are to be interpreted, they must first be combined, grouped, or in some way reduced so that their meaning can be conveyed to the human mind. This task is accomplished through the use of some general statistical techniques. Although a review of all these techniques is beyond the scope of this book, the more common ones are briefly described.

Measures of central tendency

One means of presenting the overall picture of a mass of quantitative data is by measurements of central tendency. Such measures seek to find one value in the series that best describes the whole or may be considered typical of the whole. Three measures of central tendency are most commonly used.

The first, the arithmetic mean, is the technique most people call the average. It consists simpy of dividing the total of the values in a series by the number of values in the series. As an illustration, in computing the mean weekly incomes of five men ($60, $60, $100, $105, and $150) whose total income is $475, the mean income would be $95.

The second measure of central tendency is the median—the middle value in a series of values arranged in order of magnitude. One half of the values in the series are greater than the median; the other half are lower. Thus, in the series of five incomes mentioned above, the midvalue is $100.

Third of the central tendency measures is the mode. The mode is the value most common to the series—the quantity found most frequently. Of the income figures previously illustrated, the quantity $60 occurs twice—more than any other quantity.

The obvious question following this presentation is: Which of the three measures is best? The answer to this question varies with the individual series concerned. One measure may be best to describe one series; another may be best for another series. Each measure has its limitations. For example, the mean is influenced by each of the values in the series concerned; thus, the presence of extreme values will distort the measure. And there is always the possibility that the mode of a series may be an extreme quantity. Although such distributions are rare, they sometimes occur. The median, too, may be limited in meaning, such as in series where the midvalue is removed from the points about which the values tend to congregate. Although such limitations may influence the decision to use one measure or another, usually the decision is a subjective one. That is, the investigator selects the measure that best describes the series as he sees it.

Descriptions of dispersion

Frequently, it is necessary to draw interpretations from the spread of the quantities in the series. This point is well illustrated by two series of weekly income statistics of industrial workers. One series comprises the values $50, $60, $60, $75, $75, $75, $80, $90, and $110. The second series is made up of weekly incomes of $65, $70, $70, $75, $75, $75, $80, $80, and $85. The means, medians, and modes of the two series are identical; yet, even the novice observer can see that the series differ sharply. Certainly, the central tendency measures do not completely describe the series. A need exists for a measure of the dispersion of the values.

Most of the statistical measures of dispersion (average deviation, standard deviation, and such) are too involved for treatment here, but two of the simplest and most general ones can be mentioned. Foremost of these is the range, often called the crude range. The range is simply the spread between the highest and lowest values in the series. The range of the first series in the paragraph above is from $50 to $110, or $60. In the second series the values range only $20, from a low of $65 to a high of $85. This measure may be distorted somewhat in series where an extreme value exists.

Because extreme values do tend to distort the picture of the spread of the quantities, more refined measures of the range are often used. Such a measure is the interquartile range, which is simply the spread of the middle 50 percent of the values. In other words, if all the values in the series were arranged in order of magnitude and divided into four groups of equal number, the middle two groups would comprise the interquartile range. With ungrouped[1] data, the formula for this procedure is

$$\frac{N+1}{4}.$$

The N represents the number of units in the series, and the $+$ 1 is used to adjust for the space between numbers. Applying this formula to a series of weekly incomes, $50, $55, $65, $70, $75, $75, and $80, one gets

---

[1] For the formula for computing quartiles of grouped data, see any standard statistics textbook.

$$\frac{7+1}{4} = 2.$$

This quotient means that two values are in each of the quartiles. Thus, the quartiles are marked by the second, fourth, and sixth items in the series. The interquartile range for the series in question is from $55 to $75 per week.

Comparisons by ratios

Another statistical technique that may be used as a tool to interpreting information is the ratio. By definition, ratios are simplified comparisons of quantities. One such means of simplifying comparisons is to express one quantity as a multiple of another. If, for example, 795 respondents to a survey favor one issue and 198 favor another issue, one could report that about four times as many favor the first issue as favor the second.

Also, the same comparison may be expressed as a simple ratio of four to one, or as the fraction four fifths. Oftentimes, it is best to express ratios with 100 as the base—that is, as percentages. When interpreted as a percentage, the data reviewed above may read 80 percent favor the first issue; 20 percent favor the second.

INTERPRETING FOR THE READER

After the analyst has thoroughly interpreted his problem, his interpretation chores are still not finished. He must convey these interpretations to those who will read the results of his work. He must be most thorough in these efforts, for his readers are likely to be less informed on the topic than he.

It is the report writer's duty to interpret his findings not because the reader is incapable of interpreting raw data, for such usually is not the case. Rather, he interprets for the reader because interpretation assists communication, and the communication of his findings is a major objective of the report writer.

Communication is made easier if the reader's mind is not allowed to wander but is carefully guided every step of the way. There can be little reason for allowing the reader's mind to go over the same trial-and-error route that the writer has painfully covered. The writer has worked with the information, so chances are he knows it better than anyone else. His knowledge and experience are wasted unless they are revealed in his interpretations.

ORDERLY PROCEDURE IN INTERPRETING

Even though there is no mechanical formula for the actual process of interpreting, it is possible that the interpretation efforts may
follow a general order of steps. Such an order, however, should
never be held definite and should be altered to meet the requirements of any problem. That a plan can be devised, however, should
not be assumed to mean that interpretation is wholly an objective
process. The subjective element can never be removed from interpretation.

Relate information to the problem

The first step in orderly interpretation is the simple task of relating the information collected to the phase of the problem it affects.
Sometimes, it will be found that one small bit of information may
play a paramount role in the problem. In other instances, large
quantities of information need to be combined in order to shed light
on a single minor point. On other occasions, it may be found that a
maze of comparisons and cross comparisons are necessary.

Make all practical interpretations

Next, all plausible interpretations are made of the relationships of
each bit of information to the phase of the problem it affects. No
interpretation with merit should be ignored. In many instances, a
number of interpretations may be advanced for one bit of information. Other instances will find only one interpretation deserving of
merit. The efforts here need to be orderly and thorough, for an error
or omission at this point could very well affect the problem as a
whole.

Reevaluate interpretations

In the third step, the investigator must carefully review all the
interpretations he has advanced for the information collected. Each
interpretation should be carefully evaluated in the light of existing
evidence. Possibly, the interpretations can be put to the subjective
tests previously discussed.

Select interpretations with most merit

A fourth step is to select the interpretations that appear to have most merit. The decisions here rest on an evaluation of the test results of the preceding step. Those interpretations that do not fare so well are dropped or at least qualified by explanation.

Derive conclusions from the interpretations

Finally, from the interpretations retained the solution (i.e., conclusions and recommendations) evolves.

This task of making conclusions and recommendations is yet another form of interpretation, except here the interpretations are based not on fact but on other interpretations. Thus, conclusions may be defined as interpretations of the information previously interpreted on the objective of the study. And recommendations are yet another step down this interpretation ladder, for in a sense they are interpretations drawn from the conclusions. They are the lines of action to which the conclusions logically point. They must be well supported by these conclusions, just as these conclusions must be supported by other interpretations, and these interpretations in turn must be supported by the information collected. As with any subjective process of this sort, there is no substitute for simple logic and knowledge of the field of the problem.

QUESTIONS

1. Discuss the need for interpretation in most report problems.
2. Discuss each of the major human frailties that produce interpretation error. Illustrate each with realistic examples different from those in the text.
3. Distinguish between unconscious and conscious bias. Comment on the effects of each on the interpretation of report information.
4. Explain the error of comparing noncomparable data. Illustrate with original examples.
5. What is cause-effect error. Illustrate with original examples.
6. Explain how the reliability of data is related to their representativeness. Illustrate with original examples.
7. Discuss how the selection of factors affects the quality of interpretation in a report.
8. What can one do to improve his interpretation of information.
9. Using company records covering a five-year period, a business man

concluded that most productive salesmen were in the 35-to-40 age bracket. Explain what he could do to test this interpretation.

10. What is meant by the central tendency of data? In what ways may it be measured?

11. What is dispersion? How may it be measured?

12. Give examples of appropriate uses of measures of central tendency, dispersion, and ratio.

13. Summarize the orderly form of interpretation given in the text. Comment on its limitations or shortcomings.

14. Discuss the interpretation fallacies present in the following cases.

   a) A study produced data that showed United States college students to be far behind their comparable groups in European countries. The conclusion was made that the educational systems in these European countries are superior to that in the United States.

   b) A politician concluded that in his incumbent opponent's 20 years as mayor of a city, the city's expenditures had increased an exorbitant 280 percent.

   c) The editor of a leading magazine for businessmen reported that unsolicited letters he had received from his readers justified a conclusion that the public favored stronger government controls over unions.

   d) When questioned about their feelings concerning a certain personnel policy of the company, 14 percent of the employees interviewed strongly supported the policy, 62 percent showed little or no concern about it, and 24 percent opposed it. A management report concluded that the policy should be continued, since 76 percent did not oppose it. The union objected to this conclusion.

   e) Records compiled at a certain university showed that students majoring in engineering received an average of $80 per month more than business graduates. An analyst concluded that careers in engineering are more rewarding monetarily than are careers in business.

   f) A campus survey at a midwestern university showed that 92 percent of the students of Christian faiths favored a certain issue, whereas only 33 percent of the Hindu students favored the matter. The conclusion reached was that Christians and Hindus were far apart on this matter.

   g) A top executive in a department store chain assembled statistics on sales by stores. He then concluded that those store managers who had achieved the best percentage gains were the best managers and should be so rewarded.

   h) A report writer found data showing that sales of soft drinks were correlated with vacation travel. He concluded that soft drink sales were heavily affected by vacations.

CHAPTER 9

Writing to communicate: general characteristics

After the researcher has organized his findings, he knows what the facts of his problem are, what they mean, and how he will apply them to his problem. Thus, the story his report will tell is clear in his mind. Now his task is to communicate his story to those who should receive it.

Of all the tasks he must perform, this is the one he is most likely to perform poorly. Yet, regardless of how well he has worked to this point, unless he communicates the results of his work he will fail in his objective. Research findings not communicated are really not findings at all, for they are lost to all but the researcher. The difficulty of communicating is easily explained. Of all the human activities, communicating is among the most complex. Understanding of this most vital and complex activity of communication serves as a good basis for studying the techniques involved.

THE PROCESS OF COMMUNICATION

An understanding of the complexity of communication can be gained from a close analysis of the communication process. Such an analysis is presented in the following pages. Although this description borders on oversimplification, it brings to light the major limitations, barriers, and other complexities present when one human being communicates with another. For purposes of illustration, the description builds around two people who are called Jones and Smith. Although the description generally applies to two-person oral communication, it is adaptable to written communication.

Sensory receptors and the sensory world

Analysis of what happens when Smith communicates with Jones properly begins when one of the persons, say Jones, sends a message to the other. The message sent by Jones may be in many forms—gestures, facial expressions, drawings, or, more likely, written or spoken words. The message sent enters the sensory world of Smith.

The sensory world of Smith consists of all things around him as his sensory receptors detect them. The sensory receptors, of course, are those parts of the anatomy (eyes, ears, nose) that record impressions from reality. Thus, the sensory world of Smith contains all that he feels, sees, hears, or smells. From this sensory world, Smith's receptors pick up impressions and send them to his brain.

It should be noted, however, that Smith's receptors cannot detect all that exists in the world about him. Just how much they can detect depends on a number of factors.

One determining factor is the ability of his individual sensory receptors to receive impressions. Not all receptors are equally sensitive. All ears do not hear equally well. Likewise, eyesights differ. So do abilities to smell. And so do the other senses vary from person to person.

Another determinant is Smith's mental alertness. There are times, for example, when his mind is keenly alert to all that its senses can detect. There are other times when it is dull—in a stupor, a daydream, or the like.

Still another determinant is the will of Smith's mind. In varying degrees, the mind has the ability to tune in or tune out the events in the world of reality. In a noisy room full of people at a party, for example, one can select the conversation of a single person and keep out the surrounding noises.

When Smith's sensory receptors record something from Smith's sensory world, they relay the information to his brain. The message sent by Jones probably would be recorded in this way, but it could be joined by other impressions, such as outside noises, detection of movements, facial expressions, and such. In fact, Smith's brain receives these impressions in a continuous flow—a flow that may contract or expand, go fast or go slow, become strong or become weak.

The preverbal stage

This flow of stimulations into Smith's mind begins the preverbal stage of communication. At this stage, the stream of sensory perceptions produces reactions in his mind—reactions that will be given meaning and may trigger a communication response.

Role of the filter.   It is at this preverbal stage that the most complex part of the communication process occurs. The sensory perceptions pass through the filter of Smith's mind, and they are given meaning. Smith's filter is made of all that has ever passed through his mind. Specifically, it is made up of all his experience, knowledge, bias, emotions—in fact, all that he is and has been. Obviously, no two people have precisely identical filters, for no two people have precisely the same experience, knowledge, bias, and such.

Because people's filters differ, meanings they assign to comparable perceptions also differ. One man, for example, may smile pleasantly when his filter receives the word "liberal"; another with sharply differing background may react with violent anger at the same word. In one man's filter, the word "butterball" rings a jolly note; in the filter of one who has long been troubled with weight problems a negative connotation may occur. Even a salesman's cheery "good morning" may produce sharply varying reactions. In a filter surrounded with happiness, the full positive meaning is received. A filter of a burdened, emotionally upset mind, on the other hand, may react with annoyance at these words that break into the mind's unhappy state.

The symbolizing stage

Next in the communication process is the symbolizing stage. At this stage, Smith's mind reacts to the filtered information it has received. If the filtered information produces a sufficiently strong reaction, his mind may elect to communicate some form of response by words, by gesture, by action, or by some other means.

Determination of communication form. When Smith's mind does elect to communicate, it next determines the general meaning the response will take. This process involves the innermost and most complex workings of the mind; and little is known about it. There is evidence, however, to indicate that one's ability here, and throughout the symbolizing stage, is related to his mental capacities and to the extent to which he will permit his mind to react. Especially is one's ability to evaluate filtered information and formulate meaning related to his ability with language. Apparently, ability with language equips one with a variety of symbol forms (ways of expressing meaning), and the greater the number of symbol forms in the mind, the more discriminating one can be in selecting them.

Smith ends the symbolizing stage by encoding the meaning form in his mind. That is, he converts his meaning into symbols, and he transmits the symbols. In most instances, his symbol form is words, either made as sounds or as marks on paper. He also may select gestures, movements, facial expressions, diagrams, and such.

The cycle repeated

Transmittal of the encoded message ends the first cycle of the communication process. The transmitted signals next enter the sensory world that surrounds Jones, and then begins a second cycle, identical to the first. Now Jones picks up these symbols through his sensory receptors. They then travel through his nervous system to his brain. Here they are given meaning as they pass through his individual filter of knowledge, experience, bias, emotional makeup, and the like. The filtered meanings may also bring about a response, which Jones then formulates in his mind, puts in symbol form, and transmits. The process may continue indefinitely, cycle after cycle, as long as the participants want to communicate.

The model and written communication

Although the foregoing description of the communication process applies more specifically to face-to-face communication than to other forms, it generally describes written communication as well. But some significant differences exist.

Effects on creativity. Perhaps the most significant difference between face-to-face and written communication is that written communication is more likely to be creative effort of the mind. The fact is that it is more likely to be thought out and less likely to be the spontaneous reaction to signs received by the receptors. More specifically, the message in a written communication is more likely to be a result of stimuli produced by the mind than of outside stimuli picked up by the sensory receptors.

In a report-writing situation, for example, before beginning his work the writer has decided to communicate, or perhaps someone has decided for him. Before he begins the task of communicating, he gathers the information that will form the basis of his communication. Then, through his logical thought processes he encodes the communication that will accomplish his communication objective. Thus, there is not likely to be an interchange of stimuli between communicants, nor is there likely to be any triggering of desires to communicate. The process is a creative and deliberative one.

On the other hand, a letter-writing situation can be an exception, at least to some extent. In a sense, a letter situation can be like a face-to-face situation in slow motion. Stimuli picked up by one man's receptors could produce a reaction that would bring about a communication response—in this case, a written letter. This letter could, in turn, bring about a communication response in its reader's mind. Thus, a reply would be written. This reply could then bring about another reply. And the cycle could be repeated as long as each letter brings about a communication response. Even so, letters represent more deliberate and creative efforts than face-to-face communication.

The lag of time.   Most obvious of the differences in face-to-face and written communication processes is the time factor. In face-to-face communication, the encoded messages move instantaneously into the sensory environments of the participants. In written communication, however, some delay takes place. Just how long the delay will be is indeterminate. Priority administrative announcements or telegrams may be read minutes after they are written. Routine letters require a day or two to communicate their content. Research reports may take weeks in communicating their information to the intended readers. And all such written communications may be filed for possible reference in the indefinite future. They may continue to communicate for months or years.

The lag of time also makes a difference in the return information one gets from communicating. Return information, commonly called feedback, helps greatly in determining when clear meaning is being received. In face-to-face communication, feedback is easy to get. The participants are right there together. They can ask questions. They can observe facial expressions. They can repeat and simplify whenever it appears to be necessary. In written communication, feedback is slow at best. Often it does not occur at all.

Limited numbers of cycles.   A third significant difference between face-to-face and written communication is the number of cycles that typically occur in a communication event. As previously noted, face-to-face communication normally involves multiple exchanges of symbols; thus, many cycles take place. Written communication, on the other hand, usually involves a limited number of cycles. In fact, most written communication is one-cycle communication. A message is sent and received, but none is returned. Of course, there are exceptions, such as letters and memorandums, which lead to a succession of communication exchanges. But even the most involved of these would hardly match in cycle numbers a routine face-to-face conversation.

Some basic truths

Analysis of the communication process brings out three underlying truths, which are helpful to the understanding of communication.

Meanings sent are not always received. First, meanings transmitted are not necessarily the meanings received. No two minds have identical filters. No two minds have identical storehouses of words, gestures, facial expressions or any of the other symbol forms; nor do any two minds attach exactly the same meanings to all the symbols they have in common. Because of these differences, errors in communication are bound to occur.

Meaning is in the mind. A second underlying truth is that meaning is in the mind and not in the words or other symbols used. How accurately meaning is conveyed in symbols depends on how skilled one is in choosing symbols and how accurately the person receiving the symbols is able to interpret the meaning intended. Thus, the skilled communicator looks beyond the symbols used. He considers the communication ability of those with whom he wants to communicate. When he receives messages, he looks not at the symbols alone but for the meaning intended by the person who used them.

Communication is imperfect. Third is the basic truth that communication is highly imperfect. One reason for this imperfection is that symbols, especially words, are limited and at best are crude substitutes for the real thing. The one word "man" can refer to any one of a few hundred million human males, no two precisely alike. The word "dog" stands for any one of a countless number of animals varying sharply in size, shape, color, and in every other visible aspect. "House" can refer equally well to a shanty, to a palatial mansion, and to the many different structures between these extremes. The verb "run" tells only the most general part of the action it describes; it ignores the countless variations in speed, grace, and style. These illustrations are not exceptions; they are the rule. Words simply cannot account for the infinite variations and complexities of reality.

Another reason for communication imperfection is that communicators vary in their abilities to convey their thoughts. Some find great difficulty in selecting symbols that express their simplest thoughts; others are highly capable. Variations in ability to communicate obviously lead to variations in the precision with which thoughts are expressed.

Although the foregoing comments bring to light the difficulties, complexities and limitations of communications as a whole, human beings do a fairly good job of communicating with one another. Even so, incidents of miscommunication occur frequently. Those people who attach precise meanings to every word, who feel that meanings intended are meanings received, and who are not able to select symbols well are apt to experience more than their share of miscommunication.

From the review of the communication process, certain qualities of good report writing emerge. Foremost is the fundamental quality of adaptation—of fitting the words to the mind of the individual reader concerned. A second and corollary quality is the readability of the writing. Then, other qualities help to prepare the material for maximum comprehension in the mind. These are the qualities of objectivity, logical time viewpoint, logical connection of thought, and interest. All are discussed in the following pages.

FUNDAMENTAL NEED FOR ADAPTATION

A fact often ignored by the novice report writer is that the communication abilities of reader and writer are not always equal. Probably no two people know precisely the same words; nor do they know equally much about all subject matters. This condition is a major barrier to successful communication. Obviously, if the writer uses words and concepts not known to the reader, communication does not occur. For written communication to be successful, the words and concepts used must mean the same to both writer and reader.

From this analysis, one fundamental requirement for the report writer is clear. This is the need for adapting the writing to the specific reader or readers. Unfortunately, the novice is not likely to adapt his writing to the reader without conscious effort. More than likely he finds writing such a chore that he is content to accept whatever wording first comes to mind. Such wording may communicate well with someone like the writer, but not so well with the specific reader intended.

In order to adapt his writing, the wise report writer begins by visualizing his reader. Thus, he determines such things as who his reader is, how much he knows about the subject, what is his educational level, and how he thinks. Then, keeping this image of his reader in mind, he tailors his writing to fit this one person.

The writer's task is relatively simple when he writes to a single reader or homogeneous group of readers. But what if he writes to a group with varying characteristics? What if, say, his audience comprises people ranging from college graduates to grade school graduates? The answer should be obvious. In such cases, the writer has no choice but to aim at the lowest level of the group. To aim higher would be to exclude the lower level from his message.

When the report writer is better educated or better informed on the subject area than his reader, adaptation means simplification. A company executive writing to the rank-and-file employee, for example, must write in the simple words his reader understands. Likewise, a technical man writing to a nontechnical reader must simplify his writing. But when this technical man writes to a fellow technician, he does well to use the technical vernacular easily understood and expected by such men. As the following examples show, few technical writers were better aware of this fundamental rule than the late Dr. Albert Einstein. In writing on a technical subject to a nontechnical audience, he skillfully wrote down to their level.

What takes place can be illustrated with the help of our rich man. The atom M is a rich miser who, during his life, gives away no money (energy). But in his will he bequeaths his fortune to his sons M' and M'', on condition that they give to the community a small amount, less than one thousandth of the whole estate (energy or mass). The sons together have somewhat less than the father had (the mass sum M' and M'' is somewhat smaller than the mass M of the radioactive atom). But the part given to the community, though relatively small, is still so enormously large (considered as kinetic energy) that it brings with it a great threat of evil. Averting that threat has become the most urgent problem of our time.[1]

But when writing to fellow scientists, he wrote in words they understood and expected.

The general theory of relativity owes its existence in the first place to the empirical fact of the numerical equality of the inertial and gravitational mass of bodies, for which fundamental fact classical mechanics

---

[1] Albert Einstein, *Out of My Later Years,* Philosophical Library, Inc., New York, 1950, p. 53.

provided no interpretation. Such an interpretation is arrived at by an extension of the principle of relativity to co-ordinate systems accelerated relatively to one another. The introduction of co-ordinate systems accelerated relatively to inertial systems involves the appearance of gravitational fields relative to the latter. As a result of this, the general theory of relativity, which is based on the equality of inertia and weight, provides a theory of the gravitational field.[2]

THE ESSENTIAL QUALITY OF READABILITY

Supporting the basic requirement of adapting writing to the reader is the obvious requirement that writing be readable. Readable writing is writing that communicates quickly—in a single reading. It communicates exactly—without vagueness or error. And it communicates easily—with a minimum of effort for the reader. So important is this requirement that it is the subject of detailed discussion in Chapter 10. Although the details of this complex topic are best left for Chapter 10, the fundamentals of readability are discussed here. This topic is presented through a review of various scientific studies of readability.

In recent years, various communication scientists have made exhaustive studies in the area of readability. These studies show conclusively that different levels of readability exist. More specifically, they show that for each general level of education there is a level of writing easily read and understood. Writing that is readable to one educational level can be difficult for those below that level. To illustrate, the general level of writing that is easy reading for the college graduate is difficult for those below his educational level. A level that is easy reading for the high school senior is difficult for those below him in education. Readability levels exist for each general level of education.

This finding is well known to professional writers, who long have been writing for varying levels of readership. The currently popular magazines, for example, aim at varying levels of readability. The *New Yorker* and *Harper's,* according to studies made by Rudolph Flesch, aim at about a high school graduate level of readability. Magazines like *Reader's Digest* and *Time* are easy reading for those of eighth- to tenth-grade level. Highly popular slick magazines, such as *Look* and *Ladies' Home Journal,* gauge their writing at the sixth-

---

[2] Albert Einstein, *Essays in Science,* Philosophical Library, Inc., New York, 1934, p. 50.

and eighth-grade level. And at the bottom and aiming at third- to fifth-grade level of readership are the pulp magazines. The business writer would do well to follow these professionals by adapting his work to his reader.

Development of readability formulas

In addition to generally supporting the basic need for adaptation, these studies have produced formulas for measuring readability. These formulas are based on the qualities of writing that show the highest correlation with levels of readability. In general, these qualities are two—sentence length and word difficulty.

Measuring sentence length is relatively easy, although a few complexities here and there do not meet the eye. Determining word difficulty, on the other hand, is somewhat complex. The studies show that word difficulty is traceable to many things—to historical origin, extent of usage, and such. But because normally the longer a word is the more difficult it is, word length is used in the formulas as a convenient gauge of word difficulty.

Of the various readability formulas used in business today, the Gunning Fog Index probably is the most popular. Other formulas are just as accurate in measuring readability, but this one is among the easiest to use.

The Gunning Fog Index

The ease with which the Gunning Fog Index can be used is obvious from a review of the simple steps listed below. Its ease of interpretation is also obvious in that the index computed from these simple steps is in grade level of education. For example, an index of seven means that the material tested is easy reading for one at the seventh-grade level. An index of 12 indicates high school graduate level of readability. And an index of 16 indicates the level of the college graduate.

The simple steps for computing the index are as follows.

1. *Select a sample.* For long pieces of writing use at least 100 words. As in all sampling procedure, the larger the sample, the more reliable the results can be. So, in measuring readability for a long manuscript one would be wise to select a number of samples at random throughout the work.

2. *Determine the average number of words per sentence.* That is, first count words and sentences in a sample selected. Then divide the total number of words by the total of sentences.
3. *Determine the percentage of hard words in the sample.* Words of three syllables or longer are considered to be hard words. But do not count as hard words (1) words that are capitalized, (2) combinations of short, easy words (*grasshopper, businessman, bookkeeper*), or (3) verb forms made into three-syllable words by adding *ed* or *es* (*repeated, caresses*).
4. *Add the two factors computed above and multiply by 0.4.* The product is the minimum grade level at which the writing is easily read.

Application of the Gunning Fog Index is illustrated with the following paragraph.

In *general, construction* of *pictograms* follows the *general procedure* used in *constructing* bar charts. But two special rules should be followed. First, all of the picture units used must be of equal size. The *comparisons* must be made wholly on the basis of the number of *illustrations* used and never by *varying* the *areas* of the *individual* pictures used. The reason for this rule is *obvious.* The human eye is grossly *inadequate* in *comparing areas* of *geometric* designs. Second, the pictures or symbols used must *appropriately* depict the *quantity* to be *illustrated.* A *comparison* of the navies of the world, for *example,* might make use of *miniature* ship drawings. Cotton *production* might be shown by bales of cotton. *Obviously,* the drawings used must be *immediately interpreted* by the reader.

Inspection of the paragraph reveals these facts. It has 10 sentences and 129 words for an average sentence length of 13. Of the total of 129 words, 26 are considered to be hard words. Thus, the percentage of hard words is 20. From these data, the Gunning Fog Index is computed as follows.

Average sentence length	13
Percentage of hard words	20
Total	33
Multiply by	.4
Grade level of readership	13.2

Critical appraisal of the formulas

Readability formulas are widely used in business today. Perhaps the reason for their popularity is the glitter of their apparent mathematical exactness. Or perhaps they are popular because they reduce to simple and workable formulas the most complex work of writing.

Whatever the reason, the wise writer will look at the formulas objectively.

Unquestionably, these formulas have been a boon to improving clarity in business writing. They emphasize the main causes of failure in written communication. And they provide a convenient check and measure of the level of one's writing. But they also have some limitations.

The most serious limitation of the formulas is the primer style of writing that can result from a slavish use of them. Overly simple words and a monotonous succession of short sentences make dull reading. Dull reading doesn't hold the reader's attention. And without the reader's attention, there can be little communication.

Perhaps the formulas are most useful to the unskilled writer. By intelligent use of the formulas, he may at least be able to improve the communication quality of his work. His writing style, which was poor to begin with, does not suffer. A skilled writer, on the other hand, can violate the formulas and still communicate. Charles Dickens, for example, was a master in communicating in clear yet long sentences. So was Pope. And so are some business writers. Because most business writers fall somewhere between these extreme quality groups, the wisest course for them is to use the formulas as general guides. But never will a formula replace the clear and logical thinking that is the underpinning of all clear writing.

THE ESSENTIAL QUALITY OF OBJECTIVITY

A basic quality of good report writing, objectivity concerns both the attitude of the writer and writing style. The writer maintains an objective attitude by divorcing his own prejudices and emotions from his work and by fairly reviewing and interpreting the information he has uncovered. Thus, he approaches his problem with an open mind and looks at all sides of each question. His role is much like that of a judge presiding over a court of law. He is not moved by personal feelings. He seeks truth, and he leaves no stone unturned in quest for it. He makes his decision only after carefully weighing all of the evidence uncovered.

Objectivity as a basis for believability

A report built on the quality of objectivity has another ingredient essential to good report writing. That ingredient is believability. Perhaps biased writing can be in language that is artfully deceptive and may at first glance be believable. But such writing is risky. If at any spot in the report the reader detects bias, he will be suspicious of the whole work. Painstaking objectivity, therefore, is the only sure way to believable report writing.

Objectivity and the question of impersonal versus personal writing

Recognizing the need for objectivity in their work, the early report writers worked to develop a writing style that would convey this attitude. They reasoned that the source of the subjective quality in a report is the human being. And they reasoned that objectivity is best attained by emphasizing the factual material of a report rather than the personalities involved. So they worked to remove the human being from their writing. Impersonal writing style was the result. By impersonal writing is meant writing in the third person—without I's, we's, or you's.

In recent years, impersonal writing has been strenuously questioned by many writers. These writers point out that personal writing is more forceful and direct than is impersonal writing. They contend that writing that brings both reader and writer into the picture is more like conversation and therefore more interesting. And in regard to objectivity they answer that objectivity is an attitude of mind and not a matter of person. A report, they say, can be just as objective when written in personal style as when written in impersonal style. Frequently, they counter with the argument that impersonal writing leads to an overuse of passive voice and a generally dull writing style. This last argument, however, lacks substance. Impersonal writing can and should be interesting. Any dullness it may have is wholly the fault of the writer. As proof one has only to look at the lively styles used by the writers for newspapers, news magazines, and journals. Most of this writing is impersonal—and usually it is not dull.

As in most cases of controversy, there is some merit to the arguments on both sides. There are situations in which personal writing is best. There are situations in which impersonal writing is best. And there are situations in which either style is appropriate. The writer must decide at the outset of his work which style is best for his one situation.

His decision should be based on the circumstances of each report situation. First, he should consider the expectations or desires of those for whom he is preparing the report. More than likely he will find a preference for the impersonal style, for, like most human beings, businessmen have been slow to break tradition. Next, the writer should consider the formality of the report situation. If the situation is informal, as when the report is really a personal communication of information between business associates, personal writing is appropriate. But if the situation is formal, as is so with most major reports, the conventional impersonal style is best.

Perhaps the distinction between impersonal and personal writing is best made by illustration.

Personal	*Impersonal*
Having studied the various advantages and disadvantages of using trading stamps, I conclude that your company should not adopt this practice. If you use the stamps, you would have to pay out money for them. Also, you would have to hire additional employees to take care of the increase in sales volume.	A study of the advantages and disadvantages of using trading stamps supports the conclusion that the Mills Company should not adopt this practice. The stamps themselves would cost extra money. Also, use of stamps would require additional personnel to take care of the increase in sales volume.

LOGIC OF PRESENT TIME VIEWPOINT

Maintaining a proper time viewpoint in the report is a problem for even the seasoned writer. Illogical shifts from one tense to another detract generally from the writing and mar the accuracy of the presentation. Consistency in time viewpoint is the one logical solution to the problem. But whether the consistent time viewpoint should be past or present is a matter on which opinions differ.

Some authorities favor a consistent past viewpoint. They assume that all the data collected, as well as the research and the writing of the report, are past events by the time the report is read. Thus, they conclude it is logical to report a result from the current survey in words such as "22 percent of the managers *favored* a change." And they would write a reference to another part of the report in words like these: "In chapter two, this conclusion *was* reached."

A more logical approach is to write in the present time viewpoint. In following this viewpoint, the writer presents as current all information that is current at the time of writing. For example, a presentation of the results of a recent survey may be made in words like these: "Twenty-two percent of the managers *favor* a change." Or a reference in the report to another part of the report may be in words like: "In chapter two, this conclusion *is* reached." Information clearly in the past or in the future at the time of writing, however, the writer should present in a past or future tense. For example, survey findings likely to be obsolete at the time of writing may be worded thus: "In 1939, 44.2 percent of the managers *favored* this plan." Or a predicted figure for the future may be reported in these words: "According to this projection, the value of these assets will exceed 32 million dollars by 1980." A present time viewpoint should in no way be interpreted to mean that every verb must be in the present tense. Nor should it ever result in placing a single event awkwardly in time. Adherence to this viewpoint simply involves placing all facts in their logical place in time at the time of writing.

STRUCTURAL AIDS TO REPORT COHERENCE

Smoothness in the flow of information presented is an essential characteristic of good report writing. In the well-written report, each fact is in its logical place, and the relationship of each fact to other facts and to the plan of the report is clear to the reader. Thus, the parts of the report fit together, and the report reads as a unified composition. The writing quality that gives the report this smoothness of connection is commonly called coherence.

Perhaps the one best contributor to coherence is good organization—a topic discussed in detail in an earlier chapter. By relating facts in a logical, natural sequence, some degree of coherence is given to the writing. But logical arrangement of facts alone is not always enough. Particularly is this true in the long and involved report when the relationships of the parts are complex and are not so easily grasped by the reader. In such reports, the writer needs to make special effort to structure the report so that the relationships are clear. Specifically, he can structure the report story by using concluding and summary paragraphs to mark the report's progress. He can use introductory and preview paragraphs to show major relationships. And he can use transitional sentences and words to show relationships between the lesser parts.

The use of introductory, concluding, and summarizing sections

The extent of use of introductory, concluding, and summarizing sections depends on the report. Perhaps the best rule for the report writer to follow is to use them whenever they are needed to relate the parts of the report or to move the report message along. In general, these sections are more likely to be needed in the longer and more involved reports. In such reports, the report writer is likely to follow a traditional plan of connecting structure.

This plan, as described in Figure 8, uses these special sections to tie together all the parts of the report. Because it serves to keep the reader aware of where he has been, where he is, and where he is

Figure 8. Diagram of the structural coherence plan of a long formal report

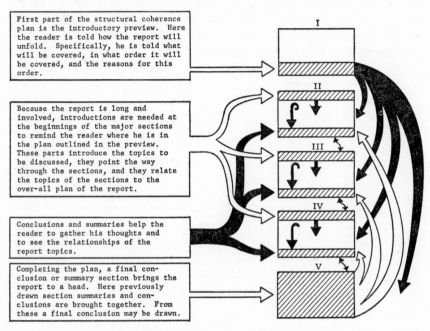

First part of the structural coherence plan is the introductory preview. Here the reader is told how the report will unfold. Specifically, he is told what will be covered, in what order it will be covered, and the reasons for this order.

Because the report is long and involved, introductions are needed at the beginnings of the major sections to remind the reader where he is in the plan outlined in the preview. These parts introduce the topics to be discussed, they point the way through the sections, and they relate the topics of the sections to the over-all plan of the report.

Conclusions and summaries help the reader to gather his thoughts and to see the relationships of the report topics.

Completing the plan, a final conclusion or summary section brings the report to a head. Here previously drawn section summaries and conclusions are brought together. From these a final conclusion may be drawn.

going, the plan helps the reader to find his way through a complex problem. Also, placement of forward-looking and backward-glancing sections permits the casual reader to dip into the report at any place and quickly get his bearing.

As noted in the diagram, three types of sections (usually a paragraph or more) may be used to structure the report. One is the introductory preview. Another is the section introduction. And still another is the conclusion or summary sections, either for the major report parts or for the whole report.

For the longer reports a section of the report introduction may be used (see Chapter 6) to tell the reader of the report's organization plan. Generally, this preview covers three things: topics to be discussed, their order of presentation, and the logic for this order. Having been informed of the basic plan, the reader is then able to quickly understand how each new subject he encounters in the following pages fits into the whole. Thus, a connection between the major report parts is made. The following paragraphs do a good job of previewing a report comparing four brands of automobiles for use by a sales organization.

The decision as to which light car Allied Distributors should buy is reached through a comparison on the basis of three factors: cost, safety, and dependability. Each of these major factors is broken down into its component parts, which are applied to each make being considered.

Because it is the most tangible factor, cost is examined first. In this section each make is compared for initial and trade-in values. Then they are compared for operating costs as determined by gasoline mileage, oil usage, repair expense, and such. In a second major section, the same comparison is used to determine the car safety. Driver visibility, special safety features, brakes, steering quality, acceleration rate, and traction are the main considerations here. In a third section, dependability of the cars is measured on the basis of repair records and salesmen's time lost because of automobile failure. In a final section weights are assigned to the foregoing comparisons and the brand of automobile best suited for the company's needs is recommended.

In addition to the introductory preview, relationships between the major report captions may be helped by introductory and summary sections placed at convenient spots throughout the report. These sections may be used occasionally to remind the reader of where he is in the progress of the report. Also, they may elaborate on the relationships between the report parts and, in general, give detailed connecting and introductory information. The following paragraph, for example, serves as an introduction to the final section of a report of an industrial survey. Note how the paragraph ties in with the preceding section, which covered industrial activity in three major geographic areas, and justifies covering secondary areas.

Although the great bulk of industry is concentrated in three areas (Grand City, Milltown, and Port Starr), a thorough industrial survey needs to consider the secondary, but nevertheless important, areas of the state. In the rank of their current industrial potential, these areas are the Southeast, with Hartsburg as its center; the Central West, dominated by Parrington; and the North Central, where Pineview is the center of activities.

The following summary-conclusion paragraph gives an appropriate ending to a major section. The paragraph brings to a head the findings presented in the section and points the way to the subject of the next section.

These findings and those pointed out in preceding paragraphs all point to one obvious conclusion. The small business executive is concerned primarily with subject matter which will aid him directly in his work. That is, he favors a curriculum slanted in favor of the practical subjects. He does, however, insist on some coverage of the liberal areas. Too, he is convinced of the value of studying business administration. On all of these points he is clearly out of tune with the bulk of big business leaders who have voiced their positions in this matter. Even the most dedicated business administration professors would find it difficult to support such an extremely practical concept. Nevertheless, these are the small business executive's opinions on the subject, and as he is the consumer of the business education product, his opinion should at least be considered. Likewise, his specific recommendation on courses (subject of the following chapter) deserves careful review.

Proper use of paragraphs such as these forms a network of connection throughout the work. The longer the report, the more effective they are likely to be.

Communication value of transition

Transition, which literally means a bridging across, may be formed in many ways. In general, transitions are made by words, or sentences, placed in the writing to show the relationships of the information presented. They may appear at the beginning of discussion on a new topic and may relate this topic to what has been discussed. They may appear at the end as a forward look. Or they may appear internally as words or phrases that in various ways tend to facilitate the flow of subject matter.

Whether a transition word or sentence should be used depends on the need for relating the parts concerned. Because the relationship of its parts may be seen merely from a logical sequence of presentation, a short report may require only a few transitional parts here and there. A long and involved report, on the other hand, may require much more transitional help.

A word of caution. Before more specific comment on transition is given, one fundamental point must be made clear. Transitions should in no way be made mechanically. They should be used only when there is a need for them, or when leaving them out would produce abruptness in the flow of report findings. Transitions should not appear to be stuck in; instead, they should blend in naturally with surrounding writing. For example, transitional forms of this mechanical type should be avoided: "The last section has discussed topic X. In the next section topic Y will be analyzed."

Transitional sentences. Throughout the report, the writer can improve the connecting network by the judicious use of sentences. They can especially be used to form the connecting link between secondary sections of the report, as illustrated in the following example of transition between Sections B and C of a report. The first few lines of this illustration draw a conclusion for Section B. Then, with smooth tie-in the next words introduce Section C and relate this topic to the report plan.

[Section B, concluded]
. . . Thus the data show only negligible difference in the cost for oil consumption [subject of Section B] for the three brands of cars.
[Section C]
Even though costs of gasoline [subject of Section A] and oil [subject of Section B] are the more consistent factors of operation expense, the picture is not complete until the cost of repairs and maintenance [subject of Section C] are considered.

Additional examples of sentences designed to connect succeeding parts are the following. By making a forward-looking reference, these sentences set up the following subject matter. Thus, the resulting shifts of subject matter are both smooth and logical.

These data show clearly that Edmond's machines are the most economical. Unquestionably their operation by low-cost gas and their record for low-cost maintenance give them a decided edge over competing brands. *Before a definite conclusion as to their merit is reached, however, one more vital comparison should be made.*

(The final sentence clearly sets up the following discussion of an additional comparison.)

. . . *At first glance the data appear to be convincing, but a closer observation reveals a number of discrepancies.*

(Discussion of the discrepancies is logically set up by this final sentence.)
Placement of topic sentences at key points of emphasis is still another way of using a sentence to improve the connecting network of the report. Usually, the topic sentence is best placed at the

paragraph beginning, where the subject matter can very quickly be related to its spot in the organization plan described in the introductory preview or the introduction to the section. Note in the following example how the topic sentences emphasize the key information. Note also how the topic sentences tie the paragraphs with the preview (not illustrated), which no doubt related this organization plan.

Brand C accelerates faster than the other two brands, both on level road and on a 9 percent grade. According to a test conducted by consumption research, Brand C attains a speed of 60 miles per hour in 13.2 seconds. To reach this same speed, Brand A requires 13.6 seconds and Brand B requires 14.4 seconds. On a 9 percent grade, Brand C reaches the 60-miles-per-hour speed in 29.4 seconds and Brand A in 43.3 seconds. Brand B is unable to reach this speed.

Because it carries more weight on its rear wheels than the others, Brand C has the best traction of the three. Traction, which means a minimum of sliding on wet or icy roads, is most important to safe driving, particularly during the cold, wet winter months. As traction is directly related to the weight carried by the rear wheels, a comparison of these weights should give some measure of the safety of the three cars. According to data released by the Automobile Bureau of Standards, Brand C carries 47 percent of its weight on its rear wheels. Brands B and A carry 44 percent and 42 percent, respectively.

Transitional words. Although the major transition problems concern connection between sections of the report, there is need also for transition between lesser parts. If the writing is to flow smoothly, there is frequent need for relating clause to clause and sentence to sentence and paragraph to paragraph. Transitional words and phrases generally serve to make these connections.

The transitional words that report writers may use are too numerous to relate, but the following review is a clear picture of what these words are and how they can be used. With a little imagination to supply the context, one can easily see how such words relate succeeding ideas. For better understanding, the words are grouped by the relationships they show between subjects previously discussed and those to be discussed.

Relationship	*Word Examples*
Listing or enumeration of subjects	In addition
	First, second, etc.
	Besides
	Moreover

Relationship	Word Examples
Contrast	On the contrary
	In spite of
	On the other hand
	In contrast
	However
Likeness	In a like manner
	Likewise
	Similarly
Cause–result	Thus
	Because of
	Therefore
	Consequently
	For this reason
Explanation or elaboration	For example
	To illustrate
	For instance
	Also
	Too

THE ROLE OF INTEREST IN REPORT COMMUNICATION

Like all forms of good writing, report writing should be interesting. Actually, the quality of interest is as important as the facts of the report, for without interest, communication is not likely to occur. If his interest is not held—if his mind is allowed to stray—the reader cannot help missing parts of the message. And it does not matter how much the reader wants to read the report message, nor is his interest in the subject enough to assure communication. The writing must maintain this interest. The truth of this reasoning is evident to the student who has tried to read dull writing in studying for an examination. How desperately he wanted to learn the subject, but how often his mind strayed away!

Perhaps writing interestingly is an art. But if it is, it is an art in which the report writer can gain some proficiency if he works at it. If he is to develop this proficiency, he needs to work watchfully to make his words build concrete pictures, and he needs to avoid the rubber-stamped jargon or technical talk so often used in business. He needs to cultivate a feeling for the rhythmic flow of words and sentences. He needs to remember that back of every fact and figure there is some form of life—people doing things, machines operating, a commodity being marketed. The secret to quality writing is to bring the real life to the surface by concrete diction and vigorous active-voice verbs insofar as it is possible. But at the same time the writer will work to achieve interest without using more words than are necessary.

Here a word of caution may be injected. Attempts to make writing style interesting can be overdone. Such is the case whenever the reader's attention is focused on how something is said rather than on what is said. To be effective, good style simply presents information in a clear, concise, and interesting manner. Possibly the purpose and definition of style can best be summarized by this objective of the report writer: Writing style is at its best when the readers are prompted to say, "Here are some interesting facts," rather than "Here is some beautiful writing." Specific suggestions for writing interestingly are presented in Chapter 10.

QUESTIONS

1. What is our sensory world? Discuss our limitations in perceiving it.
2. Describe the role of the filter of the mind in the communication process.
3. Describe the symbolizing stage. Explain how symbolizing abilities vary.
4. Discuss each of the basic truths one observes from a review of the communication process.
5. A wife spent hours describing to her husband a new house she had inspected. Later, when the two of them visited the house together, the husband remarked, "It's not bad, but it's not at all what I expected." Explain this situation from a communication point of view.
6. After reading a report written by one of his subordinates, an executive called in the subordinate to discuss some of the recommendations made. "Why do you suggest this procedure?" the executive asked at one point in the discussion. "I don't suggest that," the writer replied. "My words have been misinterpreted. I don't recommend that at all." The executive picked up a dictionary from his desk and handed it to the writer. "How can you say that? This dictionary proves that you did. Better look up your words." Discuss this situation.
7. Select five words that have several clearly different meanings. Illustrate five meanings of each word by constructing sentences that use them.

8. An angry executive had these words to say to one of his workers: "If I have told you once I've told you a hundred times not to do that. I've even put it in writing in a memorandum to you." "But boss," the worker replied, "I thought I was doing what you wanted." "The heck you did," replied the executive. Discuss.

9. When is adaptation needed in business writing? Discuss.

10. What advice concerning adaptation would you give to a writer of a report that will be read by people with a wide range of educational backgrounds?

11. Using the measure of readability given in the text, compute the readability for the first two paragraphs of this chapter. Show your computations.

12. Comment on the significance of the readability formulas.

13. Discuss the need for objectivity in report writing.

14. Summarize the arguments on the question of using personal or impersonal writing in reports. What should determine the writer's decision to use personal or impersonal writing?

15. What advice would you give a report writer on the matter of time viewpoint?

16. Using as a guide the diagram in the text, summarize the coherence plan of the report.

17. Discuss the relationship of report length to the need for introductory, concluding, and summarizing sections in the report.

18. Show your knowledge of transition by constructing three pairs of connecting sentences—one sentence in each pair ending a paragraph and one sentence beginning the following paragraph.

19. A report writer remarked that in business the reader wants the information; thus, there is no need to be concerned about holding his interest. Discuss.

CHAPTER 10

Writing to communicate: specific techniques

The ultimate goal of the report writer is to communicate the report message. Ideally, he should communicate this message as quickly, as easily, and as precisely as language will permit. As explained in Chapter 9, quick, easy, and precise communication is built on certain basic writing characteristics that the report writer should understand thoroughly. Specifically, he should understand that good report writing is adapted to the reader's level. He should know that good report writing is readable. And in this regard, he should know how to use the readability study conclusions that word difficulty and sentence length are major determinants of readability. He should know that writing should be interesting if it is to communicate—that to not make it interesting is to lull the reader and thereby defeat the communication effort.

Knowledge of all these characteristics, however, gives only a general appreciation of good report writing. The application of this general knowledge to the task of report writing requires specific knowledge of techniques. Some of the more useful techniques are presented in the following pages. They are grouped by the three basic units of writing—the word, the sentence, and the paragraph.

Before taking up these specific techniques, however, one qualifying point should be stressed. These techniques are not to be applied mechanically. Instead, they must be tempered with reason. Writing is not routine work to be done by the numbers, by rules, or by formulas. Rather it is to some extent an art. As in all forms of art, mastery of techniques is a prerequisite to good performance. In writing, perhaps more than in any other art, the techniques must be applied with good judgment.

WORD SELECTION

In general, the writer's task is to produce in his reader's mind the meanings formulated in the writer's mind. To do this, the writer uses written symbols of meaning (words). Thus, the writer's task is largely one of selecting words that exactly relate the intended meanings.

The very nature of words, however, makes this task difficult. A glance at the size of an unabridged dictionary dramatically explains this difficulty. In addition to the great volume of words in the language, the writer's difficulty is intensified by the complexity of word meaning. As pointed out in Chapter 9, words are at best inexact symbols of meanings. A single word may have a dozen dictionary definitions. In fact, it is said that the 500 most commonly used English words have a total of 14,000 dictionary definitions—an average of 28 meanings per word. No doubt, individual mental filters add to this number with countless shades of difference in meaning. Contributing further to this difficulty is the inexactness with which most people use words.

This complex nature of words makes the writer's task more difficult. Perhaps this difficulty is too much involved for even the best writers to overcome completely. But certainly any writer can improve his communication ability by understanding these limitations and by making deliberate effort to overcome them.

Selecting words the reader understands

A major requirement of writing that communicates is that the words used mean the same to both writer and reader. In many instances in business, this requirement means simplifying the writing. Certainly, simplification is justifiable in writing to intellectual inferiors. Even in writing to intellectual equals there may be some need for simplification.

This suggestion of simplifying writing, however, should in no way be interpreted as an unqualified endorsement of primer writing. In writing to technical or other learned people on subjects about which they are well informed, one should write in words they expect and understand. But even in such cases, some degree of simplification is the key to quick and correct communication. As noted in Chapter 9, the readability studies support the suggestion of simplified writing.

They show conclusively that writing communicates best when it is slightly below the comprehension level of the reader. Specifically, they show that simplification is achieved through a general preference for the familiar over the unfamiliar, for the short over the long, and for the nontechnical over the technical word. Although these distinctions between words overlap considerably, they are discussed separately for reasons of emphasis.

Use strong, vigorous words.   Like people, words have personality. Some words are strong and vigorous; some are dull and weak; and others fall in between these extremes. The skilled writer is constantly aware of these differences. He becomes a student of words, and he selects his words to produce just the right effect. He recognizes, for example, that "tycoon" is stronger than "eminently successful businessman," that "bear market" is stronger than "generally declining market," and that a "boom" is stronger than a "period of business prosperity." Usually, the skilled writer makes the strong words predominate.

Of all the forms of speech, the verb is the strongest, and it is closely followed by the noun. The verb is the action word, and action by its very nature commands interest. Nouns, of course, are the doers of action—the characters in the story, so to speak. As doers of action, they attract the reader's attention.

Contrary to what many novice writers think, adjectives and adverbs should be used sparingly. These words add length to the sentence, thereby distracting the reader's attention from the key nouns and verbs. As Voltaire phrased it, "The adjective is the enemy of the noun." In addition, adjectives and adverbs both involve subjective evaluations, and, as previously noted, the objective approach should be evident throughout the report.

Prefer the familiar to the unfamiliar word.   As a general rule, the familiar, everyday words are the best for the report writer to use. Of course, the definition of familiar words varies by persons. What is everyday usage to some people is likely to appear to be high-level talk to others. Thus, the suggestion to use familiar language is in a sense a specific suggestion to apply the principle of adapting the writing to the reader.

Unfortunately, many business writers do not use enough everyday language. Instead, they tend to change character when they begin to put their thoughts on paper. Rather than writing naturally, they become stiff and stilted in their expression. For example, instead of using an everyday word like "try," they use the more unfamiliar word like "endeavor." They do not "find out"; they "ascertain." They "terminate" rather than "end," and they "utilize" instead of "use."

Now there is really nothing wrong with the hard words—if they are used intelligently. They are intelligently used when they are clearly understood by the reader, when they are best in conveying the meaning intended, and when they are used with wise moderation. Perhaps the best suggestion in this regard is that the report writer use words he would use in face-to-face communication with the reader. Another good suggestion is that he use the simplest words that carry the thought without offending the reader's intelligence.

The communication advantages of familiar words over the formal complex ones is obvious from the following contrasting examples.

Formal and Complex	*Familiar Words*
The conclusions ascertained from a perusal of the pertinent data is that a lucrative market exists for the product.	The data studied show that the product is in good demand.
The antiquated mechanisms were utilized for the experimentation.	The old machines were used for the test.
Company operations for the preceding accounting period terminated with a substantial deficit.	The company lost much money last year.

Prefer the short to the long word.   Short words tend to communicate better than long words. Certainly there are exceptions. Some long words like *hypnotize, hippopotamus,* and *automobile* generally are well known; some short words like *verd, vie, id,* and *gybe* are understood only by a few. On the whole, however, word length and word difficulty clearly are correlated. Also, the heavier the proportion of long words to short words, the harder the writing is to understand. This is true even when the long words are understood by the reader. As the readability studies clearly show, a heavy proportion of long words tends to slow up the reading and makes understanding difficult. Thus, the wise report writer will use long words with caution. He will make certain that the long ones he uses are well known to his reader. And especially will he work to avoid using a heavy proportion of long words, even when these words are understood.

The following contrasting sentences clearly show the effect of long words on writing clarity. Most of the long words are likely to be understood by most educated readers, but the heavy proportion of long words makes heavy reading and slow communication. Without question, the simple versions communicate best.

Heavy or Long Words	Short and Simple Words
A decision was *predicated* on the *assumption* that an *abundance* of *monetary funds was forthcoming.*	The decision was *based* on the *belief* that there would *be more money.*
They *acceded* to *the proposition to terminate* business.	They *agreed* to *quit* business.
During the preceding year the company *operated at a financial deficit.*	*Last* year the company *lost money.*
Prior to accelerating productive operation the foreman inspected the machinery.	*Before speeding up production,* the foreman inspected the machinery.
Definitive action was *effected subsequent to* the reporting date.	*Final* action was *made after* the reporting date.

Use technical words with caution. Every field has its own jargon. To those in the field, much of the jargon is a part of the everyday working vocabulary. Certainly, it is logical to use this jargon in writing to members of the field. Even so, an overuse of specialized words can make reading hard for the technician. Frequently, technical jargon is made up of long and high-sounding words. When used heavily, such words tend to dull the writing and to make the message hard to understand. This difficulty seems to increase as the proportion of technical words increases. The following sentence written by a physician well illustrates this point.

It is a methodology error to attempt to interpret psychologically an organic symptom which is the end-result of an intermediary change of organic processes instead of trying to understand these vegetative nervous impulses in their relation to psychological factors which introduce a change of organic events resulting in an organic disturbance.

No doubt the length of this sentence contributed to its difficulty, but the heavy proportion of technical terms also makes understanding difficult. The conclusion that may be drawn here is obvious. The technical writer may use technical terms in writing to fellow technicians, but he should use them in moderation.

In writing to those outside of the field, the technical writer must write in layman language. A physician might well refer to a "cerebral vascular accident" in writing to a fellow physician, but he would do well to use "stroke" in writing to the layman. An accountant who writes to a nonaccountant may also need to avoid the jargon of his profession. Even though terms like "accounts receivable," "liabilities," and "surplus" are elementary to him, they may be meaningless to some people. So, in writing to such people he would be wise to use nontechnical descriptions, such as "how much is owed the company," "how much the company owes," and "how much was left over." Similar examples can be drawn from any specialized field.

Bring the writing to life with words

As noted in Chapter 9, writing must hold the undivided interest for the best possible communication result. Certainly, subject matter is a major determinant of the interest quality of writing. But even lively topics can be presented in writing so dull that even an interested reader cannot keep his mind on the subject.

To bring the writing to life and make it interesting is no simple undertaking. In fact, it involves techniques that practically defy description—techniques that even the most accomplished writers never completely master. In view of the difficulty of this undertaking, however, three simple but important suggestions for bringing writing to life can be given. In preliminary summary form, they are the preference of the concrete to the abstract, the use of action words, and the avoidance of camouflaged verbs.

Use the concrete word. Interesting report writing is marked by specific words—words that form sharp and clear meaning in the reader's brain. Such words are concrete. Concrete words are the opposite of abstract words, which are words of fuzzy and vague meanings. In general, concrete words stand for things the reader perceives—things he can see, feel, hear, taste, or smell. Concrete words hold interest, for they move directly into the reader's experience. Because concrete words are best for holding interest, report writers should prefer them to abstract words wherever possible.

To a large extent, concrete words are the short, familiar words previously discussed. In addition to being more meaningful to the reader, such words generally have more precise meaning than the other words. For example, this sentence is filled with long, unfamiliar words: "The magnitude of the increment of profits was the predominant motivating factor in the decision." Written in shorter and more familiar words, the idea becomes more concrete: "The size of the profit gained was the chief reason for the decision."

But concreteness involves more than simplicity, for many of the well-known words are abstract. Perhaps a clear distinction between concrete and abstract wording can be made by illustration. In the writeup of the results of an experiment, a chemist may refer to the bad smell of a certain mixture as a "nauseous odor." But these words do little to communicate a clear mental picture in the reader's mind, for "nauseous" is a word with many different meanings. Were the chemist to say that it smelled like "decaying fish" his words would be likely to communicate a clear meaning in the reader's mind. One of the best-known examples of concreteness is in the advertising claim that Ivory soap is "99.44 percent pure." Had the company used abstract words such as "Ivory is very pure," few would have been impressed. But they used specific words, and millions took notice. Similar differences in abstract and concrete expression are apparent in the following.

Abstract	*Concrete*
A sizable profit	A 22 percent profit
Good accuracy	Pinpoint accuracy
The leading student	Top student in a class of 90
The majority	53 percent
In the near future	By Thursday noon
A worksaving machine	Does the work of seven men
Easy to steer	Quick steering
Light in weight	Featherlight

Prefer active to passive verbs. Of all the parts of speech, the verbs are the strongest, and verbs are at their strongest when they are in the active voice. Thus, the best in vigorous, lively writing makes good use of active-voice verbs. Certainly, this statement does not mean that one should eliminate passive voice, for passive voice has a definite place in good report writing, especially when one wants to give emphasis to words other than the verb. But it does mean that the good report writer uses as much active voice as he logically can.

Active-voice verbs are those that show their subject doing the action. They contrast with the dull, passive forms that act on their subjects. The following contrasting sentences illustrate the distinction.

Active: The auditor inspected the books.
Passive: The books were inspected by the auditor.

The first example clearly is the stronger. In this sentence, the doer of the action acts, and the verb is short and clear. In the second example, the helping word "were" dulls the verb, and the doer of the action is relegated to a role in a prepositional phrase. The following sentences give additional proof of the superiority of active over passive voice.

Passive	*Active*
The new process is believed to be superior by the investigators.	Investigators believe that the new process is superior.
The policy was enforced by the committee.	The committee enforced the policy.
The office will be inspected by Mr. Hall.	Mr. Hall will inspect the office.
A gain of 30.1 percent was recorded for soft lines sales.	Soft lines sales gained 30.1 percent.
It is desired by this office that this problem be brought before the board.	This office desires that the secretary bring this problem before the board.
A complete reorganization of the administration was affected by the president.	The president completely reorganized the administration.

Avoid overuse of camouflaged verbs. Closely related to the problem of overusing abstract words and passive voice is the problem of camouflaged verbs. A verb is camouflaged when it appears in the sentence as an abstract noun rather than in verb form. For example, in the sentence "Elimination of the excess material was effected by the crew," the noun "elimination" is made out of the verb "eliminate." Although there is nothing wrong with nouns made from verbs, in this case the noun form carries the strongest action idea of the sentence. A more vigorous phrasing would use the pure verb form: "The crew eliminated the excess material." Likewise, it is stronger to "cancel" than to "effect a cancellation"; it is stronger to "consider" than to give "consideration to"; and it is stronger to "appraise" than to "make an appraisal." These sentences further illustrate the point.

Camouflaged Verbs	*Clear Verb Form*
Amortization of the account was effected by the staff.	The staff amortized the account.
Control of the water was not possible.	They could not control the water.
The new policy involved the standardization of the procedures.	The new policy involved standardizing the procedures.
Application of the mixture was accomplished.	They applied the mixture.

From these illustrations and those of the preceding discussion of passive voice, two helpful writing rules may be gleaned. The first is to make the subjects of most sentences either persons or things. For example, rather than to write "consideration was given to . . . ," one should write "we consider. . . ." The second rule is to write most sentences in normal (subject, verb, object) order and with the real doer of action as the subject. It is when other orders are attempted that involved, strained, passive structures are most likely to result.

Selecting words for precise communication

Obviously, clear writing requires some mastery of language— enough at least to enable the writer to precisely convey meaning. Unfortunately, too many writers take their knowledge of language for granted. They select words as a matter of mechanical routine. All too often, they use words without really thinking of the meanings communicated. Sometimes, they use words they really do not understand. Certainly, the resulting writing must be as fuzzy as their knowledge of language.

Thus, the good writer must become a student of words. He must learn the precise meanings of words. Especially must he learn the shades of differences in the meanings of similar words and the different meanings that various arrangements of words can bring about. For example, he must learn that "fewer" pertains to smaller numbers of units or individuals, and that "less" relates to value, degree, or quantity. He must know of the differences in connotation of similar words such as secondhand, used, and antique; slender, thin, and skinny; suggest, tell, and inform; tramp, hobo, and vagabond.

SENTENCE CONSTRUCTION

Arranging words into sentences that communicate clearly and easily is a goal of the report writer. The task is largely a mental one, for the sentence is the form man has devised to express his thought units. Since sentences are verbalized thought units, they reflect the thinking they express. Clear and orderly sentences are the product of clear and orderly thinking; vague and disorderly sentences represent vague and disorderly thinking.

The techniques of good thinking cannot be reduced to routine steps, procedures, formulas, or the like, for the process is too little understood. But the sentences that are the product of good thinking do have clearly discernible characteristics. These characteristics suggest the general guidelines for good sentence construction that appear in the following paragraphs.

Keep the sentences short

More than any other characteristic of a sentence, length is most clearly related to sentence difficulty. The longer a sentence is, the harder it is to understand. The explanation of this relationship is simple. The human mind is capable of holding at one time only a limited amount of subject matter. When an excess of information or excessive relationships are presented in a single package, the mind cannot grasp it all. At least, the mind cannot grasp it all on a single reading. Thus, like food, written material is best consumed in bite sizes.

Just what is bite size for the mind, however, depends on the mental capacity of the reader. Most current authorities agree that writing aimed at the middle level of adult American readers should have an average sentence length of about 16 to 18 words. For more advanced readers, the average can be higher. And it must be lower for those of lower reading abilities. Of course, these length figures do not mean that short sentences of six or so words are taboo, nor do they mean that one should avoid long sentences of 30 or more words. Occasionally, short sentences may be used to emphasize an important fact. And long sentences may be skillfully constructed to subordinate some less important information. It is the average that should be in keeping with the readability level of the reader.

Differences brought about by sentence length are emphatically illustrated by the following contrasting sentences. Notice how much better the shorter versions communicate.

Long and Hard to Understand	*Short and Clear*

This memorandum is being distributed with the first-semester class cards, which are to serve as a final check on the correctness of the registration of students and are to be used later as the midsemester grade cards, which are to be submitted prior to November 16.

Some authorities in personnel administration object to expanding normal salary ranges to include a *trainee* rate because they fear that probationers may be kept at the minimum rate longer than is warranted through oversight or prejudice and because they fear that it would encourage the spread from the minimum to maximum rate range.

Regardless of their seniority or union affiliation, all employees who hope to be promoted are expected to continue their education either by enrolling in the special courses to be offered by the company, which are scheduled to be given after working hours beginning next Wednesday, or by taking approved correspondence courses selected from a list, which may be seen in the training office.

This memorandum is being distributed with the first-semester class cards. These cards will serve now as a final check on student registration. Later they will be used for midsemester grades, which are due before November 16.

Some authorities in personnel administration object to expanding the normal salary range to include a trainee rate for two reasons. First, they fear that probationers may be kept at the minimum rate longer than is warranted through oversight or prejudice. Second, they fear that it would in effect increase the spread from the minimum to the maximum rate range.

Regardless of their seniority or union affiliation, all employees who hope to be promoted are expected to continue their education in either of two ways. (1) They may enroll in special courses to be given by the company. (2) They may take approved correspondence courses selected from the list, which may be seen in the training office.

Use words economically

Of the many ways in which every thought may be expressed, the shorter ways are usually the best. In general, the shorter wordings save the reader time, they are clearer, and they make more vigorous and interesting reading. Thus, the good report writer strives for economy in the use of words.

Learning to use words economically is a matter of continuing effort. The good writer is constantly aware of the need for word economy. He carefully explores and appraises the many ways of expressing each thought. And although he knows that the possibility of word economy depends on the subject matter in each case, he knows that certain ways of expression simply are not economical. These he avoids. The more common of these ways of expression are discussed in the following paragraphs.

Cluttering phrases.   Our language is cluttered with numerous phrases that are best replaced by shorter expressions. Although the shorter forms may save only a word or two here and there, the little savings over a long piece of writing can be significant. As the following sentences illustrate, the shorter substitutes are better.

The Long Way	*Short and Improved*
In the event that payment is not made by January, operations will cease.	*If* payment is not made by January, operations will cease.
In spite of the fact that they received help, they failed to exceed the quota.	*Even though* they received help, they failed to exceed the quota.
The invoice was *in the amount of* $50,000.	The invoice was *for* $50,000.

Here are other contrasting pairs of expressions:

Long	*Short*
Along the lines of	Like
For the purpose of	For
For the reason that	Because, since
In the near future	Soon
In accordance with	By
In very few cases	Seldom
In view of the fact that	Since, because
On the occasion of	On
With regard to, with reference to	About

Surplus words.   Words that add nothing to the sentence meaning should be eliminated. In some instances, however, eliminating the words requires recasting the sentence, as some of the following examples illustrate.

Contains Surplus Words	Surplus Words Eliminated
He ordered desks *which are of the* executive type.	He ordered executive type desks.
It will be noted that the records for the past years show a steady increase in special appropriations.	The records for past years show a steady increase in special appropriations.
There are four rules *which* should be observed.	Four rules should be observed.
In addition to these defects, numerous other defects mar the operating procedure.	Numerous other defects mar the operating procedure.
His performance was good enough *to enable him* to qualify for the promotion.	His performance was good enough to qualify him for promotion.
The machines *which were* damaged by the fire were repaired.	The machines damaged by the fires were repaired.
By *the* keeping *of* production records, they found the error.	By keeping production records, they found the error.

Roundabout construction.   Of the many ways of saying anything, some are direct and to the point; others cover the same ground in a roundabout way. Without question, the direct ways are usually better and should be used. Although there are many ways of making roundabout expressions (some overlap the preceding causes of excess wording), the following illustrations clearly show the general nature of this violation.

Roundabout	Direct and to the Point
The departmental budget *can be observed to be decreasing* each new year.	The departmental budget *decreases* each year.
The union is *involved in the task of reviewing* the seniority provision of the contract.	The union is *reviewing* the seniority provision of the contract.
The president is *of the opinion that* the tax was paid.	The president *believes* that the tax was paid.
It is essential that the income be used to retire the debt.	The income *must* be used to retire the debt.
It is the committee's assumption that the evidence has been gathered.	The committee *assumes* that the evidence has been gathered.

Roundabout	*Direct and to the Point*
The supervisors should *take appropriate action to determine* whether the time cards are being inspected.	The supervisor *should determine* whether the time cards are being inspected.
The price increase will *afford the* company *an opportunity* to retire the debt.	A price increase will *enable* the company to retire the debt.
During the time she was employed by this company, Miss Carr was absent once.	*While* employed by this company, Miss Carr was absent once.
He criticized everyone he *came in contact with.*	He criticized everyone he met.

Unnecessary repetition. Repetition of words or thoughts is best avoided. Exceptions to this rule, however, are justified when the writer repeats for special effect or for emphasis.

Needless Repetition	*Repetition Eliminated*
The provision of section five provides for a Union shop.	Section five provides for a Union shop.
The assignment of training the ineffective worker is *an assignment* he must carry out.	Training the ineffective worker is an assignment he must carry out.
Modern up-to-date equipment will be used.	Modern equipment will be used.
In the office they found supplies *there* which had never been issued.	In the office they found supplies which had never been issued.
He reported for work Friday *morning* at 8 A.M.	He reported for work Friday at 8 A.M.
In my opinion I think the plan is sound.	I think the plan is sound.
The *important essentials* must not be neglected.	The essentials must not be neglected.

Give the facts proper emphasis

The numerous facts, assumptions, analyses, conclusions, and such that go into a report vary in their importance to the report's objective. Some, such as conclusions, play major roles. Other areas supply supporting details. Still others are only incidental. The writer's task is to determine the importance of each bit of information in the report and then to communicate this emphasis in the writing. Giving the facts proper emphasis is largely a matter of sentence design.

The short, simple sentences carry more emphasis than longer, more involved sentences. Shorter sentences stand out and call attention to their contents. They are especially strong when placed in positions of emphasis—that is, at beginnings or ends of paragraphs.

Sentences that cover two or more items give less emphasis to the contents. Within these sentences, varying emphasis may be given each item. Those items placed in independent clauses get major emphasis. Those placed in subordinate structures (dependent clauses, parenthetic structures, modifiers, and the like) are relegated to less important roles. Thus, by skillful design, or by a lack of it, the same facts may be presented in distinctly different ways, as shown by the following illustrations.

In the first illustration, separate sentences are used to present each item of information. Each item gets special emphasis by this treatment, but because all are treated the same, none stands out. Also, the items obviously are not equally important and should not be given equal emphasis. In addition, the writing is elementary to the point of being ridiculous.

The Mann building was inspected on October 1. Mr. George Wills inspected the building. Mr. Wills is a vice-president of the company. He found that the building has 6,500 square feet of floor space. He also found that it has 2,400 square feet of storage space. The new store must have a minimum of 6,000 square feet of floor space. It must have 2,000 square feet of storage space. Thus, the Mann building exceeds the space requirement for the new store. Therefore, Mr. Wills concluded that the Mann building is adequate for the company's need.

In the next illustration, some of the information is subordinated, but not logically. The facts of real importance do not receive the emphasis they deserve. Logically, the points that should be emphasized are (1) the conclusion that the building is large enough and (2) the supporting evidence, showing that floor and storage space exceed minimum requirements.

Mr. George Wills, who inspected the Mann building on October 1, is a vice-president of the company. His inspection, which supports the conclusion that the building is large enough for the proposed store, uncovered these facts. The store has 6,500 square feet of floor space and 2,400 square feet of storage space, which is more than the minimum requirements of 6,000 and 2,000, respectively, for floor and storage space.

The next illustration gives good emphasis to the pertinent points. The short, simple sentences placed for emphasis at the beginning present the conclusion. The supporting facts that the new building exceeds the minimum floor and storage space requirements receive main-clause emphasis. Incidentals such as the identifying remarks about Mr. Wills are relegated to subordinate roles.

The Mann building is large enough for the new store. This conclusion, made by Vice-President George Wills, following his October 1st inspection of the building, is based on these facts. The building's 6,500 square feet of floor space is 500 more than the 6,000 set as a minimum. The 2,400 square feet of storage space is 400 more than the 2,000 minimum requirement.

More specific violations of logical emphasis are illustrated in the following sentences. The first shows how placing an important idea in an appositional construction weakens the idea. Notice the increased emphasis given the idea (by position and by construction) in the second sentence.

Weak Emphasis: Hamilton's typewriter, a machine which has been used daily for over 40 years, is in good condition.

Strong Emphasis: Although Hamilton's typewriter has been used daily for 40 years, it is in good condition.

The next sentence shows how an idea may be subordinated through placement in a participial construction. The idea receives more emphasis as a dependent clause in the second sentence.

Weak Emphasis: Having paid the highest dividends in its history, the company anticipates a rise in the value of its stock.

Stronger Emphasis: Because it paid the highest dividends in its history, the company anticipates a rise in the value of its stock.

Arrange the words correctly for clarity

Short and clear sentences generally conform to the conventional rules of the grammar of a language. Contrary to what many novice writers think, the rules of grammar are not merely arbitrary requirements set by detail-minded scholars. Rather, the rules are statements of logical relationships between words. Dangling participles, for example, confuse meaning by modifying the wrong word. Unparallel constructions leave erroneous impressions of the relationships of the parts. Pronouns without clear antecedents have no definite meaning. The evidence is quite clear: the business writer must know and follow the conventional standards of his language.

Unfortunately, too many business writers know very little about the conventional rules of English grammar. Why so many have avoided this subject through years of drill at all levels of education is a mystery to educators. Obviously, the area is too broad for complete coverage in this book. Some of the points with which most writers have trouble, however, are presented for quick review in Chapter 14. Their importance should not be ignored.

Place related words close together

One requisite for unmistakable clarity in writing is to keep related words as close together as practical. Of course, all related words cannot be placed exactly together, for frequently two or more words or groups of words are related to the same words. In deciding what to do in such cases, the writer must follow his good logic. He must appraise the possible meanings conveyed by the arrangement possibilities, and he must select the one arrangement that carries the one meaning intended. That placement of words makes a real difference in meaning is illustrated by the following series of sentences. In this series, the words are the same but the orders change. The order changes thoroughly alter the sentence meanings.

If at the end of this quarter the workers vote to strike, the plant will close.

As the sentence stands, the phrase "at the end of this quarter" logically relates to the verb "vote." In the following sentence, the shift of the phrase to a position between "workers" and "vote" produces confusion. Here, the phrase could modify either word.

If the workers at the end of this quarter vote to strike, the plant will close.

Similar confusion is evident when the phrase is placed between "vote" and "to strike." It could be construed to modify either the preceding or the following word.

If the workers vote at the end of this quarter to strike, the plant will close.

By moving the phrase further down the sentence, yet another form of confusion is made. Here, the phrase could modify "strike" alone or it could modify the whole group "vote to strike."

If the workers vote to strike at the end of this quarter, the plant will close.

Still another meaning is formed by moving the phrase to the end of the sentence. Here it modifies "close."

If the workers vote to strike, the plant will close at the end of this quarter.

It is quite clear, then, that the positions of words in the sentence can make a significant difference in the thoughts communicated. The good writer carefully keeps related words close together so there is no possible confusion of meaning.

CARE IN PARAGRAPH DESIGN

Clear sentences alone do not assure clear writing, for the sentences must be built logically into clear paragraphs. The techniques of building paragraphs are not easily put into words. Whether many of these techniques can be reduced to meaningful rules and instructions is questionable, for much of paragraph writing depends on the writer's mental ability to logically organize and relate facts. Nevertheless, the following concrete suggestions can be given.

Give the paragraph unity

Unity is the primary requirement of the paragraph. Unity, of course, means oneness. When applied to paragraph construction, it means that the paragraph should be built around a single topic or idea. Thus, a paragraph should include only this major topic or idea plus the supporting details that help to develop it. Exceptions to the rule of unity are the transitional paragraphs whose objectives are to relate foregoing and succeeding topics.

Just what constitutes unity is not always easy to determine. All of a report, for example, may deal with a single topic and therefore have unity. The same could be said for each major division of the report as well as for the lesser subdivisions. Paragraph unity, however, concerns smaller units than these—usually the lowest level of a detailed outline. That is, in reports written with detailed outlines, each paragraph may well cover one of the lowest outline captions.

In any event, one good test of a paragraph is to reduce its content to a single topic statement. If this statement does not cover the paragraph content, unity is not likely to be there.

Keep the paragraphs short

Short paragraphs are best for most business writing. They help the reader to follow the organizational plan of the paper. Specifically, they help him to see the beginnings and ends of the items

Figure 9.   Contrasting pages, showing psychological effects of long and short paragraphs

HEAVY PARAGRAPHS MAKE THE
WRITING APPEAR TO BE DULL
AND DIFFICULT.

SHORT PARAGRAPHS GIVE WELL
ORGANIZED EFFECT—INVITE THE
READER TO READ.

covered, and they give added emphasis to the facts covered. In addition, short paragraphs are more inviting to the eye. People simply prefer to read material that gives them frequent breaks. This is true so long as the breaks are not too frequent. A series of very short paragraphs would leave an equally offensive choppy effect.

A glance at Figure 9 quickly shows the psychological effect of paragraph length. The full page of solid type appears to be more difficult and generally less inviting than the one marked by short paragraphs. Even if both contained exactly the same words, the difference would be present. Perhaps this difference is largely psychological. Psychological or not, the difference is real.

Just how long a paragraph should be is, of course, dependent on the topic. Some topics are short; others are long. Even so, the general rule can be given on paragraph length. Most well-organized and well-paragraphed reports have paragraphs that average about 8 or 10 lines. Some good paragraphs may be quite short—even a single line. And some may be well above the 8-to-10 average.

One good rule of thumb is to question the unity of all long paragraphs—say, those exceeding 12 lines. If inspection shows that only one topic is present, no change should be made. But if inspection shows that the paragraph covers more than one topic, additional paragraphing is in order.

Put topic sentences to good use

One prominent sentence, the topic sentence, expresses the main idea of the well-written paragraph. Around this topic sentence, the details that support or elaborate the main idea build in some logical way. Exactly how a given paragraph should build from the topic sentence largely depends on the information to be covered and on the writer's plan in covering it. Obviously, much of paragraph design must come from the mental effort of the writer. He would profit, however, by being generally acquainted with the paragraph plans most commonly used.

Topic sentence first. The most widely used paragraph plan begins with the topic sentence. The supporting material then follows in some logical order. As this arrangement gives good emphasis to the major point, it is the most useful to the report writer. In fact, some company manuals suggest that this arrangement be used almost altogether. As the following paragraph illustrates, this arrangement has merit.

A majority of the economists consulted think business activity will drop during the first quarter of next year. Of the 185 economists interviewed, 13 percent look for continued increases in business activities; and 28 percent anticipate little or no change from present high level. The remaining 59 percent look for a recession. Of this group, nearly all (87 percent) believe the downcurve will occur during the first quarter of the year.

Topic sentence at end. Another logical paragraph arrangement places the topic sentence at the end, usually as a conclusion. The supporting details come first and in logical order build toward the topic sentence. Frequently, such paragraphs use a beginning sentence to set up or introduce the subject, as in the following illustration. Such a sentence serves as a form of topic sentence, but the real meat of the paragraph is covered in the final sentence.

The significant role of inventories in the economic picture should not be overlooked. At present, inventories represent 3.8 months' supply. Their dollar value is the highest in history. If considered in relation to increased sales, however, they are not excessive. In fact, they are well within the range generally believed to be safe. *Thus, inventories are not likely to have a downward drag on the economy.*

Topic sentences within the paragraph. Some paragraphs are logically arranged with the topic sentence somewhere within. These paragraphs are not often used, and usually for good reason. In general, they fail to give proper emphasis to the key point in the paragraph. Even so, they may sometimes be used with good effect, as in this example.

Numerous materials have been used in manufacturing this part. And many have shown quite satisfactory results. *Material 329, however, is superior to them all.* Built with material 329, the part is almost twice as strong as when built with the next best material. Too, it is 3 ounces lighter. And most important, it is cheaper than any of the other products.

Make the paragraph move forward

Forward movement is an essential quality of good report writing. Good report writing makes the reader feel that he is moving systematically through the subject matter—that each new idea or fact moves him progressively toward the objective. Thus, the good report writer knows how to put good movement into his writing.

Good movement is the quality of good paragraph design. Individual sentences have little movement, for they cover only single thoughts. An orderly succession of single thoughts, however, does produce movement. In addition, good movement is helped by skillful use of transition, by smoothness in writing style, and by a general proficiency in word choice and sentence design.

Perhaps the quality of movement is easier to see than to describe. In general, it is present when the reader is made to feel at the paragraph end that he has made one sure step toward the objective. Although many arrangements can illustrate good paragraph movement, the following illustration does the job quite well.

Three major factors form the basis for the decision to relocate. First, the supply of building rock in the Crowton area is questionable. The failure of recent geological explorations in the area appears to confirm suspicions that the Crowton deposits are nearly exhausted. Second, distances from Crowton to major consumption areas make transportation costs unusually high. Obviously, any savings in transportation cost will add to company profits. Third, obsolescence of much of the equipment at the Crowton plant makes this an ideal time for relocation. New equipment could be moved directly to the new site, and obsolete equipment could be scrapped in the Crowton area.

QUESTIONS

Instructions for questions 1 through 45: Revise the following sentences to make them conform with the principles discussed in the text. They are grouped by the principles they illustrate.

Using understandable words

(Assume that these sentences are written for high school level readers.)

1. Recent stock acquisitions have accentuated the company's current financial crisis.
2. Mr. Coward will serve as intermediary in the pending labor–management parley.
3. Miss Smith's idiosyncracies supply adequate justification for terminating her employment.
4. Requisites for employement by this company have been enhanced.
5. The unanimity of current forecasts is not incontrovertible evidence of an impending business acceleration.
6. Man's propensity to consume is insatiable.
7. The company must desist its deficit financing immediately.
8. This antiquated merchandising strategy is ineffectual in contemporary business operations.
9. Percent return on common stockholders equity averaged 23.1 for the year.
10. The company's retained earnings last year exceeded $2,500,000.

Selecting concrete words

11. Some years ago he made good money.
12. His grade on the aptitude test was not high.
13. Here is a product with very little markup.

14. Damage from the fire was significant.
15. We will need the new equipment soon.

Limiting use of passive voice

16. It is believed by the writer that this company policy is wrong.
17. The union was represented by Cecil Chambers.
18. These reports are prepared by the salesmen every Friday.
19. Success of this project is the responsibility of the research department.
20. Our decision is based on the belief that the national economy will be improved.

Avoiding camouflaged verbs

21. Implementation of the plan was effected by crew.
22. Acceptance of all orders must be made by the chief.
23. A committee performs the function of determining the award.
24. Adaptation to the new conditions was performed easily by all new personnel.
25. Verification of the amount is made daily by the auditor.
26. The president tried to effect a reconciliation of the two groups.

Keeping sentences short

27. The upswing in business activity that began in 1968 is expected to continue, and possibly accelerate in 1969, and gross national products should rise by $65 billion, representing an 8 percent increase over 1968, which is significantly higher than the modest 5½ percent increase of 1967.
28. As you will not get this part of medicare automatically, even if you are covered by social security, you must sign up for it and pay $3 per month, which the government will match, if you want your physician's bills to be covered.
29. Students with approved excused absences from any of the hour examinations have the option of taking a special makeup examination to be given during dead week or of using their average grade on their examinations in the course as their grade for the work missed.
30. Although we have not definitely determined the causes for the decline in sales volume for the month, we know that during this period construction on the street adjacent to the store severely lim-

ited traffic flow and that because of resignations in the advertising department promotion efforts dropped well below normal.

Using words economically

31. In spite of the fact that the bill remains unpaid, he placed another order.
32. We expect to deliver the goods in the event that we receive the money.
33. In accordance with their plans, company officials sold the machinery.
34. This policy exists for the purpose of preventing dishonesty.
35. The salesmen which were most successful received the best rewards.
36. The reader will note that this area ranks in the top 5 percent in per capita income.
37. Our new coats are made of a fabric which is of the water repellant variety.
38. Our office is charged with the task of counting supplies not used in production.
39. His salesmen are of the conviction that service is obsolete.
40. Losses caused by the strike exceeded the amount of $14,000.
41. This condition can be assumed to be critical.
42. Our goal is to effect a change concerning the overtime pay rate.
43. Mr. Wilson replaced the old, antiquated machinery with new machinery.
44. We must keep this information from transpiring to others.
45. The consensus of opinion of this group is that Wellington was wrong.
    Questions 46 through 50 are discussion and performance types.
46. Select a paragraph of at least three sentences. Alter its sentence structures in two ways to show varying emphasis in its content.
47. Write a sentence that will change in meaning when the order of its words is altered.
48. What is meant by paragraph unity?
49. Summarize the case for the short paragraph.
50. Select a paper you have written of at least eight paragraphs. Underscore the topic sentences. Criticize your paragraph designs.

CHAPTER 11

Physical presentation of a report

As far as physical appearance is concerned, the report is very much like a public speaker. When a speaker appears before a group, even before he utters a word his audience forms an initial impression of him. Such an impression is the result of what the audience sees— things such as dress, bearing, and facial characteristics. These impressions may be favorable if what is seen is pleasing, or they may be unfavorable if what is seen is not pleasing. The impressions created here set the stage for the success of the speech that follows.

Once the words begin to flow, there is, of course, the chance that the initial impressions may be altered. But even so, the chances of change coming about are related to the strength of the initial impressions. And to make it even harder for change to occur, the eyes of the listeners remain fixed on the source of the first impressions throughout the presentation.

The same story may be told of a report. A report, too, first impresses its readers with its appearance. Likewise, these first impressions are lasting ones. They, too, are made more difficult to overcome because the readers are constantly looking at what formed the first impression.

Undeniably true as this observation is, the value of an attractive report is not universally accepted by those who engage in report writing. There are writers of reports who believe the message is all that counts and that "trivial" things such as form, neatness, and general attractiveness are immaterial. But possibly because this attitude is typical of their overall thinking and ability, these people are usually found well down the organization ladder. On the other hand, the top executive who does not appreciate the importance of good physical appearance is likely to be a misfit in his position. Since it is the top executives who must be satisfied in most instances, the report writer should be thoroughly acquainted with all those mechanical considerations that go into a report's physical appearance. A general review of these considerations is presented in the following pages.

GENERAL INFORMATION ON PHYSICAL PRESENTATION

Because most business reports are typed, a general knowledge of the mechanics involved in typing manuscripts is essential to the report writer. Even if he doesn't have to type his own report, the writer should know enough about report makeup to be certain that justice is done to his work. Certainly, he cannot be assured that his report is presented in high standards unless he is familiar with such standards.

Choice of cover

The first part of any report seen by the reader is the cover. Thus, if the first impression made by the report is to be favorable, care in the selection of a cover must be exercised. Numerous types of covers are available commercially, and most of these are adequate.

In selecting a cover for use, one should consider three basic qualities: the type of fastening used, the protection offered, and the physical appearance. The fastening device used must be of the type that will hold the report pages firmly in place. As a rule, fasteners that hold through perforations in the pages do this job better than clamp-type devices. Most types of covers available furnish adequate protection for most reports, but occasionally a report may need an especially tough cover to protect it from unusual handling. For these, extra durable covers made of plastic or cloth may be used. Selection of the right cover from the standpoint of physical appearance is an easy task, for nearly all the covers available are adequate for most occasions. But there may be times when a special color or type may be best suited for a particular project.

Care in paper selection

Paper is not just paper, as many people are likely to believe. Differences in grades, sizes, weights, and such are so numerous that they defy adequate coverage here. But a few general hints should suffice to guide the report writer in his selection of paper for his own use.

Typing paper comes in two conventional sizes—8½ by 11 inches and 8½ by 13 inches. The first size is by far the more popular of the two and is used in most typed reports. The long (8½ by 13 inches) size is used principally for reports that require long tabular displays or illustrations.

There are many good grades and varieties of paper, so the writer is best guided by his own inspection. Almost any good quality typing paper is acceptable. A good quality watermarked, rag content bond is preferable to coated varieties. As a rule, a 20- or 16-pound weight is best, although quality paper of a lighter weight may be acceptable in certain circumstances. The added expense of good paper is easily justified by the appearance advantage it gives the finished work. Good paper makes typing stand out sharply, and it makes erasures easy and unnoticeable.

With little exception, white paper is used in business communications. In some companies, however, colored paper is used to identify work from certain departments or for special types of reports.

Unlike printing, typed manuscript is usually on one side of the page. Only if the heaviest type of paper is used could typing on both sides be justified, for only then would the type impressions be not likely to be seen through the sheet.

Conventional page layout

For the typical text page in the report, a conventional layout is one that appears to fit the page as a picture in a frame (see Figure 10). This eye-pleasing layout, however, is arranged to fit the page space not covered by the binding of the report. Thus, the typist must allow an extra ⅜ inch or so on the left margins of the pages of a left-bound report and at the top of the pages of a top-bound report.

As a general rule, top, left, and right margins should be equal and uniform. For double-spaced manuscripts, about an inch is recommended. From 1¼ to 1½ inches is considered ideal for single-spaced work (see Figure 11). Bottom margins are customarily made slightly larger than those at the top—about a half again as much. The left margin, of course, is easily marked by the characters that begin the line. The right margin is formed by the average lengths of the full lines. As near as is possible, this right margin should be kept straight—that is, without dips or bulges.

The typist may find it advisable to mark off in black ink a rectangle of the size of the layout he is using. Then he may place the rectangle beneath each page as it is typed so that he can see the dimensions he is using and can end his typed lines appropriately.

Special page layouts

Certain pages in the text may have individual layouts. Pages that display major titles (first pages of chapters, tables of contents, synopses, and such) conventionally have an extra half inch or so of space at the top (see Figure 12). This technique has long been followed by publishers and is illustrated in almost all published books.

Letters of transmittal and authorization also may have individual layouts. They are types in any conventional letter form. In more formal reports they may be carefully arranged to have the same general outline or shape as the space on which they appear (see Figure 16, page 275).

Choice of typing form

It is conventional to double space the typed report. This procedure stems from the old practice of double spacing to make typed manuscripts more easily read by the proofreader and printer. The practice has been carried over into typed work that is not to be further reproduced. Advocates of double spacing claim that it is easy to read because the reader is not likely to lose his line place.

In recent years, the use of single spacing has gained in popularity. The general practice is to single space the paragraphs, double space between paragraphs, and triple space above all centered heads. Supporters of this form of presentation contend that it saves space and facilitates fast reading, since it approximates the printing most people are accustomed to reading.

Patterns of indentation

Double-spaced typing should be indented to show the paragraph beginnings. On the other hand, because its paragraphs are clearly marked by extra line spacing, single-spaced typing is usually blocked.

There is no generally accepted pattern of indentation. Some

Figure 10.   Recommended layout for a double-spaced normal page

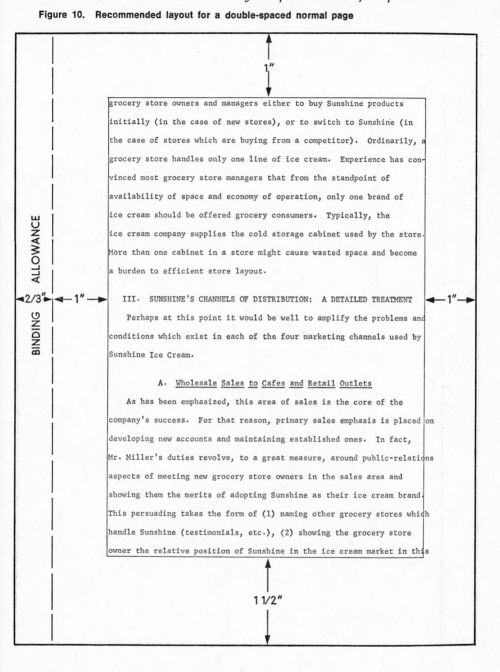

1"

ALLOWANCE

BINDING

2/3"   1"   1"

grocery store owners and managers either to buy Sunshine products
initially (in the case of new stores), or to switch to Sunshine (in
the case of stores which are buying from a competitor). Ordinarily, a
grocery store handles only one line of ice cream. Experience has convinced most grocery store managers that from the standpoint of
availability of space and economy of operation, only one brand of
ice cream should be offered grocery consumers. Typically, the
ice cream company supplies the cold storage cabinet used by the store.
More than one cabinet in a store might cause wasted space and become
a burden to efficient store layout.

III. SUNSHINE'S CHANNELS OF DISTRIBUTION: A DETAILED TREATMENT

    Perhaps at this point it would be well to amplify the problems and
conditions which exist in each of the four marketing channels used by
Sunshine Ice Cream.

            A. <u>Wholesale</u> <u>Sales</u> <u>to</u> <u>Cafes</u> <u>and</u> <u>Retail</u> <u>Outlets</u>

    As has been emphasized, this area of sales is the core of the
company's success. For that reason, primary sales emphasis is placed on
developing new accounts and maintaining established ones. In fact,
Mr. Miller's duties revolve, to a great measure, around public-relations
aspects of meeting new grocery store owners in the sales area and
showing them the merits of adopting Sunshine as their ice cream brand.
This persuading takes the form of (1) naming other grocery stores which
handle Sunshine (testimonials, etc.), (2) showing the grocery store
owner the relative position of Sunshine in the ice cream market in this

1 1/2"

Figure 11.   Recommended layout for a normal single-spaced page

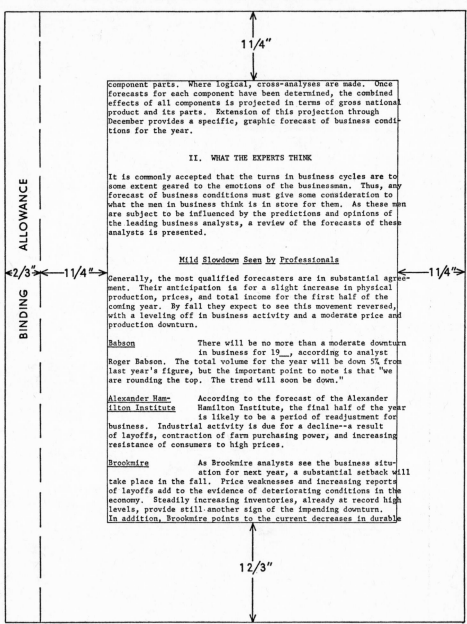

component parts. Where logical, cross-analyses are made. Once forecasts for each component have been determined, the combined effects of all components is projected in terms of gross national product and its parts. Extension of this projection through December provides a specific, graphic forecast of business conditions for the year.

II. WHAT THE EXPERTS THINK

It is commonly accepted that the turns in business cycles are to some extent geared to the emotions of the businessman. Thus, any forecast of business conditions must give some consideration to what the men in business think is in store for them. As these men are subject to be influenced by the predictions and opinions of the leading business analysts, a review of the forecasts of these analysts is presented.

Mild Slowdown Seen by Professionals

Generally, the most qualified forecasters are in substantial agreement. Their anticipation is for a slight increase in physical production, prices, and total income for the first half of the coming year. By fall they expect to see this movement reversed, with a leveling off in business activity and a moderate price and production downturn.

Babson   There will be no more than a moderate downturn
                        in business for 19__, according to analyst
Roger Babson. The total volume for the year will be down 5% from last year's figure, but the important point to note is that "we are rounding the top. The trend will soon be down."

Alexander Ham-   According to the forecast of the Alexander
ilton Institute   Hamilton Institute, the final half of the year
                        is likely to be a period of readjustment for
business. Industrial activity is due for a decline--a result of layoffs, contraction of farm purchasing power, and increasing resistance of consumers to high prices.

Brookmire   As Brookmire analysts see the business situ-
                        ation for next year, a substantial setback will
take place in the fall. Price weaknesses and increasing reports of layoffs add to the evidence of deteriorating conditions in the economy. Steadily increasing inventories, already at record high levels, provide still another sign of the impending downturn. In addition, Brookmire points to the current decreases in durable

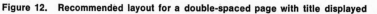

Figure 12.   **Recommended layout for a double-spaced page with title displayed**

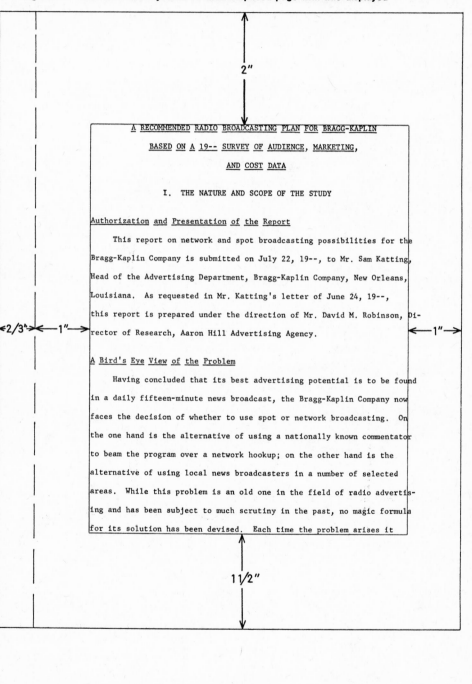

sources advocate a distance of 4 spaces; some prefer 5; some like 8; others like 10 and more. Any decision on the best distance is purely arbitrary and left up to the writer, although he would do well to follow the practice established in the office, group, or school for which he writes the report. Whatever the selection, the important rule to follow is that of consistency.

Possibilities in type selection

Should the writer have a choice of typewriters, he may profit from knowing some general information about type and typewriting. Not all typewriters present the same form of finished copy, for type forms and sizes differ. The two most widely used types are pica, which has 10 characters to the inch, and elite, which has 12 characters to the inch. Both types take up six lines to the inch; thus, the difference between the two is wholly in the width of the characters.

In addition to these two major types, numerous special sizes and styles of type may be found. There are some very small types, such as Micro Elite, Miniature Gothic, and Bank type. These types are especially useful in typing tables, forms, and such, which would crowd a full page of larger sized type. Then there are some very dark types (Boldface or Book) and some very large types (Magnatype, Bulletin, Amplitype, and Great Primer). Typewriters may even be equipped with Old English or other unusual and distinctive types. Although most of these type sizes and styles are not used for typing the text of the business report, they may serve some special need in unusual instances.

Neatness in typed work

Even with the best typewriter available, the finished work is no better than the efforts of the typist. But this statement does not imply that only the most skilled typist can turn out good work. Even the inexperienced typist can produce acceptable manuscripts simply by exercising care.

He should take care in correcting his typing mistakes, for obvious corrections (strikeovers, erasure holes in the page, and such) stand out in the manuscript like a sore thumb. With a bit of care, this operation can be done so well that the casual reader does not detect the error.

Possibly nothing detracts more from a report than type that the eye must strain to read. So the report writer should take care to see that his typewriter is equipped with a good, black ribbon—one that will make legible letters. A medium-inked ribbon is recommended for most typing work. Because the ink is likely to smear a bit on the first few pages typed with a new ribbon, it may be wise to type really important work only after a ribbon has had the excess ink worn off. Because of the sharp contrast in type it would cause, changing ribbons in the midst of a manuscript should be avoided.

For neat and clearly legible typing, the type faces must be regularly cleaned. Ink from the ribbon tends to collect and dry in the type faces. If allowed to remain, it will fill the enclosed portions of the type characters. Smudged or fuzzy typing is the result. Any small brush may be used for this purpose.

Numbering of pages

Two systems of numbers are used in numbering the pages of the written report. Arabic numerals are conventional for the text portion, normally beginning with the first page of the introduction and continuing through the appendix. Small Roman numerals are used for the pages that precede the text. Although all these prefatory pages are counted in the numbering sequence, the numbers generally are not placed on the pages preceding the table of contents. It is optional to place them on the table of contents pages.

Placement of numbers on the page varies with the binding used for the report. In reports bound at the top of the page, all page numbers are usually centered at the bottom of the page, a double or triple space below the text layout.

For the more widely used left-side binding, page numbers are placed in the upper right corner of the page, a double space above the top line of the layout and in line with the right margin. Exception to this placement is customarily made for special layout pages that have major titles and an additional amount of space displayed at the top. Included in this group may be the first page of the report text; the synopsis; the table of contents; and in very long and formal works, the first page of each major division or chapter. Numbers for such pages as these are centered a double or triple space below the imaginary line marking the bottom of the layout.

Display of captions

Captions, or headings as they are sometimes called, are titles to the various divisions of the report. They represent the organization steps worked out previously and are designed to help the reader find his way through this organization plan. Thus, it is important that the captions show the reader at a glance the importance of their part in the report.

This importance of captions may be emphasized in two ways—by type and position. Any logical combination of type and position may be used to show differences in the importance of captions. In

Figure 13.   Caption positions in order of importance

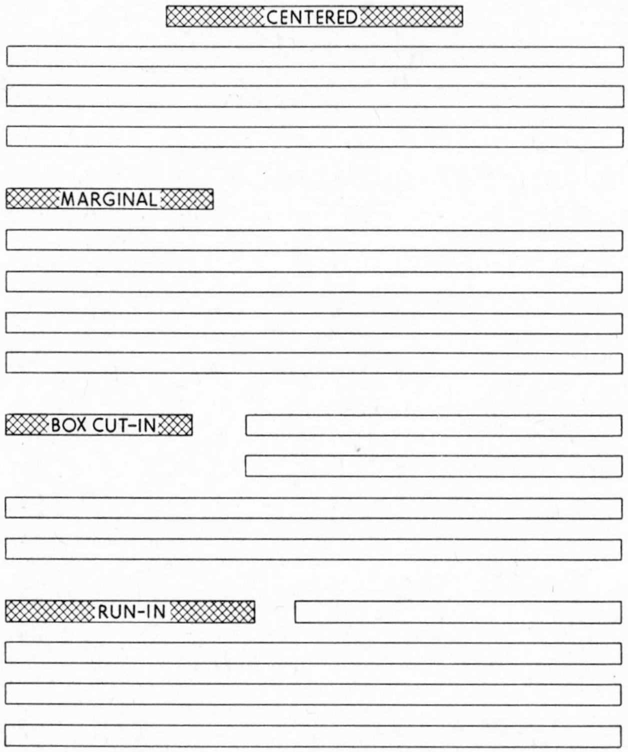

actual practice, however, a few standard orders of captions have become widely used.

There are four major positions of captions, as shown in Figure 13. Highest of these four in order of rank is the centered caption. This caption is on a line by itself and is centered between left and right margins. Next in order is the marginal caption. Beginning on the left margin, this caption is also on a line by itself. The box caption is third in this ranking, but it normally is used only in single-spaced copy. It begins on the left margin and is surrounded by a box of space formed by indenting the first few lines of the text. The box indentations are kept of equal width throughout the report, although the heights of the boxes will vary with the number of words in the captions enclosed. Fourth in importance is the run-in caption. This caption simply runs into the first line of the text it covers and is distinguished from the text only by underscoring.

Were the report to be printed, there would be a wide variety of type faces and sizes that could be used to show different degrees of importance in the captions. But most reports are typed and thereby limited by what type variations can be made with an ordinary typewriter. Except when unusual type faces are available, the report writer can show type distinctions in only two ways—by the use of capitals and by the underscore. Spacing between letters is sometimes used, although the space requirements of this technique normally eliminate it from consideration. But even though the report writer is limited to two means of showing importance by type selection, he is able to construct four distinct ranks of type.

SOLID CAPITALS UNDERSCORED

SOLID CAPITALS

Capitals and Lowercase Underscored

Capitals and Lowercase

In theory, any combination of type and position that shows the relative importance of the captions at a glance is acceptable. The one governing rule to follow in considering types and positions of captions is that no caption may have a higher ranking type or position than any of the captions of a higher level. It is permissible, however, that two successive steps of captions appear in the same type if their difference is shown by position, or in the same position if their difference is shown by type selection. Also, there is no objection to skipping over any of the steps in the progression of type or position.

Although the possibilities of variation are great, some practices have become almost conventional, possibly because they excel in showing each caption's importance at a glance. Too, these practices are no doubt widely accepted because of their simplicity of construction. One such scheme of captioning is the following, which is recommended for use in reports with three orders of division.

The first order of captions in this scheme is placed on a separate line, centered, and typed in solid capital letters. Although solid capitals underscored may be used, this high type normally is reserved for the report title, which is the highest caption in the report. Second order of captions are also on separate lines, beginning with the left margin and typed with capitals and lowercase underscored. Third-degree captions are run into the paragraph they cover. To distinguish the line from the text, underscoring is used and the caption is ended with a strong mark of punctuation, usually the period.

Other acceptable schemes include the following.

1. Centered, solid capitals.
2. Centered, capitals and lowercase underscored.
3. Marginal, capitals and lowercase underscored.
4. Run-in, capitals and lowercase underscored.

1. Centered, solid capitals.
2. Marginal, capitals and lowercase underscored.
3. Box cut-in, capitals and lowercase underscored.
4. Run-in, capitals and lowercase underscored.

1. Centered, solid capitals.
2. Centered, capitals and lowercase underscored.
3. Box cut-in, capitals and lowercase.

1. Centered, solid capitals.
2. Marginal, capitals and lowercase underscored.
3. Box cut-in, capitals and lowercase underscored.

MECHANICS AND FORMAT OF THE REPORT PARTS

The foregoing notes on physical appearance apply generally to all parts of the report. But for individual construction of specific report pages, additional special notes are needed. So that the student may be able to understand these special notes, there follows a part-by-part review of the physical construction of the formal report. Much of this presentation is left to illustration, for volumes could be written about the minute details of construction. Major points, however, are indicated.

Title fly

Primarily used in the most formal reports, the title fly contains only the report title. The title is placed slightly above the vertical center of the page in an eye-pleasing arrangement, and all its lines are centered with regard to left and right margins. It is typed in the highest ranking type used in the report (usually solid capitals underscored) and is double spaced if more than one line is required.

Title page

The title page normally contains three main areas of identification (Figure 14), although some forms present the same information in four or five spots on the page (Figure 15). In the typical three-spot title page, the first item covered is the report title. It is best typed in the highest ranking type used in the report, usually solid capitals underscored. The title is centered. If more than one line is required, the lines are broken between thought units and both lines are centered. The lines are appropriately double spaced.

The second area of identification names the individual or group for whom the report is prepared. It is preceded by an identifying phrase such as "Prepared for" or "Submitted to"—words that indicate the individual's role in the report. In addition to the name, identification by title or role, company, and address may be included, particularly if the writer and recipient are from different companies. If the information below the identifying phrase requires three or more lines of type, single spacing is recommended; fewer than three lines may be double spaced. But regardless of how this information is spaced, the identifying phrase appears best set off from the facts below it by a double space.

The third area of information identifies the report writer. It, too, is preceded by an identifying phrase. "Prepared by," "Written by," or any such wording may be used to describe this person's role in the report. The writer's title or role, company, and address may also be given here. Finally in this group of information, the date of publication is usually included. This identification information also is single spaced if four lines are required and double spaced if it involves three lines or less. Likewise, its identification phrase is set off with a double space. The dateline is preferably double spaced from the information preceding it, regardless of previous spacing. Placement of the three spots of information on the page should conform to an eye-pleasing arrangement.

One such arrangement begins the title about 1¼ inches from the top of the page. The final spot of information is ended about 2 inches from the page bottom. The center spot of information is placed so as to split the space between the top and bottom units with a two-to-three ratio, the bottom space being the larger. Line lengths of the information units, of course, are largely governed by

Figure 14.   Good layout for the three-spot title page

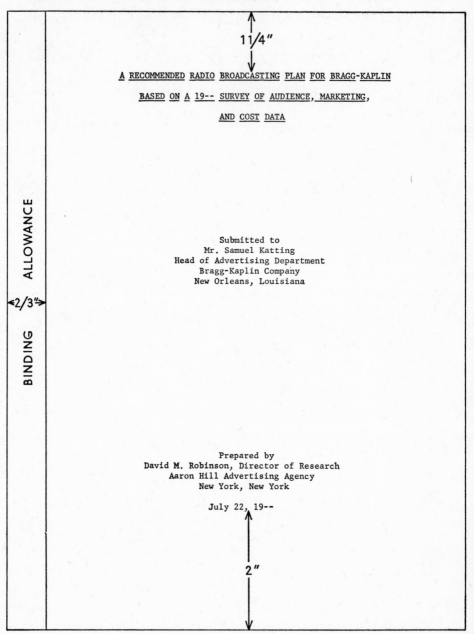

Figure 15. Good layout for the four-spot title page

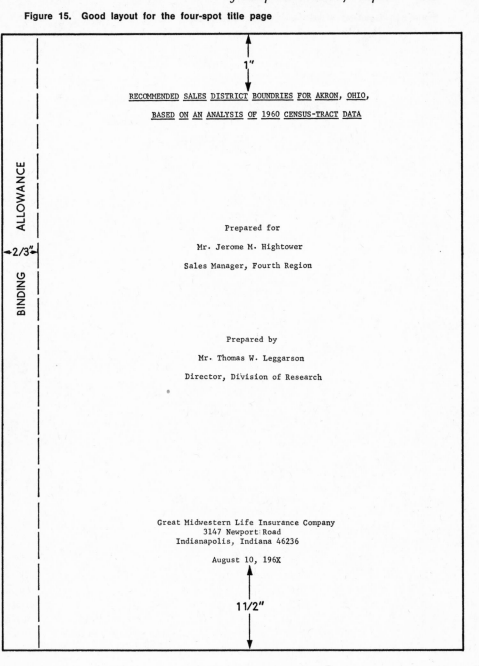

RECOMMENDED SALES DISTRICT BOUNDRIES FOR AKRON, OHIO,

BASED ON AN ANALYSIS OF 1960 CENSUS-TRACT DATA

Prepared for

Mr. Jerome M. Hightower

Sales Manager, Fourth Region

Prepared by

Mr. Thomas W. Leggarson

Director, Division of Research

Great Midwestern Life Insurance Company
3147 Newport Road
Indianapolis, Indiana 46236

August 10, 196X

1"

2/3"

BINDING   ALLOWANCE

1 1/2"

the information contained; yet, the writer will have some opportunity to combine or split units. Preferably, the lines will have sufficient length to keep the units from having an overall skinny appearance.

Letters of transmittal and authorization

As their names imply, the letters of transmittal and authorization are actual letters. Therefore, they should appear as letters. They may be typed in any acceptable letter form—pure block, modified block, or indented. A layout plan recommended for at least the more formal reports is one that fits the letter into a rectangle of the same shape as the space on which it is typed (see Figure 16). This rectangle is marked by the dateline at the top, the initial characters of type at the left, the average of the line lengths at the right, and the last line in the signature at the bottom. For the best optical effect, the rectangle should ride a little high on the page, with a ratio of top margin to bottom margin of about two to three.

Acknowledgments

When the writer is indebted to the assistance of others, it is fitting that the indebtedness be made known somewhere in the report. If the number of individuals involved is small, acknowledgment may be made in the introduction of the report or in the letter of transmittal. In the rare event that numerous acknowledgments must be made, a special section may be constructed. This section is headed with the simple capital-letter title "Acknowledgments," and is typed with the same layout as any other text page that has a title displayed.

Table of contents

The table of contents is the report outline in its polished, finished form. It lists the major report captions with the page numbers on which these captions appear. Although not all reports require a table of contents, one should be a part of any report long enough for a guide to be helpful to the readers.

The page is appropriately headed by the capital-letter caption "Contents" or "Table of Contents," as shown in Figure 17. The page layout is that used for any report page with a title displayed. Below the title, two columns are set up. One contains the captions, generally beginning with the first report part following the table of contents. The captions may or may not include the outline letters

Figure 16.   Letter of transmittal fitted to the shape of the spac

BINDING ALLOWANCE

MIDWESTERN RESEARCH

3241 MONROE STREET
CHICAGO, ILLINOIS

July 22, 19--

Mr. Joel D. Karp, President
The Munson Company
2121 Oldham Road
Cleveland, Ohio 44103

Dear Mr. Karp:

Here is the recommendation report on Munson's radio advertising policy that you requested in your May 9th letter.

As you read the report, undoubtedly you will be (as I was)
surprised to see the facts point so clearly to one decision.
The simple explanation is that this is one of those instances
in which all pertinent data lead down the same path to one
conclusion.

Perhaps you will want to question the matter of cost analysis.
It's true that the recommended plan is going to cost a bit
more initially. But the long-run outlook is much more positive. If you would like more information on the cost question, let me know and I'll rush it to you.

I am grateful to you for this assignment. And I'll be looking
forward to helping you again with other problems that you
might have.

Sincerely yours,

James W. Worthington
Director of Research

JWW:ek

and numbers. If numbers are used, the entries are arranged so the last digits of compound numbers are aligned. The other column, which is brought over to the right margin and headed by the caption "Page," contains the page numbers on which the captions may be found. These numbers are aligned on their right digits. The two columns are connected by leader lines of periods, preferably with spaces intervening.

17. **Good layout and mechanics in the first page of the table of contents**

2"

TABLE OF CONTENTS

2/3" ← 1" → | ← 1" →

1 1/2"

As a rule, all captions of the highest level of division are typed with line spaces above and below. Captions below this level may be uniformly single spaced or double spaced, depending on the overall lengths of the captions. If the captions are long, covering most of the line or extending to a second line, uniform double spacing between captions is recommended. Short captions may be typed in consistent single-spaced form. Some authorities, however, prefer to double space all the contents entries when double spacing is used in the text.

In the table of contents, as in the body of the report, variations in the type used to distinguish different levels of captions is permissible. But the contents type variations need not be the same as those used in the text typing. Usually, the highest level of captions is distinguished from the other levels, and sometimes second-degree captions are distinguished from lower captions by type differences. It is not at all wrong to show no distinction by using plain capitals and lowercase throughout.

Table of illustrations

The table of illustrations is constructed either as a continuation of the table of contents or as a separate table. This table, as shown in Figure 18, lists the graphic aids presented in the report in much the same way as the report parts are listed in the table of contents.

The table is headed with an appropriately descriptive capital-letter title such as "Table of Charts and Illustrations," or "List of Tables and Charts," or "Table of Figures." If the table is placed on a separate page, the page layout is the same as that for any text page with title displayed. And if it is placed as a continued part of the table of contents, the table of illustrations is begun after spacing four or more lines from the last contents entry.

The table is made up of two columns—one for the graphic-aid title and the second for the page on which the aid appears. Heading the second column is the caption "Page." The two columns are also connected by leader lines of spaced periods. Line spacing in the table is optional, again depending on the line lengths of the entries. Preceding each entry title is that entry's number, and should these numbers, Roman or otherwise, require more than one digit, the digits are appropriately aligned on their right member. In reports when two or more illustration types (tables, charts, maps, etc.) are used, and each has been given its own numbering sequence, the entries may be listed successively by types.

Figure 18. Good layout and mechanics in the last page of the table of contents, showing the table of illustrations attached

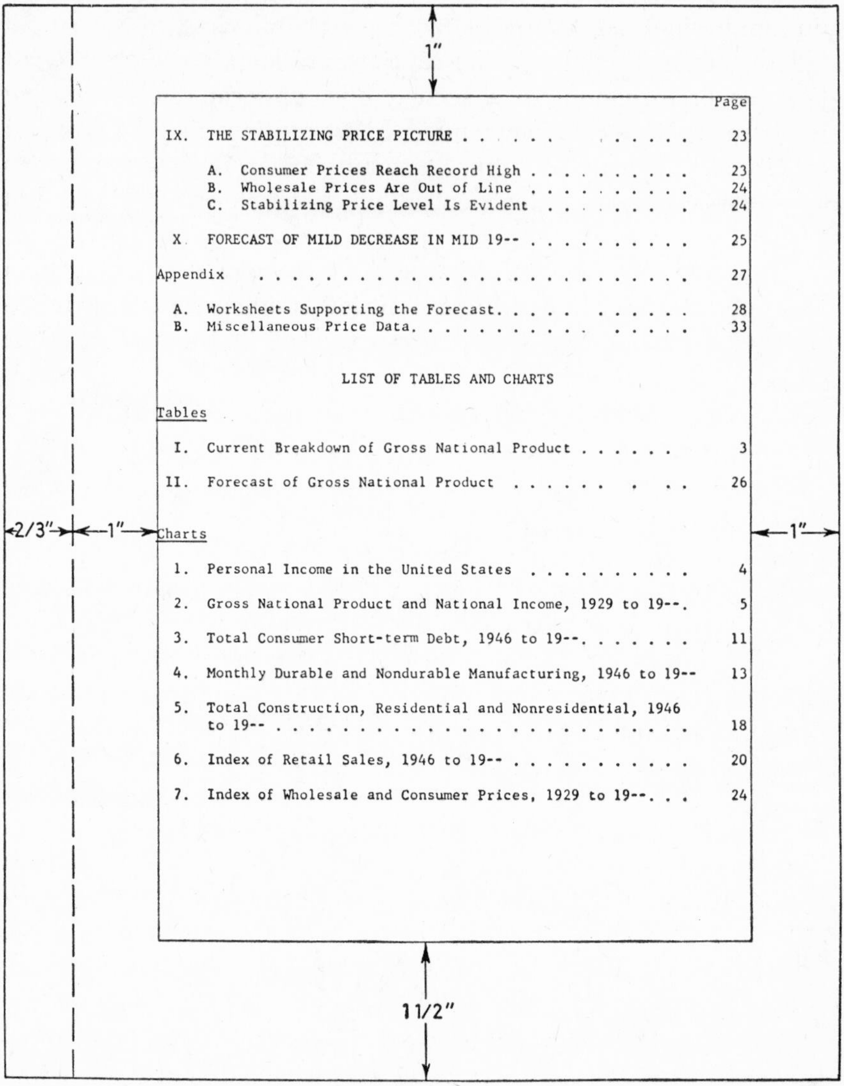

(Page layout measurements shown in margins: 1″ top margin, 2/3″ and 1″ left margins, 1″ right margin, 1 1/2″ bottom margin)

VARIATIONS IN FORMS OF REPORTS

Much of the discussion to this point has been about the long, formal report form—the form that contains numerous prefatory and appended parts in addition to a complete text. But not all reports need be of this type. In fact, most reports are not of this arrangement. Yet, they do employ much the same writing, organization, and layout principles—so much so, in fact, that a knowledge of how to prepare the longer report forms is usually adequate for the preparation of shorter types. That is, there is a close relationship in all reports, and an understanding of this relationship will allow the writer to apply the same layout, writing, and organization principles to all reports.

A general concept of report construction

This concept of report relationship, however, is only general. It does not account for all possible reports nor the countless variations in report makeup. But it does serve to help the student grasp the relationship of all reports.

To understand this relationship, one may view the whole of reports as resembling a stairway, as illustrated in Figure 5, page 124. At the top of this stairway is the formal, full-dress report. This is the form used for occasions when the problem is long and to some extent formal. It includes all the prefatory parts of the report previously discussed: title fly, title page, letters of transmittal and authorization, table of contents, synopsis, and the report proper.

As the need for formality decreases and the problem becomes smaller, this formal report form may change. The general order of these changes is vital to an understanding of the field of reports. First, the conventional but somewhat useless title fly may be dropped. Then, the synopsis (summary) and transmittal may be combined. Next, the table of contents drops out when the point is reached where the shrinking report no longer needs a guide to its contents. Still another step down, reports that are still shorter and less formal may have only the title page as a prefatory part. Below this short-report form is a report that reinstates the letter of transmittal and summary, and presents the entire report in the form of a letter—thus the letter report. And, finally, for short problems of even more informality, the memorandum (informal letter) form may be used.

Format of letter and memorandum reports

All the stages discussed in the preceding progression of report types, with the exception of the last two named, involve similar problems and instructions of physical presentation. But there is little similarity in the physical structure of the various letter-type reports.

Figure 19. Good form for a memorandum report

Campus Correspondence

LOUISIANA STATE UNIVERSITY

FROM: Committee on Courses and Curricula
         J. William Hughes, Chairman

TO: Faculty, College of   DATE: December 15, 19—
         Business Administration

SUBJECT: Report of progress and plans on the study of the business
         administration curricula

Progress for the Period October 1 to December 15

On October 10 the Committee mailed questionnaires (copy attached) to the
deans of 24 selected colleges of business administration. To date, 21 of
the deans have returned questionnaires.

Professors Byrd, Calhoun, and Creznik have tabulated the replies received
and are now analyzing the findings.

Future Plans

Professors Byrd, Calhoun, and Creznik will present their analyses to the
Committee at its February 4th meeting. At this time, the Committee expects
to study these analyses and to make final recommendations.

Professor Byrd will record the Committee's recommendations in a written
report. The Committee will distribute copies of this report to all voting
members of the faculty at least one week before the faculty meeting scheduled
for May 9.

The physical layout requirements of the letter report are the same as those for any other letter. Any conventional letter form may be used; and, as was explained in the discussion of layout of the transmittal and authorization letters, the letter report may well approximate the shape of the space in which it is typed.

Memorandum reports, although they are a type of informal letter, do not necessarily follow conventional letter format. The most popular form (see Figure 19) uses the military arrangement of introductory information: From, To, Subject. Generally, this information is followed by informal presentation of facts in organized fashion. Other forms of the memorandum vary widely. Some resemble questionnaires in that they are comprised of lists of topics or questions, with spaces provided for the written answers. Others are simply handwritten notes on standard interoffice communication forms.

QUESTIONS

1. "Business readers want facts. They could care less about the form in which the facts are presented." Comment on the logic of this evaluation.
2. Describe the layout of an ideal conventional page in a report. How does this differ from the layout of a special page?
3. Summarize the arguments on the question of whether to single or double space the report.
4. Describe the page numbering procedure of a formal report, beginning with the title fly and ending with the last page of the appended parts.
5. Discuss the two basic ways of giving emphasis to the captions in a report.
6. Work up two schemes of caption emphasis that are different from those illustarted in the text. Evaluate them critically.
7. Discuss the content and layout considerations of a title page.
8. Describe the form of the letter of transmittal.
9. In what ways may acknowledgments be handled?
10. Summarize the layout and mechanics of the table of contents.
11. Describe the structure of a letter report. Do the same for a memo report.

CHAPTER 12

Mechanics of documentation and bibliography construction

In most forms of scholarly research (excluding certain areas of the pure sciences), facts, opinions, and ideas gathered from outside sources comprise much of the information presented. Conventional techniques of handling this information should be known to all report writers.

PLACEMENT OF QUOTED AND PARAPHRASED INFORMATION

Report information from secondary sources may be used in two ways. It may be paraphrased (cast in the words of the report writer), or it may be used verbatim (exactly as the original author worded it). Paraphrased material need not be distinguished from the remainder of the report text, although its source frequently must be given. Material used verbatim, however, must be clearly distinguished from the surrounding text.

The conventional rule for marking this difference is simple. If the quoted passage is four lines or less in length, it is typed with the report text and is distinguished from the normal text by quotation marks. But if a longer quotation (five lines and more) is used, the conventional practice is to set it in from both left and right margins (about five spaces) but without quotation marks. If the text is typed with double spacing, the quoted passage is further distinguished from the report writer's work by single spacing, as illustrated in Figure 20.

Frequently, the report writer finds it best to break up or use only fragments of the quoted author's work. Because omissions may

Figure 20.   Segment of a report showing mechanics of typing a quoted passage

```
of those opposing the issue, Logan Wilson makes this penetrating ob-

servation:

            It is a curious paradox that academicians display a
            scientific attitude toward every universe of inquiry
            except that which comprises their own profession. . . .
            Lacking precise qualitative criteria, administrators
            are prone to fall back upon rather crude quantitative
            measures as a partial substitute.5

      These logical, straight-forward, and simple arguments of the pro-

ponents of teacher evaluation appear to be irrefutable.
```

distort the meaning of a passage, the report writer must clearly show such omissions. He makes these omissions clear by use of the ellipsis (a series of periods, usually three, sometimes typed with intervening spaces) at the points of omission. A passage with numerous such omissions is the following.

. . . many companies have undertaken to centralize in the hands of specially trained correspondents the handling of the outgoing mail. Usually centralization has been accomplished by the firm's employment of a correspondence supervisor. . . . The supervisor may guide the work of correspondents . . . or the company may employ a second technique. . . .

In long quotations, it is conventional to show omissions of a paragraph or more by a full line of periods, usually typed with intervening spaces.

CONSTRUCTION OF SOURCE FOOTNOTES

As great importance is placed on the honesty of the report and the validity of the information used in it, it is customary to inform the reader of the source of paraphrased and quoted material. This may be done in either of two ways—by explanation in the text or by a source footnote. Explanation within the text is normally used only for general reference to a source or authority, and not for reference to a specific passage or page in published material. For the more specific source references, the footnote is extensively used.

When to footnote

The decision to use a source footnote should be determined mainly on the basis of giving credit where credit is due. If the words and context are solely the product of the writer, no recognition is needed. But if the information presented originates from an outside source, this source should be given credit.

Following this reasoning of giving credit where credit is due, it is apparent that all material quoted should be footnoted. Such words are obviously the contribution of another and not of the author who repeats them. Failure to conform to this practice is to commit plagiarism—the highest of academic crimes.

Paraphrased material, too, is usually footnoted. Exceptions to this practice, however, are made when the material used is general knowledge in the field and is not the contribution of one particular source. For example, it is general knowledge in the field of advertising that one advantage in using sales letters is that an advertiser may pick his audience in advance. If this information were presented in written form, even though the writer had read it in the work of another writer, no footnote would be needed so long as the information were paraphrased. The writer might elect to footnote here, however, if he felt it desirable to show authority for such a statement. If the same information were quoted, recognition of the source would be imperative.

Mechanics of the footnote

Footnotes are generally placed at the page bottom, separated from the text by a 1½- or 2-inch line, which begins at the left margin. When this form is followed the typist must stop the text typing high enough on the page to allow the footnote to fit inside the page layout. A second and less popular placement of the footnote is within the text and as near as practical to the spot of citation. The note is then set off from the text by top and bottom lines, extending the full width of the page layout. This second procedure, although it does lighten the task of typing, is best used when the material is typed for the convenience of a printer. In recent years, however, it has gained in popularity with report writers.

Below the separating line, the footnote is placed. Always it is single spaced, even though the text may be double spaced. When more than one entry appear together, double spacing is used between them. If the text is typed in block form (as it may be if single spacing is used), the footnotes are also blocked. And if indented form is used (this is the rule with conventional double spacing), the footnote is also indented.

The footnotes are keyed with their text references by means of a superscript, which is an Arabic numeral typed a half line above the normal line. These numbers are first placed in the text directly after the last typed character or punctuation mark in the word or words cited. Consecutive numbering throughout the paper may be used for the superscripts, or they may begin a new series with each chapter or with each page.

Variation in footnote makeup

Unfortunately, there is no one generally accepted order that may be followed in constructing footnotes. Variations occur from school to school, from department to department, and from authority to authority. Thus, the procedures outlined below cannot be in conformity with all of these groups. They may be looked on, however, as possibly the simplest of the generally accepted arrangements. These simplified footnote arrangements have two forms—one to be used when there is a bibliography appended to the paper and the other to be used when no bibliography is present.

Footnote form with a bibliography

When a bibliography is included in the paper, the footnote references need contain only these parts: (1) author's surname; (2) title of the article, bulletin, book; and (3) page number.

[3] Wilson, *The Report Writer's Guide*, p. 44. (Book reference.)
[4] Allison, "Making Routine Reports Talk," p. 71. (Periodical reference.)

Should the reader want to know more about the source cited, he may turn to the bibliography. It is the writer's option, however, to use the complete footnote entry, regardless of the presence of a bibliography.

Form of the footnote without bibliography

A complete footnote is necessary for all first references to a source in a paper without a bibliography. But, as is pointed out in a following page, repeated references to the same source may be shortened. Because complete references to books, periodicals, articles, and such differ on certain points of their content, footnote instructions on each of these types are presented separately. All the items that could possibly be placed in each type of entry are listed in the order of arrangement. But not all these items are always available or essential to a footnote. Thus, there should be no alarm concerning items that are not present or are not essential to specific identification. These should simply be passed over. In other words, the following lists are intended to give the maximum contents and the order or arrangement of the footnote entries. In the simplified procedure recommended here, only the comma is used to separate the entries, and a period ends the list. Capitals need be used only for proper nouns. Abbreviations may be used if consistently followed.

Book entry.

1. Superscript. (Arabic numeral keyed with the text reference and placed before the first part of the entry without spacing.)
2. Name of the author, in normal order. (If two or more authors are involved, all may be presented. If the number of authors is too great to list, the first author followed by the Latin *et al.* or its English equivalent "and others" may be used.)
3. Capacity of the author. (Needed only when contribution to the publication is not truly that of the author, such as *editor,* or *compiler.*)
4. Chapter name. (Necessary only in rare instances when the chapter name helps the reader to find the source, such as in references to encyclopedias.)
5. Book name. (Book names are placed in italics. In typewritten work, italics are indicated by underscoring or by solid caps.)
6. Edition. (Only if other than a first edition.)
7. Publishing company.
8. Location of publisher. (If more than one office, one nearest the writer should be included. United States cities alone are sufficient if population exceeds 500,000; city and state are best given for smaller places.)
9. Date. (Year of publication. If revised, year of latest revision.)
10. Page or pages. (Specific page or inclusive pages on which the cited material is found.)

Examples:

(A typical book)	[1] J. H. Menning and C. W. Wilkinson, *Writing Business Letters*, rev. ed., Richard D. Irwin, Inc., Homewood, Ill., 1959, pp. 17–18.
(A book written by a staff of writers under the direction of an editor. Chapter title is considered helpful.)	[2] W. C. Butte and Amos Buchannan, editors, "Direct Mail Advertising," *An Encyclopedia of Advertising*, Binton Publishing Company, New York, 1961, p. 99.
(Book written by a number of coauthors)	[3] E. Butler Cannais and others, *Anthology of Public Relations*, Warner-Bragg, Inc., New York, 1960, p. 137.

Periodical entry.

1. Superscript.
2. Author's name. (Frequently no author is given. In such cases, the entry may be skipped, or if it is definitely known to be anonymous, the word "anonymous" may be placed in the entry.)
3. Article name. (Typed in quotation marks.)
4. Periodical name. (Placed in italics, which are made by underscoring typed work.)
5. Publication identification. (Volume number in Roman numbers, followed by specific date of publication in parentheses.)
6. Page or pages.

Examples:

[1] James C. Kinnig, "A New Look at Retirement," *Modern Business*, Vol. XXXVII (July 31, 1961), pp. 31–32.

[2] William O. Schultz, "How One Company Improved Morale," *The Business Leader*, Vol. XVII (Aug. 31, 1960), p. 17.

[3] Don Mitchell, "Report Writing Aids," *ABWA Bulletin*, October, 1961, p. 13.

Newspaper article.

1. Superscript.
2. Source description. (If article is signed, give author's name. Otherwise, give description of article, such as "United Press Dispatch" or "editorial.")
3. Main head of article. (Subheads not needed.)
4. Newspaper name. (City and state names inserted in brackets if place names do not appear in newspaper title. State names not needed in

case of very large cities, such as New York, Chicago, and Los Angeles.)

5. Date of publication.
6. Page. (May even include column number.)

Examples:

[1]United Press Dispatch, "Rival Unions Sign Pact," *The* [Baton Rouge, Louisiana] *Morning Advocate,* September 3, 1960, p. 1–A.

[2] Editorial, "The North Moves South," *The Austin* [Texas] *American,* October 3, 1961, p. 2–A.

Letters or documents.

1. Nature of communication.
2. Name of writer.   ⎫ With identification by title and or-
3. Name of recipient. ⎭ ganization where helpful.
4. Date of writing.
5. Where filed.

Example:

[1] Letter from J. W. Wells, President, Wells Equipment Co., to James Mattoch, Secretary-Treasurer, Southern Industrialists, Inc., June 10, 1961, filed among Mr. Mattoch's personal records.

The types of entries discussed in the preceding paragraphs are those most likely to be used; yet, many unusual types are likely to be found in any extensive research project. Government publications, bulletins, special publications of learned societies, essays, and the like may afford countless special problems. And there is slim chance of finding a source book that covers each of these special problems. So it is up to the writer to logically work out these problems, keeping in mind that his objective in constructing the footnote is to make it possible for the reader to find the cited source should he choose to do so. As a rule, the writer will profit by classifying each problem as either a book or a periodical, depending on which it appears to approximate. Then, he should attempt to construct the appropriate entry, leaving out the parts he feels do not help to identify the source, and inserting any additional information he feels should be included for completeness. Example:

A writer wants to make reference to a paper read at the 1961 High-Speed Computer Conference held at Louisiana State University, Baton Rouge, Louisiana, and published in the proceedings of that organization. The paper was by John S. White, Chief Accountant, Esso Standard Oil Company, and reference is to page 24 of the proceedings. As the published proceedings are written in what appears to approach periodical form (it contains a number of articles and is published annually), the following entry may be made.

[1] John S. White, "Organizing and Planning for Electronic Data Processing Systems," *Proceedings of the High-Speed Computer Conference, 1961,* held and sponsored by Louisiana State University, Baton Rouge, Louisiana, p. 24.

Double sources

Sometimes, one wants to cite a passage written by someone other than the author whose name appears on the work consulted. The passage may be a quotation that the author of the consulted work may have borrowed from another author. Or it may be that the source is a collection of papers written by various people and only edited by the one whose name appears on the publication (such as a book of readings). In such cases, the usual procedure is to make what amounts to a double reference. First is the true author's name and the identification of his work (as much as is available). Next are some appropriate relating words, such as "as quoted in" or "cited in." Finally there is the description of the reference in which the passage was found. Such a reference may look like this.

[3] John W. Benning, "How Green Were the Years," presidential address, 13th annual meeting, Academy of Social Sciences, Boulder, Colorado, 1968, as cited in Henry A. Tucker, *New Concepts in the Social Sciences,* Walthrup Press, Inc., New York, 1969, p. 314.

Standard reference forms

If it becomes necessary to cite a source more than once in a manuscript, as it frequently is, repetition may be kept to a minimum by the use of standard reference abbreviations. Although these abbreviations do serve a very worthwhile purpose in their attempt to simplify the footnote construction, it is unfortunate that they are of Latin origin and, therefore, understood only in scholarly circles. Because these forms are so little known, many writers prefer not to use them, even at the expense of repeating whole footnote entries. Possibly in time some simplified English substitutes will become generally accepted. But until that time, at least the more common of these entries should be understood by those who write research papers.

Ibid.   Literally, *ibid.* means "in the same place." It is used to refer the reader to the preceding footnote, but to a different page. The entry consists of the superscript, *ibid.*, and the page number.

Op. cit.   Meaning "in the work cited," this form is used to refer to a previously cited footnote, but not the one directly preceding. That is, the two similar citations are separated by at least one intervening footnote to another source. The entry consists of the superscript, last name of the author, *op. cit.*, and page number.

Loc. cit.   This form means "in the place cited," and its use follows its literal meaning. The form is used to refer to a preceding entry, either the one directly preceding or one farther back in the footnote series. It is used only when the page numbers of the two references to the same source are the same. If the entry refers to the footnote directly preceding, *loc. cit.* alone is used. If the form is used to refer to an entry farther back in the series, the author's last name plus *loc. cit.* make up the entry.

The following series of entries illustrates these possibilities.

[1] James Smith, *How to Write the Annual Report*, Small-Boch, Inc., Chicago, p. 173.

[2] *Ibid.*, p. 143. (Refers to Smith's book but to different page.)

[3] William Curtis, "An Experiment with Records," *Business Leader*, Vol. XIX (Dec. 5, 1960), p. 28.

[4] Smith, *op. cit.*, p. 103. (Refers to Smith's book but to different page than in footnote 2.)

[5] Curtis, *loc. cit.* (Refers to Curtis's article and to same page as in footnote 3.)

[6] *Loc. cit.* (Refers to Curtis's article and to same page as in footnotes 3 and 5.)

Other abbreviation forms are frequently used in footnote entries. Some of these are particularly useful in making reference to text passages or to other footnotes. Such references are generally made in discussion footnotes, which are quite different from the source footnotes discussed in the preceding pages. The most widely used of these abbreviations are as follows.

Cf.—compare (directs reader's attention to another passage).
Cf. ante—compare above.
Cf. post—compare below.
ed.—edition.
e.g.—for example.
et al.—and others.
et passim—and at intervals throughout the work.
et seq.—and the following.

i.e.—that is.
infra—below.
l., ll.—line, lines.
Ms., Mss.—manuscript, manuscripts.
n.d.—no date.
n.n.—no name.
n.p.—no place.
p., pp.—page, pages.
f., ff.,—following page, pages.
supra—above.
vol., vols.—volume, volumes.

DISCUSSION FOOTNOTES

In sharp contrast with source footnotes are the discussion footnotes. Through the use of discussion footnotes, the writer strives to explain a part of his text, to amplify discussion on a phase of his presentation, to make cross references to other parts of the paper, and the like. This material is not placed in the text principally because to place it there would tend to slow down or complicate the presentation. But care should be taken so that not too much of the writing is relegated to a role in a footnote. Material presented in footnote form obviously does not receive the emphasis that material presented in text form receives. Thus, unless discretion is used in selecting the points for footnote presentation, the major story of the paper will suffer.

No standard form could possibly be devised for presentation of the discussion footnote. Of course, the note should be as concise and clear as it possibly can be. But general instructions can go no further than these points, for each footnote differs because of contents. These examples illustrate some possibilities of this footnote type.

(Cross reference)   [1] See the principle of focal points on page 72.

(Amplification of discussion and cross reference)   [2] Lyman Bryson says the same: "Every communication is different for every receiver even in the same context. No one can estimate the variation of understanding that there may be among receivers of the same message conveyed in the same vehicle when the receivers are separated in either space or time." See *Communication of Ideas*, p. 5.

(Comparison)   ³ Compare with the principle of the
                                          objective: Before starting any activity, one
                                          should make a clear complete statement of
                                          the objective in view.

THE BIBLIOGRAPHY

A bibliography is an orderly list of published material on a particular subject. In a formal paper, the list covers writing on the subject
of the paper. The entries in this list very closely resemble source
footnotes, but the two must not be confused.

The bibliography normally appears as an appended part of a
formal paper and is placed following the appendix. It may be
preceded by a fly page containing the one word "Bibliography" in
capital letters. The page that begins the list is headed by the main
caption "Bibliography," usually typed in solid capital letters. Below
this title, the publications are presented by broad groups and in
alphabetical order within the groups. Usually, such groupings as
books, periodicals, and bulletins may be used. But the determination of groups should be based solely on the types of publications
collected in each bibliography. If, for example, a bibliography includes a large number of periodicals and government publications
plus a wide assortment of diverse publication types, the bibliography could be divided into three parts: periodicals, government
publications, and miscellaneous publications.

As with footnotes, variations in bibliography form are numerous.
A simplified form recommended for business use follows the same
procedure as that described above for source footnotes, with four
major exceptions.

1. The author's name is listed in reverse order, surname first, for
the purpose of alphabetizing. If coauthors are involved, however,
only the first name is reversed.

2. The entry is generally typed in hanging indention form. That
is, the second and all following lines of an entry begin some uniform
distance (usually about five spaces) to the right of the beginning
point of the first line. The purpose of this indented pattern is to
make the alphabetized first line stand out.

3. The bibliography entry gives the inclusive pages of the publication and does not refer to any one page or passage.

4. Second and subsequent references to publications of the same
author are indicated by a uniform line (see bibliography illustra-

tion). In typed manuscripts, this line may be formed by the under-score struck 10 consecutive times. But this line may be used only if the entire authorship is the same in the consecutive publications. For example, the line could not be used when consecutive entries have one common author but different coauthors.

An illustration of a bibliography is as follows.

BIBLIOGRAPHY

BOOKS

Burton, Hal, *The City Fights Back,* The Citadel Press, New York, 1954, 318 pp.

Converse, Paul D., Harvey W. Huegy, and Robert V. Mitchell, *The Elements of Marketing,* 5th ed., Prentice-Hall, Inc., New York, 1952, 968 pp.

Kiernan, Gladys M., *Retailers Manual of Taxes and Regulation,* 12th ed., Institute of Distribution, Inc., New York, 1954, 340 pp.

Koontz, Harold D., *Government Control of Business,* Houghton Mifflin Company, New York, 1941, 937 pp.

Surrey, N. M. M., *The Commerce of Louisiana During the French Regime, 1699–1763,* Columbia University Press, New York, 1916, 476 pp.

GOVERNMENT PUBLICATIONS

United States Bureau of the Census, "Characteristics of the Population," *Eighteenth Census of the United States: Census of Population,* Vol. II, part 18, United States Government Printing Office, Washington, D.C., 1961, 248 pp.

———, *Statistical Abstract of the United States,* United States Government Printing Office, Washington, D.C., 1960, 1056 pp.

United States Department of Commerce, *Business Statistics: 1961,* United States Government Printing Office, Washington, D.C., 1961, 309 pp.

———, *Survey of Current Business: 1960 Supplement,* United States Government Printing Office, Washington, D.C., 1960, 271 pp.

PERIODICALS

Montgomery, Donald E., "Consumer Standards and Marketing," *The Annals of the American Academy of Political and Social Science,* Vol. VII (May, 1940), pp. 141–49.

Phillips, Charles F., "Some Studies Needed in Marketing," *The Journal of Marketing,* Vol. V (July, 1940), pp. 16–25.

Phillips, Charles F., "Major Areas of Marketing Research," *The Journal of Marketing,* Vol. XI (July, 1958), pp. 21–26.

MISCELLANEOUS PUBLICATIONS

Bradford, Ernest S., *Survey and Directory, Marketing Research Agencies in the United States,* Bureau of Business Research, College of the City of New York, 1957, 137 pp.

Reference Sources on Chain Stores, Institute of Distribution, Inc., New York, 1959, 116 pp.

Smith, T. Lynn, *Farm Trade Centers in Louisiana,* 1901 to 1931, Louisiana Bulletin No. 234, Louisiana State University, Baton Rouge, 1933, 56 pp.

THE ANNOTATED BIBLIOGRAPHY

Frequently in scholarly writing, each bibliography entry is followed by a brief comment on the value and content of the entry. That is, the bibliography is annotated. No definite rules may be given for the composition of the annotation. The comments should, in as brief a fashion as is practical, point out the content and value of each entry. Short descriptive phrases are generally used rather than complete sentences, although sentences are acceptable. The annotation, like the bibliography entry, is single spaced, but it is separated from the entry by a double space. It, too, is indented from the initial line of the entry, as illustrated below.

Donald, W. T., editor, *Handbook of Business Administration,* McGraw-Hill Book Co., Inc., New York, 1931, 731 pp.
Contains a summary of the activities in each major area of business. Written by foremost authorities in each field. Particularly useful to the business specialist who wants a quick review of the whole of business.

Brown, Stanley M., and Lillian Doris, editors, *Business Executive's Handbook,* 3rd ed., 1947, 644 pp.
Provides answers to most routine executive problems in explicit manner and with good examples. Contains good material on correspondence and sales letters.

QUESTIONS

1. Discuss the treatment of paraphrased information in a report.
2. How should a two-line quotation be handled in a report? A seven-line quotation?
3. What should one do to show omission of three words from a passage

he is quoting? What should he do to show omission of a full paragraph?

4. What determines whether one should acknowledge a reference by a footnote?

5. Discuss the numbering sequence of footnotes.

6. From the garbled information presented below, construct (*a*) a series of footnote entries for material with a bibliography and (*b*) a series of entries for a paper without a bibliography. Assume that the entries will appear within three consecutive pages.

First entry: reference to page 107 of an article by Peter Caldwell, Joseph J. Turner, and Amos Zaleski; appearing in a periodical titled Today's Business News; dated March 7, 1969; titled Shortcomings of Today's Managers, Volume 41.

Second entry: another reference to the preceding article, but to page 111.

Third entry: reference to page 417 of the book, Space Age Management; written by Carlos Charlet; published in 1968 by Sampson Publishing Company, Boston, Massachusetts; 2nd edition.

Fourth entry: reference to page 31 of a book of readings titled Readings in Personnel; edited by Ralph Scott; published by Thomas Wells Publishing Company, Incorporated, Chicago; quoting from an article written by Henry J. Dartnell titled Three Steps to Personnel Improvement; dated 1969; 1st edition.

Fifth entry: a second reference to the article described in the first entry, this time to page 109.

Sixth entry: another reference to page 109 of the article described in the first entry.

Seventh entry: a second reference to the article by Henry Dartnell, but to page 37.

7. Select five books in your field and construct the bibliography entries for them.

8. What are discussion footnotes? How are they used?

9. Choose a hypothetical problem, and construct discussion footnotes that:
    a) Make a cross-reference.
    b) Amplify discussion.
    c) Make a comparison.

10. Discuss the purpose and form of the annotated bibliography.

11. Using the books listed in question 7, construct an annotated bibliography.

12. From the garbled information below, construct the entries as they would appear in a bibliography.

First entry: a book titled Marketing Strategy, written by Charles Mott, revised edition, published by Y. E. Brandt, Inc., New York, 1969, 549 pages.

Second entry: unsigned article in periodical titled Current Business; October 7, 1969 issue; Volume 71; covering pages 33, 47–48, and 53–54; article titled New Products for the Year; published by Davis Publishing Company, Boston.

Third entry: a booklet printed and released by the Walton Drug Company, Inc., Los Angeles; titled Twenty Years of Research Progress; unsigned; published in 1968; second printing.

CHAPTER 13

Graphic presentation

Graphic aids[1] are an essential part of most reports. Even though it is generally true that the report story is best told in words, words alone usually are not adequate. In such instances, some form of graphic aid may be used to help put over the meaning of the words. Thus, the primary function of graphic aids in the report is that of assisting the words to communicate the report contents.

In addition to their vital role in communication, graphic aids also serve to cover minor supporting detail not considered in the text words. Or they may be used to give special emphasis to certain points of coverage. Even though they should not be included for this reason alone, they serve to improve the physical appearance of the report, thereby making the report more inviting and readable.

FORESIGHT IN PLANNING THE ILLUSTRATIONS

If graphic aids are to be effective, they must be planned with foresight and care. This planning is a part of the task of organizing the report, and it is preferably done at the time the report is organized.

The task of planning the graphic presentation should never be allowed to become arbitrary or routine. Never should the writer arbitrarily select some random number of illustrations to include. Nor should the completeness of graphic presentation be judged solely on the number of illustrations used. Instead, each graphic device planned for presentation in the report should have a definite reason for being. And this reason for being should be judged by one,

---

[1] The term *graphic aids* is used here in its broadest meaning and includes all forms of illustration designed to supplement the text. By this definition, tables (which are not truly graphic) are included as graphic aids.

Figure 21. Page from a popular report, illustrating use of summary text closely helped by graphic aids

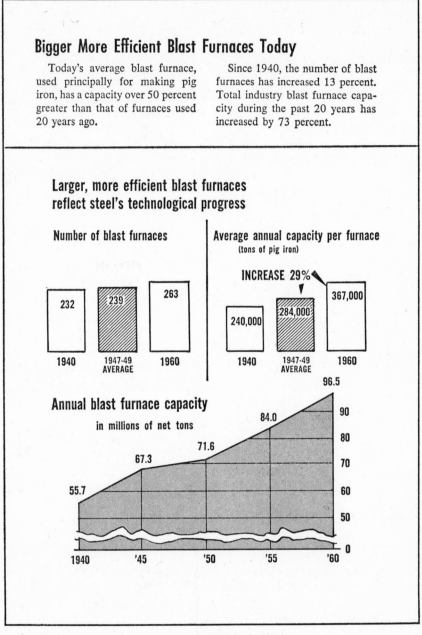

Bigger More Efficient Blast Furnaces Today

Today's average blast furnace, used principally for making pig iron, has a capacity over 50 percent greater than that of furnaces used 20 years ago.

Since 1940, the number of blast furnaces has increased 13 percent. Total industry blast furnace capacity during the past 20 years has increased by 73 percent.

Larger, more efficient blast furnaces reflect steel's technological progress

Number of blast furnaces

232	239	263
1940	1947-49 AVERAGE	1960

Average annual capacity per furnace
(tons of pig iron)

INCREASE 29%

240,000	284,000	367,000
1940	1947-49 AVERAGE	1960

Annual blast furnace capacity

in millions of net tons

55.7   67.3   71.6   84.0   96.5

1940   '45   '50   '55   '60

SOURCE: *Charting Steel's Progress*, American Iron and Steel Institute.

and only one, criterion; that criterion is need. Only if the graphic aid is needed—that is, if it helps to communicate the report story—should it be included.

RELATIONSHIP OF NEED TO THE PLAN

Just what graphic aids are needed to communicate a report story, however, is not easy to determine. Much depends on the overall plan of the writer. If the writer plans to cover the subject in detail, the role of the graphic aids is to emphasize and to supplement. Specifically, they point up the major facts discussed and present the detailed data not covered in the writing. On the other hand, if the writer plans to present the facts in summary form, he may use the graphic aids to work more closely with his text.

The first of these arrangements (complete text supplemented by graphic aids) is conventional and is best for all studies when completeness is a main requirement. The second plan (summary text closely helped by graphic aids) is gaining in importance. It is especially used in popular types of reports, such as those addressed to the general public. As illustrated in Figure 21, this plan produces fast-moving, light reading—the kind the public likes. In addition to the public, many top executives prefer this plan. With the increasing demands on their time, these executives prefer that the reports they read give them the facts quickly and easily. Short, summary reports, helped by an abundance of clear graphic aids, do this job best. Frequently, because of the need for a complete report for future reference and the need for presenting summary information to top executives, both kinds of reports are written for the same problem.

PREFERRED PLACEMENT WITHIN THE REPORT

The graphic aids designed primarily to help tell the report story are logically placed within the report text and near the text they illustrate. If the illustration is small, taking up only a portion of the page, it is best placed surrounded by the writing that covers it; if the illustration requires a full page for display, it is preferably placed immediately following the page on which it is discussed. When the discussion covers several pages, however, the full-page illustration is best placed on the page following the first reference to its contents.

Another acceptable placement of a full-page illustration is on the obverse side of a page and facing the text it supports. When this placement is used, either of two page arrangements is acceptable. The illustration page may be affixed to the preceding page so that it turns with that page and appears as its reverse side. Or the reverse side of the illustration page may be left blank. These arrangements cause some problem in numbering the pages, however. In the first arrangement, the page may be given the next number in sequence. In the second arrangement, the word "obverse" and the page number may be placed on the blank side of the page in the spot where the number normally would go.

There is some acceptance of the report arrangement in which all the illustrations are placed in the appendix. Aside from the time saved by the typist, little can be said for this practice. Certainly, it does not work for the convenience of the reader, who must flip through pages each time he wants to see the graphic presentation of a part of the text.

Graphic aids that are not designed specifically to help tell a part of the report story are best placed in the appendix. Included in this group are all graphic aids that belong within the report for completeness, yet have no specific spot of coverage within the study. As a rule, this group is largely comprised of long and complex tables that may cover large areas of information. These tables may even cover the data displayed in a number of charts and other more graphic devices generally constructed to illustrate very specific spots within the report.

Whether the illustrations are placed within or at the end of the text, they should be keyed to the text portion they cover by means of references. That is, the writer may well call the reader's attention to illustrations that cover the topic under discussion. Such references are best made as incidental remarks in sentences that state significant comments about the data shown in the illustration. Although numerous incidental wordings may be used, the following word groups are acceptable.

. . . , as shown in Chart 4, . . .
. . . , indicated in Chart 4, . . .
. . . , as a glance at Chart 4 reveals, . . .
. . . (see Chart 4) . . .

GENERAL MECHANICS OF CONSTRUCTION

In planning the illustrations, and later in the actual work of constructing them, the report writer is confronted with numerous questions of mechanics. Many of these questions must be solved through intelligent appraisal of the conditions concerned in each instance. But the mechanics fall into general groups, the most conventional of which are summarized in the following paragraphs.

Size determination

One of the first decisions involved in constructing a graphic aid is that of determining how large the illustration should be. The answer to this question should not be arbitrary, nor should it be based solely on the convenience of the writer. Instead, the writer should seek to give the illustration the size that its contents justify. If, for example, an illustration is relatively simple, comprising only two or three quantities, a quarter page might be adequate. Certainly, a full page would not be needed to illustrate the data. But if the illustration is made up of a dozen or so quantities, a larger illustration would be justified—possibly even a full page.

With extremely complex and involved data, it may be necessary to make the graphic aid larger than the report page. Such long presentations must be carefully inserted and folded within the report so that they open easily. The fold selected will, of course, vary with the size of the page, so no best fold can be recommended. The writer will do well to survey whatever possibilities are available to him.

Layout arrangement

The layout of any graphic aid is influenced by the amount of information being illustrated. But whenever practical, it is best to keep the layout of the illustration within the normal page layout.

Rules and borders

Rules and borders of any form of graphic presentation should be arranged to help display and to make clear the data presented. Thus, their use should be determined chiefly through careful planning. As a general practice, however, graphic aids of less than a page are carefully set off from the text by a line border, which completely encloses the illustration and its captions. This practice may be used for full-page illustrations as well, although with such pages the border does not serve so practical a purpose. As previously noted in the discussion of layout, the borders should not extend beyond the normal page margins. An exception to this rule is, of course, the unusual instances in which the volume of data to be illustrated simply will not fit into an area less than the normal page layout.

Color and crosshatching

Appropriate use of color or crosshatching helps the reader to see the comparisons and distinctions. In addition, they give the report a boost in physical attractiveness. Color is especially valuable for this purpose and should be used whenever practical.

Numbering

Except for minor tabular displays that are actually a part of the text, all illustrations in the report are numbered. Numerous schemes of numbering can be used, depending on the makeup of the graphic aids.

If sufficient numbers of two or more graphic aid types are used in a report, each type may be numbered consecutively. For example, if a report is illustrated by six tables, five charts, and six maps, these graphic aids might be numbered Table I, Table II, . . . Table VI; Chart 1, Chart 2, . . . Chart 5; and Map 1, Map 2, . . . Map 6.

But if the illustrations used are a wide mixture of types, they may be numbered in two groups—tables and figures. To illustrate, consider a report that contains three tables, two maps, three charts, one diagram, and one photograph. These graphic aids could be grouped and numbered as Table I, Table II, and Table III, and Figure 1, Figure 2, . . . Figure 7. By convention, tables are never grouped with other forms of presentation. *Figures* represent a sort of miscellaneous grouping, which may include all illustration types other than tables. It would not be wrong to group and number as figures all graphic aids other than tables, even if the group contains sufficient subgroups (charts, maps, etc.) to warrant separate numbering of each of these subgroups.

As the preceding examples illustrate, tables are conventionally numbered with capital Roman numerals (I, II, III, etc.). All other forms of illustration use the Arabic numerals (1, 2, 3, etc.). There is some tendency now, however, to use Arabic numerals for all forms. Obviously, the most important rule to follow in regard to numbering is that of consistency.

Construction of title captions

Every graphic aid should have a title caption that adequately describes the contents. Like the captions used in other parts of the report, the title to the graphic aid has the objective of concisely covering the illustration contents. As a check of content coverage, the report writer may well use the journalist's five W's—*who, what, where, when, why.* Sometimes he may include *how* (the classification principle). But as conciseness of expression is also desired, it is not always necessary to include all the W's in the caption. A title of a chart comparing annual sales volume of Texas and Louisiana stores of the Brill Company for the 1960–19— period may be constructed as follows.

Who—Brill Company.
What—annual sales.
Where—Texas and Louisiana.
When—1960–19—.
Why for comparison.

The caption may read, "Comparative Annual Sales of Texas and Louisiana Branches of the Brill Company, 1960–19—."

Placement of titles

Titles of tables are conventionally placed above the tabular display. Titles to all other graphic presentations usually are placed below the illustration. There is convention, too, for placing table titles in a higher type (usually solid capitals without the underscore in typewritten reports) than titles of all other illustrations. But now these conventional forms are not universally followed. There is a growing tendency to use lowercase type for all illustration titles, and to place titles of both tables and charts at the top. These more recent practices are simple and logical; yet, for formal reports the conventional way is recommended.

Footnotes and source acknowledgments

Occasionally, parts of a graphic aid require special explanation or elaboration. When these conditions come up, just as when similar explanations are made within the text of the report, a footnote is used. Such footnotes are nothing more than concise explanations placed below the illustration and keyed to the part explained by means of a superscript (raised number) or asterisk, as shown in Figure 20. Footnotes for tables are best placed immediately below the graphic presentation. Footnotes for other graphic forms follow the illustration when the title is placed at the top of the page, and they follow the title when the title is placed at the bottom of the page.

Usually, a source acknowledgment is the bottom entry on the page. By source acknowledgment is meant a reference to the body or authority that deserves the credit for gathering the data used in the illustration. The entry consists simply of the word *source,* followed by a colon and the source name. A source note for data based on information gathered by the United States Department of Agriculture might read like this: Source: United States Department of Agriculture. If the data are collected by the writer or his staff, two procedures may be followed. The source may be given as "primary"; then, the source note reads, "Source: primary." Or the source note may be omitted.

CONSTRUCTION OF TABLES

A table is any systematic arrangement of quantitative information in rows and columns. Although tables are not truly graphic in the literal meaning of the word, they are instrumental in communicating information. Therefore, they are appropriately considered a part of the graphic aids planning of a report. The purpose of a table is to present a broad area of information in convenient and orderly fashion. By such an arrangement, the information is simplified, and comparisons and analyses are made easy.

Two basic types of tables may be used—the general-purpose table and the special-purpose table. General-purpose tables are arrangements of a broad area of data collected. They are repositories of detailed statistical data and have no special analytical purpose. As a rule, general-purpose tables are placed in the report appendix.

Special-purpose tables, as their name implies, are prepared for a special purpose—to help illustrate a particular phase of the text. Usually they consist of data carefully drawn from the general-purpose tables. Only those data pertinent to the writer's analysis are selected, and sometimes these data are rearranged or regrouped to better illustrate their special purpose. Such tables are usually placed within the text near the spot they illustrate.

Aside from the title, footnotes, and source designation previously discussed, the table consists of stubs, captions, and columns and rows of data, as shown in Figure 22. Stubs are the titles to the rows

Figure 22. Good arrangement of the parts of a typical table

Stub Head	CAPTION HEAD			
	Subcaption	Subcaption	Subcaption	Subcaption
Stub	X X X	X X X	X X X	X X X
Stub	X X X	X X X	X X X	X X X
Stub	X X X	X X X	X X X	X X X
Stub	X X X	X X X	X X X	X X X
"	"	"	"	"
"	"	"	"	"
"	"	"	"	"
"	"	"	"	"
"	"	"	"	"
"	"	"	"	"
TOTAL	X X X	X X X	X X X	X X X

Footnotes

Source Note:

of data, and captions are the titles to the columns. The captions, however, may be divided into subcaptions, or column heads, as they are sometimes called.

As the text tables should be specially planned, their construction is largely influenced by their illustration purpose. Nevertheless, a few general construction rules may be listed.

1. If rows tend to be long, the stubs may be repeated at the right.

2. The dash (—) or the abbreviation "n.a.," but not the zero, is used to indicate data not available.

3. Footnote references to numbers in the table should be keyed with asterisks. Numbers followed by footnote reference numbers may cause confusion.

4. Totals and subtotals should be made whenever they help the purpose of the table. Totals may be made for each column and sometimes for each row. Usually, row totals are made at the right, but when it is desired that emphasis be given the totals they may be placed at the left. Likewise, column totals are generally made at the bottom, but they may be placed at the top of the column when emphasis of these totals is wanted. The totals are separated from their data by a ruled line, usually a double one.

5. Units in which the data are recorded must be made clear. Unit descriptions (bushels, acres, pounds, and such) are appropriately placed above the columns, as part of the captions or subcaptions. If the data are in dollars, however, the dollar mark ($) placed before the first entry in each column is sufficient.

THE SIMPLE BAR CHART

Simple bar charts are graphic means of comparing simple magnitudes by the lengths of equal-width bars. Such charts are used to show quantity changes over time, quantity changes over geographic distance, or quantitative distances.

The principal parts of the bar chart are the bars and the grid. The bars may be arranged horizontally or perpendicularly, and each has in its beginning a title to identify the quantity being illustrated. The grid on which the bars are placed is simply a field carefully ruled by line marks arithmetically scaled to the magnitudes illustrated. Usually, a finely marked grid is made as a preliminary step in constructing a bar chart, and the bars are then placed on the grid. But the final drawing of the chart is best made to show only sufficient grid lines to help the reader's eye measure the magnitudes of the bars. These scaled grid lines are carefully labeled with numerals, and the unit in which the values are measured is indicated by a scale caption that appears below the values in a vertical bar chart and above the values in a horizontal bar arrangement.

Although there are numerous acceptable variations in bar chart construction, a basic pattern should be helpful to the novice writer. Such a pattern as illustrated in Figure 23 is generally adequate.

Figure 23. Illustration of good arrangement of the parts of a simple bar chart

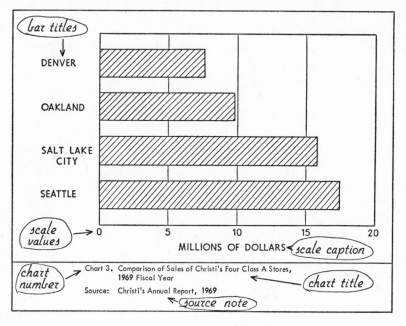

VARIATIONS OF THE BAR CHART

In addition to the simple bar chart just described, a number of other types of bar charts may be used in presenting a report. The more commonly used of these variants are the multiple bar chart, the bilateral bar chart, and the subdivided or component-part bar chart.

Multiple bar charts

Comparisons of two or three variables within a single bar chart are made possible by the use of multiple bars distinguished by crosshatching, shading or color. That is, the bars that represent each of the variables being compared are distinguished by these mechanical means, as illustrated in Figure 24. The key to the variables is given in a legend, which may be placed within the illustration or below it, depending on where space is available. Generally, it is confusing and therefore inadvisable to make multiple comparisons of this type when more than three variables are involved.

Figure 24. Multiple bar chart

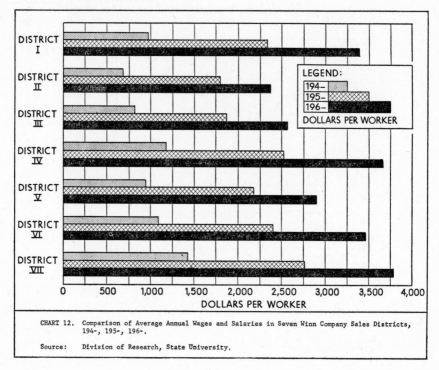

CHART 12. Comparison of Average Annual Wages and Salaries in Seven Winn Company Sales Districts, 194-, 195-, 196-.

Source: Division of Research, State University.

Bilateral bar charts

When it is necessary to show plus or minus deviations, bilateral bar charts may be used. In these charts, the bars begin at a central point of reference and may go either up or down, as illustrated in Figure 25. Bar titles may be written either within, above, or below the bars, depending on which placement best fits the illustration. Bilateral bar charts are especially good for showing percentage change, but they may be used for any series in which minus quantities are present.

Subdivided bar charts

If it is desirable to show the composition of magnitudes being compared, subdivided bar charts may be used. Crosshatchings, shadings, or colors are first assigned to each of the parts to be shown; then, the bars are marked off into their component parts, as Figure 26 illustrates. As always when crosshatching or color is used, a legend is employed to guide the reader.

Figure 25.   Bilateral bar chart

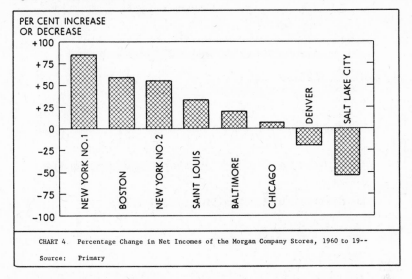

A form of the subdivided bar chart frequently is used to compare the composition of variables by percentages. This chart differs from the typical bar chart principally in that the bar lengths are meaningless in the comparisons. All the bars are of equal lengths, and only

Figure 26.   Illustration of a subdivided bar chart

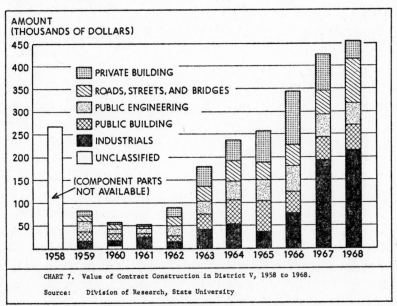

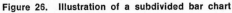

Figure 27.   Illustration of a subdivided bar chart

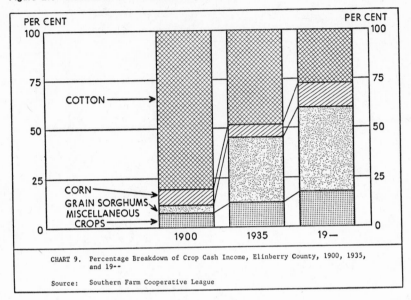

CHART 9.   Percentage Breakdown of Crop Cash Income, Elinberry County, 1900, 1935, and 19--

Source: Southern Farm Cooperative League

the component parts of the bars vary. As depicted in Figure 27, the component parts may be labeled, but they may also be explained in a legend.

PIE CHART CONSTRUCTION

Also of primary importance in comparing the percentage composition of variables is the pie chart (Figure 28). As the name implies, the pie chart illustrates the magnitude as a pie, and the component parts of this whole are shown as slices of this pie. The slices may be individually labeled, or crosshatching or coloring with an explanatory legend may be used. As it is difficult to judge the value of each slice with the naked eye, it is advisable to include the units of value within each slice. A good rule is to begin slicing the pie at the 12 o'clock position and to move around clockwise. It is usually best to show the slices in descending order of magnitude.

Pie diagrams should never be used to show comparisons of two or more wholes by means of varying the areas of wholes. Such comparisons are almost meaningless. The human eye is totally inadequate in judging the relative areas of most geometric shapes.

Figure 28. Illustration of a pie chart

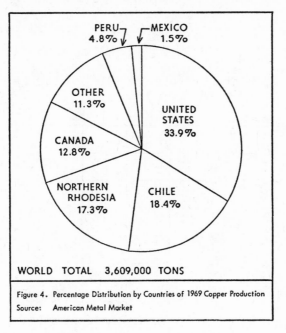

PERU 4.8%   MEXICO 1.5%

OTHER 11.3%

CANADA 12.8%

NORTHERN RHODESIA 17.3%

UNITED STATES 33.9%

CHILE 18.4%

WORLD TOTAL 3,609,000 TONS

Figure 4. Percentage Distribution by Countries of 1969 Copper Production

Source: American Metal Market

ARRANGEMENT OF THE LINE CHART

Line charts are best used to show the movements or changes of a continuous series of data over time, such as changes in prices, weekly sales totals, and periodic employment data. They may be plotted on an arithmetic, semilogarithmic, or logarithmic grid; but since the arithmetic plot is most common to business reports, it is described here.

In a line chart, the item to be illustrated is plotted as a continuous line on a grid. On the grid, time is plotted on the horizontal (X) axis; the values of the series are plotted on the vertical (Y) axis. The scale values and time periods are clearly marked on the axis lines, as shown in Figure 29.

Comparisons of two or more series (Figure 30) on the same grid may also be made on a line chart. In such a comparison, the lines should be clearly distinguished by color or form (dots, dashes, dots and dashes, and the like), and should be clearly labeled or explained by a legend somewhere in the chart. But there is a limit on the number of series that may be compared on a single grid. As a practical rule, four or five series on a single grid should be a maximum.

It is possible, also, to show component parts of a series by use of a line chart, sometimes called a belt chart. Such an illustration, how-

Figure 29.   Example of a line chart with one series

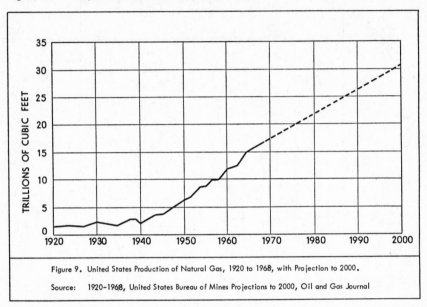

Figure 9. United States Production of Natural Gas, 1920 to 1968, with Projection to 2000.

Source: 1920-1968, United States Bureau of Mines Projections to 2000, Oil and Gas Journal

ever, is limited to one series to a chart. This type of chart, as shown in Figure 31, is constructed with a top line to represent the total of the series; then, starting from the base, the component parts are cumulated, beginning with the largest and ending with the smallest. Crosshatching or coloring may be used to distinguish the parts. The differences between the cumulative totals show the values of the last component part brought into the cumulation.

Even though the line graph is one of the simplest charts to construct, three common pitfalls should be warned against. First of these is the common violation of the rule of zero origin. The Y scale (vertical axis) must begin at zero, even though the points to be plotted are relatively high in value. If most of the points to be plotted are relatively high in value, the comparison may be made by breaking the scale somewhere between zero and the level of the lowest plotted value. Of the numerous means of illustrating scale breaks, the two techniques shown on page 314 are recommended.

Second, equal magnitudes on both X and Y scales should be represented on the grid by equal distances. Any deviation from this rule would distort the illustration, thereby deceiving the reader.

A third common violation of good line chart construction con-

Figure 30. Illustration of a line chart comparing more than one series

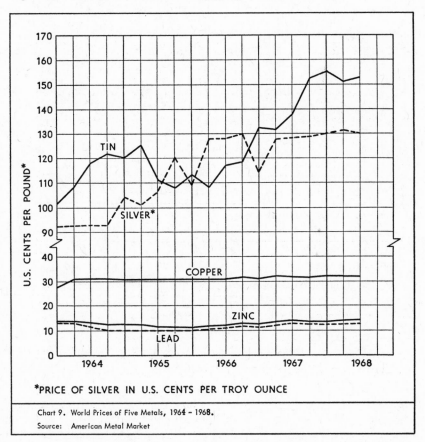

Chart 9. World Prices of Five Metals, 1964 – 1968.
Source: American Metal Market

cerns the determination of proportions on the grid. It is easy to see that by expanding one scale and by contracting the other, impressions of extreme deviation can be made. For example, data plotted on a line chart with time intervals $\frac{1}{16}$ inch apart certainly appear to show more violent fluctuations than the same data plotted on a chart with time intervals plotted $\frac{1}{2}$ inch apart. Only the application of common sense can prevent this violation. The grid distances selected simply must be such as will tend to make presentation of the data realistic.

Figure 31.   Illustration of a component-part line chart

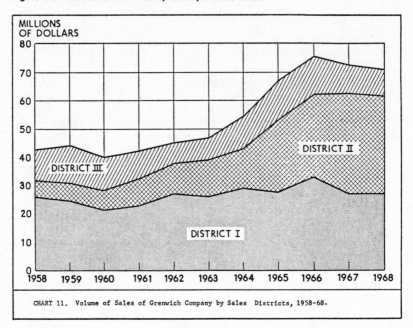

CHART 11. Volume of Sales of Grenwich Company by Sales Districts, 1958-68.

Two methods of showing scale breaks

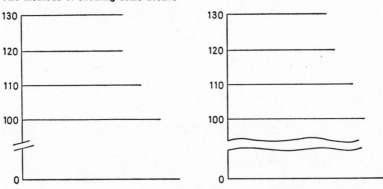

DESIGN OF THE STATISTICAL MAP

Maps may also be used to help communicate quantitative information. They are primarily useful when quantitative information is
to be compared by geographic areas. On such maps, the geographic

Figure 32. Illustration of a statistical map showing quantitative differences of areas by crosshatching

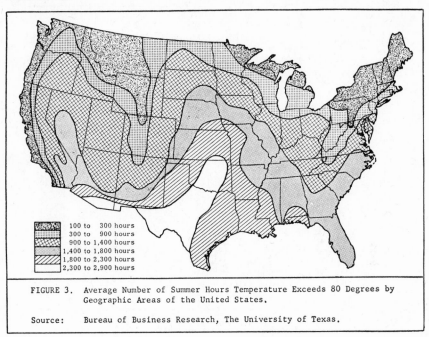

100 to   300 hours
300 to   900 hours
900 to 1,400 hours
1,400 to 1,800 hours
1,800 to 2,300 hours
2,300 to 2,900 hours

FIGURE 3.   Average Number of Summer Hours Temperature Exceeds 80 Degrees by Geographic Areas of the United States.

Source: Bureau of Business Research, The University of Texas.

Figure 33. Statistical map, showing comparisons by charts within geographic areas

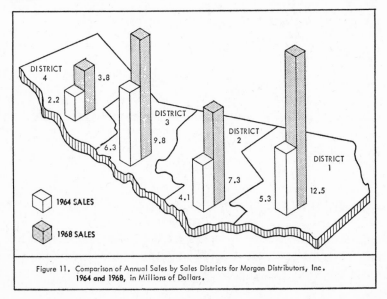

DISTRICT 4

3.8

2.2

DISTRICT 3

6.3   9.8

DISTRICT 2

7.3

4.1   5.3

DISTRICT 1

12.5

1964 SALES

1968 SALES

Figure 11. Comparison of Annual Sales by Sales Districts for Morgan Distributors, Inc.
1964 and 1968, in Millions of Dollars.

areas are clearly outlined, and the differences between areas are shown by some graphic technique. Of the numerous techniques that may be used, four are most common.

1. Possibly the most popular technique is that showing quantitative differences of areas by color, shading, or crosshatching (Figure 32). Such maps, of course, must have a legend to explain the quantitative meanings of the various colors, crosshatchings, and so on.

2. Some form of chart may be placed within each geographic area to depict the quantities representative of that area, as illustrated in Figure 33. Bar charts and pie charts are commonly used in such illustrations.

3. Placing the quantities in numerical form within each geographic area, as shown in Figure 34, is another widely used technique.

4. Dots, each representing a definite quantitiy (Figure 35), may be placed within the geographic areas in proportion to the quantities to be illustrated for each area.

CONSTRUCTION OF THE PICTOGRAM

A pictogram is a bar chart that uses pertinent pictures rather than bars to put over the information. For example, a company that seeks to graphically show its profits on the sales dollar could use a simple bar chart for the purpose. Or they could use instead of bars a line of coins equal in length to the bars. Coins may be selected because they depict the information to be illustrated. This resulting graphic form, as illustrated in Figure 36, is the pictogram.

Normally, construction of pictograms follows the general procedure used in constructing bar charts. But two special rules should be followed. First, all of the picture units used must be of equal size. The comparisons must be made wholly on the basis of the number of illustrations used and never by varying the areas of the individual pictures used. The reason for this rule is obvious. The human eye is grossly inadequate in comparing areas of geometric designs. Second, the pictures or symbols used must appropriately depict the quantity to be illustrated. A comparison of the navies of the world, for example, may make use of miniature ship drawings. Cotton production may be shown by bales of cotton. Obviously, the drawings used must be immediately interpreted by the reader.

Figure 34. Statistical map, showing quantitative differences by means of numbers placed within geographic areas

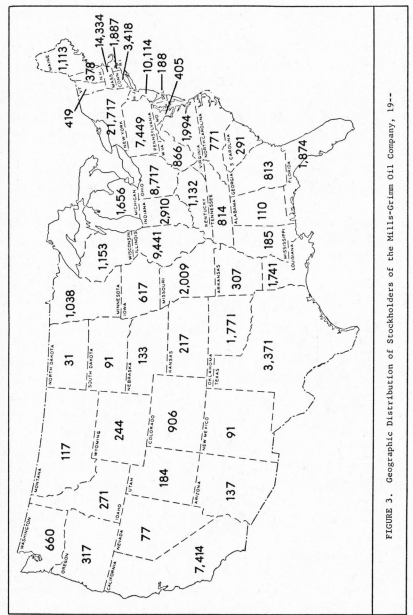

FIGURE 3. Geographic Distribution of Stockholders of the Mills-Grimm Oil Company, 19--

Figure 35. Illustration of a statistical map, using dots to show quantitative differences by geographic areas

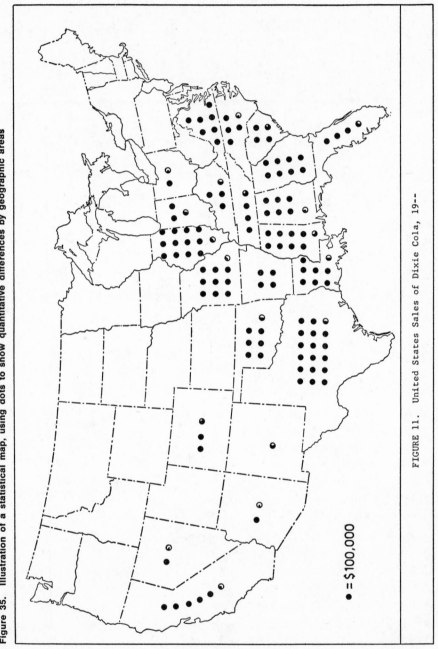

● = $100,000

FIGURE 11. United States Sales of Dixie Cola, 19--

Figure 36.   Illustration of the pictogram

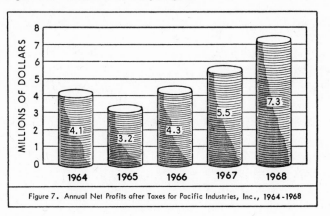

Figure 7. Annual Net Profits after Taxes for Pacific Industries, Inc., 1964-1968

MISCELLANEOUS GRAPHIC AIDS

The graphic aids discussed thus far are those most commonly used. Others are sometimes helpful in assisting in the task of communicating. Photographs and drawings may sometimes serve a useful communication purpose. Diagrams, too (see Figure 37), may help to make simple a complicated explanation or description, particularly when technological procedures are being communicated. Then there are many almost nameless types of graphic presentation, most of which are combinations of two or more of the commoner techniques. Since anything in the way of graphic design is acceptable as long as it helps to communicate the true story, the possibilities of graphic aid design are almost unlimited.

Figure 37.   Example of the use of a diagram

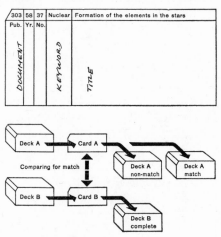

Lookup with the IBM Collator

In this system, reference cards are automatically segregated during a lookup operation. Then a bibliography may be listed directly from the cards selected.

For each keyword, there is a deck of IBM cards—one card per document indexed under that word.

When the collator finds a "match," only the card from Deck A is segregated. After the first two decks are compared, the segregated "match" cards go back into the Deck A feed and are compared with Deck C. This process continues until all decks are compared.

SOURCE: *Information Retrieval,* International Business Machines Corporation.

QUESTIONS

1. Discuss the bases for determining what graphic aids should be used in a report.
2. A report writer placed all his graphic aids in the appendix. Discuss the merits and demerits of this placement.
3. Discuss what a report writer should do to direct his reader's attention to the graphic aids. Illustrate the techniques.
4. What criterion should govern the size of a graphic aid. Justify this guideline.
5. How would you number the graphic aids in a report that has three maps, two diagrams, two charts, and five tables.
6. How would you number the graphic aids in a report that has seven charts and six tables.
7. Construct a title for a table that shows graduates of your college by major field for the past 10 years.
8. Assume that in the table prepared for question 7 you decide to use a footnote to explain that two curricula were combined in the early years covered by the report. Construct such a footnote and discuss its placement in the table.
9. Where should the titles of graphic aids be placed?
10. Distinguish between the two basic types of tables. Discuss the use of each.
11. For each of the types of graphic aids listed below, (*a*) describe its construction, (*b*) comment on what kind of information it shows best, and (*c*) give an example of some data it could present effectively.
    (1) Simple bar chart.
    (2) Multiple bar chart.
    (3) Bilateral bar chart.
    (4) Subdivided bar chart.
    (5) Pie chart.
    (6) Line chart.
    (7) Component-part line chart.
    (8) Statistical map.
    (9) Pictogram.
12. A report writer wants to present a graphic aid that shows company sales by districts and by product for the past year. (*a*) What graphic aids might he use? (*b*) Which ones should he rule out? (*c*) What is your recommendation and why?

13. What graphic aid types would be. most useful in showing total company sales, including sales by product, over a 10-year period.

14. Which of the graphic aid types would you use to show changes over a three-year period in the percentages of consumer expenditures for clothing, food, recreation, transportation, housing, and miscellaneous?

15. The writer of an annual report for a major corporation wants to use a chart to show how the company's income dollar was spent. What graphic aid form should he use?

16. What techniques may be used to show scale breaks? Why should they be used?

17. Discuss the need to take care in determining proportions on a grid.

18. What techniques may be used to show quantitative differences by area on a statistical map?

19. Discuss the strong and weak points of a pictogram.

20. *a*) What is the most appropriate graphic aid for each of the following sets of data?

   b) Defend your choices.

   c) Construct the graphic aid you select.

   (1) Percentage breakdown of assets held by United States life insurance companies for years 1949 and 1969.

Assets	1949	1969
Stocks............................	2.7	6.1
Mortgages.........................	16.8	38.1
Government bonds..................	42.5	5.8
Other bonds.......................	28.5	36.7
Other assets......................	9.5	13.3
	100.0	100.0

   (2) United States trade in steel mill products for years 1965–69, in thousands of net tons.

Year	Net Industry Shipments	Imports	Exports	Apparent Consumption
1965.............89,995		10,753	1,724	99,024
1966.............92,666		10,383	2,496	100,553
1967.............84,945		6,440	3,442	87,943
1968.............75,555		5,446	2,224	78,777
1969.............70,552		4,100	2,013	72,639

SOURCE: U.S. Department of Commerce.

(3) Share of the world's raw steel production by major consumption regions for selected years, in millions of tons.

Area	1940	1950	1965	1968
United States.....................	67	97	131	134
Western Europe...................	50	58	143	140
Eastern Europe..................	5	9	31	33
U.S.S.R..........................	20	30	100	106
Japan...........................	7	5	46	53
All others.......................	6	9	52	54
	155	208	503	520

SOURCE: American Iron and Steel Institute.

(4) Dividends paid and earnings of Howell-Mace, Inc., for years 1961–69, on per-share basis.

Year	Dividends	Earnings
1961.........................	2.00	3.16
1962.........................	2.00	2.48
1963.........................	2.00	2.64
1964.........................	2.00	2.88
1965.........................	2.10	3.10
1966.........................	2.25	2.41
1967.........................	2.40	3.78
1968.........................	2.50	3.62
1969.........................	2.55	4.03

(5) Percentage changes in sales volume by sales districts for the E. Y. Gramble Company, 1969 compared to 1968.

Sales District	Percentage Change
West Coast.........................	−11.3
Mountain..........................	+ 1.5
Southwest.........................	+18.3
Southeast..........................	− 5.1
Central............................	+ 4.7
Northeast..........................	+10.5

(6) Volume of sales by product for Baxter Cereal Company, Inc., for period 1961 to 1969, in thousands of dollars.

Year	Corn Crispies	Wheat Pops	Rice Pops	Quick Oats	Total
1961.................147		14	63	81	305
1962.................149		21	60	77	307
1963.................147		23	62	80	312
1964.................144		26	61	68	299
1965.................148		41	63	63	315
1966.................154		58	68	51	331
1967.................156		63	70	53	342
1968.................157		81	71	44	353
1969.................160		88	72	40	360

CHAPTER 14

Correctness of punctuation and grammar in reporting

The experienced report writer sees correctness in grammar and punctuation as standards that when followed will help to communicate his message. He realizes that these so-called rules of grammar and punctuation are generally accepted by learned people. More than likely, the readers of his reports will be learned people. If such people are to accept a report as coming from a learned source, the writing must conform to their standards. Thus, it stands to reason that readers of reports are apt to judge the overall standards of the writer and his work by the standards of his writing.

THE NEED FOR CORRECTNESS

The experienced writer knows, too, that his standards of writing are for the most part logical. All the conventional writing rules, he knows, serve to guard against misunderstanding and aid in presenting facts clearly and quickly. He knows that these standards have a very practical place in his work.

This practical importance of writing standards may be dramatically illustrated by any one of the numerous court cases that have centered around the changed meaning of contract words brought about by grammar or punctuation error. Possibly an even better illustration is the classic example of two sentences of directly opposing meanings. The words in the sentences are the same; only the punctuation differs. But what a difference the punctuation makes!

"The teacher," said the student, "is stupid."
The teacher said, "The student is stupid."

STANDARDS FOR CLARITY THROUGH PUNCTUATION

In the pages that follow, a review of the punctuation standards most likely to be useful to the report writer is presented. No attempt is made to include all possible points, so this presentation should in no way be considered a complete English handbook. For the finer points not included here (and every report writer at some time will run into writing situations that require such information) any one of a number of current handbooks may be consulted. The standards that follow are coded with letters and numbers that may be used as grading marks to explain the errors when they are made.

Apos 1 *Apostrophe.* The possessive case of nouns and indefinite pronouns is shown by the use of the apostrophe. If the nominative form of the word concerned does not end in *s,* an apostrophe and an *s* are added. But if the word does end in *s,* only an apostrophe is added.

Nominative form	*Possessive form*
company	company's
employee	employee's
companies	companies'
employees	employees'

However, proper names and singular nouns that end in *s* sounds are exceptions to this practice. Such words add the apostrophe and the *s* to the nominative singular; to the nominative plural, only an apostrophe is added.

Nominative form	*Possessive form*
Texas (singular)	Texas's
Joneses (plural)	Joneses'
Jones (singular)	Jones's
countess (singular)	countess's

Apos 2 The places in a contraction where letters are omitted are marked with the apostrophe.

has not = hasn't
cannot = can't
it is = it's

Apos 3 The apostrophe is used in the plural of letters, numbers, and words considered merely as words.
Examples:

There were three *17's* recorded in the final tabulation.

The first list ended with the *k's*.

If you are to achieve the conversational tone, you must use more *I's* and *you's* in your writing.

Bkts   *Brackets.*   Brackets are used to set off words the author wants to insert in a quotation. (With the typewriter, the left bracket is made by striking the diagonal, back spacing once, striking the underscore, rolling the platen up a line space, and striking the underscore again.)

Examples:

"Possibly the use of this type of supervisor [the trained correspondence expert] is still on the increase."

"At least direct supervision has gained in importance in the past decade [the report was written in 1956] during which time 43 percent of the reporting business firms that started programs have used this technique."

Cln 1   *Colon.*   The colon is used to introduce a statement of explanation, an enumeration, or a formal quotation.

Examples:

(Statement of explanation) At this time, the company was pioneering a new marketing idea: they were attempting to sell their products direct to consumers by means of vending machines.

(Enumeration) There are four classes of machinists working in this department: apprentice machinist, journeyman machinist, machinist, and first-class machinist.

(Formal quotation) President Hartung had this to say about the proposal: "Any such movement which fails to have the support of the rank-and-file worker in this plant fails to get my support."

Cln 2   The colon should not be used when the thought of the sentence should continue without interruption. If it is a list that is being introduced by a colon, the list should be in apposition to a preceding word.

Below standard: Cities in which new sales offices are in operation are: Fort Smith, Texarkana, Lake Charles, Jackson, and Biloxi.

Acceptable: Cities in which new sales offices are in operation are Fort Smith, Texarkana, Lake Charles, Jackson, and Biloxi.

Acceptable: Cities in which new sales offices are in operation are as follows: Fort Smith, Texarkana, Lake Charles, Jackson, and Biloxi.

Cln 3 Words or phrases that introduce lists, such as *namely, that is, for example,* or *i.e.,* are preceded by the colon and followed by the comma if the lists are clauses or long phrases. But a lighter mark—a dash or a comma—may precede the listing word that introduces a single item.

Example:

There is a man among us, namely Mark, who can fill the bill.

Cma 1 *Comma.* Principal clauses connected by a coordinating conjunction are separated by a comma. The coordinating conjunctions are *and, but, or, nor,* and *for.*

Examples:

Only two of the components of the index declined, and these two account for only 12 percent of the total weight of the index.
New automobiles are moving at record volumes, but used-car sales are lagging well behind the record pace set two years ago.

Exceptions may be taken to this rule, however, in the case of compound sentences made up of short and closely connected clauses.

Examples:

We sold and the price dropped.
Sometimes we profit and sometimes we lose.

Cma 2.1 Elements listed in series should be set apart by commas. In order to avoid misinterpretation in rare instances when some of the elements listed have compound constructions, it is best to place the comma between the last two items and before the final conjunction.

Examples:

Good copy must cover facts with accuracy, sincerity, honesty, and conviction.
Direct advertising can be used to introduce salesmen, fill in between salesmen's calls, cover territory where salesmen cannot be maintained, and keep pertinent reference material in the hands of prospects.
A survey conducted at the automobile show indicates that

black and cream, blue and grey, dark maroon, and black cars are favored by the public. (Note how this one illustrates the need for a comma before the final conjunction.)

Cma 2.2 Coordinate adjectives in series are separated by commas when they modify the same noun and there is no *and* connecting them. A good test to determine whether adjectives are coordinate is to insert an *and* between the words. If the *and* does not change the meaning of the expression, the words are coordinate.

Examples:

Miss Pratt has been a reliable, faithful, efficient employee for 20 years.
We guarantee that this is a good, clean car.
Light green office furniture is Mr. Orr's recommendation for the stenographic pool. (If *and* were placed between *light* and *green,* the word meaning would be changed.)
A big Dawson wrench proved to be best for the task. (The *and* won't fit between *big* and *Dawson.*)

Cma 3.1 A nonrestrictive modifier is set off from the sentence by commas. By a nonrestrictive modifier is meant a modifier that could be omitted from the sentence without changing the meaning of the sentence. Restrictive modifiers (those that restrict the words they modify to one particular object) are not set off by commas. A restrictive modifier cannot be left out of the sentence without changing the sentence meaning.

Examples:

(Restrictive) The salesman who sells the most will get a bonus. (*Who sells the most* restricts the meaning to one particular salesman.)
(Nonrestrictive) James Smithers, who was the company's top salesman for the year, was awarded a bonus. (If the clause *who was the company's top salesman for the year* is omitted, the statement is not changed.)
(Restrictive) J. Ward and Company is the firm that employs most of the physically handicapped in this area.
(Nonrestrictive) J. Ward and Company, the firm that employs most of the physically handicapped in this area, has gained the admiration of the community.

Notice how some sentences could be either restrictive or nonrestrictive, depending on the meaning intended by the writer.

Examples:

(Restrictive) All the suits that were damaged in the fire were sold at a discount. (Implies that a part of the stock was not damaged.)

(Nonrestrictive) All the suits, which were damaged by the fire, were sold at a discount. (Implies that all the stock was damaged.)

Cma 3.2 Note that *as* and *since* in their original use as time words introduce restrictive clauses and take no punctuation, but in their derived use as cause words they introduce added or nonrestrictive clauses, which require comma punctuation.

Examples:

(Restrictive—time) I have not seen him since he returned.

(Nonrestrictive—cause or reason) I shall see him Tuesday, as we shall meet at Rotary.

Cma 4.1 Parenthetic expressions are set off by commas. A parenthetic expression consists of words that interrupt the normal flow of the sentence. In a sense, they appear to be stuck in. In many instances, they are simply words out of normal order. For example, the sentence, "A full-page, black-and-white advertisement was run in the *Daily Bulletin*." contains a parenthetic expression when the word order is altered: "An advertisement, full page and in black and white, was run in the *Daily Bulletin*."

Examples:

This practice, it is believed, will lead to ruin.

The Johnston Oil Company, so the rumor goes, has cut back sharply its exploration activity.

Although the dash and the parentheses may also be used for similar reasons, the three marks differ in the degree to which they separate the enclosed words from the rest of the sentence. The comma is the weakest of the three, and it is best used when the material set off is closely related to the surrounding words. Dashes are stronger marks than commas and are used when the words set off tend to be long or contain internal punctuation marks. Parentheses, the strongest of the three, are primarily used to enclose material that helps to explain or supplement the main words of the sentence.

Cma 4.2 A comma is used to set off an appositive (a noun or a noun and its modifiers inserted to explain another noun) from the rest of the sentence. In a sense, appositives are forms of parenthetic expressions, for they do interrupt the normal flow of the sentence.

Examples:

The Baron Corporation, our machine parts supplier, is negotiating a new contract.
Saint Louis, home office of our Midwest district, will be the permanent site of our annual sales meeting.
President Carthwright, a self-educated man, is the leading advocate of our night school for employees.

But appositives that identify very closely are not set off by commas.

Examples:

The word *liabilities* is not understood by most laboring men.
Our next shipment will come on the steamship *Alberta*.

Cma 4.3 Commas are used to set off parenthetic words such as *therefore, however, in fact, of course, for example,* and *consequently.*

Examples:

It is apparent, therefore, that the buyers' resistance has been brought about by an overvigorous sales campaign.
After the first experiment, for example, the traffic flow increased 10 percent.
The company will, however, be forced to abandon the old pricing system.

Included in this group of introductory words may be interjections (*oh, alas*), and responsive expressions (*yes, no, surely, indeed, well*). But if the words are strongly exclamatory or are not closely connected with the rest of the sentence, they may be punctuated as a sentence (*No. Yes. Indeed.*).

Examples:

Yes, the decision to increase production has been made.
Oh, contribute whatever you think is adequate.

Cma 4.4 When more than one unit appears in a date or an address, the units are set off by commas.

Examples:

(One unit) December 30 is the date of our annual inventory.

(One unit) The company has one outlet in Ohio.

(More than one unit) December 30, 1906, is the date Johnston Company first opened its doors.

(More than one unit) Richmond, Virginia, is the headquarters of the new sales district.

Cma 5.1 Subordinate clauses that precede main clauses are usually set off by commas.

Examples:

Although it is durable, this package does not have eye appeal.

Since there was little store traffic on aisle 13, the area was converted into office space.

Cma 5.2 Introductory verbal phrases are usually followed by a comma. A verbal phrase is one that contains some verb derivative—a gerund, a participle, or an infinitive.

Examples:

(Participle phrase) Realizing his mistake, the foreman instructed his men to keep a record of all salvaged equipment.

(Gerund phrase) After gaining the advantage, we failed to press on to victory.

(Infinitive phrase) To increase our turnover of automobile accessories, we must first improve our display area.

Cma 6.1 The comma is used only for good reason. It is not a mark to be used indiscriminately at the whims of the writer. As a rule, use of commas should always be justified by one of the standard practices previously noted.

Cma 6.1.1 Do not be tripped into putting a comma between subject and verb.

Example:

The thought that he could not afford to fail, spurred him on.

Cma 6.1.2 Ordinarily, do not set off the second element of a compound predicate with the comma. (The compound predicate is usually a weak and unemphatic structure and needs recasting instead of bolstering with an apologetic comma.)

Cma 6.2 The only exception to the preceding notes should be in instances where clarity of expression may be helped by the insertion of a comma.

Examples:

From the beginning inventory methods of Hill Company have been haphazard. (not clear)

From the beginning, inventory methods of Hill Company have been haphazard. (clear)

Dsh   *Dash.* The dash may be used to set off an element for emphasis or to show interrupted thought. Particularly is it used with long parenthetic expressions or those containing internal punctuation. With the typewriter, the dash is made by striking the hyphen twice without spacing before or after.

Examples:

Budgets for some past years—1955, for example—were prepared without consulting the department heads.

The test proved that the new process is simple, effective, accurate—and more expensive.

Only one person—the foreman in charge—has authority to issue such an order.

If you want a voice in the government—vote.

Ex   *Exclamation mark.* The exclamation point is used at the end of a sentence or an exclamatory fragment to show strong emotion. This mark should be used sparingly; never should it be used with trivial ideas.

Examples:

We've done it again!

No! It can't be!

Hpn 1   *Hyphen.* Division of a word at the end of a line is indicated by the hyphen. The division must be made between syllables. It is generally impractical to leave a one-letter syllable at the end of a line (a-bove) or to carry over a two-letter syllable to the next line (expens-es).

Hpn 2   Hyphens are placed between the parts of some compound words. Generally, the hyphen is used whenever its absence would confuse the meaning of the words. Words hyphenated are of these groups.

Compound nouns: *brother-in-law, cure-all, city-state.*

Compound numbers under one hundred and above twenty: *thirty-one, fifty-five, seventy-seven.*

Compound adjectives (two or more words used before a noun as a single adjective): *long-term* contract, *fifty-gallon* drum, *door-to-door* selling, *end-of-month* clearance.

Prefixes (most have been absorbed into the word): *vice-president, ex-chairman, preexamine, antilabor.*

Hpn 2.1   A proper name used as a compound adjective needs no hyphen or hyphens to hold it together as a visual unit for the reader: the capitals perform that function.

Examples:

A Lamar High School student (correct).
A junior-high-school student (correct).

Hpn 2.2   Two or more modifiers in normal grammatical form and order need no hyphens. Particularly, a phrase that consists of an unmistakable adverb (one ending in *ly*), modifying an adjective or participle, which in turn modifies a noun, shows normal grammatical order and is readily grasped by the reader without the aid of the hyphen. But an adverb that does not end in *ly* should be joined to its adjective or participle by the hyphen.

Examples:

A poorly drawn chart (no hyphen needed).
A well-prepared chart (use the hyphen).

Ital 1   For the use of italics to set out book titles see QM 4 and QM 4.1 Note that this device is also used to set out names of periodicals, of works of art or music, and of naval vessels and aircraft.

Ital 2   Foreign words and abbreviations thereof should be italicized—if you must use them. Italicize standard foreign (usually Latin) words and abbreviations used in footnotes and book references. This list includes:

circa, c. (about)
et al. (and others)
ibidem, ibid. (in the same place)
idem (the same)
infra (below)
supra (above)

loco citato, loc. cit. (in the place cited)
opere citato, op. cit. (in the work cited)
passim (here and there)
sic (so, thus)
quod vide, q.v. (which see)

But the commonly used versus, or vs., or v. has become anglicized and needs no underscoring.

Ital 3   Italicizing a word, letter, or figure used as its own name or as a physical unit, instead of as a symbol of an idea, is a prime requisite for clearness. Without this device, we could not write this set of rules. Note the use of italics throughout to label name words.

Examples:

The little word *sell* is still in the dictionary.
The pronoun *which* should always have a noun as a clear antecedent. (Try reading that one without the italics: it becomes a fragment ending in midair!)

Ital 4 If your entire passage is already italicized or underlined (as a caption underlined for emphasis), how shall you distinguish a title, a foreign word, or a word normally italicized? Your best resort is to shift back to the roman type, or in typing to *omit* the underline.

Paren *Parentheses.* Parentheses may be used to set off words that are parenthetic or are inserted to explain or to supplement the principal message (see Cma 4.1).

Examples:

Dr. Samuel Goppard's phenomenal prediction (*Business Week,* June 20, 1956) has made some business forecasters revise their techniques.
Smith was elected chairman (the vote was almost two to one), and immediately he introduced his plan for reorganization.

Pd *Period.* The period is primarily used to indicate the end of a declarative sentence. But it does have some other vital uses.

Pd 1 After all abbreviations or initials the period is used. Examples: Ph.D., Co., Inc., A.M., A.D., etc.

Pd 2 The ellipsis (a series of periods) may be used to indicate the omission of words from a quoted passage. If the omitted part consists of something less than a paragraph, three periods are customarily placed at the place of omission (a fourth period is added if the omission comes at the sentence end). If the omitted part is a paragraph or more, however, a full line of periods is used. In either case, the periods are appropriately typed with intervening spaces.

Example:

Logical explanations, however, have been given by authorities in the field. Some attribute the decline . . . to the changing economy in the state during recent years. . . .

. . . .

Added to the labor factor is the high cost of raw material, which has tended to eliminate many marginal producers. Too, the rising cost of electric power in recent years may have shifted many of the industry leaders' attention to other forms of production.

Q *Question mark.* Sentences that are direct questions are ended with the question mark.

Examples:

What are the latest quotations on Ewing-Bell common stock?
Will this campaign help to sell Dunnco products?

Note, however, that the question mark is not used with indirect questions.

Examples:

The president was asked whether this campaign will help to sell Dunnco products.
He asked me what were the latest quotations on Ewing-Bell common stock.

QM 1 *Quotation mark.* Quotation marks are used to enclose the exact words of a speaker or, if the quotation is short, the exact words of a writer.

By short written quotations is meant something four lines or less. Longer quoted passages are best displayed with additional right and left margins (see Chapter 12), in single spacing (where double spacing has been used in the text), and without quotation marks.

Examples:

H. C. McVoy sums up his presentation with this statement: "All signs indicate that automation will be evolutionary, not revolutionary." (short written passage)
"This really should bring on a production slowdown," said Mr. Kuntz. (verbal quotation)

If the quoted words are broken by explanation or reference words, each quoted part is enclosed in quotation marks.

Example:

"Will you be specific," he said, "in recommending a course of action?"

QM 2 A quotation within a quotation is indicated by single quotation marks (' ').

Example:

President Carver said, "It has been a long time since I have heard an employee say 'Boss, I'm going to beat my quota today.'"

QM 3 Periods and commas are always placed inside quotation marks. Semicolons and colons always are outside the marks. Question marks and exclamation points are inside if they apply to the quoted passage and outside if they apply to the whole sentence.

Examples:

"If we are patient," he said, "prosperity will some day arrive." (comma within quotes, period within quotes)
"Is there a quorum?" he asked. (The question mark belongs to the quoted passage.)
Which of you said, "I know where the error lies"? (The question mark applies to the entire sentence.)
I conclude only this from the union's promise to "force the hand of management": violence will be their trump card. (The colon is not a part of the quotation.)

QM 4 Titles of the parts of a publication (articles in a magazine, chapters in a book, etc.) are enclosed in quotation marks. Titles of a whole publication, however, are placed in italics. Italics in typewritten material are indicated by underscoring.

Examples:

The third chapter of the book *Elementary Statistical Procedure* is entitled "Concepts of Sampling."
John Glasgow's most recent article, "A Union Boss Views Automation," appears in the current issue of *Fortune*.

SC 1 *Semicolon.* Clauses of a compound sentence that are not joined by a conjunction are separated by a semicolon.

Examples:

Cork or asbestos sheeting must be hand-cut; polyurethane may be poured into a mold.
The new contract provides substantial wage increases; the original contract emphasized shorter hours.

Covered by this standard are main clauses connected by conjunctive adverbs. Conjunctive adverbs are really not conjunctions, but are such words as *however, nevertheless, therefore, then, moreover, besides,* and so on.

Examples:

The survey findings indicated a need to revise the policy; nevertheless, the president vetoed the amendment.

Small-town buyers favor the old models; therefore, the board concluded that both models should be manufactured.

SC 1.1 Standard lists of "weak" connectives of independent clauses include the little words *so, also, hence, yet,* and *still,* and such introductory phrases as *that is, in fact, in other words,* and the like. The test of their weakness as connectives is that to perform a complete conjunctive function these words or phrases each need the support of a coordinating conjunction (*and therefore, and so, and yet, and still, but nevertheless, or in other words*). With the coordinating conjunctions, these forms would take comma punctuation, naturally; but standing alone they need the semicolon support.

SC 1.2 Note that *so that* introducing a dependent clause of purpose ("They incorporated so that they might limit liability") needs no punctuation mark because its clause is always restrictive.

SC 2 Independent clauses connected by a coordinating conjunction (*and, but, or, for, nor*) may be separated by a semicolon if the clauses are long or have internal punctuation. Sometimes, short compound sentences with coordinating conjunctions are separated in order to achieve special emphasis. The purpose of this practice is to help the reader see the break between clauses by not allowing him to be misled by the other punctuation marks.

Examples:

The FTU and the IFL, rivals from the beginning of the new industry, have shared almost equally in the growth of membership; but the FTU predominates among workers in the petroleum-products crafts, including pipeline construction and operation, and the IFL leads in memberships of chemical workers.

The market price was four dollars; but we paid seven.

SC 3 Elements in a series that contains internal commas are separated by semicolons.

Examples:

The following gains were made in the February year-to-year comparison: Fort Worth, 7,300; Dallas, 4,705; Lubbock, 2,610; San Antonio, 2,350; Waco, 2,240; Port Arthur, 2,170; and Corpus Christi, 1,420.

Elected for the new term were Amos T. Zelnak, attorney from Cincinnati; Wilbur T. Hoffmeister, stockbroker and president of Hoffmeister Associates of Baltimore; and William P. Peabody, a member of the faculty of the University of Georgia.

SC 4   Use the semicolon between coordinate units only. Do not use it to attach a dependent clause or phrase to an independent clause.

SC 5   Use punctuation marks in consistent echelons of descent—major marks for major units, smaller marks for smaller ones. Do not mix them or reverse them. To use a semicolon, colon, or dash as internal punctuation within a clause or unit already set off by commas is illogical and confusing.

> *Not this:*   His itinerary, which included New York; Portland, Main; Springfield, Ohio; and Chicago, was revised by the sales manager.
>
> *But this:*   [You'd better recast the whole thing, but this would do.] His itinerary, which included New York, Portland (Maine), Springfield (Ohio), and Chicago, was revised. . . .

Be careful also not to start a parenthetical expression with one mark and end it with another.

STANDARDS FOR CORRECTNESS IN GRAMMAR

Maintaining high standards of grammar is vital to the report writer who desires to excel at his work. Although it is not always necessary that high standards of grammar be followed in order to communicate, little can be said in favor of abandoning these standards. To illustrate, the statement "He ain't never done nothing to nobody" has little chance of not communicating its message. But doesn't it communicate more than the message intended? Doesn't it also communicate some idea about the intellectual level of the writer? Certainly, such impressions would not help the communication of a typical report.

As with the review of punctuation standards, the following summary of grammar standards is not intended to be a complete handbook on the subject. Rather, it is a summary of the major trouble spots encountered by most report writers. Mastery of these grammar principles would almost assure the report writer of achieving the high standards vital to the communication of his report.

AA *Adjective–adverb confusion.* Adjectives should not be used for adverbs, nor should adverbs be used for adjectives. Adjectives modify only nouns and pronouns, and adverbs modify verbs, adjectives, or other adverbs.

Possibly the chief source of this confusion is in statements when the modifier follows the verb. If the modifier refers to the subject, an adjective should be used. If it limits the verb, an adverb is needed.

Below standard: She filed the records *quick.*
Acceptable: She filed the records *quickly.* (Refers to the verb.)
Below standard: John doesn't feel *badly.*
Acceptable: John doesn't feel *bad.* (Refers to the noun.)
Below standard: The new cars look *beautifully.*
Acceptable: The new cars look *beautiful.* (Refers to the noun.)

It should be noted that many words are both adjective and adverb (*little, well, fast, much*). And some adverbs have two forms: one form is the same as the adjective, and the other adds the *ly* (*slow* and *slowly, cheap* and *cheaply, quick* and *quickly*).

Acceptable: All our drivers are instructed to drive *slow.*
Acceptable: All our drivers are instructed to drive *slowly.*

Agmt SV *Subject–verb agreement.* Nouns and their verbs must agree in number. A plural noun must have a plural verb form; a singular noun must have a singular verb.

Below standard: Expenditures for miscellaneous equipment *was* expected to decline. (*Expenditures* is plural, so its verb must be plural.)
Acceptable: Expenditures for miscellaneous equipment *were* expected to decline.
Below Standard: The *president,* as well as his staff, *were* not able to attend. (*President* is the subject, and the number is not changed by the modifying phrase.)
Acceptable: The *president,* as well as his staff, *was* not able to attend.

Compound subjects (two or more nouns joined by *and*) require plural verbs.

Below standard: The *welders and* their *foreman* is in favor of the proposal. (*Welders* and *foreman* are compound subjects of the verb, but *is* is singular.)

Acceptable: The *welders and* their *foreman are* in favor of the proposal.

Below standard: Received in the morning delivery *was* a *typewriter and* two *reams* of letterhead paper. (*Reams* and *typewriter* are the subjects; the verb must be plural.)

Acceptable: Received in the morning delivery *were* a *typewriter and* two *reams* of letterhead paper.

Collective nouns may be either singular or plural, depending on the meaning intended.

Acceptable: The *committee have* carefully *studied* the proposal. (*Committee* is thought of as separate individuals.)

Acceptable: The *committee has* carefully *studied* the proposal. (The *committee* is considered as a unit.)

As a rule, the pronouns *anybody, anyone, each, either, everyone, everybody, neither, nobody, somebody,* and *someone* take a singular verb. The word *none* may be either singular or plural, depending on whether it is used to refer to a unit or to more than a unit.

Acceptable: Either of the advertising campaigns *is* costly.
Acceptable: Nobody who watches the clock *is successful.*

AN   Do not use an adverbial clause as a noun clause. Clauses beginning with *because, when, where, if,* and similar adverbial connectives are not properly used as subjects, objects, or complements of verbs.

Not this:	He did not know *if* he could go or not.
But this:	He did not know *whether* he could go or not.
Not this:	The reason was *because* he did not submit a report.
But this:	The reason was *that* he did not submit a report.
Not this:	A time-series graph is *where* [or *when*] changes in an index such as wholesale prices are indicated . . .
But this:	A time-series graph is the picturing of . . .

Awk   *Awkward.*   Awkward writing attracts attention to its structure and should be avoided. Writing is awkward when its word arrangement is unconventional or uneconomical, or simply not the best for quick understanding.

Dng   *Dangling modifiers.*   Avoid the use of modifiers that do not logically modify a word in the sentence. Such modifiers are said to dangle. They are both illogical and confusing. Usually, sentences that contain dangling constructions can be corrected in either of two ways: the noun or pronoun the modifier describes may be inserted, or the dangling element may be changed to a complete clause.

> *Below standard:* Believing that the credit customers should have advance notice of the sale, special letters were mailed to them.
> *Acceptable:* Believing that the credit customers should have advance notice of the sale, we mailed special letters to them. (Improvement is made by inserting the pronoun modified.)
> *Acceptable:* Because we believed that the credit customer should have advance notice of the sale, we mailed special letters to them. (Improvement is made by changing the dangling element to a complete clause.)

Dangling modifiers are of four principal types: participial phrases, elliptical clauses, gerund phrases, and infinitive phrases.

> *Below standard:* Believing that District 7 was not being thoroughly covered, an additional salesman was assigned to the area. (Dangling participial phrase.)
> *Acceptable:* Believing that District 7 was not being thoroughly covered, the sales manager assigned an additional salesman to the area.
> *Below standard:* After hearing his convincing arguments, my vote was changed. (Dangling gerund phrase.)
> *Acceptable:* After hearing his convincing arguments, I changed my vote.
> *Below standard:* To succeed at this job, long hours and hard work must not be shunned. (Dangling infinitive phrase.)
> *Acceptable:* To succeed at this job, one must not shun long hours and hard work.
> *Below standard:* While waiting on a customer, the radio was stolen. (Dangling elliptical clause—a clause without noun or verb.)
> *Acceptable:* While the salesman was waiting on a customer, the radio was stolen.

There are, however, a few generally accepted introductory phrases that are permitted to dangle. Included in this group are *generally speaking, confidentially speaking, taking all things into consideration,* and such expressions as *in boxing, in welding,* and *in farming.*

Acceptable: Generally speaking, business activity is at an all-time high.

Acceptable: In farming, the land must be prepared long before planting time.

Acceptable: Taking all things into consideration, this applicant is the best for the job.

Frag *Sentence fragment.* The sentence fragment should be avoided. Although it may sometimes be used for effect, as in sales writing, it is best omitted by all but the skilled writer. The sentence fragment consists of any group of words that cannot stand up alone as a complete and independent statement. Probably the most frequent violation of this rule results from the use of a subordinate clause as a sentence.

Below standard: Believing that you will want an analysis of sales for November. We have sent you the figures.

Acceptable: Believing that you will want an analysis of sales for November, we have sent you the figures.

Below standard: He declared that such procedure would not be practical. And that it would be too expensive in the long run.

Acceptable: He declared that such procedure would not be practical and that it would be too expensive in the long run.

Pn 1 *Pronoun.* The antecedent of all pronouns should be unmistakably clear. Failure to conform to this standard is likely to bring about confusion. Particularly is confusion likely to come about in sentences when two or more nouns are possible antecedents of the pronoun or when the antecedent is far removed from the pronoun.

Below standard: When the president objected to Mr. Carter, he told him to mind his own business. (Who told whom?)

Acceptable: When the president objected to Mr. Carter, Mr. Carter told him to mind his own business.

Below standard: The mixture should not be allowed to boil; so when you do it, watch the temperature gauge. (*It* doesn't have an antecedent.)

Acceptable: The mixture should not be allowed to boil; so when conducting the experiment, watch the temperature gauge.

Below standard: The Model V is being introduced this year. Ads in *Life, The Saturday Evening Post,* and big-city newspapers over the country are designed to get sales off to a good start. It is especially designed for the novice boatman who is not willing to pay a big price.

Acceptable: The Model V is being introduced this year. Ads in *Life, The Saturday Evening Post,* and big-city newspapers over the country are designed to get sales off to a good start. The new model is especially designed for the novice boatman who is not willing to pay a big price.

Confusion may sometimes result from using a pronoun with an implied antecedent.

Below standard: Because of the disastrous freeze in the citrus belt, it is necessary that most of them be replanted.

Acceptable: Because of the disastrous freeze in the citrus belt, it is necessary that most of the citrus orchards be replanted.

Except when their reference is perfectly clear, it is best to avoid using the pronouns *which, that,* and *this* to refer to a whole idea of a preceding clause. Many times, the sentence can be made clear by use of a clarifying noun following the pronoun.

Below standard: (Following a detailed presentation of the writer's suggestion for improving the company suggestion-box plan.) This should be put into effect without delay.

Acceptable: This suggestion-box plan should be put into effect right away.

Pn 2   The number of the pronoun should agree with the number of its antecedent. If the antecedent is singular, its pronoun must be singular. If the antecedent is plural, its pronoun must be plural.

Below standard: Taxes and insurance are necessary evils in any business, and it must be considered carefully in anticipating profits.

Acceptable: Taxes and insurance are necessary evils in any business, and they must be considered carefully in anticipating profits.

Below standard: Everybody should make plans for their retirement. (Words like *everyone, everybody, anybody* are singular.)

Acceptable: Everybody should make plans for his retirement.

Pn 3   Care should be taken to use the correct case of the pronoun. If the pronoun serves as the subject of the verb, or if it follows a form of the infinitive *to be,* a nominative case pronoun should be used. (Nominative case of the personal pronouns is *I, you, he, she, it, we, they.*)

Acceptable: He will record the minutes of the meeting.
Acceptable: I think that it will be he.

If the pronoun is the object of a preposition or a verb, or if it is the subject of an infinitive, the objective case should be used. (Objective case for the personal pronouns is *me, you, him, her, us, them.*)

Below standard: This transaction is between you and *he*. (But *he* is nominative and cannot be the object of the preposition *between*.)
Acceptable: This transaction is between you and *him*.
Below standard: Because the investigator praised Mr. Smith and *I*, we were promoted.
Acceptable: Because the investigator praised Mr. Smith and *me*, we were promoted.

The case of relative pronouns (*who, whom*) is determined by the pronoun's use in the clause it introduces. One good way of determining which case should be used is to substitute the personal pronoun for the relative pronoun. If the case of the personal pronoun that fits is nominative, *who* should be used. If it is objective, *whom* should be used.

Acceptable: George Cutler is the salesman who won the award. (*He* [nominative] could be substituted for the relative pronoun; therefore, nominative *who* should be used.)
Acceptable: George Cutler is the salesman *whom* you recommended. (Objective case *him* would substitute. Thus, objective case *whom* is used.)

Usually, the possessive case is used with substantives that immediately precede a gerund (verbal noun ending in *ing*).

Acceptable: Our selling of the stock frightened some of the conservative members of the board.
Acceptable: His accepting the money ended his legal claim to the property.

Prl *Parallelism.* Parts of a sentence that are used to express parallel thoughts should be parallel in grammatical form. Parallel constructions are logically connected by the coordinating conjunctions *and, but,* and *or.* Care should be taken to see that the sentence elements connected by these conjunctions are of the same grammatical type. That is, if one of the parts is a noun, so should the other parts be nouns. If one of the parts is an infinitive phrase, so should the other parts be infinitive phrases.

> *Below standard:* The company objectives for the coming year are to match last year's production, higher sales, and improving consumer relations.
> *Acceptable:* The company objectives for the coming year are to match last year's production, to increase sales, and to improve consumer relations.
> *Below standard:* Writing copy may be more valuable experience than to make layouts.
> *Acceptable:* Writing copy may be more valuable experience than making layouts.
> *Below standard:* The questionnaire asks for this information: number of employees, what is our union status, and how much do we pay.
> *Acceptable:* The questionnaire asks for this information: number of employees, union affiliation, and pay scale.

Prl 1   After each member of a correlating pair of conjunctions (either . . . or . . . , both . . . and . . . , not only . . . but also . . . ,) use exactly the same grammatical form.

Prl 2   Comparisons in particular need to be kept on consistent bases. Do not fall into the ditch of jargonese shortcuts.

Prl 3   Avoid the faulty parallelism of the illogical *and which* construction. Do not tie a lone relative clause to the main clause with *and*, as if it were parallel with a minor adjective, participial modifier, or implied quality.
  Examples:

He warned of the high and frightening cost-of-living index, and which is still rising.

  Better:

He warned of the cost-of-living index, which is frighteningly high and which is still rising.

  Or:

He warned that the frighteningly high cost-of-living index is still rising.

Tns   *Tense of verb, infinitive, and participle.*   The tense of each verb, infinitive, and participle used should reflect the logical time of happening of the statement: every statement has its place in time. If this place in time is to be exactly communicated, the writer must take care in his selection of tense. Even though tense usually is determined by the subject of the statement being reported, a few trouble spots may be mentioned.

Tns 1 Statements of facts that are true at the time of writing should be worded in the present tense.

> *Below standard:* Boston was not selected as a site for the aircraft plant because it *was* too near the coast. (Boston still is near the coast, isn't it?)
> *Acceptable:* Boston was not selected as a site for the aircraft plant because it *is* too near the coast.

Tns 2 Past tense is used in statements that cover a definite past event or action.

> *Below standard:* Mr. Burns *says* to me, "Bill, you'll never make an auditor."
> *Acceptable:* Mr. Burns *said* to me, "Bill, you'll never make an auditor."

Tns 3 The time period reflected by the past participle (*having been . . .*) is earlier than that of its governing verb. For the present participle (*being . . .*), the time period reflected is the same as that of the governing verb.

> *Below standard:* These debentures are among the oldest on record, *being* issued early in 1937.
> *Acceptable:* These debentures are among the oldest on record, *having been* issued in early 1937.
> *Below standard:* Mr. Sloan, *having been* the top salesman on the force, was made sales manager. (Possible but illogical.)
> *Acceptable:* Mr. Sloan, *being* the top salesman on the force, was made sales manager.

Tns 4 Verbs in subordinate clauses are governed by the verb in the principal clause. When the main verb is in the past tense, usually the subordinate verb must also be in a past tense (past, present perfect, or past perfect). Thus, if the time of the subordinate clause is the same as that of the main verb, past tense is used.

> *Acceptable:* I *noticed* (past tense) the discrepancy, and then I *remembered* (same time as main verb) the incidents that caused it.

If the time of the subordinate clause is previous to that of the main verb in past tense, past perfect tense is used for the subordinate verb.

Below standard: In early July, we *noticed* (past) that he *exceeded* (logically should be previous to main verb) his quota three times.

Acceptable: In early July, we *noticed* that he *had exceeded* his quota three times.

The present perfect tense is used for the subordinate clause when the time of this clause is subsequent to the main verb.

Below standard: Before the war, we *contributed* (past) generously, but lately we *forget* (should be time subsequent to main verb) our duties.

Acceptable: Before the war we *contributed* generously, but lately we *have forgotten* our duties.

Tns 5   The present perfect tense does not logically refer to a definite time in the past. Instead, it indicates time somewhere in the indefinite past.

Below standard: We *have audited* your records on July 31 of 1968 and 1969.

Acceptable: We *audited* your records on July 31 of 1968 and 1969.

Acceptable: We *have audited* your records twice in the past.

WU   *Word Use.* Misused words call attention to themselves and detract from the writing. Although the possibilities of error in word use are infinite, the following list contains a few of the most common ones.

Don't Use	*Use*
a long ways	a long way
and etc.	etc.
anywheres	anywhere
different than	different from
have got to	must
in back of	behind
in hopes of	in hope of
in regards to	in regard to
inside of	within
kind of satisfied	somewhat satisfied
nowhere near	not nearly

Don't Use	*Use*
nowheres	nowhere
off of	off
over with	over
seldom ever	seldom
try and come	try to come

STANDARDS FOR THE USE OF NUMBERS

Quantities may be spelled out or they may be expressed in numeral form. Whether to use one form or the other is often a perplexing question, especially is it perplexing to the business report writer, for much of his work is with quantitative subjects. Because the means of expressing quantities is so vital to the business report writer, the following notes on the use of numbers is presented.

No *Numbers.* Although authorities do not agree on number usage, the report writer would do well to follow the rule of ten. By this rule, one spells out numbers ten and below. He uses figures for numbers above ten.

> *Correct:* The auditor found 13 discrepancies in the stock records.
> *Correct:* The auditor found nine discrepancies in the stock records.

As with most rules, this one has exceptions.

No 1 An exception to the rule of ten is made when a number begins a sentence. In this position, the number is spelled out regardless of size.

> *Correct:* Seventy-three bonds were destroyed.
> *Correct:* Eighty-nine men picketed the north entrance.

No 2 In comparisons, it is best to keep all numbers in the same form. The form used should be the one that, according to the rule of ten, would be used most often in the series.

> *Correct:* We managed to salvage three lathes, one drill, and thirteen welding machines.
> *Correct:* Sales increases over last year were 9 percent on automotive parts, 14 percent on hardware, and 23 percent on appliances.

No 3 When two series of numbers appear in one sentence, one should be spelled out and the other should be in numeral form.

> *Correct:* Three salesmen exceeded $1,500, fourteen exceeded $1,000, and thirty-one exceeded $500.

No 4 Days of the month are typed in figure form when they are preceded by the month.

> *Correct:* July 3, 1969.

When they appear alone or when they precede the month, the days of the month may be either spelled out or in numeral form, according to the rule of ten.

> *Correct:* I shall be there on the 13th.
> *Correct:* The union scheduled the strike vote for the eighth.
> *Correct:* Mr. Millican signed the contract on the seventh of July.
> *Correct:* Sales have declined since the 14th of August.

QUESTIONS

Correct any punctuation or grammar errors you can find in the following sentences. Explain your corrections.

1. Charles E. Baskin the new member of the advisory committee has been an employee for seven years.
2. The auditor asked us, "If all members of the work group had access to the petty cash fund?"
3. Our January order consisted of the following items; two dozen Norwood desk calendars, note size, one dozen desk blotters, 20 by 32 inches, and one dozen bottles of ink, permanent black.
4. The truth of the matter is, that the union representative had not informed the workers of the decision.
5. Sales for the first quarter were the highest in history, profits declined for the period.
6. We suggest that you use a mild soap for best reuslts but detergents will not harm the product.
7. Employment for October totaled 12,714 an increase of 3.1 percent over September.
8. It would not be fair however to consider only this point.
9. It is the only water-repellant snag-proof and inexpensive material available.
10. Henry Thatcher a supervisor in our company is accused of the crime.
11. Mr. Goodman made this statement, "Contrary to our expectations, Smith and Company will lose money this year."
12. I bought and he sold.
13. Soon we saw George Sweeny who is the auditor for the company.

14. Manufactured in light medium and heavy weights this razor has been widely accepted.

15. Because of a common belief that profits are too high we will have to cut our prices on most items.

16. Such has been the growth of the cities most prestigeous firm, H. E. Klauss and Company.

17. In 1968 we were advised in fact we were instructed to accept this five year contract.

18. Henrys playing around has got him into trouble.

19. Cyrus B. Henshaw who was our leading salesman last month is the leading candidate for the position.

20. The worker who completes the most units will receive a bonus.

21. The word 'phone which is short for telephone should be avoided in formal writing.

22. In last month's issue of Modern Businessman appeared Johnson's latest article What Systems Theory Means to You.

23. Yes he replied this is exactly what we mean.

24. Why did he say John it's too late?

25. Place your order today, it is not too late.

26. We make our plans on a day to day basis.

27. There is little accuracy in the 60 day forecast.

28. The pre Christmas sale will extend over twenty six days.

29. We cannot tolerate any worker's failure to do their duty.

30. An assortment of guns, bombs, burglar tools, and ammunition were found in the cellar.

31. If we can be certain that we have the facts we can make our decision soon.

32. This one is easy to make. If one reads the instructions carefully.

33. This is the gift he received from you and I.

34. A collection of short articles on the subject were printed.

35. If we can detect only a tenth of the errors it will make us realize the truth.

36. She takes shorthand good.

37. There was plenty of surprises at the meeting.

38. It don't appear that we have made much progress.

39. The surface of these products are smooth.

40. Everybody is expected to do their best.

41. The brochures were delivered to John and I early Sunday morning.

42. Who did he recommend for the job.

43. We were given considerable money for the study.

44. He seen what could happen when administration breaks down.

45. One of his conclusions is that the climate of the region was not desirable for our purposes.

46. Smith and Rogers plans to buy the Bridgeport plant.

47. The committee feels that no action should be taken.

48. Neither of the workers found their money.

49. While observing the workers, the assembly line was operating at peak perfection.

50. The new building is three stories high, fifteen years old, solid brick construction, and occupies a corner lot.

51. They had promised to have completed the job by noon.

52. Jones has been employed by the Sampson Company for twenty years.

53. Wilson and myself will handle the job.

54. Each man and woman are expected to abide by this rule.

55. The boiler has been inspected on April 1 and May 3.

56. To find problems and correcting them takes up most of my work time.

57. The carton of canned goods were distributed to the workers.

58. The motor ran uneven.

59. All are expected except John and she.

60. Everyone here has more ability than him.

A report checklist

The following list of the most common violations in report construction may serve two purposes. First, it may be useful as a guide to one preparing a report. Second, it may serve as a convenient grading aid. As a grading aid, it permits the grader to point out violations merely by writing symbols rather than by writing out longhand comments. Although the checklist covers the longer, more formal types of reports, it can easily be adapted to other forms.

1. *Report title*
    a) Is this title complete? The title should tell the reader what he may expect to find in the contents, and it should rule out what he may not expect to find. Although requirements differ with the case, these aspects of the problem should be considered in constructing the title.
        (1) Who.
        (2) What.
        (3) Where.
        (4) When.
        (5) Why.
        (6) How.
    b) This title is too long. Try to be more economical with words.
    c) This title is too short. A scant title is broad and usually covers too much ground.
    d) In typing the title, break it at convenient breaking points—that is, at the ends of thought units rather than in the middle of thought units.

2. *Title page*
    a) For best optical effect, center the parts between left and right margins. Here the lines are off center.
    b) Too much or too little space between the parts detracts from the

appearance of the page. Check the text illustrations for better placement of the parts.

c) For better balance, use (1) fewer and longer lines (by combining some of the items) or (2) more and shorter lines.

d) Check this part for completeness. Usually, the recipient and the writer should be identified by name, title, company or organization, and address.

e) Date the report specifically—by month, day, and year, if possible, but at least by year.

f) Preferably single space units of three lines or less. Double space longer units.

3. *General layout and mechanics*

a) Fit the layout of the page to the space available (see instructions in Chapter 11). This page is:
(1) Too fat.
(2) Too low, high, or off-center (as marked).
(3) Too tall and thin.

b) Neat typing? Strikeovers, smudges, and erasures detract from the report's message.

c) Keep the right margins relatively straight. Successive lines falling under or over the right margin boundary offend the eye.

d) The spacing could be improved here.
(1) Too much space used here.
(2) Not enough space here.

e) Follow the conventional system of page numbering.
(1) Use small Roman figures (i, ii, etc.) for the prefatory pages.
(2) Use Arabic figures (1, 2, etc.) for all other pages.
(3) No numbers are needed on the pages preceding the table of contents. But these pages are counted in the numbering sequence.

f) This page is choppy. Consider lengthening or combining the paragraphs for more logical organization and better appearance.

g) This page is too heavy. Consider breaking down these paragraphs into shorter ones.

h) Your system of captioning could be improved. The captions should tell the reader at a glance the relative importance of each part. Better check the instructions in Chapter 11.

i) Don't let a caption appear at the bottom of the page without at least two lines of text. Captions placed this way appear to be headings to nothing.

4. *Letter of transmittal*

a) Begin the letter with a direct presentation of the report. The primary objective of the letter is to transmit the report, and there is no reason for delaying the message with slow explanation or other material.

b) Refer incidentally to the authorization by date and nature (oral, written) somewhere early in the letter.

c) (For combination transmittal-synopsis letters.) Move smoothly into a review of the highlight facts and conclusions of the report. (For additional checklist points on this type of letter, use the appropriate notes under item 5.)

d) (For letters that do not serve also as a synopsis.) A digest of the report findings is better left for the synopsis.

e) Your choice of subject matter for the letter could be improved. Perhaps the best choice is some appropriate talk about the report—comments that will help the reader to understand or appreciate the report.

f) A statement of your personal attitude toward the assignment is appropriate. It may well come at the close of the letter.

g) Make this part sound more sincere. It is easy to overdo words of appreciation, and it is easy to make them sound like rubber stamps. You are most likely to avoid these pitfalls by making your words fit this one case and by writing in good conversational language.

h) A friendlier, livelier style would improve this letter. Except in the more formal situations, the transmittal letter is best written in good personal language (with personal pronouns *I, we, you,* and such). This is your one chance to personally address the recipient.

5. *Synopsis*

a) (If direct order assigned.) Begin with a statement of your main finding, conclusion, or recommendation.

b) (If indirect order assigned.) Begin with a brief orientation to the study.

c) Briefly summarize the essential introductory facts. Consider these for completeness: for, by whom, when, what about, and how solved.

d) Summarize the parts in the order treated in the report.

e) Coverage of this part is out of proportion.

   (1) This coverage is scant. Highlight more of the supporting facts. The synopsis is not just a review of conclusions. It includes all the foundation facts, their analyses, and the conclusions—in summary form.

   (2) This coverage is too much in detail. The task of the synopsis is to summarize.

f) Your writing is not so concise as it should be. The objective of a synopsis is to cover the important ingredients of the report in a minimum of space. Economy in the use of words is a main requirement.

g) This writing tends to be dull. Try not to let your efforts to write concisely deaden your writing style. Your objective is to summarize concisely without sacrificing good writing style.

6. *Table of contents*

a) Be consistent in the use of type and capitals. Although you may choose from a number of type forms (capitals, capitals and lowercase underscored, and such), consistency is a logical requirement.

b) This spacing is not the best for eye-pleasing effect.

(1) These parts are crowded. Better double space here.

(2) Here the parts are strung out too much. Single spacing would be better.

c) Use leader lines (preferably periods with spaces intervening) to relate the part to the page number.

d) Keep the parts in line. Captions on the same level should begin at the same spot. Roman numerals in the outline and page numbers should be aligned on their right digits. Periods in the leader lines should be lined up.

e) Elements that precede the contents table need not be listed. Thus, the only prefatory part listed in the contents table of the conventional long, formal report is the synopsis.

f) Do not give the appendix or the epitome Roman number status in the outline. They are appended parts of the report and are not part of the report message.

g) These parts are not arranged in the best order of coherence. Review the logic of your plan for a better sequence.

h) These topics overlap. In general, each section of the report should be mutually independent. Although some repetition and relating of points may be in order, too much of this is a sign of illogical organization.

i) Do not let one major section account for the entire body of the report. Except in the very minor problems, it is a rare case in which more than one aspect of the problem need not be discussed.

j) One-item subdivisions are illogical. You cannot divide an area without coming up with at least two parts.

k) More control captions are needed here. Subcaptions to this caption would show better organization.

l) The subcaptions, in good order, should cover all the territory fenced in by the major captions—no more or less.

m) This organization plan is not the best. Restudy the problem for a more logical plan of presenting this report.

n) These parts are not equal in importance. So do not treat them as being equal in the development of the problem.

o) (If talking captions assigned.) These captions do not talk so well as they might. Talking captions not only state the subject but also tell what is said about the subject.

p) Coordinate headings should be parallel in grammatical structure. That is, if caption A is a noun phrase, so should captions B and C be noun phrases. If 1 under A is a sentence, so should 2 and 3 be sentences.

q) These captions tend to be too long. Good captions use the minimum wording that will convey the meanings intended.

r) Avoid monotonous repetition in the captions. Vary the wording or the construction patterns.

7. *Introduction*

a) Although the reader's needs for orientation will change with the problem, these areas generally need to be covered in the report introduction.

(1) How the report came about: time and nature of the origin of the problem, identification of the participants, and the like.

(2) What the problem is: objective, scope, definitions, background information, and so on.

(3) How the problem is solved: description of the sources of information or research procedure employed in solving the problem.

(4) How the information is presented in the report: a preview to the organization of the report.

b) Work for a smooth, natural writing style in this part.

8. *Coherence and tight connection*

a) For the long, formal reports, short summary-previews are needed at important stages of the progress. These parts complement the preview section, which typically ends the introduction of a formal report. Summary-preview parts are useful to let the reader know periodically where he is in the report plan.

b) Your transition is weak here. Avoid abrupt changes of thought.

c) Here you could improve your paragraph construction by selecting a topic sentence and leading from it.

d) Don't lean heavily on the captions. A well-written report should read clearly, even if all captions are taken out.

e) This section ends abruptly. A summary or concluding statement would help.

9. *Writing the report*

a) Is this writing adapted to the audience? It appears to be (1) too heavy or (2) too light for your reader. In general, this criticism concerns the lengths of your sentences and your choice of words. Better test your writing for readability.

b) Avoid overuse of passive voice.

c) This writing style is dull. Work for a fast-moving and interesting writing style—one that is alive with concrete and action words.

d) Your writing should be more concise. Be economical. Try to cut down on words without sacrificing meaning.

e) (If conventional formality is required.) Write in the third person. Avoid these slips from impersonal to personal writing.

f) Be consistent in time viewpoint. Illogical shifts from past to present and from present to past confuse the report message. Preferably write in the present time viewpoint, treating all things as they relate to the time of writing.

10. *Miscellaneous*

a) The text must tell the story, so don't just refer the reader to a chart or table and let it go at that.

b) Supporting facts are necessary for any conclusions. Your presentation is (1) lacking in supporting fact or (2) cluttered with too much detailed fact. (Minute detail may well be presented in summary tables.)

c) Don't lose sight of your objective. You must do more than present information. Adapt this information to the problem.

d) Beware of unsupported, unqualified statements. Back up these parts with fact.

e) Opinions and facts should be clearly differentiated. Label opinions as such.

11. *Graphic display*

a) The layout arrangement appears to be crowded or awkward at the points indicated. Particularly don't crowd the illustration or table with the text. It is well to triple-space (at least) before and after it.

b) Here the layout appears to be needlessly spaced out.

c) If you have three or more of one type of illustration (charts, tables, maps, etc.), group them together for the numbering sequence within the report. For example, a report with three charts, four maps, and three illustrations would have these graphic aids numbered: Charts 1, 2, and 3; Maps 1, 2, 3, and 4; and Illustrations 1, 2, and 3. If you have a mixture of types, with only one or two of each, refer to them as Figures and number them all in the same series. For example, a report with one chart, two maps, and three illustrations would be numbered Figures 1, 2, 3, 4, 5, and 6.

d) Titles for all tables are appropriately placed above the table. Titles for all other graphic devices conventionally appear below the illustration.

e) The table or graphic display number may appear either on the line with the caption or on a line by itself and centered above the caption.

f) It is conventional to number tables with Roman numerals and all other displays with Arabic numerals. There is convention, too, for placing the caption of tables in a higher type than the titles of other forms of graphic display.

g) You have too much here for one clear picture. Consider (1) breaking it into logical parts for regular display or (2) placing it in the appendix section.

h) If the table or chart cannot be considered essential to a clear understanding of the context, it should be placed in appendix section.

i) Tables are useful, but tables alone are not enough. They are not in the true sense graphic; they don't tell the story instantly.

j) Place each graphic aid as near as is practical to the spot where you talk about it. Placing all graphic aids in the appendix is easy for the writer but hard on the reader who must flip pages back and forth for reference.

k) The type of illustration chosen here is not the most appropriate one to display this set of factors.

l) Possibly this is your very best work, but it falls down in overall appearance and quality. Clear, straight-inked lines neatly drawn, possibly with the use of crosshatching or color, are necessary for the best graphic display.

m) Overlarge illustrations break the continuity of the reading. Couldn't you have reduced the size here without hurting the effectiveness?

n) Tie together the illustration and text by referring the reader to the illustration, and do it when you want him to look at it.

o) Make incidental your references to illustration material. Instead of using a separate sentence, use statements such as "as shown in Figure 2," or "(see Chart 5)."

Statistical techniques for determining sample size and reliability

The reliability of sample results as well as the adequacy of sample size may be measured by statistical and some less technical techniques (as described in Chapter 3). Although a thorough review of sampling statistics would require more space than is available in this summary, two of the basic measures are described in the following paragraphs. Both are special adaptations of the standard deviation, which is a measure of the spread of the normal distribution.

Each of these two basic formulas contains a symbol for the numbers in the sample and a measure of error. Thus, the formulas may be worked for either of these values when the value is unknown. Also, each application of the formulas tests only one characteristic of the study at a time. Thus, in determining the desired size of a sample many applications may need to be made. In a study involving a questionnaire of 10 questions, for example, 10 separate applications could be made—one for each question. Although it is seldom necessary to test every question in the study, enough should be tested to assure a reasonable degree of reliability for the whole.

The first of these formulas is the standard error of the percentage. As its name implies, it is a measure used when the findings are recorded in percentage form. It is expressed in the following formula:

$$\sigma_p = \sqrt{\frac{pq}{N}}.$$

Explanation of the symbols is as follows.

σ_p is the standard error of the percentage (the maximum allowable error either way in percentage points).

p is the frequency of occurrence of the phenomenon measured expressed as a percentage of the whole.

q is $1 - p$

N is the number of cases in the sample.

When used to obtain the number required for a given allowable error rather than the standard error, the formula becomes:

$$N = \frac{pq}{\sigma_p^2} .$$

The sample size computed by this formula gives results within the limits of error specified about 68 out of 100 times. For greater accuracy, the investigator could work the formula for two standard errors, which ensures that the answer has a 95 out of 100 chance of being within the error allowed. The formula then becomes:

$$N = \frac{pq}{\left(\frac{\sigma_p}{2}\right)^2} .$$

As an illustration of its practical application, a consumer-preference study of a new soap may be used. Any of the questions in this study could be tested individually; and one such question might be "Do you like the odor of ——— soap?" The investigator, possibly by observing the first returns as they come in, estimates the probable ratio of answers. Possibly for the question on soap odor preferences, such an estimate could be 60 percent yes and 40 percent no or don't know. Thus, p expressed in decimal form would be .60, and q $(1 - p)$ would be .40. The investigator would then have to decide the percentage of error that he would tolerate. In this instance, a 5 percent (.05 in decimal form) error (σ_p) might be selected. If the investigator wants to be about 95 percent confident that his results will be within the error he will tolerate, the problem becomes:

$$N = \frac{.60 \times .40}{\left(\frac{.05}{2}\right)^2} = \frac{.24}{.000625} = 384 .$$

The second formula used is the standard error of the mean. It is used to determine error of findings expressed as means as well as the sample size needed in obtaining such findings. It is expressed in this formula:

$$\sigma_{\bar{x}} = \frac{\sigma}{\sqrt{N}} .$$

N is the size of the sample.

σ is the standard deviation of the items in the sample.

$\sigma_{\bar{x}}$ is the standard error of the mean.

In working the formula, the investigator must first find values for the two unknowns, the standard deviation (σ) and the standard error of the mean ($\sigma_{\bar{x}}$). If he is statistically inclined, he can compute this value by using the conventional statistical formula.[1] But if he does not know statistics, he can make a rough but usually satisfactory approximation of the standard deviation. He can estimate the standard deviation to be one-sixth of the range (R) of the values—that is, one-sixth of the difference between the largest and smallest items in the sample. Thus, his formula becomes:

$$\sqrt{N} = \frac{\frac{R}{6}}{\sigma_{\bar{x}}} .$$

For the standard error of the mean $\sigma_{\bar{x}}$, he simply decides how much error (in units in which the data are given) he can permit and still have satisfactory results.

A study of average weekly incomes of factory workers illustrates this technique. In a preliminary survey, the investigator finds incomes ranging from $60 to $150. Although this information is scant, it gives the investigator something to work with. So he assumes a range of $90 ($150 less $60). Next, the investigator decides that he wants the mean value of the sample to be no more than $1 away from the true mean value. With these quantities determined, he then applies them to the formula:

$$\sqrt{N} = \frac{\frac{R}{6}}{\sigma_{\bar{x}}} = \frac{\frac{90}{6}}{1} = \frac{15}{1}$$

$$N = 15^2 = 225 .$$

Thus, the investigator needs a sample of 225 to get the accuracy he wants. This size of sample will produce the accuracy desired in about 68 cases out of 100. If the investigator wants to be more than 68 percent certain, he can work the formula for an N with 95

---

[1] The formula for the standard deviation is

$$\sigma = \sqrt{\frac{\Sigma x^2}{N}} .$$

$\Sigma_x{}^2$ is the summation of the deviations from the mean squared. N is the number of units.

percent certainty. This he may do by dividing the standard error by 2—in this case, 1 divided by 2, or .5. The computation with this new value produces an N of 900.

From the illustrations used for the two measures, two general observations may be made. First, in both cases the estimates of sample size were based on scant preliminary information. The investigator would do well to apply the formula again after more of the survey information has been collected. Second, to cut in half the range of error in a sample, one must quadruple the size of the sample. That is, if the range of error of a sample is to be improved from 4 percent to 2 percent, the sample must be increased 4 times.

TABLE FOR DETERMINING SAMPLE SIZE*

(Sample size necessary to ensure, with 95 percent certainty, that the survey proportions are within a given number of percentage points of the true value)

Maximum Percentage Error Either Way	Frequency with Which Phenomenon Occurs					
	5 or 95 Percent	10 or 90 Percent	20 or 80 Percent	30 or 70 Percent	40 or 60 Percent	50 Percent
0.5	7,600	14,400	25,600	33,600	38,400	40,000
1.0	1,900	3,600	6,400	8,400	9,600	10,000
2.0	475	900	1,600	2,100	2,400	2,500
3.0	211	400	711	933	1,067	1,111
4.0	119	225	400	525	600	625
5.0	76	144	256	336	384	400
10.0	19	36	64	84	96	100

* When findings are expressed in percentage form.

Report problems

SHORT PROBLEMS (MEMORANDUM AND LETTER REPORTS)

1. *Should the Baker Manufacturing Company begin the practice of gift-giving?* The management of the Baker Manufacturing Company is considering giving presents to its industrial customers, just as many of its competitors do. In fact, corporate gift-giving has become so commonplace in the industry that Baker officials have begun to question the wisdom of continuing to avoid this practice. They have asked you, an administrative assistant to the president, to do some research on the matter. As you know, the practice of corporate gift-giving consists of giving presents to certain officials of the organizations with which a firm does business. Usually, the gifts have nominal value, consisting of such goods as wines, liquors, golf balls, cheeses, fruits, and leather goods. They are intended as good-will gestures—as expressions of appreciation for business. Although some officials (including some at Baker) look on the practice as a mild form of bribery, most consider it to be ethical as long as the gift values are kept low and the gifts are uniformaly given.

In getting information to guide you in making your recommendation, you used the facilities of your research staff to conduct a small survey of other companies in the field. Using your industry's trade directory, you mailed questionnaires to 484 companies. You received an even 100 returns. Your tabulations to the various questions on the questionnaire appear at the end of the assignment.

Your report will present your survey findings with whatever analyses and applications to your problem you feel are appropriate. Even though you have all these survey results, you will arrive at your recommendation somewhat subjectively. The facts are not all that clear. Regardless of how you recommend, your report will present all the survey statistics for whatever possible future use they may have.

Because the problem is not an involved one, you will use your company's short-form report (including only title page and text). You will write the text in direct order, beginning with your recommendation and immediately supporting it with the major evidence.

ANSWERS TO SURVEY QUESTIONS IN PERCENTAGES

1. Has your company ever given business gifts?
   yes   72%   no   38%
2. Does business gift-giving help build your business?
   yes   53%   no   47%
3. Did you send more gifts this year than last year?
   more   52%   fewer   48%
4. How much did they cost?
   a) under $5   38%
   b) $5–$9.99   33%
   c) $10–$14.99   17%
   d) $15–$19.99   5%
   e) $20–$25   6%
   f) more   1%
5. Did everyone receive the same gift or a different gift?
   same   58%   different   42%
6. Who received the business gifts?
   a) customers/clients   58%
   b) suppliers   22%
   c) other   20%
7. Why do you give business gifts?
   a) goodwill   46%
   b) appreciation   54%
8. Do you give business gifts on the same occasions every year?
   yes   78%   no   22%
9. If yes, on what occasions?
   a) Christmas   84%
   b) birthday   15%
   c) wedding   0
   d) other   11%
10. How does your company distribute business gifts?
    a) mail   49%
    b) in person 45%
    c) messenger 6%
11. What location are they sent to?
    home   45%   office   55%

12. Have you ever received a business gift?

 yes 88%   no 12%

2. *Pointing out customer irritation to Consolidated Restaurants.* Assume the role of restaurant consultant and take on the problems of your newest client, Consolidated Restaurants, Inc. This major restaurant organization owns and operates two nationwide chains. One, the Big Dollar chain, caters to low-income and middle-income families with economy-priced meals. The other, The Steak House, aims at a slightly higher clientle, mainly middle-income and upper-middle-income families. At the moment, Consolidated's directors are unhappy about both of their organizations. Sales have been dropping and are well below national averages. That is why you have been called in.

 With your usual thoroughness, you have made a careful study of kitchen operations, menu designs, purchasing, and such. These

QUESTION: WHICH THREE OF THE THINGS ON THIS LIST IRRITATE YOU MOST WHEN EATING OUT IN A RESTAURANT?

		Income				
Customers' Complaints	Entire Sample	$10,000 and over	$7,000– $9,999	$5,000– $6,999	$3,000– $4,999	$3,000– and under
Can't get attention of waiter or waitress	% 46	% 55	% 50	% 52	% 36	% 36
Paying extra for second cup of coffee	42	46	47	43	40	30
Menu run outs early in meal period	21	26	24	23	21	12
Paying extra for substitutions	20	20	21	22	19	18
Menu hard to read	19	14	17	20	25	20
Paying extra for toasted bread in a sandwich	18	18	17	16	18	20
Having separate tabs put on one check	11	13	11	13	10	9
Paying extra for Roquefort cheese salad dressing	9	13	10	8	9	4
Being given a small plate to use at a buffet table	8	8	7	7	10	7
Being given a small salad bowl	5	8	5	5	4	4
Not especially irritated by any of them	20	18	21	22	16	20
Don't know	13	7	8	10	20	26
Totals*	232	246	238	241	228	206
Number of interviews	1681	363	399	345	291	251
			(Income Undesignated—32)			

* Totals exceed 100% because of multiple responses.

areas are a major part of your investigation and will comprise the bulk of the final report you will write for Consolidated Restaurants.

In addition, however, you have been working on the matter of customer satisfaction. In fact, you and your research staff have conducted a survey of 1,681 people who eat in restaurants at least once a month in an effort to learn what, if anything, they do not like about the service they get. Your findings here will also be a part of your final report. But because this information can be helpful to Consolidated's management right away you decide to present it now in short-report form. Your report will cover the survey findings, of course, but also it will point out any recommendations for change that may be apparent. The data for your presentation are summarized in the table on page 365.

3. *Recommending job termination for Mr. Kennedy.* You are the office manager for the Houghton and Smith Wholesale Grocery Company, and today you must write a personnel action report on one of your subordinates. It is a chore you had hoped not to do, but the actions of Christopher A. Kennedy leave no other choice.

Six months ago, Mr. Kennedy began work as an order clerk, a position for which he was qualified by seven years of experience with the Midville Grocery Wholesale Company. Although he was given a good recommendation from a Midville executive, rumors you have heard recently indicate that it was a courtesy recommendation. The rumors indicate that during the last two years at Midville Kennedy developed an alcoholism problem and had to be dismissed. Apparently, the Midville executive who wrote the recommendation felt that the man deserved another chance—but with another company.

Anyway, you now have the problem. For the first two months, Kennedy appeared to be trying hard to do a good job. He did not miss a single day of work. Although he made a few errors, some of them costly for the company, you attributed them to his newness on the job. In the third month, however, he made a sharp turn for the worse. In this month, he missed work four days, each one explained by a claim of illness. He was late for work six times, once by over two hours. His errors increased, too, although you failed to keep a record of them.

In the third month, you sensed a problem, so you began to keep a log on his attendance and work record. Absences for these three months were three, three, and five. His times tardy were six, two, and five. Errors in his work have been numerous and have affected over 6 percent of the orders he has handled. (You expect something near zero.) You can attribute at least three lost accounts to his errors.

He is a friendly fellow who tries hard to do his job. But it is apparent that he is drinking heavily. In the three conferences you have had with him, he admitted he had a drinking problem, and each time he promised to quit. But you have not noticed any change, except for the worse. In fact, after your last conference with him he reported for work the following morning in a drunken condition and had to be sent home.

As today ends the six-month probationary period all company employees go through before being given a permanent appointment, you must make your recommendation on Mr. Kennedy. You must recommend that he be dismissed, and you will support the recommendation with adequate facts. (You may use your imagination to supply additional details so long as they do not change the general image set in the problem description.) Write your report in memorandum form. Use the direct-order.

4. *Reporting an errant subordinate for good reason.* As much as you dislike doing such things, today you must report Roger A. Tucker for improper conduct and neglect of duty.

Mr. Tucker joined your sales force about 8 months ago after over 18 years of sales experience with your rival company, Temple Brothers, Inc. At first, Tucker did a reasonably good job for you, making his quotas each of the first five months. Since that time, however, sales have dropped. In fact, last month he sold only 44 percent of quota, as compared with 68 percent the month earlier and 76 percent the preceding month.

About six weeks ago, you learned from an old customer in Tucker's territory that this customer had apparently been dropped from Tucker's route without explanation. Further investigation revealed that at least five other customers were also dropped, apparently without cause.

You called in Tucker, talked with him, and learned that marital trouble was to blame. Tucker admitted not making many of his regular calls, and promised to do better, saying his troubles were behind him.

In following weeks, he showed no improvement. In fact, his work deteriorated more. Three additional talks with the man produced only promises for improvement, but improvement never occurred. His sales continued to drop, and you continued to hear about lost and dissatisfied customers.

You really do not know just how many customers have been lost or the exact extent of the damage done. But you know that something has to be done soon. So you will recommend that Tucker be relieved of his sales duties. As basically he is a capable man with problems, you will recommend that the company keep him in some other capacity—if he is willing.

Using standard memorandum form, write a report, stating your recommendaton and backing it up with supportable reasoning. Use your imagination to supply details not given.

5. *Choosing a retail outlet for Tachert suits.*   Assume the position of administrative assistant to Gregory A. Huddleston, sales manager for A. R. Tachert, Incorporated, manufacturers of men's quality suits. You have been sent to Hill City to investigate two retail outlets as possible dealerships for Tachert Suits. Each of the two stores has indicated an interest in handling your line, but one to a town the size of Hill City is Tachert's policy.

For the past three days, you have been in Hill City, getting all the pertinent information on the two stores. As you analyzed your findings, you kept in mind Tachert's reputation as a prestige product. As Tachert suits are somewhat conservatively styled and in the higher price range, they appeal primarily to the successful professional man.

Quality customers, however, are not your only consideration in selecting an outlet. You want one that can bring about quantity sales. And you want one that gives the kind of service that is consistent with Tachert quality. Also, you will need to consider such factors as store location, growth potential, and the physical facilities.

Now you are ready to begin your analysis of the facts you have assembled (see summary below). You will present your report to Mr. Huddleston in the company's standard memorandum report form.

COMPTON CLOTHIERS

Located on Main Street in the heart of the business district. New men's store (one year old) in modern, spacious (80 × 120 feet sales area) building. Bright, well-lighted interior, neatly arranged stock. Owned by Henry T. Compton, a dynamic and young businessman who makes use of aggressive marketing technique. Store has 4 salesmen, 3 under 30 and 1 about 40. All use aggressive sales approaches. Store carries wide range of clothing from medium to high priced and for young and old. Handles four brands of men's suits: R. E. Allen (middle priced), Wall Street (middle priced), J. H. Conrad (upper middle priced), and I. A. Chapman (high priced). Advertises heavily—about one and one-half pages per week. Annual sales about $650,000.

HILL CITY MEN'S STORE

Oldest store in town (1887) and in original building located one block off main business street. Building is in excellent repair and store is attractive and elegant, although obviously old. Store area is small (35 × 60 feet). Owner is Theodore E. Krutcher, about 60 and a grandson of the founder. Mr. Krutcher is an easygoing, gregarious type who greets many of his customers by name. Two salesmen employed, ages over 50. Use soft-sell approach. Stresses service. Carries conservative upper middle (J. H. Conrad, Baxter Brothers) and high priced (Ross and Baker, C. Kaperton) brands. Light advertiser (total of about one-half page a week). Annual sales of $300,000.

Analyze these facts and make your recommendation to Mr. Huddleston. Present your report to him in a direct-order memorandum report.

6. *Selecting a site for a National service station.* As a junior executive in charge of site selection for the National Oil Company, you must select one of three sites that have been recommended for a new service station in Springville. You have collected the following data on these prospective locations.

HILL AVENUE AND 37TH STREET

Commercial area. Lot 150 × 100 feet. Corner location. Cost of $25,000. Traffic count per day (7 A.M. to 9 P.M.), 4,200 cars. Distance from nearest company station, 3.1 miles.

311 DELMONT STREET

Commercial area. Lost 200 × 100 feet. Noncorner location. Cost of $24,000. Traffic count per day, 9,000 cars. Distance from nearest company station, 3.9 miles.

AVENUE G AT INDEPENDENCE STREET

Commercial area. Lot 150 × 150. Corner location. Cost of $30,000.

Traffic count per day, 6,500 cars. Distance from nearest company station, 2.1 miles.

All the sites have relatively the same amount of competition in the immediate area. Each has one competing station within a distance of five blocks. Your task is to evaluate these alternative sites and to recommend one. Present your recommendation and analysis in a memorandum report. Write it in the direct order.

7. *Selecting the best laundry service for Maxwell Cafeterias.* Assume the position of a management consultant hired by the Maxwell Cafeterias of Saint Louis. One of the many problems you have been asked to solve for this company is how it should handle its linen and laundry. Specifically, should they own their own cloth equipment and have it laundered? Or should they rent this equipment?

According to information you have gathered, the Maxwell people will need about $2,500 worth of such equipment from the beginning, and its life expectancy is about 2 years. You can get a monthly laundry rate of $60, including pickup and delivery. Weekly costs of renting the comparable equipment needed are as follows.

540.............	54″ tablecloths	@ $ .12 each
2,100...........	napkins	@ $1.75 per 100
175.............	aprons	@ $ .15 each
84.............	dresses	@ $ .50 each
35.............	coats (waiters)	@ $ .45 each
140.............	dish towels	@ $ .03 each

Your task is to prepare the alternative possibility and to write a recommendation for the Maxwell people. Do it in standard memorandum form, using direct style order of presentation.

8. *Recommending a store manager for Econo-Mart's new store.* Next month in Camp City, Econo-Mart, a regional chain of food stores, will open its newest outlet. It is now looking for someone to manage that store, and you, an interviewer in the organization's personnel department, have completed screening applicants in the Camp City area. From the nine who applied, you have narrowed the field down to three. Now you must evaluate them and rank them for the job. You will write your recommendations in a conclusion-first order memorandum addressed to Conrad Carlisle, personnel manager.

A summary of the basic biographical data on the three is as follows.

	Philip S. Towne	Bill A. Sweet	Ralph T. Story
Personal details	Age 45, married, 6 children, good health.	Age 36, married, no children, service-connected disability but otherwise good health.	Age 28, single, good health.
Experience	21 years with Ero Gro., Co., duties as stock clerk, cashier, assistant manager (2 years). 3 years as manager White's Drive-In Grocery.	12 years U.S. Army, rank master sergeant, duties in food services and supply 5 years with Dugan Grocery Co., duties as cashier, manager of produce department (3 years).	3 years as route salesman for Matron Baking Co. 3 years with H & H Super Market, duties as stock clerk, cashier, and assistant manager (1 year).
Education	High school, 3 years State University, major in education.	High school, Teague Business College 6 months.	High school, 2 years State University (mainly night school), major in business administration
Score on management potential test*	78	81	89
Major comments made by references	Hard-working, steady, and loyal Honest beyond question. Well liked by all who know him. Easygoing.	A hard worker. Friendly but has quick temper, honest. Drives subordinates hard.	Hard-working. Extremely ambitious. Occasionally has run-ins with other workers. Honest. Works subordinates hard.

* Scores: grade of 60, passing; 75, average; 85 and above, outstanding.

9. *Recommending an office manager for Econo-Mart.* Using the same general instructions given in the problem above, evaluate and rank the following three applicants for the position of office manager for the home office of Econo-Mart Stores, Inc. For varying reasons, the organization has decided to hire from the outside rather than to promote from within.

	Warren T. Childs	*Tim T. Terrell*	*Adolph A. Raska*
Personal details	Age 42, single, good health.	Age 35, married, three children.	Age 32, divorced, one child.
Experience	4 years with Case Brick Co. as office clerk. 9 years with Ross Wholesale Co. as order clerk (6 years), chief of shipping and orders department (3 years). 9 years as office manager, Hess Wholesale Grocery Company.	3 years U.S. Army, rank sergeant, duties primarily in office administration. 11 years with Butler Bros. Food Stores as records clerk (3 years), chief records section (5 years) and assistant office manager (3 years).	4 years U.S. Army, rank first lieutenant, Adjutant General Corps, duties in office administration. 7 years with Crow Mfg. Co., duties of management trainee (1 year), personnel assistant (3 years), chief of records section (3 years).
Education	High school, 1 year Moss Business College.	High school, 3 years Eastern University, major in accounting.	High school, B.S. from Eastern University, major in marketing.
Scores on aptitude tests			
Office procedures	76	81	89
Management potential	87	82	76
Comments by references	A hard-working, self-made man. Handles subordinates well. Strong character.	Well liked and easygoing. Dependable but not highly ambitious.	Not a strong personality, but intelligent. Works hard. Well liked by those who know him, but is not gregarious.

10. *A progress report on Global's new sales district.* One month ago, you were transferred by Global Insurance, Hartford, Connecticut, to Boon City to expand Global's sales coverage to this area. It is time now to make a progress report to the home office. Frankly, you do not have much to show in the way of real sales results, but you have put in a lot of work, and you think you have made good progress. As you recall, Geoffrey Curtis, district manager and recipient of your report, assured you that Global did not expect profits right off—that moving into a new territory requires time and patience.

In preparing your report, you first make random notes of the various things you have done during the month. Garbled as they are, your notes look like this.

Rented three-office suite, Hall Building, $210 per month.

Hired secretary (Miss Cleo Struble) at $450 per month. Picked from 11 applicants. Appears to be highly efficient—good work so far.

Visited two local newspapers. Bought space to announce Global's entry to area—cost $212 and $180 for 4-column, 8-inch ads in *Daily Herald* and *Evening Star,* respectively. Got free publicity in business news sections of both papers. (You will attach clippings of ads and articles.)

Bought office furniture: 3 executive desks at $205 each; 3 swivel chairs at $45 each; 7 straight chairs at $26 each; 1 stenographic desk at $145; 1 typist's chair at $28; 1 manual typewriter at $178; office supplies (stationery, stamps, paper clips, etc.), $67; 5 metal 3-drawer file cabinets at $117 each; 2 coat-trees at $13 each; 3 bookshelves at $54 each.

Visited Chamber of Commerce. Got names of 17 business leaders likely to help in finding agents. Visited all 17. Got names of seven prospects. Interviewed all seven. Four not interested. One ruled out—short on personality. Two were interested.

George Smathers: Took Global's aptitude test—made 97 (exceptional). Has 13 years' sales experience, but not in insurance. Sold business machines, securities, and industrial chemicals. Hired him. Have spent much time training him both in office and on sales calls. Man is eager—a born salesman. Good personality, high morals, intelligent. No sales yet, but several good prospects lined up. This man will go places.

William A. Tucker: A proved insurance salesman, with nine years of experience. Now with Central Life, but is considering a change. Hasn't yet taken Global's aptitude test. Have discussed employment possibilities with him three times. Is definitely interested. Will continue discussion. Good chance of hiring him.

These are the major facts you have to report, although you may think of additional minor details as you write the report. You will use Global's conventional memorandum report form.

11. *Investigating a personnel problem in department 3–N.* Today's assignment in your role as special assistant to George B. Dymkus, director of employment relations of Southwestern Aircraft, Inc., takes you to department 3–N. Your objective is to investigate charges brought to you by Karl Connerly, the union steward who represents the men of this department. According to Connerly, union members in department 3–N have been discriminated against in the awarding of overtime work. Nonunion workers have been getting the lion's share of overtime.

On arriving at the department, you discuss the matter with Wilfred Knudson. Knudson's version of the story goes like this: Of the eight workers in the department, five are members of the union and three are not. The three nonunion men have had more overtime than the others, but they deserve it. Knudson claims that he gives overtime on the basis of seniority and productivity—nothing else. This policy, he points out, is permitted in the contract with the union. If the nonunion men got most of the overtime, Knudson says, it is because they have seniority and are better workers.

After talking to Knudson, you go to the files that contain the department's records. Here you find data that should prove or disprove Knudson's claim and, in fact, should point to the solution of the whole problem. After an hour or more of poring over these records of the past six months, your summary notes look like this.

Employee and Union Status*	Hours of Overtime Work	Years Employed	Productivity (Average Daily Units Performed)	Percent Rejection (Not Meeting Inspection)
George Graves (U)	0	14	30	0.08
W. Wilson Davis (U)	0	1	21	0.09
Kermit Crowley (U)	10	3	32	0.07
Walter H. Quals (U)	60	8	26	0.01
Hugo Detresanti (U)	60	7	30	0.03
Ralph A. Andrews (NU)	40	35	26	0.02
Will O. Rundell (NU)	70	17	35	0.03
Thomas A. Baines (NU)	90	12	43	0.03

* U, union; NU, nonunion.

Now your task is to analyze these data and to present your finding to Dymkus in the form of the standard memorandum report used by the company. In addition to analyzing the data, you will recommend a course of action on the problem.

12. *Will contest bring profits to Food King?*   John H. Gromman, newly appointed advertising and promotion manager for Food King, Inc., has an idea to increase sales, and thereby increase profits, for the chain of 142 stores. He thinks that contests at each store, with an abundance of prizes, would more than pay off. Such contests, he concludes, have been tried by other stores, and they appeared to work.

George Clemmons, however, does not think very much of the plan; and George Clemmons happens to be Food King's president. So to prove or disprove the value of contests, Clemmons suggests that the company conduct an experiment. You, as director of research, get the assignment.

The first step is to devise a contest for the experiment. With

Gromman's assistance, you settle on a contest involving a simple drawing for prizes. With each purchase of $10 or more, the customers receive entry blanks, which they endorse and deposit in a large box. Drawings are made weekly to determine the winners of such prizes as washing machines, radios, electric mixers, and toasters.

For your experiment, you select two comparable and homogeneous groups of five stores—one as the experimental group and the other as a control group. In one group of stores (group A) contests are held; none are held in the other stores (group B). After one month of contests, with weekly drawings and prizes galore, the contests are stopped. Because you believe the contests may have some long-run effect on sales, you decide to analyze operations for the following months. You later find three months to be adequate. Now you assemble the data in preparation for your analysis.

Although you considered using a variety of data (traffic flow, size and number of purchases, cost of the contests), you conclude that net profits tell the whole story in summary fashion. Here are the profit figures you assembled.

NET PROFITS
(In hundreds of dollars)

Group	Store	Month before Contests	Month of Contests	Month after	Second Month after	Third Month after
A...............	1	32	29	39	34	32
	2	31	27	38	33	30
	3	30	27	33	31	31
	4	33	25	37	34	33
	5	30	28	38	31	29
B...............	6	29	30	31	30	32
	7	30	32	31	30	30
	8	31	31	30	30	32
	9	33	34	33	32	32
	10	30	31	31	30	30

Write up your analysis of these data, and then draw conclusions from your analysis. Write up your work in a form that is appropriate for this situation.

INTERMEDIATE LENGTH PROBLEMS

13. *Analyzing last year's activity in the soft drink industry.* Move the calendar back to 1967 and take over as administrative assistant to the president of the Seven-Up Company. Although the

company has had a reasonably good year, it is nevertheless curious to know what has happened in the industry in general, and especially how its own operations compare with industry figures. It is particularly concerned in view of the apparent inroads of its market made by Coca-Cola's Fresca.

Specifically, you have been asked by President William A. Bass to review the year's activities for the industry and to analyze them for any trends that may be evident. In the process, you will point up all developments of significance to Seven-Up.

As the report is formal but of moderate length, you will use your company's standard short-report form. It will have only a title page preceding the report. The report you will write in the direct order,

Sales of major soft-drink companies

(All case estimates are 24 unit case of 8-oz. units.)

Company	1965† Cases (millions)	1966 Cases (millions)	Percent change
Coca-Cola	790	895	+13.3%
Pepsi-Cola	550	595	+ 8.2
Royal Crown	230	260	+13.0
Seven-Up	185	200	+ 8.1
Canada Dry	160	165	+ 3.1
Nesbitt Food Products	70	80	+14.3
Dr Pepper	70	80	+14.3
Beverages Intl.**	70	80	+14.3
Cott***	60	61	+ 1.7
Shasta	25	30	+20.0
Squirt	22	24	+ 9.1
Nu Grape	20	22.5	+12.5
Sub total	2,252	2,492.5	+10.7%
All others	348-448	307.5-407.5	—
Grand total	**2,600-2,700***	**2,800-2,900***	**+ 8.0%**

... and the smaller competitors

Company	Cases (millions) 1965	1966
Mason's	NA	18.5
Grapette Co.‡	17.0	18.0
White Rock	17.0	17.5
Vernors	14.5	16.0
Frank's	9.0	14.0
Dad's	11.0	13.5
Cragmont (Safeway)	NA	11.0
No Cal	10.0	11.0
Schweppes	NA	10.0
Faygo	7.5	9.0
Bireley's	6.0	6.5
Yukon (A&P)	NA	6.0
Cotton Club Chek (Winn Dixie)	5.0	5.0

Company	Cases (millions) 1965	1966
Big K (Kroger)	4.0	5.0
Yoo-Hoo	3.0	4.5
Bubble-Up	4.0	4.0
Del Monte	3.0	4.0
Hoffman	NA	3.0
Tru-Ade	2.0	2.5
Uptown	2.0	2.0+
Mayfresh (Mayfair)	1.0	1.0+
Dixi Cola	1.0	1.0+
Sun Drop	1.0	1.0
HoJo (Howard Johnson)	—	1.0
Grand total	**122.0**	**190.0**

Estimated market shares by flavors

Type	1964	1965	1966
Cola	62%	63%	63%
Lemon-lime	16	17	17
Orange	8	9	10
Root beer	4	4	5
All others	10	7	5
	100%	100%	100%

Diet drinks' volume continues strong

Company	1965 Cases (millions)	1966 Cases (millions)
Royal Crown	95	100
Coca-Cola	50	95♦
Pepsi-Cola	50	55
Sub total	195	250
All others	135	160
Grand total	**330**	**410**

Cola and lemon-lime: Leaders' sales

Company	Cola market†† 1965 Cases (millions)	1966 Cases (millions)	Lemon-lime market‡‡ 1965 Cases (millions)	1966 Cases (millions)
Coca-Cola	615	685	50	65
Pepsi-Cola	490	525	20	15
Seven-Up	—	—	170	170
Royal Crown	190	210	10	10
All others	360	370	200	220
Grand total	**1,655**	**1,790**	**450**	**480**

*John C. Maxwell Jr. estimates.
**Includes Hires and Orange Crush.
***Includes all brands—Cott, Clicquot Club, Mission of California and Big Giant Cola.
†Revised figures.
‡Includes Grapette, Mr. Cola, Sunburst beverage flavors, Old Red Eye.
♦Includes Fresca.
††Includes diet colas.
‡‡Does not include "hillbilly" drinks or Fresca.

leading with the major findings and the implications they have for Seven-Up. Because all of the report is based on statistics, you will want to use some carefully chosen graphic aids to display your major findings.

The bases for your analyses come from *Soft Drink Industry* magazine, which is the authoritative collector of such information in the field. A summary of their findings and estimates for the past two years is found on page 376.

14. *Answering the question of threat of apparel imports.* As consulting economist for the American Apparel Manufacturers Association, you are assigned the task of determining the seriousness of the apparel import threat. According to some members of the industry, imports are threatening to make damaging inroads into the United States market. With their lower prices (in spite of tariffs and other import costs) and improved quality, imports are giving domestic manufacturers good cause to be alarmed.

In your efforts to determine the seriousness of the threat, you have assembled the data the association has compiled over the years. Based on Department of Commerce figures for overall production and imports, and the association's own information for breakdowns (shown on page 378), the data available give you just what you need. It appears that they will permit you to answer your basic questions; and equally important, they will permit you to point out the trouble areas—if there are any.

You will direct the report to the association's directors. And even though it is relatively short, the formality of the situation prompts you to give the report the preparatory trappings of a title page and letter of transmittal. Because of the report's short length, you do not feel it will require a table of contents or a synopsis; but probably you will present the text in the direct order.

15. *Reporting next year's capital expenditures for the nation.* As economic analyst for Hahnn-Dreyfus, Inc., write a report covering next year's planned capital spending for the nation. Hahnn-Dreyfus is one of the nation's largest construction and equipment installation firms, and it is quite naturally interested in the prospects for its activities for the year ahead. That is why each year your office gathers Department of Commerce and Securities and Exchange Commission data for the past year, and the McGraw-Hill Economics Department's projection for the coming year, and presents a

U.S. Production and Imports of Apparel Products for Selected Calendar Years
(Figures in millions)

		Unit	Domestic Production Quantity	Imports for Consumption Quantity	Ratio Imports to Domestic Production
Men's and boys' separate trousers and shorts, not knit, all fibers	1961	no.	117.1	4.3	3.6
	1964	no.	164.0	13.0	7.9
	1966	no.	194.5	21.5	11.0
	1967	no.	208.1	24.0	11.5
	1968	no.	225.5	28.6	12.6
Men's and boys' dress and sport shirts, including uniform shirts, not knit, all fibers	1961	doz.	28.0	1.44	5.1
	1964	doz.	29.9	1.95	6.5
	1966	doz.	33.5	3.11	9.2
	1967	doz.	35.7	3.73	10.4
	1968	doz.	39.2	4.10	10.4
Women's, girls', and children's blouses, not knit, all fibers	1961	doz.	17.1	2.8	16.3
	1964	doz.	18.5	2.4	12.9
	1966	doz.	20.9	3.5	16.7
	1967	doz.	21.6	4.1	18.9
	1968	doz.	20.2	4.5	22.2
Women's, girls', and children's trousers, slacks, and shorts all fibers	1961	doz.	7.5	1.7	22.6
	1964	doz.	10.5	3.0	28.5
	1966	doz.	12.7	4.3	33.8
	1967	doz.	14.0	4.5	32.1
	1968	doz.	n.a.	4.2	...
Nightwear, all types all fibers	1961	doz.	11.2	n.a.	...
	1964	doz.	14.0	0.78	5.5
	1966	doz.	14.7	0.80	5.4
	1967	doz.	n.a.	1.02	...
cotton	1968	doz.	11.8	0.77	6.5
Body supporting garments, all fibers	1961	doz.	19.7	2.0	10.1
	1964	doz.	23.3	2.6	11.1
	1966	doz.	23.8	2.6	10.9
	1967	doz.	26.2	2.8	10.6
	1968	doz.	27.1	2.6	9.5
Raincoats, ¾ length or longer, not knit	1961	doz.	0.65	0.06	9.2
	1964	doz.	0.91	0.11	12.0
	1966	doz.	1.14	0.09	7.8
	1967	doz.	1.25	0.11	8.8
	1968	doz.	1.49	0.13	8.7

summary report for top management. Quite obviously, such information is of vital concern to Hahnn-Dreyfus in evaluating its results and in making its plans.

The data that will form the basis of your report are presented in the table that follows. You will present them in Hahnn-Dreyfus short-report form (title page and direct-order report).

REPORTING CAPITAL EXPENDITURES FOR NATION
(In billions of dollars)

Industry	Last Year Actual	Next Year Planned	% Change
Iron and steel.................................	$ 2.31	$ 2.40	+ 4%
Nonferrous metals.............................	.90	.93	+ 3
Machinery....................................	2.95	3.37	+14
Electrical machinery..........................	1.24	1.45	+17
Autos, trucks, and parts......................	1.66	1.66	0
Aerospace....................................	.77	.75	− 3
Other transportation equipment (RR equipment, ships)......................................	.32	.32	0
Fabricated metals and instruments..............	1.56	1.84	+18
Stone, clay, and glass.........................	.73	.76	+ 4
Other durables...............................	1.25	1.55	+24
Total Durables..........................	13.69	15.03	+10
Chemicals....................................	$ 2.88	$ 2.79	− 3
Paper and pulp...............................	1.64	1.51	− 8
Rubber.......................................	.49	.64	+30
Petroleum and coal products...................	4.65	5.12	+10
Food and beverages...........................	1.41	1.58	+12
Textiles......................................	.89	.82	− 8
Other nondurables............................	1.04	1.04	0
Total Nondurables.......................	13.00	13.50	+ 4
All Manufacturing......................	$26.69	$28.53	+ 7
Mining.......................................	$ 1.42	$ 1.56	+10
Railroads....................................	1.53	1.35	−12
Airlines......................................	2.16	2.94	+36
Other transportation..........................	1.73	1.83	+ 6
Communications...............................	5.91	6.26	+ 6
Electric and gas utilities......................	9.88	11.07	+12
Commercial...................................	12.34	12.96	+ 5
All Business...........................	$61.66	$66.50	+ 8%

SOURCE: U.S. Department of Commerce; Securities and Exchange Commission.

16. *Presenting the growth pattern for radio and television.* Continental Communications, Inc., an owner of a number of television and radio stations in the United States, wants information about the industry they are a part of. In general, they want a word picture of the growth patterns—past and projected—in these two areas; and in the process they want a review of the components of growth.

You, an administrative assistant in the office of Roger T. Beale, chairman of the board, have drawn the assignment. Presently, you have conducted most of the research involved. From annual releases, you have collected sales data for radio dating back to 1935 and for television dating to 1948 (see tables below). These two series, with their components, give you the information you need for measuring past growth. Your projections for the future will be simple, freehand extensions of the trend lines established.

You will write the report in the logical order. You will use only a title page and a combination letter of transmittal and synopsis as prefatory elements.

RADIO TIME SALES 1935-1966

Year	National Network	% change from previous year	Regional	% change from previous year	National Non-Network	% change from previous year	Local	% change from previous year	Total	% change from previous year
1935[1]	$ 39,737,867		1	-------	`$ 13,805,200	-----	$ 26,074,476	-----	$ 79,617,543	-----
1936[2]	--------------	-----	--------------	-----	--------------	----	--------------	-----	--------------	----
1937	56,192,396	+41.4	$2,854,047	-----	23,177,136	+67.4	35,745,394	+37.1	117,908,973	+48.1
1938	56,612,925	+ 0.7	2	-----	28,109,185	+21.6	32,657,349	— 8.7	117,379,459	— 0.6
1939	62,621,689	+10.6	2	-----	30,030,563	+ 6.8	37,315,774	+14.2	129,968,026	+10.7
1940*	71,919,428	+13.1	1,869,583	-----	37,140,444	+23.8	44,756,792	+20.0	155,686,247	+20.5
1941	79,621,534	+10.7	2,752,073	+47.2	45,681,959	+23.0	51,697,651	+15.5	179,753,217	+15.4
1942	81,744,396	+ 2.7	3,444,581	+25.2	51,059,159	+11.8	53,898,916	+ 4.2	190,147,052	+ 5.8
1943	99,389,177	+21.6	6,256,508	+81.6	59,352,170	+16.2	64,104,309	+18.9	228,102,164	+20.0
1944	121,757,135	+22.5	7,612,366	+21.7	73,312,899	+23.5	84,960,347	+20.3	287,642,747	+26.1
1945	125,671,834	+ 3.2	8,301,702	+ 9.1	76,696,463	+ 4.6	99,814,042	+17.5	310,484,046	+ 7.9
1946	126,737,727	+ 0.8	8,043,381	+ 3.1	82,917,505	+ 8.1	116,380,301	+16.6	334,078,914	+ 7.6
1947	127,713,942	+ 0.8	7,012,689	—12.8	91,581,241	+10.4	147,778,814	+27.0	374,086,686	+12.0
1948	133,723,098	+ 4.5	7,329,255	+ 4.3	104,759,761	+14.4	170,908,165	+ 15.6	416,720,279	+11.4
1949	128,903,467	— 3.6	5,994,858	—18.2	108,314,507	+ 3.4	182,144,301	+ 6.5	425,357,133	+ 2.1
1950	124,633,089	— 3.3	6,897,127	+15.0	118,823,880	+ 9.7	203,210,834	+11.6	453,564,930	+ 6.6
1951	113,984,000	— 8.5	8,481,000	+23.0	119,559,000	+ 0.6	214,519,000	+ 5.6	456,543,000	+ 0.6
1952	102,528,000	—10.0	7,334,000	—13.5	123,658,000	+ 3.4	239,631,000	+11.7	473,151,000	+ 3.6
1953	92,865,000	— 9.4	5,192,000	—29.2	129,605,000	+ 4.8	249,544,000	+ 4.1	477,206,000	+ 0.9
1954	78,917,000	—15.0	4,767,000	— 8.2	120,168,000	— 7.3	247,478,000	— 0.8	451,330,000	— 5.4
1955	60,268,000	—23.6	3,809,000	—20.1	120,393,000	+ 0.2	272,011,000	+ 9.9	456,481,000	+ 0.7
1956	44,839,000	—25.6	3,585,000	— 5.9	145,461,000	+20.8	297,822,000	+ 9.5	491,707,000	+ 7.7
1957	47,951,000	+ 6.9	3,709,000	+ 3.5	169,511,000	+16.5	316,493,000	+ 6.3	537,664,000	+ 9.3
1958	42,786,000	— 8.7	3,733,000	+ 0.6	171,939,000	+ 1.4	323,207,000	+ 2.0	541,665,000	+ 0.9
1959	35,633,000	—23.4	.... **	-----	188,143,000	+ 9.4	359,138,000	+11.1	582,914,000	+ 7.6
1960	35,026,000	— 1.7	....	-----	202,102,000	+ 7.4	385,346,000	+ 7.3	622,474,000	+ 6.8
1961	35,837,000	+ 2.3	....	-----	197,352,000	— 2.4	384,053,000	— 0.3	617,242,000	— 0.9
1962	37,326,000	+ 4.2	....	-----	208,455,000	+ 5.6	419,468,000	+ 9.2	665,249,000	+ 7.8
1963	41,797,000	+12.0	....	-----	220,227,000	+ 5.6	449,717,000	+ 7.2	711,741,000	+ 7.0
1964	43,783,000	+ 4.8	....	-----	232,038,000	+ 5.4	487,947,000	+ 8.5	763,768,000	+ 7.3
1965	44,602,000	+ 1.9	....	-----	247,942,000	+ 6.9	535,238,000	+ 9.7	827,782,000	+ 8.4
1966†	46,999,000	+ 5.4	....	-----	283,631,000	+14.4	595,388,000	+11.2	926,018,000	+11.9

[1]Nationwide and regional networks combined.
[2]Data not available.
†1966 figures estimated by BROADCASTING. All others are from FCC.

*Figures prior to this date not comparable in all categories.
**Regional network calculations discontinued in 1959.

TELEVISION TIME SALES 1948-1966

Year	National Network	% change from previous year	National Non-Network	% change from previous year	Local	% change from previous year	Total	% change from previous year
1948*	$ 2,500,000	-----	-------------	-----	$ 6,200,000	-----	$ 8,700,000	-----
1949	10,796,000	-----	$ 7,275,000	-----	9,460,000	-----	27,530,000	-----
1950	35,210,000	+226.1	25,034,000	+244.1	30,385,000	+221.2	90,629,000	+229.2
1951	97,558,000	+177.1	59,733,000	+138.6	51,304,000	+ 68.8	208,595,000	+130.2
1952	137,664,000	+ 41.1	80,235,000	+ 34.3	65,171,000	+ 27.0	283,070,000	+ 35.7
1953	171,900,000	+ 24.9	124,318,000	+ 54.9	88,474,000	+ 35.8	384,692,000	+ 35.9
1954	241,224,000	+ 40.3	176,766,000	+ 42.2	120,131,000	+ 35.8	538,122,000	+ 39.9
1955	308,900,000	+ 28.1	222,400,000	+ 25.8	149,800,000	+ 24.7	681,100,000	+ 26.6
1956	367,700,000	+ 19.0	281,200,000	+ 26.4	174,200,000	+ 16.3	823,100,000	+ 20.8
1957	394,200,000	+ 7.7	300,500,000	+ 6.9	174,000,000	− 0.1	868,700,000	+ 5.5
1958	424,500,000	+ 7.7	345,200,000	+ 14.9	181,300,000	+ 4.2	951,000,000	+ 9.5
1959	445,800,000	+ 5.0	424,200,000	+ 22.9	200,600,000	+ 10.6	1,070,600,000	+ 12.6
1960	471,600,000	+ 5.8	459,200,000	+ 8.3	215,800,000	+ 7.6	1,146,600,000	+ 7.1
1961	480,300,000	+ 1.2	468,500,000	+ 2.0	211,200,000	− 2.1	1,160,000,000	+ 1.2
1962	521,500,000	+ 8.6	539,500,000	+ 15.2	242,500,000	+ 14.8	1,303,500,000	+ 12.4
1963	537,900,000	+ 3.1	600,700,000	+ 11.3	256,100,000	+ 5.6	1,394,700,000	+ 7.0
1964	563,400,000	+ 4.7	689,500,000	+ 14.8	297,000,000	+ 16.0	1,549,900,000	+ 11.1
1965	585,100,000	+ 3.9	764,500,000	+ 10.9	324,100,000	+ 9.1	1,673,700,000	+ 8.0
1966†	604,554,000	+ 3.3	821,330,000	+ 7.4	370,439,000	+ 14.3	1,796,323,000	+ 8.2

*In 1948 FCC reported only "total revenues" (from time, talent and services) from "network programs" and from business "sold directly by stations." Hence figures for that first year of television financial reporting are not comparable with figures for time sales in ensuing years.
†1966 figures estimated by BROADCASTING.

17. *Reporting the stability and growth of the food brokerage business.* At the last meeting of the National Food Brokers Association, the membership voted to conduct a survey of its members to determine its stability as well as its past and present growth. As a staff research analyst for the group, the work fell on your shoulders.

First, you designed a somewhat simple questionnaire. Then, you mailed it to all of the association's 2,115 members. Of this number, 1,073 returned the questionnaire—a response of better than 50 percent. Next, you tabulated your responses and compiled them in a form suitable for your analysis (see tables on page 382). It is now time to begin analyzing the data and to construct a report that will convey your findings.

As the project is neither major nor highly formal, you have been instructed to write it up in the form of a memorandum report. The report will be duplicated by mimeograph and mailed to all the cooperating members. You will write the report in the direct order, beginning with a quick review of major findings. Even though the report is somewhat short and informal, you may find need for some graphic aids.

Questionnaires received, 1,100 (52 percent of the membership).
Age of the brokerage firm (1,073 firms reporting):

Total number of years in business, 32,481.

Average age, 30.27 years.

Oldest company reporting, 120 years old.

Number of years in business by age groups (1,073 firms reported):

Age Group	Number of Firms	%
1 to 10 years	159	15
11 to 20 years	317	29
21 to 30 years	169	16
31 to 40 years	154	14
41 to 50 years	95	8.8
51 to 60 years	73	7
61 to 75 years	60	6
76 to 100 years	33	3
100 years or more	13	1.2

Length of service of accounts (1,073 firms reported):

Age Group	Number of Accounts	%
5 years or less	7,886	35
6 to 10 years	5,069	23
11 to 15 years	3,617	16
16 to 20 years	2,366	10
21 to 30 years	1,839	8.2
31 years or more	1,647	7.8

Accounts served for 21 years or more, total 3,486:

Length of Service	Number of Accounts
21 to 30 years	1,839
31 to 40 years	1,114
41 to 50 years	344
51 to 60 years	135
61 to 75 years	41
76 to 100 years	11
Over 100 years	2

18. *Evaluating industry sales and promotion for the Bellcamp Soup Company.* Industry reports on sales and promotion of soups have just been compiled from industry sources by the Bellcamp Soup Company (see tables at end of problem). You have drawn the assignment of writing a quick appraisal of these new data for Bellcamp top management.

In a nutshell, your task is to review the newly compiled data, to compare it with data for past years, and to point out the significant developments Bellcamp executives should be acquainted with. As you see the data before you, the sales figures should give you a fair idea of what has happened. From the promotion data, you may be able to find some explanation of why it happened.

As usual, you will write the report in the company's traditional short-report form, which includes only title page as a prefatory part. You will write it in the direct order, leading off with a summary of your major observation. Because the report is primarily quantitative, you will make some use of graphic aids.

SHARE OF U.S. SOUP MARKET, BY COMPANY 1966–68

	3 Years Ago			2 Years Ago			1 Year Ago		
	Total Market	Dry Market	Wet Market	Total Market	Dry Market	Wet Market	Total Market	Dry Market	Wet Market
Bellcamp............	82%	14%	90%	82%	97%	90%	82%	8%	90%
Tonlip..............	6	50	...	6	56	...	6	57	...
Freing..............	4	...	5	4	...	5	4	...	5
Doarr..............	3	22	...	2	14	...	1	12	...
Siler's..............	1	10	...	1	13	...	2	16	...
J. I. Green..........	...	2	...	...	2	...	...	3	...
Subtotal......	96%	98%	95%	95%	94%	95%	95%	96%	95%
All others..........	4	2	5	5	6	5	5	4	5

SOURCE: J. C. Merrill and Associates.

Advertising Media	Bellcamp	Tonlip	Freinz	Doarr	Siler's	J. I. Green	Others
Magazines							
1 year ago...............	7,379	1,225	...	1,339	...	...	...
2 years ago...............	6,219	1,773	9	764	114	...	38
Newspapers							
1 year ago...............	668	60	393	345	13	15	43
2 years ago...............	953	...	...	14	...	19	44
Spot TV							
1 year ago...............	1,664	1,763	1,026	921	...	89	155
2 years ago...............	1,791	1,441	705	185	292	307	66
Network TV							
1 year ago...............	5,632	327	...	261	...	...	...
2 years ago...............	6,447	394	...	38	...	...	63
Spot Radio							
1 year ago...............	1,490	...	...	40	34	76	...
2 years ago...............	3,210	...	...	92	...	27	57
Network Radio							
1 year ago...............	551	...	...	...	453	...	...
2 years ago...............	744	...	...	...	117	...	...
Total							
1 year ago...............	17,384	3,375	1,419	2,906	500	180	198
2 years ago...............	19,364	3,608	714	1,093	523	353	268

SOURCE: Bureau of Advertising Sources; Publishers Information Bureau.

19. *Determining the need for a restaurant in your university community* (requires research). Warren's, Inc., a national food service chain, is considering placement of one of its eating facilities in your university community. It has hired you to analyze the need for such a facility and to recommend the appropriate action.

The Warren organization actually consists of two food service systems. One is made up of 327 short-order stands, bearing the name The Dog House. As the name implies, The Dog House specializes in a variety of hot dogs, although it handles a well-rounded assortment of sandwiches, ice creams, and soft drinks. The other chain consists of 132 small-scale cafeterias, bearing the name Serve'nSave. These restaurants offer a streamlined menu of typical, tasty American food at low prices. They operate on a self-service plan.

From you, the Warren people want recommended answers to two basic questions: First, is there need for additional eating facilities in the university community? Second, if there is a need, which of the two types of Warren's operations would be best?

In answering these questions, you will survey the eating facilities in the area, evaluating each as to its menu offering, prices, service, and convenience of location. From your analysis, you will base your recommendation.

You will write the report in typical short-report form, consisting of title page and text. The text you will begin in direct order, leading off with your recommendations and following them with a quick summary of supporting information. The more detailed presentation of the report material will follow. Address the report to Mr. Kenneth A. Warren, president.

20. *Analyzing the consumer market for the months ahead.* Move the calendar back to mid-1968. Charles H. Buckham, president of the Continental Credit Corporation, has asked you (his administrative assistant) to digest for him the most recent data released on consumer buying. The data you will use are compiled quarterly by the Bureau of the Census, U.S. Department of Commerce. They cover both recent past purchases and projected future purchases. The Bureau obtains these data for past periods by samples of actual sales reports. The projection, however, it makes by a somewhat unique method.

In summary, this projection method consists of obtaining from a survey of 15,000 households from all 50 states probability judgments concerning future purchases. Each respondent is asked to rate his likelihood of purchasing automobiles, houses, household appliances, and furniture on a 0–100 scale, and to state the price they expect to pay. The most recent survey results are summarized in the tables that follow.

Largely, your report for Mr. Buckham will be informational. Because Continental extends credit primarily for automobile and household durables, you will limit your report to the data concern-

PAST AND PROJECTED CONSUMER EXPENDITURES FOR DURABLES
(Seasonally adjusted—at annual rates; in billions of dollars)

	Past									Projected		
	1966				1967				1968			
					Quarter							
	1st	2nd	3rd	4th	1st	2nd	3rd	4th	1st	2nd	3rd	4th
Consumer durables...........	71.6	68.2	70.9	70.6	69.4	72.5	72.7	73.8	78.4	79.2	81.0	83.2
New automobiles...........	31.4	28.5	29.8	29.6	27.3	29.7	29.9	30.1	33.2	32.4	32.9	33.9
Major appliances and furniture................	29.4	29.1	30.6	30.6	31.4	31.9	32.1	32.6	34.2	35.2	36.0	36.9
Other durables............	10.8	10.6	10.5	10.4	10.7	10.9	10.7	11.1	11.0	11.6	12.1	12.4

EXPECTATION OF BUYING DURABLES AND HOUSING, BY REGION AND RACE
(12-month expectation, not seasonally adjusted)

	Oct.'66	Jan.'67	Apr.'67	July'67	Oct.'67	Jan.'68	Apr.'68
New cars (chances in 100)							
By region							
Northeast..........	10.2	10.0	9.0	10.5	9.3	9.4	9.3
North Central......	11.5	11.3	10.2	10.6	10.0	10.7	10.3
South............	9.0	8.3	7.6	8.9	8.4	8.1	7.7
West.............	9.1	8.8	8.2	9.8	9.7	9.2	10.2
By race							
White............	11.2	10.9	9.7	10.9	10.2	10.4	10.3
Negro............	6.8	6.5	6.7	7.0	6.0	5.4	5.3
Used cars* (chances in 100)							
By region							
Northeast..........	7.1	7.2	7.4	7.8	7.7	7.4	7.7
North Central......	8.3	8.5	8.3	7.6	8.1	8.6	8.6
South............	7.2	7.1	6.7	5.9	6.6	6.9	6.5
West.............	9.3	9.1	9.4	9.9	9.6	10.0	10.5
By race							
White............	8.5	8.6	8.4	8.4	8.4	7.9	8.6
Negro............	9.4	8.6	8.9	6.3	8.1	9.0	8.5
Household durables (average in dollars)							
By region							
Northeast..........	$238	$224	$239	$256	$222	$230	$246
North Central......	220	245	217	226	214	225	223
South............	194	199	189	187	180	188	192
West.............	239	253	236	255	253	239	256
By race							
White............	$223	$230	$221	$231	$214	$220	$230
Negro............	213	204	191	197	204	195	181

* Although not a part of the consumer expenditures data (preceding table), used car sales are important in Continental s loan program.

AVERAGE PROBABILITY OF BUYING AN AUTOMOBILE WITHIN 12 MONTHS
(Chances in 100; not seasonally adjusted)

Households Classified	Chances in 100					
	Jan.'67	April'67	July'67	Oct.'67	Jan.'68	Apr.'68
By family income						
Under $3,000......	7.8	7.5	7.1	6.7	7.4	7.1
3,000–4,999.......	15.0	14.3	13.9	14.7	13.6	14.3
5,000–7,499.......	21.3	19.2	20.0	18.8	20.0	18.5
7,500–9,999.......	24.6	23.0	24.8	22.7	23.6	23.6
10,000–over.......	30.4	28.9	30.8	29.4	29.0	30.1

AVERAGE EXPECTED EXPENDITURES FOR NEXT 12 MONTHS,
MAJOR HOUSEHOLD DURABLES AND HOME IMPROVEMENTS
(Not seasonally adjusted; in dollars)

Family Income	1966	1967				1968	
		Quarter During Which Survey Was Taken					
	4th	1st	2nd	3rd	4th	1st	2nd
Under $3000.............$	77	$ 75	$ 71	$ 75	$ 75	$ 80	$ 84
$3000–4999.............	153	147	136	153	145	145	143
$5000–7499.............	233	244	208	225	212	220	202
$7500–9999.............	300	297	298	301	259	276	297
$10,000 and over.........	422	424	430	418	399	391	414
All income groups.........$	222	$227	$218	$227	$213	$218	$226

ing these items. You will present the data in clear written form, emphasizing the highlights you find. You will want to emphasize any regional developments that may be of importance in planning for the organization's 512 branches. As a final goal, you will arrive at a general conclusion of prospects for the credit business in the months ahead.

Because Mr. Buckham will take this report with him to the board of directors meeting next week, you will present your report in the company's standard short-report form (title page plus report body). You will write the report in the direct order, beginning with your major observations or conclusions. In addition, you will make good use of graphic aids whenever they help tell the statistical story.

21. *Analyzing performance of the Bay City Store.* As an administrative assistant to President Frederick B. Green, American Stores, Incorporated, you have been assigned the task of reviewing the year's operating record of each of the food chain's 36 stores. Your objective is to compare each store's performance, by department, with the all-store averages. Then, you will inform each store manager of his store's performance.

The report that you will write to each store manager will be in memorandum form, with a copy for President Green and two other top executives. You will organize each report in the direct style of presentation, with the major observations at the beginning. As you will try hard to be objective in your work, you will take care to point out good as well as bad performances.

First of the 36 stores you will work on is the Bay City Store. Its performance summary and the all-chain average are as follows.

PROFIT AND LOSS, BAY CITY STORES BY DEPARTMENTS

	Total Store	Gro-ceries	Meats	Prod-uce	Dairy	Baked Goods	Frozen Foods	H&BA	Other Non-foods
Sales	100%	100%	100%	100%	100%	100%	100%	100%	100%
Margin on sales	18.1	16.7	18.8	23.2	14.4	16.4	27.1	31.3	25.8
Expenses:									
Personnel	7.2	5.9	11.8	14.1	3.2	4.5	6.6	7.2	4.0
Wrapping supplies	.7	.4	1.4	.7	.5	.5	.3	.3	.2
Utilities	.4	.2	.4	.8	.7	.1	2.4	.2	.3
Laundry	.1	...	.1	...	...	...	...	...	...
Insurance, outside service, telephone, bad checks, over–short miscellaneous	.2	.2	.2	.2	.2	.1	.2	.2	.2
Repairs, maintenance	.2	.1	.2	.3	.4	.1	2.5	.1	.1
Rent, depreciation of leasehold improvements	1.8	1.6	1.2	2.8	1.4	1.2	2.1	1.2	1.5
Licenses, taxes	.2	.2	.2	.2	.2	.2	.2	.2	.3
Depreciation equipment	.5	.4	.6	1.3	.9	.3	3.3	.3	.2
Advertising, promotion	.4	.8	.5	.5	.4	.5	.3	.5	.7
Stamps	2.1	2.0	2.0	2.0	2.0	2.0	2.0	2.0	2.0
All other overhead	1.1	1.3	1.2	1.2	1.2	1.2	1.2	1.2	1.2
Total Expenses	14.9	13.1	19.8	24.1	11.1	10.7	21.1	13.4	10.7
NOP (before taxes)	3.2	3.6	(−1.0)	(−.9)	4.3	5.7	6.0	17.9	15.1

AVERAGE FOR ALL AMERICAN STORES
PROFIT AND LOSS STATEMENT BY DEPARTMENTS

	Total Store	Gro-ceries	Meats	Prod-uce	Dairy	Baked Goods	Frozen Foods	H&BA	Other Non-foods
Sales	100%	100%	100%	100%	100%	100%	100%	100%	100%
Margin on sales	18.8	16.7	18.3	28.9	15.2	16.1	25.7	32.1	26.0
Expenses:									
Personnel	6.0	4.9	8.3	12.8	3.8	4.9	5.7	3.8	3.1
Wrapping, supplies	.7	.4	1.5	.8	.5	.5	.3	.2	.2
Utilities	.5	.2	.5	.9	.7	.1	2.4	.2	.3
Laundry	.1	...	.1	...	...	...	...	...	...
Insurance, outside service, telephone, bad checks, over–short, miscellaneous	.2	.2	.2	.2	.2	.1	.2	.2	.2
Repairs, maintenance	.2	.1	.2	.3	.4	.1	1.6	.1	.1
Rent, depreciation of leasehold improvements	1.4	1.4	1.0	2.7	.9	1.0	1.8	1.2	1.6
Licenses, taxes	.2	.2	.2	.2	.2	.2	.2	.2	.3
Depreciation equipment	.7	.4	.7	1.4	1.0	.3	3.2	.3	.2
Advertising, promotion	.8	.6	.9	1.0	.9	.8	.5	1.0	1.3
Stamps	2.0	2.0	2.0	2.0	2.0	2.0	2.0	2.0	2.0
All other overhead	1.2	1.2	1.2	1.2	1.2	1.2	1.2	1.2	1.2
Total Expenses	14.0	11.6	16.8	23.5	11.9	11.2	19.0	10.4	10.5
NOP (before taxes)	4.8	5.1	1.5	5.4	3.3	4.9	6.6	22.0	15.5

22. *Solving a problem on your campus* (requires additional research). On all college campuses, some common problems exist. At least, they exist in the minds of many of the faculty, students, and staff. From the list of problem areas that follows, select one you regard as a problem at your institution.

For the problem that you select, you will first gather all the significant information that concerns it. When you are thoroughly acquainted with the facts of your problem, you will gather whatever authoritative information you can concerning how it may be solved. Perhaps your research will involve looking through bibliographical sources to find out what has been done on other campuses. It may involve getting information or opinions from the various people on campus who are involved in the problem. When you have all this information, you will carefully analyze your problem in the light of all available knowledge. Then you will arrive at a recommended solution.

So that the situation will appear to be realistic, you may assume the appropriate role or position at your college. Present your work in suitable report form.

Your problem area possibilities are as follows (some are broad and will need to be made specific).

Library operation
Campus security
Athletic ticket sales policies
Administration regulation of social
    activities
Dress regulations
Student government
Registration procedure
Faculty–student relations

Orientation program for freshmen
Curriculum improvement
Increasing enrollments
Cheating
Improving cultural atmosphere on
    campus
Class attendance policies
Scholastic probation policies
Parking

23. *Recommending an equipment purchase for Campbell's home office.* As office manager in charge of a staff of 18 at the home offices of Campbell Department Stores, Inc., 3371 Parkwood Avenue, Baltimore, you have just had a visit from Vice President Lester A. Bridges, your immediate superior. Bridges reported that funds have been made available for purchasing new——(typewriters, dictating machines, duplicating equipment, or the like—your instructor will specify). He wants you to collect information on the major brands available and to recommend the brand to be purchased.

Your procedure will be to collect all pertinent information on what you conclude to be the three best buys. Then, you will set up what you believe to be the logical bases for comparison of the products, make the comparisons, and then arrive at your recommendation. You will present your evaluations and your recommendation to Bridges in Campbell's standard memorandum report form. Because you believe Bridges may accept your recommendation without question, you will place it at the report beginning. But in the event that he does not, you will present the supporting evidence in thorough detail.

24. *Recommending a writing improvement program for Huggins Engineering, Inc.* In the role of chief consultant on the staff of Writing Improvement, Inc, you must now recommend a writing improvement program for a prospective client, Huggins Engineering, Inc. Yesterday, Elija P. Huggins, president, called you in to hear his problem. From him, you learned that Huggins engineers, like most engineers, have writing problems. In a nutshell, the engineers simply cannot express themselves clearly. Their reports, Huggins says, are masterpieces of gobbledygook. They are filled with long and involved sentences. They are poorly organized. Huggins thinks it is high time that something should be done, and that is why you have been called in.

Your organization is not new at writing improvement work. In fact, it has for about 10 years conducted short courses and clinics, prepared manuals and other literature, provided individual consulting and instruction, and the like for 75 of the nation's blue-chip firms. To do this work, you have a staff of about 15 writing experts.

In spite of your experience, however, Huggins presents a quite different problem. Huggins' operations are almost global. Its 371 engineers are currently working on projects in the United States and 17 foreign countries. Only 32 to 40 of the engineers work at the firm's central office in New York City, and from 6 to 8 normally are assigned to each of the regional offices (Atlanta, Houston, Chicago, Denver, Los Angeles, and Seattle). The remaining engineers work from temporary field offices scattered over the areas where the company operates. Usually, these field offices are staffed with from two to five engineers.

Your plan now is to design a program for Huggins—one that will fit the company's unusual organization. Because of the company's far-flung operations, you see some real problems in conducting classes. Perhaps you can handle the work by mail. Or maybe you can get the engineers to rotate in coming to the main office for instruction. Will you prepare a manual for their use? How will you keep up interest in the writing program over time? These and dozens of other questions cross your mind as you begin to prepare your plan.

Once you have your plan in mind, you write it up in a report to Huggins. You will want to tell him enough about your proposal (including cost) to permit him to accept or reject your plan. But you will not want to cloud his thinking with so many details that he will be confused or bored.

You plan to present your proposal in good report form. In addition to the normal text, you will have a title page and a combination letter of transmittal and summary. If your report becomes long enough to justify a table of contents, you will include one.

25. *Reporting on last year's volume of advertising.* Assume that you are executive director of the American Association of Advertising Agencies, and write a summary report of the year's changes in advertising volume.

Each year you write such a report for AAA members. It is a report that presents in summary form the changes in advertising volume by medium from the preceding year. The report is primarily informational, although it does call attention to any significant changes or trends that are evident.

The data below have been collected by the association's own statistical department and are confidentially treated by association members. That is why the report will not be printed in volume. Instead, it will be set up in good typewritten form and will be reproduced by multilith. As the report will be moderately long and somewhat formal, you will give it the appropriate prefatory trappings.

First, you will have a title page. Next, you will have a letter of transmitttal, addressed generally to the association members. Because the information in the report is confidential, somewhere in your letter you will remind your reader of the security they should give the report. Your third prefatory part will be a table of contents, including a list of illustrations. Because your report will be written in logical order, ending with a summary of highlights, you will not use a synopsis.

ADVERTISING VOLUME IN THE UNITED STATES, LAST THREE YEARS

	3 Years Ago		*2 Years Ago*			*Last Year*		
Medium	*Millions*	*Percent of Total*	*Millions*	*Percent of Total*	*Change from Year before*	*Millions*	*Percent of Total*	*Change from Year before*
Newspapers								
Total............	$ 4,456.5	29.2%	$ 4,876.0	29.5%	+ 9.4%	$ 4,900.0	29.1%	+ 0.1%
National........	869.4	5.7	956.0	5.8	+10.0	940.0	5.6	− 3.6
Local...........	3,587.1	23.5	3,920.0	23.7	+ 9.3	3,960.0	23.5	+ 1.0
Magazines								
Total...........	1,198.8	7.9	1,295.0	7.8	+ 8.0	1,281.0	7.6	− 0.8
Weeklies........	610.0	4.0	671.0	4.1	+10.0	651.6	3.9	− 1.0
Women's........	269.0	1.8	279.6	1.7	+ 4.0	282.0	1.7	+ 0.7
Monthlies.......	282.4	1.9	307.6	1.8	+ 8.9	312.4	1.8	− 1.2
Farm national....	37.4	0.2	36.8	0.2	− 1.6	35.0	0.2	− 4.4
Television								
Total...........	2,515.0	16.5	2,765.0	16.7	+ 9.9	2,923.0	17.4	+ 3.5
Network........	1,237.0	8.1	1,373.0	8.3	+11.0	1,476.0	8.8	+ 6.0
Spot............	866.0	5.7	931.0	5.6	+ 7.5	947.0	5.6	− 1.4
Local...........	412.0	2.7	461.0	2.8	+11.9	500.0	3.0	+ 6.1
Radio								
Total...........	917.0	6.0	1,001.0	6.1	+ 9.2	1,027.0	6.1	+ 1.7
Network........	60.0	0.4	64.8	0.4	+ 8.0	64.2	0.4	+ 1.0
Spot............	268.0	1.7	294.2	1.8	+ 9.8	297.2	1.8	− 1.0
Local...........	589.0	3.9	642.0	3.9	+ 9.0	665.6	3.9	+ 3.0
Farm publications								
(Regional).......	33.5	0.2	34.2	0.2	+ 2.1	32.8	0.2	− 2.1
Total farm pubs.....	(70.9)	(0.5)	(71.0)	(0.4)	+ 0.1	(67.8)	(0.4)	− 3.3
Direct mail........	2,324.0	15.2	2,454.0	14.8	+ 5.6	2,478.0	14.7	+ 0.7
Business papers.....	671.0	4.4	711.5	4.3	+ 6.0	712.0	4.2	+ 0.1
Outdoor								
Total...........	180.0	1.2	181.0	1.1	+ 0.6	188.8	1.1	+ 6.2
National........	120.1	0.8	119.0	0.7	− 0.9	124.8	0.7	+ 6.0
Local...........	59.9	0.4	62.0	0.4	+ 3.5	64.0	0.4	+ 6.7
Transit								
Total...........	33.0	0.2	34.2	0.2	+ 3.7	36.8	0.2	+ 9.5
National........	17.4	0.1	17.8	0.1	+ 2.6	17.8	0.1	+ 7.2
Local...........	15.6	0.1	16.4	0.1	+ 4.8	19.0	0.1	+11.8
Miscellaneous								
Total...........	2,926.2	19.2	3,193.1	19.3	+ 9.1	3,264.6	19.4	+ 1.0
National........	1,733.3	11.4	1,858.7	11.2	+ 7.2	1,896.0	11.3	+ 0.5
Local...........	1,192.9	7.8	1,334.4	8.1	+11.9	1,368.6	8.1	+ 1.7
Total								
National........	9,365.0	61.4	10,075.0	60.9	+ 7.6	10,234.0	60.8	+ 0.6
Local...........	5,890.0	38.6	6,470.0	39.1	+ 9.8	6,610.0	39.2	+ 1.8
Grand Total.......	$15,255.0	100.0%	$16,545.0	100.0%	+ 8.5%	$16,844.0	100.0%	+ 1.0%

LONG PROBLEMS

26. *Interpreting television industry statistics for the Becker Advertising Agency.* Take the job of research specialist for the Becker Advertising Agency, and analyze the data President Elton W. Becker placed in your hands today. The data are the annual statistics for the television industry, compiled by the Advertising Associations of America.[1] "These statistics," Becker stated, "no doubt are

---

[1] Actually, these data were compiled by the advertising agency, Batten, Barten, Durstine and Osborne, Inc., but the fictitious association is used to make the problem realistic.

useful to us in planning the ads of our clients. And they will help us to answer some of the questions some of them ask. But there are so many important facts here that I can't take the time to study them. You do it for me."

So, with these words, he assigned you the task of reviewing the statistics and bringing to light the significant observations that are evident from them. You will not be able to cover every little detail —just the most significant parts. Becker concluded his assignment by specifying that he wants you to present your work in a report that will serve him as a reference source for the significant information on the television industry.

In sifting through the voluminous data you have assembled, you must make some early selection decisions. As you see Becker's needs, certain areas appear to have greater significance than others. These you select for your report. For example, the data on television usage you believe would be useful to Becker in convincing clients of the value of this medium. For similar reasons, television costs, especially with the constantly changing pattern of recent years, need to be known from time to time. Thus, a knowledge of time variations (both hours of the day and seasonal) and popularity of program types are vital in planning campaigns. It is this information that you decide to make the heart of your report.

Although your finished report will be to some extent informational, it will also be analytical. For this reason, you plan to write it in the logical order conventional for such reports. And because it is one of your major undertakings for Mr. Becker, you plan to present the report in formal fashion, with a full compliment of prefatory parts.

TELEVISION, GENERAL

I. Definitions.

   Penetration—the percent of total households in a given area owning one or more TV sets.

   Households using TV (HUTV)—the percent (or number) of total TV households tuned in during the average minute for a particular time period.

   Viewers per household—the average number of persons viewing per household using TV.

II. TV ownership in Continental United States.

	Total HH (000)	TV		Multisets		Color Sets	
		HH (000)	Pene-tration %	HH (000)	TV HH Pene-tration %	HH (000)	TV HH Pene-tration %
Total.............	58,240	54,900	94	13,720	25	8,100	15
New England.......	3,350	3,230	96	900	28	430	13
Met. N.Y..........	5,040	4,840	96	2,060	43	700	14
Mid. Atlantic.......	6,650	6,400	96	1,840	29	790	12
East Central........	9,310	8,950	96	2,300	26	1,440	16
Met. Chicago........	2,230	2,150	96	620	29	310	14
West Central........	8,330	7,860	94	1,700	22	870	11
Southeast...........	8,740	7,900	90	1,090	14	1,020	13
Southwest..........	5,770	5,270	91	890	17	650	12
Met. L. A..........	2,740	2,590	95	800	31	730	28
Pacific.............	6,080	5,710	94	1,520	27	1,160	20

Note: UHF penetration is 35–40 percent of TV households, and CATV penetration is about 4 percent.

III. Television usage.

SEASONAL VARIATIONS IN HOUSEHOLD TV USAGE BY DAY PART

	% of Total TV Households Tuned in during the Average Minute				
	Annual Average	Jan.– Mar.	Apr.– June	July– Sept.	Oct.– Dec.
Monday–Friday					
10 A.M.–12 noon................	19	22	19	19	18
12 noon–3 P.M...................	26	28	25	25	25
3 P.M.–5 P.M...................	28	32	27	24	27
5 P.M.–7:30 P.M................	41	48	36	31	44
All evenings					
7:30 P.M.–9 P.M.................	56	67	53	44	62
9 P.M.–11 P.M..................	56	61	56	49	58
11 P.M.–1 A.M..................	25	28	24	23	24

AVAILABLE AUDIENCE BY DAY PART (ANNUAL AVERAGE)

	% of People Viewing during the Average Minute			
	Men (18+)	Women (18+)	Teens (12–17)	Children (2–11)
Monday–Friday				
10 A.M.–12 noon................	4	12	3	12
12 noon–3 P.M..................	6	20	4	8
3 P.M.–5 P.M...................	6	19	9	16
5 P.M.–7:30 P.M................	23	29	22	35
All Evenings				
7:30 P.M.–9 P.M................	40	46	37	46
9 P.M.–11 P.M..................	39	46	29	18
11 P.M.–1 A.M..................	16	19	6	1

ANNUAL AUDIENCE COMPOSITION DURING AVERAGE QUARTER HOUR BY DAY
PART (VIEWERS PER HOUSEHOLD)

	Men (18+)	Women (18+)	Teens (12-17)	Children (2-11)	Total Viewers
Monday–Friday					
10 A.M.–12 noon............20	.75	.05	.40	1.40
12 noon–3 P.M..............25	.95	.05	.20	1.45
3 P.M.–5 P.M...............25	.80	.15	.40	1.60
5 P.M.–7:30 P.M............50	.70	.20	.60	2.00
All Evenings					
7:30 P.M.–9 P.M............65	.85	.20	.55	2.25
9 P.M.–11 P.M..............70	.90	.20	.25	2.05
11 P.M.–1 A.M..............65	.85	.10	.05	1.65

IV. Index of seasonal variations in household TV usage.

The following table provides a fast indication of seasonal changes in household TV usage levels by time zone and day parts.

In many smaller markets, rating reports appear only twice a year, usually during the spring and fall. This table permits ready estimates of seasonal audience differences in these local markets. For instance, a fall rating in early fringe time (5 P.M.–7:30 P.M.) in a market in the eastern time zone would probably be 35 percent lower during the summer.

INDEX OF HOUSEHOLDS USING TV TO FALL LEVELS

	Local Time in Each Zone		
	Eastern	Central	Pacific
Monday–Friday			
10 A.M.–12 noon			
Fall....................100	100	100
Winter..................130	110	125
Spring.................. 85	90	110
Summer..................100	100	130
12 noon–3 P.M.			
Fall....................100	100	100
Winter..................110	100	130
Spring.................. 75	80	105
Summer.................. 85	95	135
3 P.M.–5 P.M.			
Fall....................100	100	100
Winter..................115	120	145
Spring.................. 75	80	120
Summer.................. 75	90	120
5 P.M.–7:30 P.M.			
Fall....................100	100	100
Winter..................120	115	135
Spring.................. 70	75	90
Summer.................. 65	70	85

	Local Time in Each Zone		
	Eastern	Central	Pacific
All Evenings			
7:30 P.M.–9 P.M.			
Fall..................100	100	100	
Winter...............110	105	110	
Spring............... 70	80	90	
Summer.............. 60	70	75	
9 P.M.–11 P.M.			
Fall..................100	100	100	
Winter...............105	110	105	
Spring............... 90	90	95	
Summer.............. 80	85	85	
11 P.M.–1 A.M.			
Fall..................100	100	100	
Winter...............110	110	110	
Spring............... 95	90	100	
Summer..............100	115	115	

NETWORK TELEVISION

I. Definitions.

Average minute households—the number of TV households tuned to the program during the average minute of that program.

Average minute rating—the average minute households tuned to the program as a percent of all TV households.

Cost per minute—the cost of one minute of commercial time.

CPM (cost per thousand) households—the cost to reach 1,000 households with 1 minute of commercial time.

Average minute people (adults, women, etc.)—the number of people (adults, women, etc.) viewing the program during the average minute of that program.

CPM (cost per thousand) viewers (adults, women, etc.)—the cost to reach 1,000 viewers (adults, women, etc.) with 1 minute of commercial time.

Demographic peaks of appeal—indicates the pattern of rating performance within key market groups.

II. Nighttime.

COST AND AUDIENCE TRENDS, AVERAGE NIGHTTIME NETWORK SHOW

	Cost/Min.	Avg. Min. Rtg.	Avg. Min. HH (000)	Avg. HH CPM	Avg. Min. People (000)	Avg. Viewer CPM
1955–56........\$18,500		18.0%	6,000	\$3.10	18,000	\$1.05
1960–64........ 28,000		18.0	8,000	3.50	18,000	1.50
1965–66........ 36,000		17.5	9,000	4.00	19,500	1.85
1966–67........ 38,500		17.5	9,500	4.05	20,500	1.90

III. Daytime.

COST AND AUDIENCE DELIVERED

	Cost/Min.	Avg. Min. Rtg.	Avg. Min. HH (000)	Avg. HH CPM	Avg. Min. Women (000)	Avg. Women CPM
ABC						
11 A.M.–5 P.M.	$ 5,100	5.5%	3,000	$1.70	2,400	$2.15
CBS						
Morning plan	$ 4,450	5.5	3,000	$1.50	2,100	$2.10
11:45 A.M.–4:30 P.M.	$10,000	12.0	6,600	$1.50	5,900	$1.70
NBC						
10 A.M.–4:30 P.M.	$ 5,600	6.5	3,600	$1.55	3,200	$1.75

DEMOGRAPHIC PEAKS OF APPEAL BY PROGRAM TYPE
(A, above average; B, average; C, below average)

		Female Viewer Characteristics								
		Income			Age			County Size		
Program Type	Women	L	M	U	Y	M	O	A	B	C/D
Comedy	B	A	C	C	A	C	C	C	C	A
Serials	A	A	C	C	A	C	B	C	B	A
Quiz and audience participation	A	A	B	C	C	C	A	C	A	A

IV. Sports.

COST AND AUDIENCE DELIVERED

	Cost/Min.	Avg. Min. Rtg.	Avg. Min. HH (000)	Avg. HH CPM	Avg. Min. Adult Men (000)	Avg. Men CPM
Football:						
NFL	$70,000	15.0%	8,200	$8.55	7,800	$ 8.95
AFL	38,000	7.5	4,100	9.25	3,900	9.75
NCAA	47,500	12.0	6,600	7.20	5,100	9.30
Bowl games	41,500	20.0	11,000	3.75	10,500	3.95
Baseball:						
Saturday afternoon	17,500	8.0	4,400	4.00	3,200	5.45
Specials:						
All Star	35,000	14.0	7,700	4.55	6,000	5.85
World Series	62,000	26.0	14,300	4.35	11,400	5.45
Golf:						
Series	22,000	4.5	2,500	8.80	2,200	10.00
Specials	26,000	6.0	3,300	7.90	2,900	8.60
Bowling	12,000	6.0	3,300	3.65	2,400	5.00
General sports series:						
ABC Wide World of Sports	18,100	9.0	5,000	3.60	3,300	5.50
CBS Sports Spectacular	22,000	6.5	3,600	6.10	2,900	7.60

V. Children (Saturday morning).

COST AND AUDIENCE DATA (ANNUAL AVERAGE)

Cost/minute...................................$6,500
Avg. household rating........................ 7.5%
Avg. min. households (000).................... 4,100
Avg. household CPM........................... $1.60
Avg. children 2–5 years (000)................. 2,300
Avg. children 2–5 years CPM.................. $2.85
Avg. children 6–11 years (000)............... 3,400
Avg. children 6–11 years CPM................ $1.90

VI. Other network programs.

COST AND AUDIENCE DELIVERED (ANNUAL AVERAGE)

	Cost/Min.	Avg. Min. Rtg.	Avg. Min. HH (000)	Avg. HH CPM	Avg. Min. Adults (000)	Avg. Adult CPM
Today	$ 9,500	4.0%	2,200	$4.30	2,800	$3.40
Tonight (M–F)	16,100	6.5	3,600	4.45	5,400	3.00
Early network news:						
ABC	$12,000	7.0	3,800	$3.15	5,000	$2.40
CBS	25,000	14.0	7,700	3.25	12,300	2.05
NBC	22,800	14.0	7,700	2.95	12,300	1.85

DEMOGRAPHIC PEAKS OF APPEAL BY PROGRAM TYPE
(A, above average; B, average; C, below average)

Program Type	Adult Viewer Characteristics										
	Sex		Income			Age			County Size		
	M	W	L	M	U	Y	M	O	A	B	C/D
Today	B	A	B	B	B	C	B	A	C	A	C
Tonight	B	A	C	B	A	B	B	B	A	B	C
Early network news	B	B	A	B	B	C	B	A	C	B	B

SPOT TELEVISION

I. Definitions.

TV market coverage—the number of TV households tuning at least once a week to one or more stations originating in a given TV market. The table in item III shows the percent of U.S. TV households viewing stations in each group of markets. The top 10 markets combined cover 38 percent of the U.S.; the top 20, 50 percent; and so on.

Time periods—the time periods used in this section are defined as follows.

Prime evening—7:30–11 P.M., Monday to Sunday.
Early fringe—5–7:30 P.M., Monday to Sunday.
Late fringe—11 P.M.–sign-off, Monday to Sunday.
Daytime—Sign-on to 5 P.M., Monday to Friday.

Note: Ten- and twenty-second commercials are available during all time periods for network and independent stations. Sixty-second commercials are available only on independent stations during prime time when sponsored network programs are broadcast. Central time zone classifications are one hour earlier, local time.

II. Commercial television stations.

	1962	1963	1964	1965	1966
VHF.....................	443	446	453	458	464
UHF.....................	85	85	86	93	108
Total...............	528	531	539	551	572

III. TV market coverage and costs.

Markets	% U.S. TV HH Covered	Day "60" 9 A.M.– 5 P.M.	Early Fringe "60" 5–7:30 P.M.	Prime "20" 7:30– 11 P.M.	Late Fringe "60" 11:30– 1 P.M.
1–10..............	38%	$2,800	$ 6,100	$11,800	$ 4,900
1–20..............	50	4,000	8,400	15,800	6,500
1–30..............	60	5,000	10,700	19,100	7,700
1–40..............	67	5,900	12,600	21,700	8,700
1–50..............	74	6,700	13,900	23,800	9,500
1–60..............	80	7,400	15,200	25,900	10,200
1–70..............	84	7,900	16,300	27,400	10,800
1–80..............	88	8,400	17,300	28,600	11,200
1–90..............	92	8,900	18,100	29,700	11,700
1–100.............	95	9,400	18,900	30,800	12,100

Note: Although spot TV prices have gone up, the prices in the above table are lower than those reported in previous editions. This is due to a change in the base used to compute costs.
Costs are based on the average of all network stations in each market. Five plan rates were used when they were available; otherwise 6, 10, or 26 plan rates were used.

IV. Average rating levels for spot TV announcements in the top 100 markets by program type (fall).

| Program Type | HUTV | Avg. Rating Levels | | | | | |
		HH	Men	Women	Teens	Children	Total Viewers
Daytime.............22%							
Local movie.........		5.0	1.5	3.0	2.0	3.0	2.5
Network...........		6.0	1.5	4.5	1.0	2.5	2.5
Early fringe...........37%							
News..............		13.0	9.0	9.5	5.0	4.0	7.5
Movie.............		7.5	3.5	4.5	6.0	5.0	4.5
Syndicated.........		8.5	5.0	5.0	5.5	7.0	5.5
Prime time...........55%							
Network...........		18.5	13.0	15.0	10.0	8.0	12.0
Independent........		5.0	3.5	3.5	2.5	2.0	3.0
Late fringe...........23%							
News..............		11.5	8.0	9.0	2.0	.5	6.0
Movie.............		5.5	3.5	4.0	1.5	..	2.5
Tonight...........		6.0	3.5	4.5	.5	..	3.0

27. *Determining the profile of luggage and leather goods dealers.*
Assume the role of a research specialist for *Leather and Luggage Goods,* the trade publication for the industry. At the oral request of Mike M. Henning, managing editor, you conducted a survey of dealer-subscribers to your publication. Now you are ready to write up your findings.

The objective of your research, as Mr. Henning worded it, is to "get a profile of leather and luggage good dealers." A description of their operation, Mr. Henning reasoned, would be most helpful for organizations engaged in selling to the retailers as well as for the retailers themselves. The manufacturers, and in some instances their wholesale representatives, would be able to use such information in planning and assessing their sales efforts. Retailers would find such information helpful in comparing the various phases of their operations with others.

So it was with this general objective in mind that you designed the survey that would get you the information you feel is needed. From the publication's list of dealer-subscribers, you mailed 700 questionnaires. You got a return of 116—a percentage of over 16, which you feel is good, considering the work involved in supplying the answers. Of this total, however, 15 turned out to be not usable for one reason or another. Counting branches of the 101 companies in the sample, 196 stores are represented.

As questionnaires are somewhat useless in their initial form, you tabulated them and you worked up some summary statistics from your tabulation. There may be still more to do, but at the moment your tabulations and statistical treatment of the data for the questions are as they appear at the end of this problem description.

You are now faced with the task of preparing a comprehensive write-up of your findings. You will use formal report form, and you will prepare the report for Mr. Henning. This report will form the permanent record of your investigation, and it will serve as the source of an article that will summarize the research for readers of your publication. With perhaps only minor change, the report probably will be duplicated and made available at cost to subscribers who want more details than the article will provide.

Q. How many stores are you operating at present?

Number	*Number of stores operated*
56	1
22	2
10	3
6	4
3	5
2	6
1	7
1	8

Q. What is the size of your main store in square feet?

Number of Stores	*Square Feet of Space*
7	Under 2,000
14	2,001–4,000
36	4,001–6,000
22	6,001–8,000
9	8,001–10,000
7	10,001–12,000
5	Over 12,000

Average size: 6,160 square feet
High: 20,000
Low: 1,200

Q. How many square feet of space in your main store are devoted to selling, warehousing, and administration functions?

	1,000 and under	*1,001– 2,000*	*2,001– 3,000*	*3,001– 4,000*	*4,001– 5,000*	*5,001– 6,000*	*Over 6,000*
Number of stores:							
Selling	6	12	31	28	15	5	4
Warehousing	7	13	35	24	12	6	5

	200 and under	201– 400	401– 600	601– 800	Over 800

Number of stores:

Administration......5   15   48   30   3

Average:

Selling space......................3,009

Warehouse space...................2,688

Administration space................ 613

Q. What is (are) the size(s) of your branch store(s) in square feet?

1,000 and under	1,001– 2,000	2,001– 3,000	3,001– 4,000
16	29	38	12

Average: 2,144 square feet

Q. How many employees (full-time equivalent) do you have (other than stock voting officers of the firm) in your main store?

NUMBER OF STORES REPORTING, BY AREA OF EMPLOYMENT

Number Employees	Selling	Adminis- tration	Warehouse* and Other
0	4	17	17
1	14	38	31
2	27	33	37
3	27	11	7
4	13	1	4
5	7	1	2
6	4	..	1
7	2	..	2
8	..	..	..
9	2	..	..
10	1	..	..

* Large number of warehouse workers reported in stores supporting branch stores.

Q. How many employees (full-time equivalent) are employed at each branch store?

Number Employees	Selling	Adminis- tration	Warehouse* and Other
0	0	81	62
1	37	14	33
2	45	..	..
3	10	..	..
4	2	..	..

* In some cases, administration and warehouse functions performed at main stores.

Q. What was your total payroll to employees last year?

Payroll	Number of Stores
Under $10,000	5
$10,001–$20,000	9
$20,001–$30,000	17
$30,001–$40,000	31
$40,001–$50,000	24
$50,001–$60,000	7
$60,001–$70,000	3
$70,001–$80,000	2
Over $80,000	3

Average: $ 38,431
High: $112,400
Low: $ 3,600

Q. What was your gross sales volume?

SALES ALL STORES, INCLUDING BRANCHES

Gross Volume	Number of Stores
$200,000 and under	17
$200,001–$400,000	42
$400,001–$600,000	29
$600,001–$800,000	8
$800,001–$1,000,000	3
Over $1,000,000	2

Average: $ 394,450
High: $1,700,000
Low: $ 60,000

SALES OF BRANCH STORES

Gross Volume	Number of Stores
Under $100,000	53
$100,001–$200,000	24
$200,001–$300,000	9

Average: $108,500
Low: $ 40,000
High: $284,000

Q. What percentage of gross sales volume was done in luggage, briefcases, personal leather goods, and gifts.

	Main Store	Branches
Luggage	33.14%	31.00%
Personal leather goods	19.19	14.33
Gift items	17.13	26.20
Handbags	16.02	7.41
Briefcases	14.52	21.16

Q. What percentage of your total sales volume was done in each of the 12 months last year?

Monthly Average for All Reporting Stores

January	5.44%
February	4.73%
March	6.17%
April	5.72%
May	7.54%
June	9.12%
July	6.46%
August	7.37%
September	10.11%
October	6.15%
November	10.09%
December	21.10%
	100.00%

Q. What percent of sales do you spend on promotion?

Percent of Sales	Number of Stores
Under 2	7
2–4	49
4–6	35
6–8	5
8–10	3
Over 10	2

Average: 4.4%
High: 11.0%
Low: 0.5%

Q. What is your average gross margin, including all discounts, in luggage, briefcases, personal leather goods, and gift items?

	Luggage	Briefcases	Personal Leather Goods	Gifts
Number of Stores				
Under 35%	5	5	2	3
35%–40%	18	16	12	14
40%–45%	42	43	31	39
45%–50%	27	29	41	36
50%–55%	9	7	12	7
Over 55%		1	3	2
Average Gross Margin	42.56%	43.94%	49.07%	47.07%
High	54 %	55 %	58 %	58 %
Low	32 %	35 %	37 %	37 %

Q. How many manufacturers are represented in your luggage, briefcase, personal leather goods, and gift lines?

		Number of Stores		

	Under 5	6–10	11–15	16–20	21–25
Luggage.......................	8	39	47	7	
Briefcases.....................	44	48	9	...	
Personal leather goods...........	3	17	49	17	15

			Number of Stores			

	Under 20	21–40	41–60	61–80	81–100	Over 100
Gifts..........................	8	13	28	37	11	4

Average:
Luggage.......................11.15
Briefcases..................... 5.10
Personal leather goods...........13.00
Gifts..........................79.00

Q. What percentage of your merchandise is imported?

Percentage	Number of Stores
Under 5.......................	65
6–10.........................	27
11–15........................	5
16–25........................	3
Over 20......................	1

Average: 5.7%
High: 28 %
Low: 1 %

28. *Determining the profile of a corporate executive.* Write a report for the American Association of Manufacturers, presenting a profile of its top executives. Such a study, the association directors reason, should be most interesting, and it should also serve as a guide to executive manpower planning for the years ahead. It is with this planning point in mind that you will develop your report.

As a research specialist for the association, you have been working on this assignment for the past eight weeks. First, from 183 cooperating companies you obtained the personnel records of 220 recently promoted executives at the presidential or vice presidential levels. Of the 220, 68 had been promoted to president, 30 to executive vice president, and 122 to various vice presidential positions. Then, from these records you extracted the information you feel will be needed in your report (see summary table at end). Now, you are ready to begin the task of organizing and analyzing the data for the final task of presenting them in report form.

Because your report will be published and made available to association members who request it, you will take care to present it in appropriate form. Its formality and moderate length suggest some prefatory parts—perhaps a title page and preface (or an impersonal letter of transmittal addressed to all members). Whether you will need a table of contents and a synopsis will depend on the length of the finished report. If you find that a synopsis is not justified, you will be wise to begin your report in the direct order with a quick review of highlights.

SUMMARY TABULATIONS OF SURVEY STATISTICS

Ages	Presidents	Executive Vice Presidents	Vice Presidents
Under 35	1	0	3
35–39	5	0	9
40–44	12	5	17
45–49	25	7	44
50–54	14	13	26
55–59	8	2	18
60–65	3	1	5

Compensation*	Presidents	Executive Vice Presidents	Vice Presidents
Under 30	2	2	39
30–49	16	6	62
50–69	22	9	17
70–89	17	8	3
90–109	6	3	1
110–129	3	2	0
Over 130	2	0	0

* Base annual salaries in thousands of dollars.

Company Size of Promoted Executives*	Number of Executives (all types)
Under 10	9
10–24	8
25–49	15
50–74	15
75–99	12
100–199	26
200–499	53
500–749	13
750–999	14
1000 and over	18

* Annual sales in dollars; 000,000 omitted.

FUNCTIONAL AND CORPORATE EXPERIENCE

Principle Work Area	*Presidents*	*Number of Vice Presidents*	*Total*
Marketing	18	30	48
Administration	18	26	44
Finance	6	28	34
Operations	15	13	28
Manufacturing	3	11	14
Engineering	3	10	13
Corporation planning	3	7	10
Personnel	0	5	5
Research and development	0	3	3
Legal	1	5	6
International	0	4	4
Public relations	0	3	3
Other	1	7	8
Total	68	152	220

Years with Present Employers*	*Percent*
Hired from outside	4.2
Less than 1 year	13.7
1–5 years	13.1
6–10 years	9.2
11–15 years	14.6
16–20	15.3
21–25 years	11.0
Over 25 years	18.9

* All executives.

Years in Immediate Past Position	*Percent*
1 year or less	21.1
2 years	14.6
3 years	15.6
4 years	8.2
5 years	9.2
6 years	7.3
7 years	4.1
8 years	2.7
More than 8 years	17.0

Education (Highest Level Completed)	*Presidents*	*Vice Presidents*	*Total*
H. S. graduates		9	9
Attended college	3	17	20
Bachelor degree	43	86	129
Attended graduate school	6	17	23
Advanced degree	16	23	39

Undergraduate Major	*Presidents*	*Vice Presidents*
Business administration	32	61
Engineering	17	45
Liberal arts	7	15
Others	12	31

Advanced Degree	*Presidents*	*Vice Presidents*
M.B.A.	7	11
M.A.	2	2
LL.B.	2	4
M.S.	4	6
Others	1	..

29. *What does the future hold for the glass container industry?* As a business research specialist with Greer and Osborne Management Consultants, Incorporated, you have been assigned a special study for Kelton and Fenston, Incorporated, an investment company with main offices in Chicago. It seems that Kelton and Feston is considering the purchase of Essex Glass Works, a small but old glass container manufacturer with primary manufacturing facilities in Minneapolis.

The financial aspects of the proposed purchase Kelton and Fenston can study with their own staff specialists. What they want from you is an analysis of the container industry. Primarily, they want to determine from the past just what the future holds for the glass container industry in general. Then, more specifically, they want to know what is happening in each of the major segments of manufacturing. Although at present the Essex Glass Company is principally engaged in manufacturing containers for various industrial chemicals, almost their total output is produced under contract to a few large manufacturers in the chemical industry. But if the Kelton and Fenston organization takes over, shifts to other container types can well occur. Thus, your report should not only analyze growth patterns in general but should also point out lucrative areas that the new management might look into.

Your investigation brings up a storehouse of current and historical data from the U.S. Department of Commerce (see following tables, pages 408–11). Perhaps you will want to supplement it with additional data, but it appears to be adequate for your purpose. You will write the report in the formality that is required in this business situation, and you will make the analyses and recommendations your client needs.

U.S. Glass Container Shipments, for All Uses
(In thousands of gross)

	Total	Domestic	Export	Domestic per Capita (Units)
1966	206,299	204,093	2,206	150
1965	198,131	195,924	2,207	146
1964	186,741	184,773	1,968	139
1963	177,886	176,298	1,588	135
1962	174,195	172,240	1,955	133
1961	165,656	164,010	1,646	129
1960	156,799	154,685	2,114	124
1959	153,102	150,463	2,639	123
1958	143,366	140,469	2,897	117
1957	143,467	140,448	3,019	119
1956	140,890	137,924	2,966	119
1955	137,278	134,474	2,804	118
1954	124,649	121,870	2,779	109
1953	127,516	124,404	3,112	113
1952	114,102	111,427	2,675	103
1951	114,738	111,676	3,062	105
1950	107,897	105,254	2,643	100
1949	89,827	87,450	2,377	85
1948	97,333	93,964	3,369	93
1947	110,170	105,681	4,489	106
1946	116,084	113,547	2,537	117
1945	106,318	104,007	2,311	113
1944	97,109	95,304	1,805	103
1943	96,655	95,518	1,137	102
1942	80,667	79,685	982	86
1941	70,780	69,408	1,372	75
1940	53,391	52,494	897	57
1939	50,031	49,366	665	54
1938	44,099	43,528	571	48
1937	50,929	50,243	686	56
1936	n.a.	45,575	n.a.	51
1935	n.a.	37,642	n.a.	43

U.S. Domestic Shipments of Glass Containers by End Use
(In thousands of gross)

	Total	Food	Beverage	Drug and Cosmetic	Chemical
1966	204,093	74,914	83,601	39,766	5,812
1965	195,924	76,555	73,690	38,797	6,882
1964	184,773	72,971	67,672	36,764	7,366
1963	176,298	69,946	61,819	35,661	8,872
1962	172,240	69,920	56,091	36,795	9,434
1961	164,010	66,555	49,550	35,820	12,085
1960	154,685	63,812	42,919	34,808	13,146
1959	150,463	62,488	39,606	34,998	13,371
1958	140,469	60,199	35,231	33,526	11,513
1957	140,448	58,299	34,649	35,230	12,270
1956	137,924	56,718	35,958	33,371	11,877
1955	134,474	55,908	34,061	32,794	11,711
1954	121,870	50,609	30,072	30,058	11,131
1953	124,404	49,657	34,834	28,924	10,989
1952	111,427	45,842	31,001	25,259	9,325
1951	111,676	43,375	33,783	25,419	9,099
1950	105,254	44,530	26,280	25,706	8,738
1949	87,450	37,241	21,982	21,165	7,062
1948	93,964	39,542	26,412	21,311	6,699
1947	105,681	42,838	35,687	20,766	6,390
1946	113,547	51,647	27,668	25,963	8,269
1945	104,007	44,289	27,790	23,629	8,299
1944	95,304	38,776	26,347	21,633	8,548
1943	95,518	41,365	22,869	23,360	7,924
1942	79,685	30,271	25,256	18,983	5,175
1941	69,408	23,586	20,941	19,966	4,915
1940	52,494	17,968	15,557	15,447	3,522
1939	49,366	17,498	13,354	15,225	3,289
1938	43,528	15,466	12,257	13,067	2,738
1937	50,243	17,266	15,382	14,991	2,604
1936	45,575	16,414	12,232	14,304	2,625
1935	37,642	14,712	8,336	12,420	2,174

U.S. Domestic Shipments of Glass Containers, Percentages of Major End Uses to Total

Year	Food	Beverage	Drug and Cosmetic	Chemical
1966	36.7	41.0	19.5	2.8
1965	39.1	37.6	19.8	3.5
1964	39.5	36.6	19.9	4.0
1963	39.7	35.1	20.2	5.0
1962	40.6	32.6	21.3	5.5
1961	40.6	30.2	21.8	7.4
1960	41.3	27.7	22.5	8.5
1959	41.5	26.3	23.3	8.9
1958	42.8	25.1	23.9	8.2
1957	41.5	24.7	25.1	8.7
1956	41.1	26.1	24.2	8.6
1955	41.6	25.3	24.4	8.7
1954	41.5	24.7	24.7	9.1
1953	39.9	28.0	23.2	8.9
1952	41.1	27.8	22.7	8.4
1951	38.8	30.3	22.8	8.1
1950	42.3	25.0	24.4	8.3
1949	42.6	25.1	24.2	8.1
1948	42.1	28.1	22.7	7.1
1947	40.5	33.8	19.7	6.0
1946	45.5	24.3	22.9	7.3
1945	42.6	26.7	22.7	8.0
1944	40.7	27.6	22.7	9.0
1943	43.4	23.9	24.4	8.3
1942	38.0	31.7	23.8	6.5
1941	34.0	30.2	28.8	7.0
1940	34.2	29.7	29.4	6.7
1939	35.4	27.1	30.8	6.7
1938	35.6	28.1	30.0	6.3
1937	34.4	30.6	29.8	5.2
1936	36.0	26.8	31.4	5.8
1935	39.1	22.1	33.0	5.8

U.S. Domestic Shipments of Glass Containers for Foods (In thousands of Gross)

Year	Total Foods	Packers Ware			Dairy	Home Canning
		Total	Narrow Neck	Wide Mouth		
1966	74,914	73,773	21,605	52,168	1,141	*
1965	76,555	75,290	21,548	53,742	1,265	*
1964	72,971	71,550	20,829	50,721	1,421	*
1963	69,946	68,424	19,225	49,199	1,522	*
1962	69,920	68,309	18,989	49,320	1,611	*
1961	66,555	64,849	17,904	46,945	1,706	*
1960	63,812	61,999	17,628	44,371	1,813	*
1959	62,488	60,494	16,239	44,255	1,994	*
1958	60,199	58,276	15,422	42,854	1,923	*
1957	58,299	56,027	15,265	40,762	2,272	*
1956	56,718	54,106	15,032	39,074	2,612	*
1955	55,908	53,117	14,337	38,780	2,791	*
1954	50,609	47,831	12,745	35,086	2,778	*
1953	49,657	46,290	12,614	33,676	3,367	*
1952	45,842	42,692	11,917	30,775	3,150	*
1951	43,375	39,858	11,528	28,330	3,517	*
1950	44,530	40,835	11,061	29,774	3,695	*
1949	37,241	32,167	8,835	23,332	3,311	1,763
1948	39,542	34,178	9,852	24,326	3,247	2,117
1947	42,838	36,772	10,679	26,093	3,891	2,175
1946	51,647	45,156	10,479	34,677	3,897	2,594
1945	44,289	38,223	8,887	29,336	3,608	2,458
1944	38,776	33,709	7,550	26,159	2,966	2,101
1943	41,365	33,881	7,240	26,641	3,126	4,358
1942	30,271	24,936	5,552	19,384	3,316	2,019
1941	23,586	19,048	4,826	14,222	3,248	1,290
1940	17,968	14,790	3,800	10,990	2,456	722
1939	17,498	14,146	3,695	10,451	2,394	958
1938	15,466	12,338	3,172	9,166	2,201	927
1937	17,266	13,407	3,573	9,834	2,581	1,278
1936	16,414	13,062	3,491	9,571	2,466	886
1935	14,712	11,288	3,084	8,204	2,067	1,357

* Home canning jars and glasses are included in the wide-mouth food container data.

U.S. Domestic Shipments of Glass Containers for Beverages
(In thousands of gross)

	Total Beverages	Wine and Liquor			Beer	Soft Drinks
		Total	Wine	Liquor		
1966	83,601	17,608	5,341	12,267	38,895	27,098
1965	73,690	17,273	5,447	11,826	36,134	20,283
1964	67,672	16,756	5,446	11,310	33,252	17,664
1963	61,819	16,186	5,233	10,953	29,438	16,195
1962	56,091	15,638	4,953	10,685	26,213	14,240
1961	49,550	15,495	5,077	10,418	21,974	12,081
1960	42,919	14,911	5,047	9,864	16,507	11,501
1959	39,606	15,360	4,914	10,446	12,950	11,296
1958	35,231	13,992	4,538	9,454	11,297	9,942
1957	34,649	14,086	4,610	9,476	10,837	9,726
1956	35,958	14,821	4,706	10,115	10,710	10,427
1955	34,061	13,864	4,590	9,274	10,455	9,742
1954	30,072	12,951	4,242	8,709	9,854	7,267
1953	34,834	13,411	4,206	9,205	11,570	9,853
1952	31,001	12,200	3,682	8,518	10,456	8,345
1951	33,783	12,864	3,219	9,645	14,341	6,578
1950	26,280	13,455	3,746	9,709	6,366	6,459
1949	21,982	11,661	3,421	8,240	4,996	5,325
1948	26,412	10,942	3,182	7,760	7,665	7,805
1947	35,687	12,320	2,418	9,902	12,991	10,376
1946	27,668	14,430	4,017	10,413	6,782	6,456
1945	27,790	10,625	2,364	8,261	10,359	6,806
1944	26,347	9,362	2,738	6,624	10,080	6,905
1943	22,869	8,984	n.a.	n.a.	8,319	5,566
1942	25,256	11,184	n.a.	n.a.	9,277	4,795
1941	20,941	10,757	n.a.	n.a.	4,636	5,548
1940	15,557	8,788	n.a.	n.a.	2,942	3,827
1939	13,354	7,867	n.a.	n.a.	2,339	3,148
1938	12,257	7,376	n.a.	n.a.	2,136	2,745
1937	15,382	7,936	n.a.	n.a.	4,313	3,133
1936	12,232	7,447	n.a.	n.a.	2,674	2,111
1935	8,336	5,663	n.a.	n.a.	1,346	1,327

U.S. DOMESTIC SHIPMENTS OF GLASS CONTAINERS, RETURNABLES AND
NONRETURNABLES FOR BEER AND SOFT DRINKS
(In thousands of gross)

	Beer			Soft Drinks		
	Total	*Returnable*	*Non-returnable*	*Total*	*Returnable*	*Non-returnable*
1966	38,895	4,003	34,892	27,098	13,351	13,747
1965	36,134	3,493	32,641	20,283	13,294	6,989
1964	33,252	2,882	30,370	17,664	13,275	4,389
1963	29,438	2,693	26,745	16,195	12,303	3,892
1962	26,213	2,453	23,760	14,240	10,930	3,310
1961	21,974	2,602	19,372	12,081	9,290	2,791
1960	16,507	2,994	13,513	11,501	9,771	1,730
1959	12,950	3,021	9,929	11,296	9,830	1,466
1958	11,297	2,693	8,604	9,942	8,608	1,334
1957	10,837	2,343	8,494	9,726	8,452	1,274
1956	10,710	2,478	8,232	10,427	9,239	1,188
1955	10,455	2,444	8,011	9,742	8,565	1,177
1954	9,854	2,125	7,729	7,267	6,304	963
1953	11,570	2,934	8,636	9,853	8,980	873
1952	10,456	2,258	8,198	8,345	7,898	447
1951	14,341	4,525	9,816	6,578	6,398	180
1950	6,366	3,155	3,211	6,459	6,291	168
1949	4,996	1,995	3,001	5,325	5,274	51
1948	7,665	4,100	3,565	7,805	7,792	13
1947	12,991	9,952	3,039	10,376	10,376	
1946	6,782	5,904	878	6,456	6,456	
1945	10,359	5,940	4,419	6,806	6,806	
1944	10,080	5,809	4,271	6,905	6,905	
1943	8,319	6,562	1,757	5,566	5,566	
1942	9,277	6,181	3,096	4,795	4,795	
1941	4,636	3,676	960	5,548	5,548	
1940	2,942	2,608	334	3,827	3,827	
1939	2,339	2,108	231	3,148	3,148	
1938	2,136	2,136		2,745	2,745	
1937	4,313	4,313		3,133	3,133	
1936	2,674	2,674		2,111	2,111	
1935	1,346	1,346		1,327	1,327	

30. *What is happening to hospital costs?*   Move the calendar back to the year 1965. Place yourself in the position of a research specialist for the National Consumer League. The league, which is an organization dedicated to the task of fighting the consumers' battles on matters of price, merchandise, quality, service, and such, has been receiving complaints about the spiraling costs of medical care. So numerous have these complaints become that the organization has decided to look into the matter. And you draw the assignment.

As outlined to you by your superior, Dr. Charles F. Cory, your objective is to determine whether the complaints are justified. In the process, you will need to analyze the components of medical cost and of the consumers ability to pay them. Hopefully, you will be able to pinpoint any problem area that may exist.

You begin your research by going to the local university library. After long and exhaustive research, you come up with some data you think will fill your needs (see tables that follow, pages 413–18). How much of these data you will use and just how you will use them you have not yet determined. But you see them as a suitable basis for the analytical reports you will want.

As the problem is somewhat long and the problem's situation is somewhat formal, you will need to give your report the prefatory trappings traditional to such reports (letter of transmittal, title page, table of contents, and synopsis). Address the report to Dr. Cory, chairman, board of directors.

PERSONAL CONSUMPTION EXPENDITURES FOR MEDICAL CARE AS A PROPORTION
OF DISPOSABLE PERSONAL INCOME AND GROSS NATIONAL PRODUCT
1935–1962

Year	Total Private Expenditures for Medical Care (Millions)	Disposable Personal Income (Billions)	Gross National Product (Billions)	Private Medical Care Expenditures as a Percent of	
				DPI	GNP
1935	$ 2,288	$ 58.3	$ 72.5	3.9%	3.2%
1936	2,493	66.2	82.7	3.8	3.0
1937	2,672	71.0	90.8	3.8	2.9
1938	2,688	65.7	85.2	4.1	3.2
1939	2,848	70.4	91.1	4.0	3.1
1940	3,018	76.1	100.6	4.0	3.0
1941	3,298	93.0	125.8	3.5	2.6
1942	3,735	117.5	159.1	3.2	2.3
1943	4,189	133.5	192.5	3.1	2.2
1944	4,705	146.8	211.4	3.2	2.2
1945	5,042	150.4	213.6	3.4	2.4
1946	6,104	160.6	210.7	3.8	2.9
1947	6,790	170.1	234.3	4.0	2.9
1948	7,749	189.3	259.4	4.1	3.0
1949	8,051	189.7	258.1	4.2	3.1
1950	8,741	207.7	284.6	4.2	3.1
1951	9,440	227.5	329.0	4.1	2.9
1952	10,172	238.7	347.0	4.3	2.9
1953	11,072	252.5	365.4	4.4	3.0
1954	11,925	256.9	363.1	4.6	3.3
1955	12,827	274.4	397.5	4.7	3.2
1956	14,126	292.9	419.2	4.8	3.4
1957	15,417	308.8	442.8	5.0	3.5
1958	16,645	317.9	444.5	5.2	3.7
1959	18,189	337.1	482.7	5.4	3.8
1960	19,508	349.9	502.6	5.6	3.9
1961	20,716	364.4	518.2	5.7	4.0
1962	22,001	384.4	554.9	5.7	4.0

Data for 1960, 1961, and 1962 include Hawaii and Alaska. Data are for expenditures by the private sector and exclude governmental health expenditure for military, veterans, welfare, etc. Ratios computed by the Commission staff.

SOURCES:

Tables 1 (I–1), 4 (II–1), 14 (II–4), *Survey of Current Business*, 43:12, 14, 20, July 1963.]

Table 14 (II–4), *Survey of Current Business*, 42:14, July 1962.

U.S. Office of Business Economics, *U.S. income and output, a supplement to the Survey of Current Business*, Washington, D.C., 1958. Table I–1, p. 118–19; Table II–1, p. 144–45; Table II–4, p. 150.

————, *National income, 1954 edition, a supplement to the Survey of Current Business*, Washington, D.C., 1954. Table 30, p. 206–7.

HOSPITAL UTILIZATION IN THE UNITED STATES*
1946–1962†

Year	Hospital Beds		Average Daily Census		Admissions during Year	
	Number (in Thousands)	Per 1,000 Population‡	Number (in Thousands)	Per 1,000 Population‡	Number (in Thousands)	Per 1,000 Population‡
1946........473		3.4	341	2.5	13,655	98.7
1947........465		3.3	354	2.5	15,908	111.6
1948........472		3.3	361	2.5	15,072	103.8
1949........477		3.2	352	2.4	15,428	104.5
1950........505		3.4	372	2.5	16,663	110.9
1951........516		3.4	378	2.5	16,677	110.4
1952........531		3.5	385	2.5	17,413	113.5
1953........546		3.5	394	2.5	18,098	116.0
1954........553		3.5	393	2.5	18,392	115.6
1955........568		3.5	407	2.5	19,100	117.7
1956........586		3.5	425	2.6	20,107	121.6
1957........595		3.5	438	2.6	21,002	124.7
1958........610		3.6	451	2.6	21,684	126.5
1959........620		3.6	462	2.6	21,605	123.7
1960........639		3.6	477	2.7	22,970	128.9
1961........659		3.6	489	2.7	23,375	129.0
1962........677		3.7	509	2.8	24,307	132.3

* Excludes newborn infants and nursery accommodations.

† Nonfederal short-term general and other special hospitals. Excludes psychiatric and tuberculosis hospitals.

‡ Refers to the civilian population.

SOURCE: Health Insurance Institute, *Source book of health insurance data, 1963*, New York, The Institute, 1963, p. 71.

TOTAL EXPENDITURE ON MEDICAL CARE AS A PROPORTION OF NATIONAL INCOME AND
GROSS NATIONAL PRODUCT
1929–1963

Year	Total Medical Care Expenditures Selected Fiscal Years, 1928–29 through 1962–63 *(In Millions)*						Total Medical Care Expenditure as % of	
	Public		Private		Total		*NI*[2]	*GNP*[1]
	(Millions)	*(%)*	*(Millions)*	*(%)*	*(Millions)*	*(%)*		
1928–29.....	$ 509.5	14%	$ 3,112	86%	$ 3,621.5	100%	4.1%†	3.6%
1934–35.....	558.5	18	2,580	82	3,138.5	100	5.9	4.6
1939–40.....	858.4	22	3,023	78	3,881.4	100	5.0	4.0
1944–45.....	2,568.9	33	5,335	67	7,903.9	100	4.3	3.7
1949–50.....	3,086.0	25	9,065	75	12,151.0	100	5.3	4.6
1954–55.....	4,358.0	24	13,517	76	17,875.0	100	5.7	4.7
1955–56.....	4,757.8	24	14,731	76	19,488.8	100	5.7	4.8
1956–57.....	5,244.9	25	16,160	75	21,404.9	100	6.0	4.9
1957–58.....	5,591.5	24	17,505	76	23,096.5	100	6.3	5.2
1958–59.....	6,116.8	24	18,875	76	24,991.8	100	6.5	5.4
1959–60.....	6,362.0	24	20,427	76	26,756.4	100	6.6	5.4
1960–61.....	7,039.7	24	21,835	76	28,874.7	100	6.9	5.7
1961–62.....	7,583.7	25	23,153	75	30,736.7	100	7.0	5.7
1962–63.....	8,316.1*	25	24,650*	75	32,966.1*	100	7.2‡	5.8

* Preliminary estimates.
† 1928–29 based on 1929 only.
‡ 1962–63 based on average of third and fourth quarters of 1962.
Computations by the Commission staff.
[1] U.S. Social Security Administration, Division of Research and Statistics, *Public and private expenditures for health and medical care, fiscal years 1928–29 to 1962–63* (Research and Statistics Note No. 10–1963, September 25), Washington, D.C., 1963.
[2] U.S. Office of Business Economics, *U.S. income and output, a supplement to the Survey of Current Business*, Washington, D.C., 1958. Table I–8, p. 127.
SOURCES:
Table 8 (I–12), *Survey of Current Business*, 42:11, July 1962.
Table 8 (I–12), 11 (I–11, I–14), *Survey of Current Business*, 43:17, 18, July 1963.

Average Charge per Patient Day, Average Length of Stay, and Average Charge per Patient Stay in Nonfederal Short-Term General and Other Special Hospitals 1946–1962

Year	Average Charge per Patient Day	Average Length of Stay (Days)	Average Charge per Patient Stay
1946	$ 9.39	9.1	$ 85.45
1947	11.09	8.0	88.72
1948	13.09	8.7	113.88
1949	14.33	8.3	118.94
1950	15.62	8.1	126.52
1951	16.77	8.3	139.19
1952	18.35	8.1	148.64
1953	19.95	7.9	157.61
1954	21.76	7.8	169.73
1955	23.12	7.8	180.34
1956	24.15	7.7	185.96
1957	26.02	7.6	197.75
1958	28.27	7.6	214.85
1959	30.19	7.8	235.48
1960	32.23	7.6	244.95
1961	34.98	7.6	265.85
1962	36.83	7.6	279.91

Source: Health Insurance Institute, *Source book of health insurance data, 1963,* New York, The Institute, 1963, p. 67.

Number of People with Health Insurance Protection in the United States, by Type of Coverage*
1940–1962
(In thousands)

End of Year	Type of Coverage† Hospital Expense	Surgical Expense	Regular Medical Expense	Major Medical Expense	Loss of Income
1940	12,312	5,350	3,000	...	n.a.
1941	16,349	6,775	3,100	...	n.a.
1942	19,695	8,140	3,200	...	n.a.
1943	24,160	10,069	3,411	...	n.a.
1944	29,232	11,713	3,840	...	n.a.
1945	32,068	12,890	4,713	...	n.a.
1946	42,112	18,609	6,421	...	26,229
1947	52,584	26,247	8,898	...	30,574
1948	60,995	34,060	12,895	...	32,700
1949	66,044	41,143	16,862	...	33,626
1950	76,639	54,156	21,589	...	37,793
1951	85,348	64,892	27,723	108	38,035
1952	90,965	72,459	35,670	689	38,373
1953	97,303	80,982	42,684	1,220	39,571
1954	101,493	85,890	47,248	2,198	39,397
1955	107,662	91,927	55,506	5,241	39,513
1956	115,949	101,325	64,891	8,876	41,688
1957	121,432	108,931	71,813	13,262	42,939
1958	123,038	111,435	75,395	17,375	41,870
1959	127,896	116,944	82,615	21,850	42,665
1960	131,962	121,045	87,541	27,448	42,436
1961	136,522	126,940	94,209	34,138	43,055
1962	141,437	131,185	98,204	38,250	44,902

* Net total of people protected—eliminates duplication among persons protected by more than one kind of insuring organization, or more than one insurance company policy providing the same type of coverage.

† For hospital, surgical, and regular medical expense includes coverage provided by insurance companies, Blue Cross, Blue Shield, and medical society-approved plans, and independent plans. For major medical expense, includes insurance companies only. For loss of income includes insurance companies, formal paid sick leave plans, and coverage through employee organizations.

n.a. indicates that data were not available.

Source: Health Insurance Institute, *Source book of health insurance data, 1963,* New York, The Institute, 1963, p. 11.

DISPOSITION OF THE PRIVATE CONSUMER'S MEDICAL CARE DOLLAR,
SELECTED YEARS, 1929–1962

Year	Total Medical Care	Physi- cians	Dentists	Ophthalmic Products and Orthope- dic Appli- ances	Privately Controlled Hospitals and Sani- tariums	Other Profes- sional Services	Medical Care and Hospitali- zation Insurance	Drug Prepara- tions and Sundries
1929............100%	32.7%	16.4%	4.5%	13.7%	8.5%	3.7%	20.6%
1930............100	32.6	16.3	4.7	14.3	8.2	3.9	20.0
1932............100	31.1	14.7	4.4	18.1	7.2	3.4	21.1
1935............100	31.9	13.2	5.7	17.7	6.6	4.1	20.7
1940............100	30.3	13.9	6.2	17.5	5.7	5.5	21.0
1945............100	27.2	12.3	6.9	18.3	5.3	7.4	22.6
1950............100	29.4	10.5	5.8	23.9	5.8	7.7	17.0
1955............100	24.9	11.8	5.3	25.2	5.1	8.5	19.3
1956............100	24.9	11.5	5.8	24.9	5.0	7.6	20.3
1957............100	24.6	11.3	6.4	25.2	4.8	7.8	19.9
1958............100	25.3	11.1	6.0	25.7	4.7	7.3	19.9
1959............100	25.3	10.4	6.5	25.8	4.6	7.6	19.7
1960............100	24.8	10.2	6.2	26.6	4.5	7.6	20.0
1961............100	24.4	10.1	6.0	27.5	4.5	8.1	19.4
1962............100	24.1	9.9	6.2	28.2	4.4	8.2	18.9

SOURCES:
Table 14 (II–4), *Survey of Current Business*, 43:20, July 1963.
Table 14 (II–4), *Survey of Current Business*, 42:14, July 1962.
U.S. Office of Business Economics, *U.S. income and output, a supplement to the Survey of Current Business*, Washington, D.C., 1958. Table II–4, p. 150.
———, *National income, 1954 edition, a supplement to the Survey of Current Business*, Washington, D.C., 1954. Table 30, p. 206–7.

PERSONAL CONSUMPTION EXPENDITURES BY MAJOR CLASSES,
SELECTED YEARS, 1929–1962
(In millions)

Year	Personal Consump- tion Expendi- tures	Medical Care	Food (Less Tobacco)	Clothing (Less Jewelry)	Housing and Household Operation	Liquor and Tobacco	Recreation and Foreign Travel	Transpor- tation	All Other
1929.....$ 78,952	$ 2,937	$19,535*	$10,633	$22,181	$ 1,695†	$ 5,130	$ 7,612	$ 9,229
1930..... 70,968	2,835	17,964*	9,200	20,600	1,450†	4,746	6,147	8,026
1932..... 49,306	2,127	11,382*	5,790	15,781	1,322†	2,909	3,981	6,014
1935..... 56,289	2,288	13,632	6,777	15,377	3,989	2,982	5,281	5,963
1940..... 71,881	3,018	16,740	8,443	19,806	5,483	3,984	7,143	7,264
1945..... 121,699	5,042	34,116	18,463	27,937	10,457	7,760	6,845	11,079
1950..... 195,013	8,741	47,448	22,425	50,201	12,222	12,360	24,654	16,962
1955..... 256,940	12,827	59,242	26,595	67,260	14,050	16,508	35,341	25,117
1956..... 269,917	14,126	62,244	27,812	71,622	14,628	17,633	33,987	27,865
1957..... 285,164	15,417	65,184	28,843	75,425	15,204	18,593	36,475	30,023
1958..... 293,198	16,645	67,389	29,138	78,934	15,610	19,463	33,565	32,454
1959..... 313,538	18,189	68,074	31,005	83,800	16,545	21,106	39,157	35,662
1960..... 328,232	19,508	69,660	31,807	87,869	17,163	22,555	41,116	38,554
1961..... 336,828	20,716	70,896	32,321	91,270	17,786	23,599	39,617	40,623
1962..... 355,360	22,001	73,555	33,599	96,233	18,419	24,932	44,082	42,539

* Includes alcoholic beverages.
† Tobacco only.
SOURCES:
Table 14 (II–4), *Survey of Current Business*, 43:20, July 1963.
Table 14 (II–4), *Survey of Current Business*, 42:14, July 1962.
U.S. Office of Business Economics, *U.S. income and output, a supplement to the Survey of Current Business*, Washington, D.C., 1958. Table II–4, p. 150–51.
———, *National income, 1954 edition, a supplement to the Survey of Current Business*, Washington, D.C., 1954. Table 30, p. 206–8.

CONSUMER PRICE INDEX—UNITED STATES CITY AVERAGE: INDEXES OF SELECTED ITEMS AND GROUPS, ANNUAL AVERAGES, 1935–1963
(1957–59 = 100 UNLESS OTHERWISE INDICATED)

Year	All Items	Services	Medical Care	Hospitalization Insurance	Physicians' Fees	Dentists' Fees	Optometric Examination and Eye glasses	Hospital Daily Service Charge*	Surgical Insurance† (Dec. 1958 = 100)	Hospitalization Insurance‡	Prescriptions and Drugs
1935	47.8	53.2	49.4	58.0	53.9	52.0	69.0	23.8	...	...	69.2
1936	48.3	53.8	49.6	58.2	54.2	52.1	69.2	24.0	...	...	69.0
1937	50.0	55.4	50.0	58.7	54.5	53.3	69.6	24.6	...	...	69.4
1938	49.1	56.5	50.2	58.8	54.4	53.4	69.7	25.2	...	...	69.8
1939	48.4	56.6	50.2	58.8	54.5	53.5	70.2	25.3	...	...	69.6
1940	48.8	56.8	50.3	58.8	54.5	53.5	70.8	25.4	...	...	69.3
1941	51.3	57.5	50.6	59.1	54.7	53.6	71.0	25.9	...	...	69.9
1942	56.8	59.3	52.0	60.5	55.8	55.0	71.9	28.0	...	...	71.5
1943	60.3	60.4	54.5	63.1	59.4	57.5	75.0	30.2	...	...	72.0
1944	61.3	61.9	56.2	65.0	61.8	60.7	76.8	31.5	...	...	72.7
1945	62.7	62.7	57.5	66.6	63.3	63.3	77.8	32.5	...	...	73.2
1946	68.0	63.9	60.7	69.6	66.4	67.0	79.3	37.0	...	...	74.6
1947	77.8	66.5	65.7	74.4	70.7	72.6	82.4	44.1	...	...	80.1
1948	83.8	70.7	69.8	77.8	73.5	76.5	85.9	51.5	...	...	84.3
1949	83.0	74.0	72.0	79.7	74.8	79.6	88.7	55.7	...	...	85.6
1950	83.8	76.4	73.4	81.0	76.0	81.5	89.5	57.8	...	...	86.6
1951	90.5	80.4	76.9	83.9	78.8	84.6	93.6	64.1	...	59.4	89.1
1952	92.5	84.0	81.1	86.3	82.3	86.4	94.7	70.4	...	67.3	89.9
1953	93.2	87.5	83.9	88.1	84.5	89.2	93.7	74.8	...	72.7	90.7
1954	93.6	89.8	86.6	89.7	87.0	92.2	92.5	79.2	...	78.0	91.7
1955	93.3	91.4	88.6	91.5	90.0	93.1	93.8	83.0	...	80.1	92.7
1956	94.7	93.4	91.8	94.1	92.7	94.9	95.3	87.5	...	85.1	94.7
1957	98.0	97.0	95.5	97.1	96.7	97.2	99.0	94.5	...	90.1	97.2
1958	100.7	100.1	100.1	100.2	100.0	100.2	100.0	99.9	...	99.4	100.6
1959	101.5	102.7	104.4	102.6	103.4	102.7	101.1	105.5	100.5	110.5	102.2
1960	103.1	105.6	108.1	104.8	106.0	104.7	103.7	112.7	102.3	120.9	102.3
1961	104.2	107.6	111.3	106.7	108.7	105.2	107.0	121.3	106.9	130.0	101.1
1962	105.4	109.5	114.2	108.9	111.9	108.0	108.6	129.8	107.9	136.0	99.6
1963	106.7	111.5	116.7	110.5	114.4	111.1	109.3	138.0	108.8	140.7	98.7

* This designation changed from "Hospital Room Rates" as of December 1961. Same items priced.
† Also includes hospitalization insurance in West Coast cities.
‡ This designation changed from "Group Hospitalization" in 1958.
SOURCES:
U.S. Bureau of Labor Statistics, *Consumer Price Index. Price indexes for selected items and groups; annual averages, 1935–61, . . .* Washington, D.C., September 1962, p. 3–5, 9–14.
————, *Quarterly price indexes for selected items and groups, December 1962 to December 1963*, Washington, D.C., February 1964, p. 3, 5–6.

31. *Determining competition's advertising for a local retailer* (requires research). You have been hired by a local retailer (a department, grocery, drug, or other store to be selected by your instructor) to construct a summary of the advertising done by the store's competition and to compare this advertising with the store's own efforts. Your goal, in general, is to inform the store management of its relative position with its competition and to inform it of any conditions that may be of value to it in its competitive effort. More specifically, your study will cover what the competition advertises, how much they advertise, and when and how often they advertise.
To get this information, you will collect the local newspapers for

one full week. Then, you will go through them, page by page, recording the advertising information on forms you will design for the purpose. You will record the volume of the advertising, probably in columns (eight to the page) and inches. You will record the information on the merchandise advertised, prices, appeals, and such. Just how you will classify this information you will have to think out, but you know you will need such information for your report. The time (morning, evening) and position placement of the ad may also be of importance. In the end, you have sufficient information to give the company a good profile of the advertising of its competition in relation to its own.

After you have collected the data, you will tabulate it. Then you will analyze it and prepare it for presentation in a meaningful report for the store's management. The report will be dressed in formal style with all the prefatory elements.

32. *A study of the import and export toy market.*   The American Association of Toy Manufacturers has employed you, a business analyst with the management consulting firm of H. Y. Larry and Associates, to conduct a study of the import-export market for toys.

Understandably, AATM is concerned with the continuing threat of toy imports. From time to time in the past, they have conducted studies to determine the extent of the import-export toy trade. The last study was made only two years ago, but according to talk in the trade it is now obsolete. Things are changing fast, they say.

So it was that AATM hired you to study the import and export toy business over the past two years. In general, they want a summary picture of what has happened in toy imports and exports over this period, with an emphasis on any changes that may have come about. More specifically, they want this summary to show from what countries we import what toys. And they want to know the same thing for our exports. As a general conclusion, they want to know the severity of our changes in import-export balance.

From the U.S. Department of Commerce, you quickly find the data that will form the basis of your study (see tables pages 420–22). You will need to study them for their meanings, and to organize them for the most effective order of presentation. Then, you will write them up in the form of a formal report, using all the conventional prefatory pages. Address the report to the association's board of directors, which authorized the study.

UNITED STATES TOY IMPORTS FOR CONSUMPTION BY MAJOR COUNTRIES,
LAST TWO YEARS
(Foreign value in U.S. dollars)

Country of Origin	Dolls and Doll Clothing		Toys and Games		Wheeled Goods		Total	
	Last Year	This Year	Last Year	This Year	Last Year	This Year	Last Year	This Year
Canada	7,060	5,010	980,914	928,876	190,081	367,897	1,178,055	1,301,783
Mexico	8,164	21,848	135,268	205,206	...	...	143,432	227,054
Panama, Rep. of	...	802	1,803	76,866	...	...	1,803	77,668
Haiti	...	...	5,173	6,738	...	...	5,173	6,738
Peru	...	...	6,221	2,464	...	...	6,221	2,464
Sweden	1,791	1,896	305,938	363,975	4,705	1,472	312,434	367,343
Norway	1,841	2,293	23,715	6,935	36,729	28,868	62,285	38,096
Finland	2,307	2,849	89,858	79,185	...	...	92,165	82,034
Denmark	2,699	1,195	164,654	138,957	16,512	14,741	183,865	154,893
United Kingdom	247,156	255,651	5,166,345	8,324,674	431,486	396,975	5,844,987	8,977,300
Ireland	5,374	440	5,561	1,599	...	...	10,935	2,039
Netherlands	4,202	2,058	51,323	94,080	16,614	59,912	72,139	156,050
Belgium & Luxembourg	2,218	373	9,844	13,553	12,402	11,625	24,464	25,551
France	87,715	75,143	503,050	671,563	2,777	1,585	593,542	748,291
West Germany	186,121	158,128	3,729,686	4,039,421	22,524	35,437	3,938,331	4,232,986
East Germany	5,760	4,249	9,087	8,513	...	...	14,847	12,762
Austria	3,844	3,762	139,071	156,296	...	406	142,915	160,464
Czechoslovakia	3,293	2,807	16,105	23,670	378	6,552	19,776	33,029
Hungary	11,949	...	7,117	13,844	...	...	19,066	13,844
Switzerland	23,900	2,370	94,207	94,353	1,390	1,322	119,497	98,045
Poland	102,161	144,376	28,023	34,569	...	...	130,184	178,945
U.S.S.R.	410	1,260	877	2,666	...	...	1,287	3,926
Spain	100,954	66,878	190,259	317,853	25,836	9,745	317,149	394,476
Portugal	32,919	61,361	467,781	299,041	...	273	500,700	360,675
Italy	470,850	456,115	2,020,164	3,595,081	311,003	772,060	2,802,017	4,823,256
Yugoslavia	2,285	284	120,190	251,219	...	...	122,475	251,503
Greece	12,210	2,955	5,099	10,239	...	...	17,309	13,194
Israel	4,740	2,001	3,354	9,984	...	...	8,094	11,985
India	9,786	2,029	15,864	8,314	...	...	25,650	10,343
Indonesia, Rep. of	150	...	6,038	...	...	...	6,188	...
Korea, Rep. of	1,825	13,256	61,811	66,063	...	...	63,636	79,319
Hong Kong	6,054,644	7,104,406	13,867,337	15,959,433	3,595	4,027	19,925,576	23,067,866
Taiwan	19,959	84,800	419,438	538,989	...	...	439,397	623,789
Japan	14,471,366	14,962,524	29,685,514	35,054,027	37,734	11,094	44,194,614	50,027,645
Nansei + Nanpo Island	5,783	...	666	280	...	...	6,449	280
Australia	337	547	62,973	71,281	...	...	63,310	71,828
Other countries	9,058	6,444	22,097	30,265	...	...	31,155	36,709
Total	21,904,831	23,450,110	58,422,525	71,500,072	1,113,766	1,723,991	81,441,122	96,674,173

UNITED STATES FOREIGN TRADE IN TOYS WITH MAJOR COUNTRIES OF ORIGIN
AND DESTINATION
(Value in U.S. $1,000)

Countries	Last Year		This Year		Percentage Change	
	U.S. Imports	U.S. Exports	U.S. Imports	U.S. Exports	U.S. Imports	U.S. Exports
Japan	44,195	6,183	50,028	3,784	+13.2%	−38.8%
Hong Kong	19,926	302	23,068	562	+15.8	+86.1
United Kingdom	5,845	2,224	8,977	2,235	+53.6	+ 0.5
Italy	2,802	783	4,823	1,056	+72.1	+34.9
West Germany	3,938	1,480	4,233	1,888	+ 7.5	−27.6
Canada	1,178	8,084	1,302	8,756	+10.5	+ 8.3
Venezuela	...	4,218	...	3,277	...	−22.3
Australia	63	880	72	1,404	+14.3	+59.5
France	594	745	748	1,122	+25.9	+50.6
Other countries	2,900	9,304	3,423	11,234	+18.0	+20.7
Total	81,441	34,203	96,674	35,318	+18.7	+ 3.3

UNITED STATES TOY EXPORTS BY KIND AND BY MAJOR COUNTRIES, LAST TWO YEARS

(Value in U.S. dollars)

Country of Destination	Dolls		Indoor Games		Toys		Wheeled Goods		Total	
	Last Year	This Year	Last Year	This Year	Last Year	This Year	Last Year	This Year	Last Year	This Year
Canada	551,472	438,045	1,063,509	1,103,267	5,950,117	6,491,000	519,095	723,421	8,084,193	8,755,733
Mexico	80,113	109,456	205,019	32,273	523,648	619,227	107,166	105,750	915,946	866,706
Guatemala	42,325	31,224	26,479	7,161	205,175	220,615	86,860	45,204	360,839	304,204
El Salvador	25,568	18,217	10,047	10,344	151,733	121,275	32,039	40,781	219,387	190,617
Honduras	8,433	5,648	8,486	5,435	98,870	85,331	29,224	32,990	145,013	129,404
Nicaragua	7,305	8,653	10,620	4,743	119,591	100,485	81,737	59,595	219,253	173,476
Costa Rica	29,850	13,122	3,528	6,049	124,573	124,565	39,216	47,108	197,167	190,844
Panama	49,011	73,249	68,992	52,980	410,444	314,587	55,683	63,396	584,130	504,212
Bermuda	18,216	12,366	12,129	8,642	102,277	128,415	12,059	13,700	144,681	163,123
Bahamas	15,841	30,033	121,785	46,911	116,485	152,275	19,229	19,709	273,340	148,928
Jamaica	4,100	10,918	2,087	5,124	119,612	87,009	7,766	4,382	133,565	107,433
Dominican Republic	8,612	17,345	3,894	16,425	92,683	137,798	18,871	31,262	124,060	202,830
Trinidad	5,952	2,710	2,452	22,218	28,133	21,501	1,770	3,765	38,307	50,194
Netherlands Antilles	12,767	7,436	24,586	18,779	45,526	112,505	16,959	7,117	99,838	145,837
Colombia	3,520	18,802	2,243	558	8,350	32,722	600	4,626	14,713	56,708
Venezuela	277,691	277,218	863,409	515,711	2,600,760	2,113,605	476,167	370,843	4,218,027	3,287,377
Ecuador	3,233	1,474	4,616	3,164	93,669	109,258	18,054	13,093	119,572	126,989
Peru	90,453	130,310	59,057	18,592	292,608	433,641	101,045	150,718	543,163	733,261
Bolivia	13,600	6,487	3,853	57,732	30,513	23,848	730	1,758	48,696	89,825
Chile	7,234	9,765	2,400	45,597	22,512	32,354	1,156	915	33,302	88,631
Brazil	404	2,848	200	...	2,678	21,219	350	1,191	3,632	25,258
Argentina	116,378	159,296	1,830	3,604	90,200	102,948	...	1,382	208,408	262,928
Iceland	2,569	1,517	...	684	23,421	76,257	3,105	...	29,095	82,760
Sweden	35,203	10,494	61,706	182,730	442,200	395,963	1,158	2,750	540,267	591,938
Norway	10,350	6,402	5,341	6,784	58,913	104,687	850	...	75,454	117,873
Finland	2,450	1,006	6,076	3,442	82,424	79,375	...	...	90,950	83,822
Denmark	6,347	...	9,968	1,959	95,937	114,111	...	...	112,252	116,070
United Kingdom	105,074	193,882	871,972	588,388	1,215,066	1,402,499	31,420	49,960	2,223,532	2,234,729
Ireland	...	...	56,402	125,517	11,992	288,056	...	332	68,394	413,905
Netherlands	20,852	17,752	31,070	37,360	524,523	789,265	4,692	4,628	581,137	849,005
Belgium	13,390	7,214	95,909	72,435	370,198	267,661	2,461	...	481,958	347,310
France	62,078	136,947	50,451	140,495	631,402	843,945	1,224	505	745,155	1,121,892
West Germany	143,402	271,068	389,369	254,541	901,802	1,358,166	45,845	3,849	1,480,418	1,887,624
Austria	657	6,869	1,080	1,686	35,728	145,662	...	...	37,465	154,217
Switzerland	31,315	22,439	28,372	113,784	348,671	502,895	2,291	592	410,649	639,118
Spain	51,571	109,705	244	4,258	76,699	125,680	212	...	128,726	240,235
Portugal	646	5,655	15,891	554	53,414	164,179	...	1,052	69,951	171,440
Italy	77,508	44,191	59,342	105,213	640,200	901,423	5,459	5,078	782,509	1,055,905
Greece	2,703	4,270	...	...	...	22,479	...	1,770	2,703	28,519

UNITED STATES TOY EXPORTS BY KIND AND BY MAJOR COUNTRIES (CONTINUED)

Country of Destination	Dolls		Indoor Games		Toys		Wheeled Goods		Total	
	Last Year	This Year	Last Year	This Year	Last Year	This Year	Last Year	This Year	Last Year	This Year
Lebanon	2,076	2,169	6,116	6,307	57,318	41,536	14,460	16,334	79,970	66,346
Saudi Arabia	...	...	7,419	22,016	11,584	15,357	3,235	5,611	22,238	42,984
Thailand	...	...	77,480	107,772	10,323	24,777	4,727	10,244	92,530	142,793
Malaysia	2,596	1,630	64,288	3,908	105,031	26,699	4,110	458	176,025	32,695
Singapore	...	3,409	...	23,524	...	137,820	...	2,314	...	167,067
Philippines, Rep. of	4,211	852	47,443	99,693	182,810	171,928	6,525	17,576	240,989	290,049
Korea, Rep. of	...	...	...	43,678	623	600	...	...	623	44,278
Hong Kong	13,102	94,636	36,776	153,210	221,230	296,929	31,109	17,715	302,217	562,490
Taiwan	...	...	3,450	93,696	218	2,065	...	...	3,668	95,761
Japan	180,486	391,808	5,086,226	2,962,374	882,685	388,606	33,214	40,840	6,182,611	3,783,628
Nansei + Nanpo Island	458	...	345,739	348,631	6,768	7,431	912	581	353,877	356,643
Australia	37,248	26,456	52,763	94,900	773,870	1,273,133	15,996	9,802	879,877	1,404,291
New Zealand	5,293	4,416	...	1,198	120,655	98,450	648	238	126,596	104,302
French Pacific Islands	1,255	1,726	384	532	36,775	43,162	3,787	3,942	42,201	49,362
Libya	764	...	15,614	49,694	3,716	8,691	494	364	20,588	58,749
Spanish Africa	894	628	...	376	6,176	26,858	...	...	7,070	27,862
Liberia	911	368	1,041	2,949	20,311	39,206	5,817	4,635	28,080	47,158
Rep. of South Africa	110,825	57,509	23,877	12,790	581,736	700,261	2,935	1,028	719,373	771,588
Other Countries	17,556	17,497	70,223	88,696	218,159	313,464	29,141	19,245	335,079	438,902
Total	2,315,868	2,827,137	10,023,253	7,741,083	19,982,735	22,785,458	1,881,603	1,964,149	34,203,459	35,317,827

33. *Recommending an advertising plan for Universal Mills.* Move back to the year 1967 and place yourself in the position of research specialist for Universal Mills, Kansas City, Kansas. Although the company dates back to the early 1900's, its venture into the cereal manufacturing business is a new experience.

At the moment, the company has completed plans for manufacturing a short line of breakfast cereals. The line will include Corn Krispes (a corn flake), Rice Puffs and Wheat Puffs (puffed rice and wheat), Honey Crisps (a sugar-coated rice cereal), Jiffy Oats (oatmeal), and Cream-o-malt (a hot wheat cereal). Now, it must work on the marketing phase of launching the new products, and this is where you come in. Specifically, it will be your job to recommend an advertising plan for the new product—one that will get the new line off the ground.

Although Universal Mills is small compared with the other cereal manufacturers, it nevertheless seeks to crash the cereal market. Its products will be of a high quality, costing more and tasting better than any of its competitor's products.

To launch this new line, it will budget $3.2 million for the first year of advertising, which is a small amount when compared with the Kellogg, General Mills, and General Foods expenditures, but large for a company like Universal Mills. With this amount, the company hopes to cover the nation, and they hope to do it as thoroughly and effectively as possible.

As you begin your planning, you are painfully aware that Universal Mills has had little experience in this area of advertising. So after discussing the matter at length with Henry Booth, director of advertising, you agree that Universal Mills may well learn from the experiences of your competition. Their experiences are a matter of public record, you reason, for summary data on them are available in a recent issue of a trade magazine. As you and Booth reason, these companies have learned from experience, so why not learn from them?

So you gather the most recent statistics on advertising expenditures of the cereal manufacturers (see tables pages 424–25). As Booth suggested, you will analyze these figures, looking for industry patterns. Then, you will use your analysis in determining what Universal Mills should do. Specifically, from your analysis you will base your recommendation on how to apportion the budgeted amount by advertising medium and by product type.

You will, of course, write up your analysis and your recommenda-

ADVERTISING EXPENDITURES, BY MEDIA, OF SIX MAJOR UNITED STATES CEREAL MANUFACTURERS, 1965–66
(All figures in thousands of dollars)

	Spot TV		Network TV†		Magazines (General and Farm)		Newspapers (Incl. Supplements)		Spot Radio*	
	1965	1966	1965	1966	1965	1966	1965	1966	1965	1966
Kellogg 1965 total; $36,406.3; 1966 total; $36,549.2										
All Bran	...	...	495.3	329.0	109.5	...	12.6	...	...	...
Apple Jacks	...	...	...	1,763.2	...	...	45.5	472.2	...	...
Bran Buds	...	...	495.3	407.3	198.1	...	...	...	...	...
Cocoa Krispies	...	...	347.7	285.2	28.8	44.5	...	...	...	...
Concentrate	...	...	...	...	170.2	...	...	...	...	...
Corn Flakes	...	...	4,057.1	3,804.6	1,179.6	...	574.0	...	...	...
Corn Flakes & Fruit	...	...	...	...	...	...	259.3	...	...	...
Fruit Loops	...	...	316.1	326.6	20.0	...	...	...	...	...
OKs	...	...	...	...	2.2	...	...	...	...	...
Product 19	...	...	...	...	...	145.6	...	174.7	..	...
Raisin Bran Flakes	...	...	996.9	945.3	28.1	7.5	70.7	54.0	...	...
Rice Krispies	...	...	2,605.0	2,377.1	536.4	57.2	...	...	...	...
Special K	...	...	2,434.2	2,941.8	612.4	614.3	...	...	...	...
Stars	...	...	362.2	133.5	...	...	139.5	...	...	...
Sugar Frosted Flakes	...	...	1,401.9	1,880.4	526.5	...	320.5	...	...	...
Sugar Pops	...	...	295.6	423.7	...	...	...	...	...	...
Sugar Smacks	...	...	319.7	440.1	...	...	...	...	...	...
Contest	...	...	...	...	21.6	...	...	...	...	...
Triple Snack	...	...	95.2	14.0	...	...	282.7	148.2	...	...
Handi Pak	...	...	160.4	...	...	...	...	...	...	...
Jumbo Assortment	...	...	38.0	...	...	...	98.9	72.5	...	...
Request Pak	...	...	200.8	8.2	...	...	...	...	...	...
Snack Pak	...	...	324.8	33.4	...	...	...	...	...	...
Variety Pak	...	...	725.4	572.9	312.6	...	...	...	...	...
Unclassified	...	...	523.2	479.6	345.6	356.4	143.2	372.6	1,033.0	118.0
Totals	13,140.0‡	16,273.6‡	16,194.8	17,165.9	4,091.6	1,225.5	1,946.9	1,294.2	1,033.0	118.0
General Mills 1965 total, $26,103.7; 1966 totals, $26,209.8										
Buttercup	58.5	6.3	...	...	...	6.7	...	...	...	...
Cheerios	1,079.0	850.6	4,748.5	5,095.2	...	...	...	...	...	...
Cocoa Puffs	87.3	136.5	398.1	569.9	...	...	...	...	...	...
Country Corn Flakes	960.6	343.7	389.8	416.9	3.8	...	18.4	...	...	...
Frosted Corn Bursts	...	39.0	...	...	...	...	...	...	...	...
Frosty O's	81.3	61.3	313.5	256.6	...	...	...	...	...	...
Good News	99.8	38.2	...	...	5.3	...	...	1.6	...	...
Kix	54.5	63.8	499.7	510.2	...	...	...	3.5	...	...
Lucky Charms	346.4	110.5	1,050.8	575.6	...	...	0.2	...	...	...
Protein Plus	...	...	...	...	...	26.0	...	...	...	...
Raisin Bran	3.1	...	...	...	241.3	...	...	...	...	...
Smiles	...	51.5	...	...	...	10.7	...	...	...	...
Sugar Jets	55.8	55.4	148.5	200.7	...	...	...	...	...	...
Total Cereal	398.2	412.2	2,752.2	3,083.5	280.3	280.7	...	86.5	...	...
Trix	117.0	100.2	889.2	771.8	...	...	...	...	...	...
Twinkles	66.8	...	190.5	...	...	...	...	...	...	...
Wackies	438.5	...	...	...	...	...	49.5	...	...	...
Wheat Hearts	...	...	...	...	...	26.0	...	...	...	...
Wheat Stax	182.4	922.2	...	1,550.7	...	154.0	...	...	...	...
Wheaties	2,089.9	1,469.8	987.1	1,930.3	...	...	...	...	...	...
Unclassified	6,491.2	4,821.9	43.7	137.6	...	...	...	...	238.0	334.0
Totals	12,610.3	9,483.1	12,411.6	15,099.0	530.7	504.1	68.1	91.6	238.0	334.0
General Foods 1965 total, $17,332.2; 1966 total, $22,604.3										
Alpha Bits	597.9	670.9	183.9	544.3	...	...	...	...	...	...
Bran Flakes	138.3	0.4	129.3	...	...	598.6	...	...	...	...
Bran & Prune Flakes	624.3	90.9	457.4	136.0	12.0	...	57.5	...	...	...
Corn Flakes & Fruit	1,881.8	1,588.4	...	580.7	0.7	23.5	...	...	...	...
Corn Flakes & Blueberries	...	...	426.7	255.6	76.0	53.4	117.0	70.4	...	...
Corn Flakes & Peaches	...	...	179.8	305.8	...	...	105.5	104.8	...	...

	Spot TV		Network TV†		Magazines (General and Farm)		Newspapers (Incl. Supplements)		Spot Radio*	
	1965	1966	1965	1966	1965	1966	1965	1966	1965	1966
Corn Flakes & Strawberries	...	...	586.9	160.0	185.2	92.2	210.2	74.2	...	...
Crispy Critters	877.5	247.6	239.7	304.4	...	...	...	...	...	...
Fortified Oat Flakes	54.2	1,053.4	...	340.2	...	...	9.0	139.8	...	...
Grape-Nuts & Flakes	825.0	924.8	665.8	1,404.0	...	24.4	...	45.3	...	...
Honeycomb	1,543.0	3,091.4	557.3	1,592.2	...	...	...	...	...	...
Post Toasties	327.7	711.5	846.3	877.9	...	...	99.1	4.8	...	...
Puffed Corn Flakes	1,023.2	1,183.3	...	19.5	220.5	15.5	122.5	139.1	...	...
Rice Krinkles	...	...	118.7	153.8	...	...	...	...	...	...
Raisin Bran	380.5	1,020.4	212.6	355.1	...	...	...	...	...	...
Sugar Crisps	593.9	531.9	197.9	1,297.8	...	...	1.9	...	...	...
Sugar Sparkles	0.2	...	...	...	...	...	...	...	...	...
Post Tens	...	...	442.4	5.4	...	...	75.1	...	...	...
Treat Pak	...	...	120.9	24.7	...	...	...	...	...	...
Unclassified	1,409.8	1,155.7	244.2	235.3	...	...	147.9	345.0	5.0	10.0
Totals	10,277.3	12,270.6	5,609.8	8,592.7	494.4	807.6	945.7	923.4	5.0	10.0

Quaker Oats
1965 total, $12,185.2; 1966 total, $11,563.3

	Spot TV		Network TV†		Magazines (General and Farm)		Newspapers (Incl. Supplements)		Spot Radio*	
	1965	1966	1965	1966	1965	1966	1965	1966	1965	1966
Cap'n Crunch	2,938.0	1,599.5	1,625.4	1,385.8	...	3.3	4.1	2.1	...	...
Life	6.6	845.0	854.8	1,124.2	139.0	61.2	...	...	...	...
Mother's Oats	2.3	0.3	191.0	...	...	...	...	...	...	...
Muffets	2.0	...	...	...	...	...	16.9	...	...	...
Puffed Rice	255.3	0.8	374.0	41.6	15.1	...⎫	17.5	...	...	...
Puffed Wheat	222.4	0.8	586.6	24.0	15.1	...⎭	...	...	...	...
Quake	4.8	337.9	...	...	...	...	...	...	...	...
Quaker Diet Frosted Puffs	777.5	12.8	255.3	...	285.3	162.7	...	97.6	...	...
Quaker & Aunt Jemima Grits	...	172.2	...	...	...	17.3	13.0	...	...	...
Quaker Instant Oatmeal	140.3	844.9	412.1	2,233.8	...	309.4	105.1	67.2	...	...
Quaker Oats	511.4	201.9	642.2	20.8	1,067.6	926.9	1.1	0.1	...	...
Quisp	4.8	356.3	...	...	...	...	...	...	...	...
Shredded Wheat	...	78.2	...	...	...	...	...	281.9	...	...
Unclassified	625.7	207.2	47.9	116.4	...	12.2	...	...	25.0	17.0
Totals	5,491.1	4,657.8	4,989.3	4,946.6	1,522.1	1,493.0	157.7	448.9	25.0	17.0

National Biscuit
1965 total, $7,790.8; 1966 total, $7,392.2

	Spot TV		Network TV†		Magazines (General and Farm)		Newspapers (Incl. Supplements)		Spot Radio*	
	1965	1966	1965	1966	1965	1966	1965	1966	1965	1966
Cream of Wheat	65.0	29.6	896.9	937.5	70.6	68.5	...	...	361.0	317.0
Grambits	...	69.0	...	...	...	8.8	...	26.2	...	...
Hi-Graham hot cereal	46.5	84.1	...	...	...	...	3.7	3.6	...	...
Nabisco 100% Bran	475.2	...	...	298.3	...	...	...	...	...	...
Nabisco Puppets	...	7.1	...	...	...	...	...	...	...	...
Shredded Wheat	491.0	452.3	1,447.9	1,511.2	88.0	51.6	183.6	136.7	1.0	...
Shredded Wheat contest	...	...	...	...	77.7	...	...	...	...	...
Shreddies	...	...	...	...	8.4	19.3	...	3.6	5.0	24.0
Team Flakes	1,691.5	677.0	483.1	1,490.0	499.6	104.0	...	223.0	...	...
Wheat & Rice Honeys	640.0	550.3	209.3	176.0	...	...	...	...	...	...
Unclassified	45.8	123.5	...	...	...	...	...	...	...	...
Totals	3,455.0	1,992.9	3,037.2	4,413.0	744.3	252.2	187.3	393.1	367.0	341.0

Ralston Purina
1965 total, $5,249.0; 1966 total, $6,309.7

	Spot TV		Network TV†		Magazines (General and Farm)		Newspapers (Incl. Supplements)		Spot Radio*	
	1965	1966	1965	1966	1965	1966	1965	1966	1965	1966
Chex Sweepstakes	...	...	...	...	...	207.9	...	...	...	...
Chexmates & Strawberries	0.5	...	...	...	...	...	...	...	...	...
Corn Chex	644.7	809.2	252.5	134.0	...	...	...	...	...	...
Mr. Waffles	...	387.7	...	...	...	...	...	32.6	...	...
Rice Chex	412.7	569.8	234.7	146.1	...	...	...	...	...	...
Wheat Chex	388.8	539.7	234.4	220.5	...	...	...	...	...	...
Ralston Chex	...	...	2,372.3	2,262.7	161.4	85.5	105.9	227.8	...	...
Ralston Hot Cereals	325.7	550.4	...	...	...	...	...	...	...	...
Ralston Cereals	7.8	121.7	...	12.1	...	...	12.4	...	...	...
Unclassified	...	...	73.2	...	...	...	...	...	22.0	2.0
Totals	1,780.2	2,978.5	3,167.1	2,775.4	161.4	293.4	118.3	260.4	22.0	2.0

* In network radio, Kellogg Co. invested $472,000 in 1966; General Mills, $245,000 in 1965 and $698,000 in 1966.

† Network television figures are estimated net time and talent costs.

‡ Since a major portion of this company's spot TV investment is unclassified, posting of the available investments for individual products may be misleading.

Sources: Television Bureau of Advertising/N. C. Rorabaugh; Leading National Advertisers/Broadcast Advertisers Reports; Bureau of Advertising, ANPA; Publishers Information Bureau; Radio Advertising Bureau.

tion in the form of a formal report. Address it to Warren H. Belton, president.

SUBJECTS FOR LIBRARY RESEARCH REPORTS

The following topic suggestions may be used for library research reports. For most of the topics, the specific facts of the case must be created through the student's (or perhaps the instructor's) imagination before a business-type problem exists.

Accounting

Should Company X lease or buy capital equipment?

How can Company X use a CPA firm to aid them in decision making?

Establish a bad debts policy and design a collection system for Company X.

What are the recent trends in the use of accounting data for decision making?

Determine the feasibility of a consolidated delivery service for City Y.

What are the liabilities and responsibilities of a CPA firm?

What is the most feasible way to finance a newly formed Company?

Handling the state sales tax on Company X's books.

Design an inventory control plan for Company X.

The use of the flexible budget as a management tool for control.

The use of cash-flow statements for decision making.

The use of standard cost for control and pricing purposes.

The validity of return on investment as a measure of performance.

The use of sunk cost in decision making.

The use of statistics in cost accounting.

The effect of the corporate income tax on corporate decision making.

The use of opportunity cost in decision making.

What are the methods Company X can use in handling errors that affected net income in prior years?

What are the rights of stockholders relative to dividends?

How should Company X handle its patents and copyrights on its books?

How should Company X handle a long-term construction contract that will be partially completed from year to year?

What are the recent trends in the area of long-term leases on the financial statements?

What are the criticisms of and arguments against conventional accounting?

The controller of today and his position in management.

How should Company X account for R.&D.?

What are the recent trends in responsibility accounting?

The history and present status of management accounting.

Recent developments in marketing cost analysis.

History and trends in union accounting.

Value of internal auditing to management.

Recent developments in break-even analysis for profit planning and control.

The use of risk and uncertainty in decision making.

The use of operations research as a decision making tool for accountants and managers.

The use of accounting data for replacement decisions.

The use of probability theory in decision making.

The use of variance analysis as a guide in decision making.

How should Company X use cash-flow analysis as a guide in and for profit planning?

Alternative methods of measuring return on investments.

The development and status of internal auditing.

Trend in the design of annual reports.

Professional ethics in public accounting.

Recent trends and developments in accounting theory.

The effect of electronic computers on accounting.

The allocation of income taxes on financial statements.

Direct costing for external reporting.

Determining priorities for cash distributions in partnership liquidations.

Accounting for management control.

Depreciation provisions in standard costs.

Usefulness and limitations of accounting data adjusted for price level changes.

Income tax considerations in the selection of a form of business organization.

Advantages and disadvantages of uniform cost accounting system.

The accountant's concept of business income.

The influence of governmental administrative agencies on accounting.

The effect of tax laws on accounting principles and practices.

Should the X Company use an accelerated method of depreciation?

Recommending the proper disclosure of long-term leases in the financial statements of the X Company (or industry).

Should scientific sampling be used in auditing?

Accounting contributions to the effective management of a business.

The accountant's role in cost reduction and analysis.

Accounting for pension costs.

Basic considerations in organizing a forecast and budget program.

Problems and progress of bank accounting.

Business education

Should business teachers be unionized?

The present status of business education teaching as a true profession.

Historical developments of business education.

What are the advantages and disadvantages of national business teacher organizations?

A comparison of business teacher training to the B.B.A. degree.

The ideal certification program for business teachers.

Placement responsibilities of business education in secondary schools.

Coordinating distributive education programs.

The function of career guidance in business education.

The ideal education for careers in business.

Financing business education programs at the secondary level.

Job training as a supplement of creating better consumers.

Supervision of business education in secondary schools.

The ideal training program for business education teachers.

Coordinating research efforts in business education.

Should a program for exceptional youths be developed in business education?

Effects of automation and data processing on teaching business subjects in secondary schools.

The emerging role of the junior college in business education.

Setting standards of achievement in the business education curriculum.

The role of economics education at the secondary level.

Evaluating student achievement in course X.

Audio-visual aids as a supplement to teaching business subjects.

Various theories of learning applied to the teaching of business subjects.

Management techniques in the office.

The place of student opinions and evaluations in curriculum revisions.

Work measurements in the office.

Ideal testing procedures in business education.

Should business education be offered in the public secondary school or in a technical-vocational school?

Should the business curriculum be specialized or should it provide a generalized, well-rounded education?

Trace the development of federal aid to business education.

General management

Investigate the use of air express for Company X.

How should Company X go about establishing or developing a favorable public image?

Recent labor–management rulings and their significance to Company X.

Establish a plan to introduce a quality control department in Company X that will maintain satisfactory human relations.

Establish a complete suggestion system for Company X.

The use of probability theory to increase profits for Company X.

Government regulation of the drug industry and an evaluation of recent rulings and regulations.

How the Small Business Administration can aid Company X.

How can Company X use management consultants?

The feasibility of a community computer center for small businesses.

The impact of the Common Market on product X.

The civil and criminal liabilities of corporate executives.

The value to Company X of membership in organization Z.

What are the procedures of incorporation in ———— (state)?

How can Company X measure the value of its executives?

The ethics of the corporate executive.

Recommending a profit-sharing plan for X Company.

Determining a code of ethics for a sales company.

Possibilities for use of operations research by X Company.

Can X Company profitably use an electronic computer?

Would hiring the handicapped workers be charity or good business for X Company?

Designing an executive development program for X Company.

How can Company X increase the creativity of its management and workers?

The nature and role of leadership.

The nature and significance of morale—a study of the psychology of morale and its organizational effects.

A program for achieving optimum discipline in X Company.

Organization and placement of a personnel (or other) department.

Business outlook for ———— industry (or X Company).

The importance of sales forecasts.

Should Company X use milestone budgeting.

The use of game theory in management.

The profit maximization concept.

Management as a cybernetic system.

The effect of white collar unionization.

The problems of office security at Company X.

Develop a plan to measure office costs for Company X.

Should Company X use outside marketing research consultants or set up its own staff?

An analysis of staff-line relationships at Company X.

Antitrust laws and corporate mergers.

How companies can combat student disenchantment with business.

How companies determine executive pay.
Can companies control water and air pollution?
The problems of product pricing.
Methods of creating company loyalty.

Labor

How have union contracts limited the area of decision making?
Ramifications of the union and the white collar worker.
Trends and implications of teachers' organizing.
Recent trends relative to the older worker and the stand taken by unions in this area.
The problem of automation and the unions' reactions to it.
Status and effects of the right-to-work law.
Unions in business for themselves.
Plans for unionizing Company X.
Recommending a grievance system for Company X.
Should antitrust laws apply to unions?
Discrimination in unions.
The union and government employees.
The power structure of unions and its implications.
The future of process unionism.
Unionism in retail stores and its effect on prices.
Labor regulation in State S.
Are unions monopolistic?
How should X Company respond to an attempt by Z Union to organize workers?
Now that the workers at X Company have been organized, what official attitude should management assume toward the union?
How should Company X prepare for upcoming contract negotiations with the union?
Causes of industrial war and peace.
Should Company X join an employers' association?
Determinants of wages.
Recommending a formal salary scale for X Company.
Do public employees have a right to strike?
Fringe benefits versus wage increases as motivational compensation.
Structural organization of the X union.
Feasibility of importing skilled workers.
Should blue collar workers be salaried?
The history and present status of labor unions.
The need for labor–management communication and understanding.
The effect of strikes on the economy.
A critical appraisal of labor leaders.
Project the future occupational opportunities for skilled labor.

Will a labor shortage eventually occur due to increased college enrollment?

Personnel administration

Design a safety training program for Company X.

Develop a method to test morale in Company X.

A management retirement program for Company X.

Recent developments in personal administration.

Design a retirement plan that will properly adjust the employee to retirement.

The importance of employees' wives to employers.

Set up a secretary selection plan.

Recent trends in the employment of women.

The use of teaching machines in training programs.

The use of management games for training.

What do applicants most want to know about Company X?

Validity of the accident proneness concept.

The effect of age and experience on production and accidents.

Developing a personnel testing program for Company X.

Developing a merit rating system for X Company.

Recent experiments and developments in remuneration.

A safety program for X Company.

Should Company X offer its employees a guaranteed annual wage?

Should Company X permit women to hold executive positions?

How can Company X maximize the productivity of its managers and workers?

The importance of a manpower inventory.

The use of constructive criticism.

Recommend a training program for new employees of Company X.

The use of teams in personnel management.

Develop a fringe benefit program for Company X.

Methods of manager appraisal education versus previous experience as a basis for employee selection.

Methods of evaluating various group insurance contracts.

Design an employment brochure for Company X.

How to deal with resistance-to-change problems.

The importance of employee participation in community activities.

Marketing

Design a promotion campaign for the opening of Company X.

Explore various selling methods and recommend the best method for Company X.

Recent trends in point-of-purchase advertising.

Determine the best method of selling a new issue of stock for well-established Company X.

The use of contests to boost efforts of Company X salesmen.

The use of computers in marketing.

The successful salesman of today and how he has changed.

The changing trends in the services offered by department stores.

Comparison of marketing systems in the United States and Russia.

The liabilities involved in manufacturing Product X.

The history and present status of the drive-in grocery.

Compare and contrast the college graduate and high school graduate in the marketing field.

The use of credit cards to increase the business of Company X.

The use of pallet warehousing to reduce marketing costs.

Should Company X use centralized or decentralized warehousing?

Should Company X rent or lease trucks for distribution of Product A.

Opportunities for a college graduate in marketing.

The ethical and social aspects of pricing for the market.

The use of statistics in marketing.

The case for and against advertising.

The need for regulating advertising.

Types of control on advertising, direct and indirect.

What should Company X look for in an advertising agency?

What bases can Company X choose from in order to determine the amount of money to allocate to advertising?

Should Company X use its own advertising department or an agency?

The growing problem of television commercials, with a recommended solution.

A promotional program for the introduction of product X.

The changing consumer.

Where in your area should Company X locate its next supermarket (or any other type of outlet)?

How can motivation research help Company X to make its decisions?

The nature and role of fashion in modern merchandising.

How can Company X measure the effectiveness of its advertising?

How downtown merchants can cope with suburban shopping centers.

Trends in packaging for ——— type products.

A market study of Z town to determine whether it is a suitable location for a chain discount house outlet.

Should X Company establish its own sales force, use manufacturers' agents, or use selling agents?

Should X Petroleum Company attempt to increase its share of the market by engaging in active price competition?

Factors involved in determining whether a department should be fully self-service, semi-self-service, or not self-service.

Determining the best channel of distribution for ———— product line.

The problem of evaluating salesman performance.

Develop a systems approach to marketing.

Design a marketing mix for Company X.

The effect of world-of-mouth promotion as an advertising medium.

Importance of brand image to the consumer.

Should Company X vertically integrate?

Comparison of commodity cost and convenience cost from the consumer point of view.

Should Store X scramble merchandise?

The problem of measuring consumer satisfaction.

The effect of legislation on pricing policy.

The effect of trading stamps and games on price.

The use of mathematics in marketing.

Design a compensation package that will motivate salesmen for Company X.

Consumer attitudes toward chain stores.

Advertising and the U.S. Supreme Court.

The use of public relations in marketing.

The effect of a declining birth rate on marketing.

Selection of a target market for product X.

The future for wholesalers in the distribution system.

Does marketing cost too much?

The need for consumer protection through government regulation.

Determining the effectiveness of advertising.

Index

This book has been set in 11 and 10 point Caledonia, leaded 2 points. Chapter numbers are 10 point Helvetica Bold and chapter titles are 14 point Helvetica Medium. The size of the type page is 27 by 46 picas.